The Royal Marines Band Service

by

John Ambler

Foreword written by HRH The Duke of Edinburgh, Captain General Royal Marines

To celebrate the 100th Anniversary of the founding of the Royal Naval School of Music at Eastney and the commencement of the modern
Royal Marines Band Service.

Special Publication Number 28.
Series Editor: Captain Derek Oakley MBE, RM

Published by
The Royal Marines Historical Society

Printed by Holbrooks Printers, Norway Road, Portsmouth, Hants PO3 5HX

ISBN 0 9536163 2 0

Dedicated to the memory of my father,

John Mayer Ambler

First published in the UK by:

The Royal Marines Historical Society
The Royal Marines Museum
Southsea
Hants
PO4 9PX

ISBN 0 9536163 2 0

Book layout and graphic design by Sgt Bug Mark Snell RM of the Blue Band Magazine, Royal Marines Band Service.

Contents

Chapters

Appendices

Acknowledgements

The acknowledgements for assistance with this book are many since not only have I received a great deal of help, encouragement and assistance but many people have been inconvenienced whilst I gave time and effort to this task. Firstly, I would thank the following for supplying specialist information: LtCdr Brian Witts (HMS Excellent Museum), Bugle Major Martin Williams (Plymouth Band), BdCSgt Ian Davies (Portsmouth Band), Maj Gordon Turner, Colin Bowden and the serving members of HQ RMBS and the staff of the Royal Marines School of Music. Thanks are also due to Lt Col Ewen Southby-Tailyour for permission to use his eloquent and forceful view on the worth of the Band Service to the Corps and to Matthew Sheldon of the Royal Naval Museum for permission to reproduce the Simpkin prints.

Proof readers can make an enormous difference to a book and I would thank the following for their patience and their diligence with what is a very difficult task: My wife Margaret, Pat Chambers of the International Military Music Society, Liz LeGrove of the Royal Marines School of Music and especially Major Alastair Donald of the Royal Marines Historical Society. In addition I would thank Lt Col Paul Neville, Lt Col Jim Mason, Lt Col Graham Hoskins, Lt Col John Ware and Lt Col Chris Davis. All have not only read and checked the drafts covering their periods of service but have also encouraged me in the writing of this book. Special thanks to Lt Col Richard Waterer who has encouraged the project from the start, has offered and given assistance and has always been available to provide comment, guidance and encouragement.

Additionally, for their support as part of the RMHS Publications team, I would thank Tony Brend who leads the team so well, Capt Derek Oakley as Executive Editor and Capt Andy Henderson who represented the Principal Director of Music and the RMBS. Two friends and colleagues deserve special mention not only for their knowledge, skills and encouragement but also for accepting the Band Service as virtually my only topic of conversation for the past two years! They are Susan Lindsay and Matthew Little, Assistant Curator and Archivist/Librarian respectively at the Royal Marines Museum. Matthew also administered the reproduction rights for photographs from the Royal Marines Museum collection and elsewhere.

My special thanks go to my good friend 'Tommy' Lawton, the Corps Bugle Major, for not only suggesting that I write this book but also for all the encouragement and in particular, the research into the historical records of the Buglers Branch.

Apologies to Ken Mann and the Emsworth Band for not being around to help much in the past two years. Apologies also to the UK Branch of the International Military Music Society for having to stand down as Chairman due to the demands of a new job and, in particular, this book. If it is any consolation I also gave up my regular trips to Twickenham for the rugby!

Two other thanks are necessary. First of all Sgt Bug Mark Snell of HQRMBS who has done such a professional job of arranging my words and pictures into this book. I hope that he is proud of the finished article, he certainly should be. Last, but certainly not least, my wife Margaret, daughters Janette ('Biggles') and Elizabeth and son-in-law Ian. All have not only allowed me time and space for this project but have also been encouraging and understanding.

BUCKINGHAM PALACE.

The Corps of Royal Marines had its own military bands since the 18th century, but then in 1903 the Royal Naval School of Music was established in the Royal Marines Barracks at Eastney, Portsmouth, and the Corps became responsible for providing musical support for the Royal Navy. In 1950 the School moved to Deal and became the Royal Marines School of Music. In 1996 it moved back to Portsmouth, where it presently occupies the old Naval Detention Quarters.

Anyone who has had any experience of service life is only too well aware of the value of military bands. They are indispensable for ceremonial occasions and the entertainment they provide at times of operational stress does wonders for morale. Royal Marines Musicians and Buglers are highly skilled in their primary musical role, but their secondary duties are no less demanding and frequently carried out in dangerous conditions both at sea and on land. They carried stretchers at Gallipoli, they worked in fire control Transmitting Stations, in the depths of battleships and cruisers during both world wars and they have served as peacekeepers and reconcilers in Kosovo.

Royal Marines Bands have performed on parade and in concert all over the world. They have 'flown the flag' for this country with style wherever ships of the Royal Navy and the Royal Yachts have taken them. This book is a tribute to this unique service.

Author's General Introduction

Throughout the writing of this book one thing has become very clear. It is not possible, in a book of this size, to tell the complete story. The modern Royal Marines Band Service is derived from a number of separate strands that, during the last one hundred years, have gradually been woven together. To write the story of all of these strands has not been easy. It has been attempted before. John Trendell wrote '*A Life on the Ocean Wave*' – a labour of love that I do not seek to replace. John's book still has a place on the bookshelf of anyone who has an interest in military music or in the Royal Marines. It needed updating because it is over thirteen years since it was published and hopefully this book will accomplish that need.

The Royal Naval School of Music, Royal Marines Bands, Buglers Branch, RM Divisional Bands and the modern Royal Marines Band Service each deserve a book of their own - and some could fill a very large one.

Some readers may feel that, at times, I have 'gone off at a tangent' but I wanted to portray as much of the detail of life with the Bands or Corps of Drums as possible and one of the most effective ways of doing this was to use anecdotal accounts of events. The selection of such events was, to some extent, governed by available reports and correspondence. I have included as many stories of personal experiences, especially about life in the Royal Naval School of Music and with Royal Marine Bands, as possible. Those days are long gone and the words of those who were there and who took part add colour and warmth to a bare historical and factual account. I have also had to bear in mind that readers of this book will range from those with an intimate knowledge of the history of the Band Service to those who know nothing about them other than that they wear white helmets and play wonderful music.

Like John Trendell, the late Capt A C Green has done the Royal Marines Band Service a great favour, for it was he who, albeit inadvertently, provided me with much information through his interviews and correspondence with members of Royal Marines Bands.

With space at a premium it is essential that I avoid duplication of the work of others. For this reason I do not intend to repeat the story of Sir Vivian Dunn. Derek Oakley has written a splendid and very detailed account of his life called '*Fiddler on the March*' and I would draw the attention of readers to this book, and commend it to them. Similarly, John Trendell also wrote an account of the life of Major Ricketts (Kenneth Alford) as '*Colonel Bogey on Parade*'.

The temptation to dwell on the 'personalities' of the Band Service has been resisted since that would invite comparison and would also dilute the story of the Band Service itself. Details of the modern history of the Buglers Branch are difficult to find but, in many ways, their story is completely interwoven with that of the bands themselves.

I hope that I have managed to take the work of the two great chroniclers of the Royal Marines Band Service, John Trendell and Capt A C Green, and to build upon the foundations that they have provided for me. There is still much to write about. Uniform, for instance, is a complex, and difficult, subject but a definitive reference book is required. One day, perhaps...

John Ambler,
Emsworth
June 2003

Introduction

The history of the Royal Navy and the history of the British Army have many parallels. However a major organisational difference has resulted in the bands of each service developing in very different ways. The Army Regimental and Corps system has, until very recently, allowed its bands to evolve in a manner that is firmly rooted in the continuity of the Regiment or Corps, its custom and its traditions. This system is mirrored in the Royal Marines, a Corps whose history and operation was, and to some extent still is, part of a similar system.

Sailors on the other hand have, over many centuries, been part of a commission system that has seen a crew formed for the length of a voyage, or a 'commission', only to be disbanded when the ship returned to its homeport. This does not mean that the pride in the ship's name, and its battle honours, are not as strong as in the Army, for they are, and a name will be passed from one ship to another as time goes by. Royal Navy Bands were part of the same commission system and would be brought together to join a particular ship only to be either disbanded, or kept together in part or in total, when the commission was completed.

Abbreviations

Any book on a military subject is bound to include many abbreviations. Although these are explained within the text or in the footnotes the following list of the more commonly used abbreviations may be helpful.

Adjt	Adjutant	DAG	Deputy Adjutant	RAM	Royal Academy
AGRM	Adjutant General,		General		of Music
	Royal Marines	DofM	Director of Manning	RMA	Royal Marine Artillery
AFO	Admiralty Fleet Order	DoM	Director of Music	RMB	Royal Marine Band
Asst Comdt	Assistant	Fl BM	Fleet Bandmaster	RMBS	Royal Marines Band
	Commandant	GD	General Duties		Service
BB	The Blue Band	G&L	The Globe and Laurel	RMHS	Royal Marines
	Magazine.		Journal		Historical Society
BdCpl	Band Corporal	Hon Lt	Honorary Lieutenant	RMLI	Royal Marines Light
Bdr	Bombardier	HO	Hostilities Only		Infantry
BM	Bandmaster	HQ	Headquarters	RMM	Royal Marines
Capt	Captain	KR & AI	Kings Regulations and		Museum
CBM	Corps Bandmaster		Admiralty Instructions	RMRO	Royal Marines
Cdo	Commando	Musn	Musician		Routine Order
Cd BM	Commissioned	NCO	Non Commissioned	RNB	Royal Naval Barracks
	Bandmaster		Officer	RNSM	Royal Naval School
CDM	Corps Drum Major	OCRM	Officer Commanding		of Music
CGRM	Commandant General,		Royal Marines	Temp Lt	Temporary Lieutenant
	Royal Marines	OIC	Officer in Command	TS	Transmitting Station
C-in-C	Commander-in-Chief	PTI	Physical Training	WO RM	Warrant Officer
CO	Commanding Officer		Instructor		Royal Marines
Col Comdt	Colonel Commandant	QMS	Quartermaster		
CPO	Chief Petty Officer		Sergeant		

The Development of the Royal Marines Band Service 1900-2003

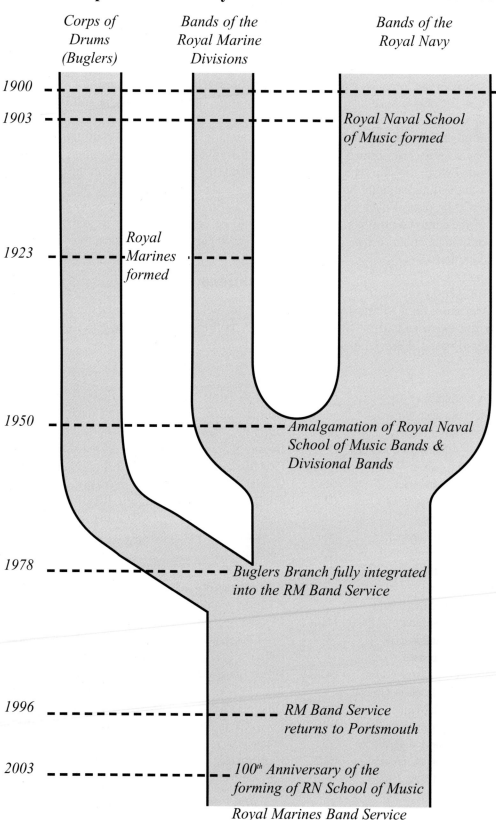

Corps of Drums (Buglers)

Bands of the Royal Marine Divisions

Bands of the Royal Navy

1900

1903 — *Royal Naval School of Music formed*

Royal Marines formed

1923

1950 — *Amalgamation of Royal Naval School of Music Bands & Divisional Bands*

1978 — *Buglers Branch fully integrated into the RM Band Service*

1996 — *RM Band Service returns to Portsmouth*

2003 — *100th Anniversary of the forming of RN School of Music*

Royal Marines Band Service

CHAPTER ONE

Ships' Bands at the Turn of the Twentieth Century

Bands were started in the Royal Navy by private enterprise. During the Napoleonic Wars most flagships and many battleships had them but it was not until the middle of the nineteenth century that the Admiralty began to show an official interest in, and to encourage, bands. The rating of Bandsman was introduced in 1847 and in 1856 new scales of complements for HM Ships included eighteen Bandsmen for each First and Second Rate ship of the line with fifteen Bandsmen allowed for each Third and Fourth Rate ship. The Admiralty stated that foreigners might be entered into the bands and indeed they were, in great numbers. They were mainly Italian or Maltese, especially in the Mediterranean Squadron.[1]

The first step, albeit rather small, towards training of Naval Bands was taken when, in 1863, a few Band Boys were entered in wooden walled Boys' Training Ships. The next eleven years saw the Admiralty take an effective grip upon, and responsibility for, Naval Bands. In 1867 it made grants for the purchase of instruments and then, in 1868; it established Bandmasters with the rating of Petty Officers followed three years later by the establishment of Band Boy and Bandsman 2nd Class ratings. Chief Bandmasters were introduced into the Training Ships in May 1874.[2] In the same year the connection of Naval Bands with the Royal Marines began as a result of the Adjutant General Royal Marines (AGRM) being directed to order the Bandmasters of the Royal Marines Divisions to inspect Training Ship Bands twice a year and to issue Certificates of Competence to Royal Navy Chief Bandmasters.[3]

In 1884 the Commander of the Channel Squadron, Vice Admiral HRH Prince Alfred, Duke of Edinburgh, recognised that the standard of musicianship of bandsmen awaiting draft deteriorated as a result of lack of opportunity to practise whilst they were held in Depot Ships. He suggested that bandsmen awaiting draft should be attached to the band of the Commander-in-Chief (C-in-C) at one of the Home Ports. He went even further and suggested that a rota system be set up so that all men took their turn at sea service. The latter suggestion did not endear the Duke to the Cs-in-C at the Home Ports since they were cultivating their own bands on the pattern of the Guards, the Royal Artillery and the Royal Marine Divisions - stable bands that offered inducements and privileges to the finest players, such as teaching or performing in leisure hours. His third suggestion was for a training school for music for the training and qualification of Bandmasters. The Duke of Edinburgh's thoughts about the problem of bandsmen awaiting draft caused[4] Continuous Service Bandsmen to be attached to Training Ships where they would be able to practise, using Admiralty supplied instruments.[5]

Charles Sanderson[6] was a Band Boy at the turn of the century. Children were recruited from the various orphanages to join the Boys' Training Ships. He joined the Training Ship *Exmouth* at Grays, Essex in 1900 and gravitated to the Band that was part of the Naval Band Service. The boys were destined to join adult bands when they reached the age of eighteen. Practice took place in the sand lockers of the ship; these were the ballast rooms located above the bilges - ballast being required to keep the vessels upright. The sand was floored over to prevent the lads sinking and light was provided by candle, each boy being issued with an 'eight-hour candle' for this purpose. Practice was from 9am until 11am and from 1pm until 3pm each day. Charles would descend each day into this blackness carrying his double bass or his bombardon.

Commander-in-Chief Plymouth's Orchestra c1891-1899. Some of these men appear to have served in the Crimea, Egypt and/or Sudan and also China.

Another ex-Musician, (J N Squire) wrote that a Training Ship Band was the responsibility of the Chief Bandmaster (Ch BM) who was assisted by a 1st Class Bandmaster (1st Cl BM) and a Band Corporal (BdCpl) who, by courtesy, was called Band Sergeant (BdSgt) and who was allowed to wear three stripes. The Chief BM was paid eight shillings and ten pence a day plus a further shilling per day instruction money if he was in a Training Ship. Out of that he had to pay for messing in the Chief Petty Officers (CPO) Mess and for every bit of his uniform.

Their Naval colleagues did not hold Naval Musicians in great esteem; they were regarded as 'idlers' and often given other work to do on board ship - such as Midshipmen's servants.[7] Ships' Bands were the cause of growing unrest in Wardrooms at the turn of the century. RN Officers were responsible for the financial upkeep of the bands, and in some cases the Bandmaster as well, except for pay and part of the cost of musical instruments. In addition, many of the foreign Bandmasters and musicians were disinclined to take part in, or notice of, RN custom, tradition and discipline. Bandmasters such as Pellela, Fontanezzi, Lochatelli, Licari and de Robertis[8] were all volatile characters - another trait that did little to endear them to the RN Officers.

In 1899 the rating of Chief Bandmaster (Chief BM) and Bandmaster (BM) was substituted by Bandmaster and Band Sergeant but, in 1890, this was rescinded and the old titles restored.

The normal band of 1889 comprised eleven players who would provide a band and an orchestra, the instruments being (for a band) one piccolo and flute, three clarinets, two cornets, two saxhorns, one baritone, one euphonium and one bombardon. Orchestral instrumentation would be four violins, one viola, one violincello, one double bass, one flute, one cornet and one euphonium. Some of the Bandsmen obviously had to be double handed.[9]

By 1897 the numbers borne were twenty Chief Bandmasters and Bandmasters, eighty-four Band Corporals and Musicians, four hundred and ninety-six Bandsmen and two hundred and twenty Boys. 'Musicians' were very often violinists and usually very few of these would be on board ship. Very often the 'Musicians' were "…so inferior and objectionable a class as to be entirely unfit to hold the rating of Petty Officer"[10] Small ships were not allowed a band but were allowed to carry "a Musician".

A Naval Band with group of Royal Navy and Royal Marine personnel c1900

In October 1902 a letter was written from the Training Ship '*Mercury*' moored in the River Hamble:

> Boys are sent from here into the Army Bands in preference to the Navy Bands. One of the reasons being that the prospects for a Military Bandsman is far in advance of that of the Navy. Kneller Hall which is a military Institution is a great advantage and there is no similar Institution in the Navy. Again, the station of a Military Bandmaster is far in advance of the Naval man. The two Services will not compare until the Bandsman afloat is placed on a similar footing to those on shore. I do not suppose this, or any like Institution would send their boys into the Navy Bands. The individual boy or man has many opportunities of improving his knowledge of music, not only by general but private practice. The Bandsman on board is generally an annoyance to everyone except just at the time he is taking part in the band. The Army Band Boy is far better looked after and cared for. Also there are many opportunities for private engagements, which never come in the way of the Naval men. Bands should be supplied to ships by the Marines, they would then have no difficulty in obtaining men who would ensure a really good Band.

So, at the end of the nineteenth century the Admiralty and the Royal Navy had endorsed the need for ships' bands only to discover that it had an organisation with a very crude and basic method of training young musicians; the support of the Royal Marines through an auditing system for both musicians and Bandmasters; a nucleus of Bandmasters who, in the main, were hard-working and indoctrinated into, and part of, the Royal Navy system; or, in the case of the foreign contingent, hard working but volatile and unsympathetic towards the Royal Navy and who, most importantly, had alienated the Officers. Changes were needed and it was probably this final point that set the wheels in motion.

CHAPTER TWO

The Royal Naval School of Music
1903-1950

Part 1 -The Royal Naval School of Music 1903 - 1914

The bands of the Royal Marine Light Infantry Divisions (RMLI) and the Royal Marine Artillery (RMA) were, at the turn of the twentieth century, well trained, well-led and very skilled and so it was not surprising that the Royal Navy looked to them as a means of improving the calibre of ships bands. A Memorial from the Right Honourable the Lords Commissioners of the Admiralty was presented to the King at Buckingham Palace on the 20th of May 1903. The King approved the Memorial, which included the following:

> Whereas we have had under our consideration the regulations which govern the organisation and maintenance of Bands on board Your Majesty's Ships. And whereas we are of opinion that it is desirable to improve the efficiency of Naval Bands and to reduce the expense, which at present falls upon the officers of Your Majesty's Naval Service. We beg leave humbly to recommend that Your Majesty may be graciously pleased by Your Order-in-Council to sanction the following scheme for the entry, training and pay of Bandsmen in Your Majesty's Fleet:
>
> In future Band ratings to be entered as Royal Marines and form part of Your Majesty's Royal Marine Force, the total number of that force being correspondingly increased.
>
> So far as possible Naval Band ratings now serving to be gradually transferred to the Royal Marines or otherwise disposed of under such arrangements as the Admiralty may direct.[1]

A scale of Rates of Pay was included. The new Band ratings would be Chief Bandmaster (Warrant Officer); 1st Class Bandmaster with over three years experience; 1st Class Bandmaster with less than three years experience; 2nd Class Bandmaster; Band Corporal; Musician and Band Boy. Band Corporals and Musicians would be paid a daily instrument allowance for maintaining their instruments in good condition and Chief Bandmasters and Bandmasters would receive a higher daily allowance if they were well maintained. In addition to this all ranks below Bandmaster, when serving on a sea-going ship, would receive a coaling allowance.

The Admiralty was prepared to act swiftly. On the 25th May 1903, a Naval Band was paid off from HMS *Impregnable* and on the 22nd of July 1903 Bandmaster H Lidiard led the thirty-four strong band of HMS *Impregnable*, which included a few of the older boys from HMS *St Vincent* - a Training Ship moored in Portsmouth harbour,[2] through the gates of Eastney Barracks and the band became the Royal Marine Band (RMB) of the Royal Naval School of Music (RNSM). A few days prior to this, on the 10th July, the ship's band of HMS *Leviathan* had become the first to transfer from the Royal Navy to the Royal Marines. This occurred whilst the ship was at Plymouth and the Colonel Commandant of Plymouth Division RMLI signed the Attestation Papers. The first man to sign his papers was Arthur William Shepard, a Royal Navy Bandsman who, overnight, became a Royal Marine Musician with the number 'RMB1'[3]. It is evident from Attestation Papers that each man had received a 'Notice' from Major Slessor at the RNSM. From this time all ships' bands, upon being paid off, would be discharged to the RNSM. Bandmaster Lidiard, after twenty-six years service, was promoted Warrant Officer, Royal Marines (WO RM) and appointed Chief BM RM[4]. 'Second Fiddle' wrote the following for Globe and Laurel:

July 22 1903 saw the birth of what is now known as the Royal Marines Band Service at RMA Barracks Eastney. The State for that day gives the total strength, exclusive of Staff, as one Chief Bandmaster and thirty four boys [5]

On the 22nd July 1903 the band of HMS Impregnable (Bandmaster H Lidiard) became the first band to march into the new Royal Naval School of Music at Eastney.

A course of training at the School of Music would be taken by all Bandsmen and the School itself would be staffed by a Commandant (Royal Marine Major) - Major Herbert Slessor RMA; a Musical Director (RNSM) of WO rank - Mr E C Stretton (Bandmaster, 1st Battalion The York and Lancaster Regiment was brought from India. He was subsequently promoted WO RM); a Superintending Clerk - Mr J M Mitchell RMLI who was promoted Quartermaster and Acting Adjutant RNSM with rank of Honorary Lieutenant[6] (Hon Lt); two Bandmaster-Instructors of 1st Cl BM rank (who would also receive a daily Instruction Allowance in addition to the Instrument Allowance) and a Schoolmaster who would be a Sergeant, RM[7] (Sgt RM). Whilst the Commandant reported directly to the Deputy Adjutant-General RM (DAG RM) regarding the administration of the School, all matters of discipline were to be referred to the Colonel Commandant (Col Comdt)RMA.

The "raison d'être" of the RNSM was to form and train bands for service in His Majesty's Fleets and Naval shore establishments and the bands, known as Royal Marine Bands (RMBs) were not to be confused with the Divisional Bands of the Royal Marines. The object of the School was to provide efficient small military bands, orchestras and dance combinations. So the Admiralty had recognised the shortcomings of ships' bands, examined the Royal Marine model, prepared a scheme that addressed the deficiencies in musical training, discipline and leadership and then made the Royal Marines responsible for raising the standards to that of their own bands. From this time the Royal Marines were to be totally responsible for, and representative of, Royal Navy music in all its forms.

Over the next few months many discussions took place between the infant school and its hosts, the RMA, particularly with regard to uniform detail. Buttons were to be RMLI pattern but with 'Royal Marines' instead of 'Royal Marine Light Infantry'; helmet plates were to be as the RMLI pattern but with the bugle omitted, whilst collar badges were to be embroidered lyres. The DAG, RM wrote to the Col Comdt of the RMA on the 27th June 1903 authorising the sealing of the uniforms and insisting that the uniforms for the Band of HMS *Leviathan* be made forthwith[8]. This indicates that it was known that this ship would be the first to have its band transferred.

The Divisional BM, RMA was despatched to the Admiralty to assist in the examination of instruments for the RNSM.

A letter[9] dated August 1903 was sent by the Admiralty to all 'Commanders-in-Chief, Captains, Commanders, and Commanding Officers of HM Ships and Vessels at Home and Abroad' outlining the structure of the school but including, for the first time, 'and a limited number of visiting professors with a knowledge of the requisite instruments'. This document also mentions that relocation to Chatham was highly likely but, whilst at Eastney, the school would be considered as being temporarily attached to the RMA Division and under the disciplinary control of the Col Comdt, RMA. Furthermore the Admiralty undertook to supply, free of charge, a ceremonial band, instruments, music stands, accessories and music to all those ships and RN establishments that were allowed a band. If the Officers of a ship or shore establishment also required a string band then the Officers were expected to contribute towards the supply, on loan, of the required instruments. New entries to the School would be recruited under the supervision of the Royal Marines. It was anticipated that a higher standard of musical knowledge and ability would be required of recruits.

The transfer of band ratings from ships' and shore establishments and of boys under training on Boys Training Ships was expected to be a gradual one with the Commandant making arrangements with the various ships' Captains on an individual basis.

Formalised training at both the School of Music (SoM) and upon return to ships was to include physical training, elementary infantry and rifle drill and swimming, all concurrent with the musical training. Courses for first aid and stretcher drill were carried out on board ship and eligibility for promotion was dependent upon certificates being awarded for these courses. The foundation of the modern Royal Marines Band Service (RMBS) can be seen to be emerging in these arrangements. However the practice of Musicians and Band Corporals serving as personal servants to Officers whilst afloat or in Depots was to continue but, from now on, Officers were obliged to pay gratuities as set out by the Admiralty.

The standard composition of bands was also set out in this letter. Senior Flagship bands of the Home, Channel, Mediterranean and China Fleets would have a 1st Cl BM, a BdCpl and twenty-two Musicians[10]. Other Flagships, Schools and Depots would have a 1st Cl BM, a BdCpl and fifteen Musicians. The existing bands of the Port Admirals would be reduced to a 1st Cl BM, a BdCpl and eleven Musicians[11]. Battleships and 1st Class Cruisers would have a 2nd Cl BM, a Bd Cpl and thirteen Musicians whereas other ships allowed bands also had a 2nd Cl BM and a BdCpl but only nine Musicians.

A limited number of Chief Petty Officers (CPO) holding the rating of Chief Bandmaster (Ch BM) were to be selected for promotion to the new rank of Chief Bandmaster (Warrant Officer), Royal Marines (Ch (WO) BM), and were to be borne in lieu of the new rating of Bandmasters, 1st Class[12] (BM 1st Cl).

This letter would have left all RN Officers in no doubt about the shake-up that the Admiralty was applying to music in the Senior Service.

The complements of these bands together with the need to play as a military band, an orchestra and a dance band demanded great versatility on the part of individual musicians and the smaller the number the greater was the efficiency demanded from each member.

In the autumn of 1903 Lt G Miller of the RMLI Portsmouth Band started a debate concerning the band embarked upon the Royal Yacht that involved the Admiralty and the King himself. As a result the Admiralty wanted to remove both Lt Miller's band and the RMA Band and use the Band of the RNSM as the permanent Yacht Band. This was a bit unfair since the School had not been operational long enough to have attained the same standard as the Divisional Bands. However, if this occurred it is possible that the current band service would still have 'Royal Naval' as part of its title.[13]

Early in 1904 the RNSM was visited by HM King Edward VII who was impressed by their smartness on parade. A month later the Prince and Princess of Wales visited Eastney to lay the foundation stone of the Barracks Church and also inspected "…that new limb of the Corps at present known as The Naval School of Music".[14]

A General Order, Royal Marines[15] (GORM) stipulated that recruits entering Royal Naval Bands were subject to the same requirements for physical fitness as other Royal Marines recruits.

HMS *Crescent*, a Second-Class cruiser, had one of the first bands from the School to be sent abroad, leaving in 1904 for a three-year commission as the Flagship on the South Africa Station. On the 25th February the RMB under Ch BM Smith led the ship's company from their barracks down to the dockyard, which they reached at 8.55am. At 9.00am the Colours were hoisted and the commissioning Pennant broke at the masthead whilst the guard presented arms and the band played "God Save the King". Stores were taken aboard on the 26th and then on the 27th, when storing was completed the band played on the upper deck for the crew for one hour, this being a regular Saturday evening routine in the Royal Navy.[16]

Less than a year after it had opened, cracks were starting to appear in the structure that was the RNSM. The administrative and support staffing levels of the School were obviously much too low. Clerks could not cope with the number of bandsmen and musicians being processed through the school; the Adjutant (Adjt) was able to deal with the stores, clerical and accounts part of his duties but was unable to carry out the duties of the Company Officer such as inspections. This situation had repercussions upon the RMA since its staff were becoming more and more involved in the work of the school. Col Comdt RMA petitioned the Admiralty for an increase to the staffing levels pointing out that he was providing three Sgts, and seven Cpls and Bombardiers (Bdr) to the school. He estimated that the school needed another Quartermaster Sergeant, (QMS) two clerks, one storeman, an assistant marker and six tailors to prevent a reduction in the number of men and boys being passed through the school. En route to the Admiralty the DAG, RM endorsed the request, adding that he felt that the additional staff should include a Captain, (Capt) or Subaltern, as Assistant Commandant (Asst Comdt) and Examiner of Accounts. The DAG also supported the suggestion of the RNSM's Commandant, Major Slessor, that the initial training be decanted to the Divisions whilst final training and the forming of ships' bands would be retained at the School. School staff would also be responsible for monitoring the musical training at the Divisions. The expectation of relocating the School to Chatham had been abandoned when it was realised that there was far less space at Chatham than at Eastney - which was struggling to cope with the situation.[17]

The Admiralty approved of the plan in principle and, after correspondence and discussion had taken place between the Admiralty and the Treasury, the DAG, RM received a letter dated 8th October 1904 from the Admiralty that set out the new arrangements for the RNSM[18]. The main points were:

Instead of a comprehensive school at Eastney there would be a small central school with local Branches at the Head Quarters (HQ) of each Royal Marine Division including Eastney and the Depot, Deal.

The Eastney Central School would remain under the Comdt of the SoM and would receive Band ratings prior to completion of training; when being formed into bands for embarkation and when qualifying for higher ratings. It was to become the Depot where all higher training was to take place to fit men for soloists and the higher ratings of the Band Service.

Branches to be placed under the immediate control of the Royal Marine Divisional Bandmaster assisted by one of the new scheme BMs. They would be under the superintendence of the Comdt of the SoM. Recruits would go to these schools to undergo training before being transferred to the central school for completion of their musical education. Band ratings would return to these schools from Service afloat in the same manner as Marines return to their Divisions. They would assist with instructional duties as required. Maximum number under training at each Division other than Eastney at any one time would be about 100.

The Staff allowed to the central RNSM were to be located at Eastney and also at the Divisional Schools at Forton, Eastney, Plymouth, Chatham and Deal. The Central School and the Eastney Divisional School had an Administrative Staff comprising of a Commandant (Major), an Assistant Commandant (a Captain or a Subaltern), an Adjutant who was a Quartermaster and Honorary Lieutenant, a Gymnastic Instructor (Sergeant), a Sergeant Major and a Senior Clerk (Sergeant) with three NCO or Gunner Clerks. The Instructional Staff were the Musical Director (a Warrant Officer) and two Bandmasters who could be either Chief Bandmasters or 1st or 2nd Class Bandmasters. The Divisional Adjutants with two Sergeants were responsible for the administration of the Divisional Schools whilst Musical Instruction was the responsibility of the Divisional Bandmaster and men of the Divisional Bands who were employed on instructional duties.

Following this, instructions were given for the renumbering of men and boys to reflect their joining the Royal Marine Bands by the prefix RMB to their number. Rates were set out for civilian musical instructors and for allowances to be paid to NCOs and men of the Royal Marines Divisional or Depot Bands.

It would appear that Chatham Division soon found itself up to complement (100) whilst the 25 boys who had been sent to Forton were returned to Eastney for instruction because of the lack of instructors in the area.[19]

In the 1904 Navy Estimates the Corps strength was increased by 850 to allow for the Naval Band complement.

The first report received from a ship's band to be published by the Corps journal 'Globe and Laurel' appeared at the end of 1904 when HMS *Euryalus* arrived at Suva, Fiji, and a Guard and Band paraded. Next day the new Band of the Flagship played at a ball given at Government House.

On the 8th June 1905 the Admiralty issued another circular letter[20] to all Commanders-in-Chief, Captains, Commanders and Commanding Officers of HM Ships and Vessels at Home and Abroad, detailing the revised structure and operation of the RNSM. As well as

The requirements for promotion to BM, 1st and 2nd Class, were:

(a) a service afloat of not less than six months as a confirmed NCO;

(b) a Second Class Certificate of Education.

Once examinations for the rank of Cpl were introduced the Boards would comprise the Comdt, SoM as President; and a Capt RM. The examination would be held at the School. For a First Class Certificate, 50% of the marks in each subject must be obtained, with an aggregate of not less than 260. For a Second Class Certificate, 50% of the marks in each subject must be obtained, with an aggregate of not less than 225.[21] Four subjects would be taken. They would be Music (practical), Music (theory), First Aid and Infantry Drill (Practical and detail).

Special arrangements could be put in place to allow those afloat to take the course and the examination.

Band Instruments and Music:

Admiralty to supply to the Officers of ships and shore establishments that were allowed bands, through the School of Music and free of charge, all usual instruments and cases, music stands, and other accessories for a brass and reed (ceremonial) band and would bear the cost of repairs.

Music to a value according to the class of ship would be provided.

An allowance paid for the good upkeep of instruments to continue to be paid to Bandsmen and Bandmasters.

Until such time as Marine Bandsmen were available to all ships, instruments would be provided to ships not having Marine Bandsmen if requested. Non-Marine Bandsmen would not be paid the allowance for looking after the instruments and so the SoM would require payment from the Ships' Officers to cover any damage.

If a ship required to maintain a String Band, the necessary instruments would be supplied, on loan, from the SoM and an annual charge would be levied on the Officers, the Captain being responsible for the use of the instruments and the collection of the money.

Some alterations to King's Regulations and Admiralty Instructions (KR&AI) were necessary to accommodate the above. They included:

Band Rank and Buglers RM - Efficiency Allowance and Musical Proficiency Allowance payable to all provided certain conditions were met.

Marine Bandsmen were listed with their equivalent rank, viz:

Bandmaster 1st Class (Colour Sergeant)

Bandmaster 2nd Class (Sergeant)

Band Corporal (Corporal)

Musician (Private)

Band Boy

Herbert Wright enlisted as a Band Boy at Eastney on the 5th August 1905 as a flautist and, after a few months he was also put on violin. A further few months went by and he began training as a drummer as well. He recalled that the Boy's early morning routine was rise at 6.15am, make beds for inspection, clean their area and then wash. Breakfast was at 07.00 - toast supplied but butter or margarine had to be purchased by the individual. 8.15 Parade and infantry drill until 9.00.

At Eastney the whole School had to turn out every Saturday morning on a recruiting march around Portsmouth.[22] It was also in 1905 that the white helmet was introduced for fulltime use of band ranks.[23] Up until that time the blue pattern was worn in England and the white one was worn only in warm climates. (This was not the current helmet, the Wolseley Pattern, which was not introduced until 1912)

Educational training of Boy Buglers, Band Boys and Recruits was carried out by RM Schoolmasters who also assisted in the schools for the children of the ranks serving at the RMA Barracks. They also organised voluntary evening classes and, where necessary, day classes for the various Service Certificates of Education. Possession of this was necessary for promotion. The most senior of the schoolmasters at Eastney was a Chief Schoolmaster. Later the Children's Schools were transferred to the Local Education Authority and then a Headmaster replaced the Chief Schoolmaster. At sea RN Schoolmasters were available for the assistance of those needing help. The Chief Schoolmaster (later the Headmaster) was responsible for the educational testing of all applicants for entry to the RNSM; for organising the classes in which the Band Boys were prepared for the examinations for their Third, Second and First Class Certificates of Education; and for arranging the necessary voluntary day and evening classes for those other ranks wishing to attend[24].

Bombardon, Bass and Euphonium Class RNSM 1905. Instructor is Professor Rich. A C Green (later Captain) is seated on floor at right; S Fairfield (later RNSM Musical Director) is seated on bench at left; W E Faithfull (later served at Gallipoli and became first RNSM Band Boy to be commissioned) was one of the original band of HMS Impregnable and is in the rear rank carrying the circular bombardon.

In 1905 the RNSM assembled a band of over forty for HMS *Renown*, which was preparing for a Royal Tour to India and Burma. Her escort was HMS *Terrible* with Bandmaster T Porteous. *Renown's* band was under the direction of the RNSM Musical Director E C Stretton who was made a Temporary Lieutenant (Temp Lt) for the duration of the tour. He wrote a march called *The Royal Tour* to mark the occasion. The Leader of the Orchestra was Maltese Bandmaster Paul Grosso and amongst the band of forty-one were future notables such as Bandmaster Gilbert Dowell, Comm BM Sparrow, BM Barham (who was later killed on board HMS *Indefatigable* at the Battle of Jutland) Lt E W Faithfull and Musical Directors S Fairfield and A C Green. A second Maltese Bandmaster, de Robertis, had played oboe in Verdi's orchestra. Major H S Neville White in his report[25] included the following:

They [the band] have reached a high pitch of excellence and, as a string band, certainly they need not fear comparison with some of our finest military bands. It has been an education to listen to them, and the only regret expressed on all sides is that so fine a band should now be scattered to the four winds.

Throughout the history of the RNSM many fine bands must have suffered a similar fate. When a ship returned home and went out of commission its band returned to the School and its members were granted leave according to their service afloat. When they returned from leave they were drafted to other ships as they were commissioned. The opportunity was taken to mix the older, experienced men with the younger men when a band was being formed for service in a ship.

RNSM Band formed for HMS Renown. This was the first band selected from the School for a Royal Tour and was under the direction of Temporary Lieutenant E C Stretton, the RNSM Musical Director.

In August 1905 the Second Cruiser Squadron under HRH Prince Louis of Battenberg went to Canada. A 'Display Party' was landed for a Naval and Military Tournament in Quebec, Montreal and other cities. This party consisted of 200 seamen and 100 Royal Marines and was accompanied by the massed bands of the Squadron. A Sergeant (RMLI) was appointed temporary Drum Major and carried a staff that was made in the Squadron. The head was made in the engine-room of HMS *Drake* and the ferrule in the engine-room of HMS *Cumberland*. These metal parts were fitted on a boathook shaft, which was later replaced by a Malacca cane and the staff was presented by LtCol H C Evans to the RMLI Portsmouth Division in 1912.[26]

By January 1906, the strength of the Royal Marines Bands had grown from the inception of the School less than three years earlier to 946 with 34 bands embarked. HMS *King Alfred* was typical of a ship's band complement having ten from Chatham, five from Plymouth, four from Forton and five from Eastney.

Ships' bands normally served afloat for a period of two to three years before returning to the School. However, drastic changes were needed to ensure that standards of ships' bands, and of the shore establishments, would be raised. In 1907 the C-in-C Plymouth's Band was severely shaken when a Bandmaster from the RNSM took over. Set in their ways for many years the ex-Army and Navy musicians suddenly found that they had to arrive much earlier for practice and had to clean their own practice area.

The Band of the Boys' Training Establishment, HMS *Ganges* at Shotley - ten miles from Ipswich, became a Royal Marine Band in 1906. Classed as a ship's band its strength was normally between eighteen and twenty. Its function was to assist the instruction of young entrants of fifteen or sixteen years of age through their basic training period. Apart from these duties the band provided concerts throughout the East Anglian region.

The Admiralty issued instructions for the care and preservation of musical instruments on board ship in July 1907. This was issued to all Commanders-in-Chief, Captains and Commanding Officers of HM Ships and Vessels at home and abroad.

When Bandmaster Stretton transferred to the Royal Artillery (RA) in 1907, Charles Franklin, who had been serving with the Egyptian Army, was appointed Musical Director of the RNSM. In 1908, the Lords Commissioners of the Admiralty directed that all RN Band ranks undergoing training at Chatham and Plymouth should be transferred to Eastney for completion of training.[27] In 1908 the first class of BdCpls took the examination of the Royal Academy of Music.

The first RM Band to serve on the Mediterranean Station was that of HMS *Queen*, the Flagship of the Mediterranean Fleet during 1907/1908. A C Green was in the band at the time. The second was HMS *Bacchante*, all the other ships of the Fleet still having Maltese or Italian Bands[28].

In 1907 the King inspected the Naval Brigade which numbered three thousand Seaman and one thousand Royal Marines. Following his passage through the ships of the Mediterranean Fleet the King left the Royal Yacht and his procession drove through streets lined by the men of the Naval Brigades. All Buglers and Drum and Fife Bands had been disembarked from the ships of the Fleet. Five battleship bands under the Fleet Bandmaster were at the Custom House with the Guard of Honour and a further six battleship bands and the Drum and Fife Band were with the Battalions along the route. On the day of the inspection the Naval Brigade took position on the Marsa. The King inspected the Brigade, which then marched past, reformed, Advanced in Review Order, halted and gave three cheers[29].

The Austrian Fleet visited Malta in March 1908 and on Tuesday the 3rd two hundred and forty officers and seamen of the British and Austrian Fleets sat down to dinner. The combined bands of HMS *Lancaster* and HMS *Implacable* were under the direction of Mr Quaranta who must have been one of the last of the foreign bandmasters. The bands were in the adjoining billiard room and during dinner they played *Entry of the Gladiators* (Fincke); *Light Cavalry* (Suppé); *Veronique* (Messager); *Unrequited Love* (Lincke); *Faust* (Gounod); and *Mad Music from Monsieur Beaucaire* (Rosse).

A GORM[30] announced that musical training at Forton Barracks would cease on 30th November 1908 and that all Band ranks at Forton on that day would transfer to Eastney.

In 1909 the augmented band of HMS *Inflexible* under Ch BM Welsh of the RNSM played *The Star Spangled Banner* and *God Save the King* as the *Lusitania* overhauled them in mid-Atlantic. Upon arrival in New York the band massed with bands of the Squadron, HMS *Drake*, *Duke of Edinburgh*, *Argyle* and *Inflexible*, at the head of the Royal Naval Brigade as it marched through the streets of New York as part of the Hudson Fulton celebrations. Sgt G W Chant of Portsmouth Division, who was serving in HMS *Duke of Edinburgh's* Detachment, acted as Drum Major and, "By his fine appearance and masterly manipulation of the Drum Major's staff he won the hearts and the applause of the New York populace".

One of the features of serving in a Royal Marine Band at sea during this period was coaling ship. Thousands of tons of coal would be taken aboard with monotonous regularity from docks and coaling ships strategically placed around the world. When Musn John Allen joined his first ship, HMS *Russell*, a 13,000ton battleship en route to Malta for a major refit, he kept a diary. One day in May 1909 at Dover he noted, "Coaled 1,466 tons from 6.00 am until 01.00 am next morning. The Band started at 05.45 am and finished at 10.30 pm. Had to play four pieces an hour. During the intervals played on the quarterdeck. Band had 7 days' leave stopped for being two minutes adrift from playing a double for coal ship morning when the call sounded *Fall in Hands for Coaling*". Herbert Wright described his first experience of joining ship as follows:

I left there [HMS *Victory* - Portsmouth shore base, now HMS *Nelson*] April 1909 and put straight into another band for RM Barracks Plymouth, and left there the next day to commission HMS *Temeraire* in Devonport Dockyard. The ship was alongside and directly we got there we had to change into working rig and help to take in stores. This went on for several days. Finally, when ready for sea, the band got the usual job in the depths of the ship working the fire control instruments. In addition to this we had our stations for 'in' and 'out' torpedo nets. When taking in ammunition we were kept busy. Our worst job was when taking in coal. Two thousand tons at a time was nothing unusual, our job being running the sacks of coal as they were hoisted on board on to barrows and cast them onto bunker chutes halfway along the ship.

Unlike the Captain of HMS *Russell* who was happy for his band to entertain the crew whilst they coaled ship the Captain of HMS *Temeraire* obviously believed in using all hands for the purpose of coaling.

During this period the damage to musical instruments taken on board ship started to become a real problem for the Admiralty. They issued circular letters[31] reminding Musicians of their responsibilities with regard to instrument condition and making the Bandmaster responsible for all of the accessories including music stands and music. Musicians were also reminded of their obligation to take care of their instruments or forfeit their Instrument Allowance.

A GORM[32] confirmed that all RM Band ranks (WOs, NCOs, Men and Boys) allocated to RMLI and RMA Divisions for training should return to the Central School of Music at Eastney.

On the 21st July the band of the RNSM under Lt Charles Franklin played at the Guildhall, London, when the Corporation of London hosted a "Visit of the Men of the Fleet"

By 1910 all foreign musicians had been eliminated from the system and band ranks stood at 1,300 with 900 in the Fleet's 53 bands. The remainder, aged fifteen to twenty-three years, were at the School - which was producing about 120 musicians and boys each year. By this time the School was operating smoothly with a well-defined curriculum for recruits, for Band Corporals and for Bandmasters. Twenty-three Professors were responsible for ensuring that all pupils received the training necessary to enable them to play an orchestral and a wind instrument to a high standard. In addition pupils were taught music theory, first aid, infantry drill, physical training, swimming, musketry and English education in classrooms within two huge buildings. The Corporal's Course took each of these topics further and culminated in examinations. Bandmasters' Classes included elements of music, harmony, practical knowledge of all wind and string instruments used in bands and orchestras, scoring for military band and for small orchestra and being able to show proof of intelligence as a conductor. A minimum of 75% in all subjects had to be achieved to pass the RAM examination. It was in this year that the award for the Best Student of the Year presented by the Worshipful Company of Musicians (WCM) was instituted. The Company began awarding a Silver Medal in 1889 on a triennial basis at the Royal Academy of Music, Royal College of Music and the Guildhall School of Music in rotation to the most distinguished student. In 1908 this gift was extended to the Royal Military School of Music, Kneller Hall, and in 1910 to the RNSM.[33] The award was made annually to both military schools. The cost of the medal for the RNSM was provided through an endowment given to the Company by Mr Hugh Wyatt, a Past Master of the Company.[34]

Cd BM (WO) H Lidiard succeeded Lt J McFarlane Mitchell as the Quartermaster, RNSM, and was then appointed Honorary Lieutenant and Quartermaster RMLI.

HRH the Duke of Connaught visited South Africa in the SS *Balmoral Castle* in 1910 accompanied by an RM Band under Mr A M Moffatt. The following year the King and Queen visited Dublin with the 1st and 2nd Battle Squadrons and the 2nd Cruiser Squadron, and six bands totalling 180 musicians played for them. No 1 Band comprised the RM Bands of *Neptune* (23), and *Vanguard* (7); No 2 Band was from *St Vincent* (10), *Bellerophon* (10) and *Collingwood* (10); No 3 Band came from the *King Edward VII* (23) and *Hindustan* (7) whilst No 4 Band came from *Hibernia* (17) and *Britannia* (13). *Superb* (14) and *Temeraire* (14) formed No 5 Band whilst the bands of *Shannon* (10), *Agamemnon* (10) and *Lord Nelson* (10) were No 6 Band. All were under BM (WO) G Clarke. The King and Queen reviewed the Naval Brigade in Dublin Park and the bands played *Coburg* during the King's inspection; *Heart of Oak* as the field guns went past; *They All Love Jack* for the 1st and 2nd Seaman Battalions march past and *Nancy Lee* for the 3rd and 4th Seaman Battalions. The Royal Marines marched past to *A Life on the Ocean Wave* and the Brigade marched back to *Red, White and Blue*.

In the same year a band from the RNSM, including representatives of the Students' Classes, under BM George Robertson was sent to Caernarvon for the Investiture of the Prince of Wales. They were in the Guard of Honour for the King and Queen at Holyhead Station as well as for the Prince of Wales as they joined the Royal Train for Caernarvon. On arrival the Band marched the RN contingent to the castle where they camped in the grounds.[35]

A rather odd incident occurred in 1911 when Horace de Vere Cole, a well-known hoaxer, and a group of friends masqueraded as an Abyssinian Prince and his retinue and not only convinced the RN of his authenticity but boarded their newest battleship, HMS *Dreadnought*. Welcomed by Guard and Band he and his retinue even managed to have the Sunset ceremony delayed by a half-hour so that they could perform their 'devotions' on the quarterdeck! BM Reely was given a particular problem since his book of National Anthems did not include one for Abyssinia. Taking a chance he played the first eight bars of *Dover Castle*. Such was the level of mickey-taking that *Dreadnought's* crew had to endure after the de Vere Cole hoax that the Admiral took the Fleet to sea for exercises to stop the incessant fights that took place ashore each night.

A year later the members of the band of the RNSM suggested a concert on South Parade Pier, Southsea, in aid of the Titanic Disaster Fund and as a tribute to the heroic conduct of the liner's musicians. An orchestra of a hundred under Lt Franklin was used for this and the programme included *The Land of the Mountain and the Flood* and *A Day in Naples*. A Naval and Marine Tournament was held at the United Services Ground, Portsmouth in late August and an RNSM band of eighty augmented by the bands of HMS *Victory* and HMS *Excellent* performed under Lt Franklin. Admiral Lord Charles Beresford was given the Freedom of Weymouth and the massed bands of the ships that happened to be in Portland Harbour took part in the ceremony. HMS *Hercules* was the Flagship and her Bandmaster was therefore in charge of the event. Whilst each Divisional Band had a Bugle Major and a Drum Major (CSgt or Sgt) no RM Band had either of these appointments. Drum Majors would be found from within either the band or the RM Detachment. A Drum Major was necessary for such a massed bands display so BM Read prevailed upon BdCpl G C Weinrich to assume the responsibility and he made a magnificent job of it.

Total strength had reached 1,450 by 1913 and embarkation and disembarkation were now very frequent. HMS *Highflyer* was commissioned for the East Indies putting a British band on that station - previous bands being Goanese. Naval manoeuvres were being planned and HMS *Euryalus*, the flagship of the Umpire-in-Chief[36], was sent a special band of twenty-four.

An International Peacekeeping Force consisting of British, German, Austrian, French and Italian forces with the British in command was sent to occupy Scutari (Albania) in 1913 to protect the Muslim inhabitants from ethnic cleansing by the Montenegrins. This area would soon become Yugoslavia. The band of HMS *King Edward VII* went ashore with the marines and sailors. The entire force was billeted together and the only other band was with the Austrian contingent. The two bands could not be massed since the pitch of the instruments was different. The band played every other evening throughout the stay and impressed all, especially the Mallisori tribal chiefs who attended a reception given by Vice-Admiral Burney, in charge of the International Force. The King's Birthday was celebrated by a parade that all Forces attended. The Band with the RM and Seaman Detachments returned to HMS *King Edward VII* when the West Yorkshire Regt (The Prince of Wales's Own) relieved them.[37]

The lighter side of the life of a RM Musician at sea was apparent through the Concert Party. Open to all this provided the opportunity for talent and, in particular, imagination to shine. The band of HMS *Minotaur* on the China Station at Wei-Hai-Wei opened the ship's concert party on the 12th September with an overture. Whilst the Glee party were very popular the band claimed the honour of providing the chief feature - a gymnastics display by members of the band! Proceeds from the concert party went to the Seamen's and Marine's Orphan's Home[38]. The part played by RM Bands afloat cannot be over-emphasised. As a Military and Ceremonial Band it was constantly used for moving men about their duties in an orderly manner; the ship's daily routine which included the Morning Colours Ceremony, Divisions, Prayers, physical training and Evening Colours was much more impressive to a ship's company when a band was aboard. There was also the frequent need for parades ashore and since many ships were 'flying the flag' appearance was most important not only to those watching but also for the morale of the ships' crews. The Band was also used to give an impressive welcome when Foreign Royalty or Foreign Officials visited the ship. At all sporting occasions the Military Band was employed and frequent variety programmes were played on board to help relieve the monotony of long voyages and routine.

As an orchestra the musicians were used to provide music for luncheon and dinner parties when visitors were aboard. Orchestral and variety concerts for the ship's company were often held and the band also played each Sunday at Church Service. During a ship's commission scarcely a week would go by without a performance by the ship's dance band or without its support of the Ship's Concert Party. Thus it was generally accepted that a band helped increase the efficiency of the ship, raised the morale of its crew and was very important to the daily business of showing the might of the British Navy to friend and potential foe alike.

Back in Portsmouth the Divisional Band of the RMA and the Band of the RNSM both played at the funeral of Captain G V Wildman-Lushington, one of the first Royal Marines to qualify as a pilot and serve in the Naval Wing of the Royal Flying Corps.[39] The pilot was buried in Christchurch Cemetery on Portsdown Hill overlooking Portsmouth with full military honours.

As the year came to an end BM C T Leeder, who had been a bass player in the band of HMS *Impregnable* in 1903, was given an unusual posting. He was sent to the Gold Coast in West Africa as the bandmaster of the Gold Coast Regiment, part of the West African Frontier Force. His band was formed from native musicians.

Two of the larger and more important RN establishments had their own bands at this time. One was the Band of Nore Command and the other was that of HMS *Excellent*. Nore Command itself was formed in 1547 and covered the Thames Estuary and River Medway area. This was an area that might bear the brunt of any attacks and invasions upon the country or, conversely, would be one of the launching points for raids or invasions against our enemies. The first recorded Bandmaster of the Band of the C-in-C The Nore was BM G Welsh in 1912. HMS *Excellent* was the RN's School of Gunnery Training on Whale Island, a man-made island in Portsmouth Harbour. This establishment also dealt with the ceremonial training of officers and men in the Royal Navy. For these reasons, and because of the importance of its very large officers' mess, HMS *Excellent* was given its own band in 1895. In 1904 the Bandmaster, W C Windram, and the active service members of his band were absorbed into the RNSM organisation and they became an RM Band. The band was seldom drafted to sea and it retained its permanent nature until World War I.

1913 saw the Tenth Anniversary of the RNSM. In that ten year period the numbers who had passed through the School were:

11 Warrant Officers,
26 Bandmasters 1st Class
38 Bandmasters 2nd Class
112 Corporals
966 Musicians
246 Band Boy.

The Naval Bandsman's Nightmare in the Transmitting Station.

Cartoon drawn by Charles Ingle in 1917. Ingle served in RM Bands in HMS King Edward VII until she was sunk and then HMS Royal Oak at Jutland.

17

Part 2 - The Royal Naval School of Music 1914 - 1918

The war years 1914-1918 brought forth many tales of hardship, valour, and humour about musicians. Band ranks were particularly at risk on board ship because of their specialist duties. They were trained in gunfire control and were responsible for manning the Transmitting Station. This was located in the very bowels of the ship. When closed up and at Action Stations the bandsmen knew that there was little chance of escape. Why were the men of the bands chosen for this particularly dangerous task? One theory[1] is that the Bandsmen at this time were designated as Lower Quarter Ratings and this meant that, along with Chefs, Writers and others, they were to be part of the gunnery system of the ship. The logical use for these 'spare hands' would be ammunition handling but since this could have put hands and fingers in danger they were given the task of working in the Transmitting Stations.

On the 18th July the Reserve Fleet had assembled for a review at Spithead as a test mobilisation. Prince Louis of Battenberg, the First Sea Lord, countermanded the order for the dispersal of the Fleet on completion of the Review. As a result the Reserve was well prepared for mobilisation. On the 1st August 1914 Buglers were sounding the recall all over Portsmouth and Gosport. Within a matter of hours all ships from the Reserve Fleet had bands detailed to them by the staff of the RNSM.

Those who had not been allocated to ships were called the 'Ready-men'. A few days later a band of twenty-four under BM Faithfull was formed from the ready-men. There were five BdCpls (one of whom was John Allen who earlier recalled the HMS *Russell* coaling ship episode) twelve Musicians and six Band Boys[2]. This band was needed for the Royal Naval Division on the orders of the First Lord of the Admiralty, the Rt Hon Winston S Churchill who, whilst issuing instructions for the complement of the Brigade noted: "A band must be provided. The quality is not important. There must be sufficient pupils at the Naval School of Music to provide for this. The Band is to join on Saturday next". It is ironic that the first bands from the RNSM to see action were involved not at sea but on land in Belgium. BM Faithfull's band acted as a Red Cross Party at the siege of Antwerp until the town was evacuated, the band losing all its instruments in the process and narrowly avoiding capture. The Bandmaster and sixteen of his band were with Benbow Battalion of the 1st Naval Brigade when it mistakenly crossed into Holland but, being non-combatants, the band was allowed to continue to England. One of its members, Musn Alley, was captured by the Germans but escaped, managed to find civilian clothes at a Belgian farmhouse and returned to England via Flushing. The Dutch released the remaining members of the band in time for them to be back in Eastney by the end of the year.[3] A Depot for the RND had been formed at the Crystal Palace. Whilst preparing for its next task at HMS *Crystal Palace* known, for obvious reasons, as 'The Glasshouse' this band, now known as the Royal Marine Band of the Royal Naval Division, was selected to lead the Lord Mayor's Procession through London. Music was very important at Crystal Palace since it was a Training Establishment and, as such, particularly practised the Colours ceremony and Divisions. A second band was formed which became known as simply the Band of the Royal Naval Division. This was a brass band and comprised Royal Navy ratings with a few Royal Marine Musicians. It regularly led route marches and provided musical entertainment during the lunch period[4].

From there, now as part of the Drake Battalion of the Royal Naval Division, they moved to Duns in Berwickshire on the 23rd November where they lived in stables at Duns

Castle before leaving, during January, for the newly built Blandford Camp in Dorset, where they lived in huts.

On the 28th February Drake Battalion, now the 1st Battalion of the 1st Brigade of the Royal Naval Division, left Blandford for Avonmouth where they embarked in the SS *Franconia*. It would appear that instruments were not taken on board - they were certainly not taken ashore, unlike Antwerp.

Whilst the *Franconia* was making her way towards the Dardanelles the Royal Navy launched an attempt to force the Dardanelles passage. An Allied fleet of seventeen battleships and one battle cruiser entered the Straits and advanced to the start line. Five hours after the force moved off a third of the capital ships had either been sunk or put out of action by Turkish mines. The only band casualty was Musn C Lower of HMS *Inflexible*.

On the 24th April the *Franconia* was ordered at full speed to Cape Helles where the Division, including the band as first aid party and stretcher-bearers, went ashore at about 0800hrs on the 26th. Between the 26th April and the 24th December 1915, when it was recalled for Sea Service, the band members were part of the Mediterranean Expeditionary Force in the Dardanelles. Drake Battalion formed up on the beach then, in silence, marched in single file to a place on the cliffs about a mile away. It was very cold and little sleep was had. Next morning they were bombed by two Turkish planes but this was ineffective. The Turkish artillery was also shelling the position. There was no shelter from either shell or shrapnel since orders had been given not to dig-in for fear of digging up dead men. Bodies were strewn all over the cliffs. John Allen's own words best describe what it was like during that period:

28th April. At noon we set off in artillery formation for the firing line, collecting wounded on the way. Our Battalion acted as supports to the King's Own Scottish Borderers and the Border Regiment. Jack Hucknall and Major Barker killed this evening. At 9pm it was raining heavily and we all huddled together like a rugby scrum, heads to the centre to try and sleep. About 10pm we were called to go to the firing line to collect wounded. We dressed the wounds of about 8 men and carried them away, a very difficult task as there were no roads and we had to find our way through heather, gorse and brushwood to 'X' Beach where they were taken on board ship. We finished about 3am, wet through, and lay down in an old Turkish trench to sleep.

29th April. 6am. Again called to collect wounded about two miles from the beach and by the time we had found our Battalion again, it was time for breakfast at 1.30 pm. We were now about 200 yards behind the firing line and made our post on top of one of the banks of the Great Dongha (now known as Gulley Ravine) amongst shrubs and heather and trees, and each stretcher party in turn kept watch for two hours, the country being full of snipers. During the two days since leaving camp, we only had 'iron rations', but on the morning of the 30th the Borderers supplied us with food, which wasn't up to our usual ration, but thankfully received by us. After two days of heavy shelling by the Turks, the Doctor decided that it was too dangerous for us to continue on the one and only road from Krithia, so we had to make our way round the coast; at times walking on the edge of precipitous cliffs and at other times waist deep in water. When we did eventually find the so-called rest camp (stores) of the Battalion, the Quartermaster was only prepared to issue two days rations for four men, instead of 24, as he had been informed that all were killed except four

7th May. Drake Battalion left for the trenches and for the next few days the stretcher party was kept busy as there was plenty of fighting. Throughout the next two weeks there was continuous shelling.

17th May. We had fresh meat for dinner for the first time since leaving the *Franconia*, and with preserved onions and potatoes, it made a fine stew.

19th May. We went for a bathe in the Dardanelles. Quite safe, as there was an aeroplane overhead.

24th May. Whit Monday. Ought to be wet Monday, for everything wet through and the trenches thick with mud. Major Wilson shot through the head and died in half an hour. I had to fetch his body from advanced trenches, too narrow for a stretcher. Had to lift him over our heads; couldn't keep our feet for mud.

25th May. Heavy rain swamped the trenches, so plenty of gravy for those who were cooking. All the time a heavy dose of shrapnel which was well answered by our artillery. Decided now that it was much safer in the trenches than in the Rest Camp. Violent artillery duel in the evening and Maxim and rifle fire at night. Drake Battalion retired to the Rest Camp through mud two feet deep.

A composite Brigade comprising the Drake and Plymouth Battalions and the 1st Lancashire Fusiliers was formed in May 1915 and, for a short time, they served with Australians and New Zealanders brought to Helles from Anzac Cove:

10th June. Strong wind and plenty of dust and Turks artillery firing all day. Covered in dust from head to foot for three days.

13th June. Issue of fresh potatoes and onions today (first time). With fresh meat it was splendid, but flies are thick on everything now.

16th June. Heavy bombardment. Bandmaster Faithfull wounded for the second time so I have taken over his duties.

Throughout June and July the bombardment increased and by mid-July the trenches we now occupied were literally strewn with dead of both sides, Turks in great majority. We had to wear respirators in the trenches owing to the stench from dead bodies

24th July. Report that Kinsey is dead. (Wounded 14th) [Musician Bertram Kinsey, RMB/1803]

7th August. Too busy with sick to keep daily diary now. (Reached 150)

5th September. The most awful night one could imagine; shells bursting of all kinds near to us. Worst night we have had.

27th September. Telegram from Kitchener of big advance in France. At 7pm a Bugler sounded the Royal Salute, then simultaneously every gun in the Peninsula fired 21 rounds, after which all troops gave three cheers. The Turks thinking we were attacking, wasted no end of all sorts of ammunition to stop us.

20th October. I visited our machine gunners in "MacTurk Alley", where last time there was dead of both sides all around. The Chief and I were rather exposed, and were sniped at. Saw a skeleton with a bandage still round its skull.

Bitterly cold in the trenches in November and December.

16th December. Officially told we were being recalled to England. The trench where our 'Aid Post' is situated this time is the worst shrapnelled and shelled (high explosive) we have yet been in.

21st December. Rained heavily all night and we were flooded out in our dug-out. Wounded casualties every night.

22nd December. Returned to the Rest Camp through water and mud up to the waist.

24th December. Left camp for V-Beach at 8pm. On arrival there 'Asiatic Annie' said goodbye to us by dropping one very close. Lucky for us it didn't burst. French Commander arranged passage for us in one of their boats and we were all on deck to see the last of Cape Helles when we steamed away at midnight.

25th December. Arrived Mudros early on Christmas morning. After a lot of trouble managed to get nicely settled on SS *Aragon*. (HQ ship)

31st December. Left Aragon today and embarked SS *Grampian*

1st January. Steamed out of Mudros.

3rd January. Arrived Alexandria.

Whilst at Alexandria we were accommodated in tents at Mustapha Barracks while awaiting passage to England. BM Faithfull was here as Acting Quartermaster and Supply Officer of the RND Transit Camp

16th January. Left Alexandria in the SS *Manitou*

29th January. Arrived Eastney[5]

On the 31st July 1915 both John Allen and BM Faithfull were Mentioned in Despatches - "Behaved in a gallant and courageous manner in action at Cape Helles 17th May to 31st July". Three musicians from Drake Battalion (Billings, Kensey and Harper) died of wounds or disease at Gallipoli. The Royal Naval Division was to remain at Helles until the very end, the last of its units leaving on the night of the 8th/9th January 1916; only two weeks after the band were withdrawn.[6]

The men of the RM Band of the Royal Naval Division on their return from Gallipoli where they served as stretcher-bearers. Cpl John Allen seated centre. January 1916 - the men look tired and drawn after their ordeal.

1st November 1914 had brought the first heavy loss to the Band Service when the entire band of twenty-four (BM 2nd Cl Barber) died when HMS *Monmouth* was sunk at the Battle of Coronel off the coast of Chile. HMS *Good Hope*, the Flagship of Admiral Cradock, was also sunk but she was not carrying her band because she had left the Reserve Fleet Review on August 2nd before the band had gone aboard. In the same month another complete band was lost when HMS *Bulwark*, an ancient battleship moored off Sheerness, blew up. This band, led by the School's Senior Bandmaster WO E Scofield, had been the band of HMS *Excellent* at Whale Island for many years and all its members were well known in Portsmouth[7].

The band of HMS *Iron Duke*, Flagship of the Home Fleet, was detailed to provide music for the Consecration of the Naval Cemetery on Scapa during late 1914. The Home Fleet spent a great deal of time under steam, but moored, in the great natural port of Scapa during the early part of the war. Poised to respond to any threat from the German Navy this represented a stand off that meant both sides had thousands of servicemen effectively removed from other theatres of war. Two musicians serving in the band of HMS *King Edward VII* decide to edit and publish "The North Sea Times" which eventually attained a circulation of 5,000. The editor of the 'Globe and Laurel' wrote,

> Glancing through its pages it is apparent that the men of the Fleet are anything but low-spirited and down-hearted, and the paper is highly creditable to its editors. This is another instance of the Musician as a handy man.

The Band of HMS Dreadnought entertain the ships company sometime during the First World War.

Each Wednesday afternoon the Flagship's band would play on the deck of the Hospital Ship *Maine*. On Wednesday the 30th December 1915, whilst *Iron Duke's* band was performing on board the *Maine*, BM 2nd Cl Parker was conducting the band of HMS *Natal*, moored about three hundred yards away, in a programme for her Officers and guests. A huge underwater explosion was heard and HMS *Natal's* 9.2" turret was hurled into the air. All fifteen members of the band were killed.

At the RNSM Lt Lidiard reached the age of compulsory retirement but, because of the war, he was retained on the Active List. Capt C Franklin and the RNSM Band continued to give concerts throughout the year in aid of war charities and for the winter clothing and comforts fund for bands afloat. The Band of the RMA paid BM S Fairfield a compliment during a concert on South Parade Pier, Southsea when they played his overture *Colossus* which he had composed whilst serving in the ship of that name in 1912. It was reported to be

> very difficult and only possible with a first-class orchestra. In some parts it was quite masterly in tone, colour and effects and was rendered by the band in their usual artistic manner and the bold opening bars soon claimed the attention of the audience who enjoyed what proved to be a work of exceptional merit.

The official establishment (1915) of the School and its bands was 1,500 men and boys made up as follows: one Quartermaster; one Musical Director; one Sergeant-Major: one Superintending Clerk; eleven Bandmasters (WO); two Company Sergeants-Majors; thirty-two Bandmasters 1st Class; forty-seven Bandmasters 2nd Class; one hundred and four Band Corporals; one thousand two hundred and seven Musicians and ninety-three Band Boys.

The seventeen members of the band of HMS *Russell* were saved when that ship was sunk after hitting a mine off Malta then, in May 1916, the Battle of Jutland took place. The mightiest Fleet that the world had ever seen left Scapa, Cromarty and the Forth Bridge area and by midnight on May 30th was sailing across the North Sea[8]. The Fleet carried forty-seven bands - a total of almost seven hundred Musicians - almost half of the RNSM strength and about twice the total strength of the current Royal Marines Band Service. The British and German Fleets made contact in the afternoon and HMS *Lion* (Admiral Beatty's Flagship) and HMS *Princess Royal* immediately became engaged with the German battleship SMS *Lutzow*. Within an hour *Lion* had received two direct hits from *Lutzow* and, a little later, she received another, much more serious blow when 'Q' turret, manned by the RM Detachment, received a direct hit[9]. Musn J H Hoad was the only member of the band of HMS *Lion* to be killed.

The Band of HMS Indefatigable (BM2[nd]Cl G Barham) 1912. With the exception of BdCpl C Mansfield (euphonium player on left) and Musn A White, all of these men plus two others were killed at Jutland.

Meanwhile SMS *Von der Tann* scored three devastating hits on HMS *Indefatigable* in one salvo causing one of her magazines to explode. Seconds later she was hit by another salvo from the German battleship that caused her to blow up and sink[10]. All but two of her crew including BM 1st Cl Barham, BdCpl Schummacher and thirteen Musicians perished.

HMS *Queen Mary* had been firing at the SMS *Seydlitz* and inflicting a good deal of damage when she came under fire from not just *Seydlitz* but *Derfflinger* as well.

Renowned for her accurate gunnery the *Queen Mary* was making little impact upon the *Seydlitz* because of the effective German armour. Like *Indefatigable* the *Queen Mary* was unable to withstand the heavy and accurate bombardment. Five hits prefaced a massive explosion that split the ship in two. Further explosions tore her apart and she sank, taking 1,266 of her crew to their deaths. Included amongst the dead were the entire RM Band - BM 1st Cl J Taylor, BdCpls T Smith and A Wood and twelve Musicians. The battle continued during the afternoon. HM Ships *Invincible, Inflexible* and *Indomitable* were hitting the German battle cruisers but, once the range closed sufficiently, the Germans replied and *Derfflinger* and *Lutzow* concentrated their fire on Admiral Hood's Flagship, the *Invincible*. She was hit by a full salvo and the Royal Marines' 'Q' turret received a direct hit that caused the turret magazines to explode. Unlike the *Lion*, nobody was able to take action to prevent the flash from reaching the main magazines and with a shattering explosion the ship split into three and sank immediately. Only two officers and three ratings survived the sinking that took the lives of BM 1st Cl G Deacon, BdCpls Chance and Jamieson and fourteen Musicians.

Musn G Moody was on board Admiral Jellicoe's Flagship, HMS *Iron Duke*, during the Battle of Jutland. He later described his recollections of the battle as follows:

> The *Iron Duke*, having a band of 24, most of us were stationed in the 13.5" transmitting station in the bowels of the ship, four were also in the decoding office. I was stationed in the Voice Pipe Control, also in the stomach of the ship, with a seventeen year old Midshipman and a sailor boy of the same age. I was close on 20.
>
> Abaft the messdecks and close to the Bandmaster's cabin, was a watertight door with six cleats. Opening from this door was a shaft, about 4feet square which went two decks down. On the bulkhead was an iron-runged ladder which you descended to an iron grid in two sections, each section hinged. When closed the grid could be lifted from above. When open, one descended another iron runged ladder to the Voice Pipe Control. The Control was just a huge steel box approximately 20ft x 20ft x 20ft amongst the coal bunkers. The only furniture in it was six voice-pipes and a five foot form for our comfort. The Voice Pipe control would come into use should the electrical system fail in which case all orders would be sent to all turrets from the TS.
>
> On the 30th May the ship's company were in their action stations all through the day. At last we received the order to 'Secure'; so back to our mess decks to attend to our respective duties. The Band had 7 o'clock supper and then rigged up for a wardroom programme.
>
> Morning of 31st May 1916. Sunny morning and a calm sea. Same routine as yesterday. "Close all watertight doors". "Batten Down". The grid of the 'Black Hole' dropped and watertight doors secured. Having my ear to the TS voice-pipe I could hear all the 'goings-on'. Testing tubes, firing circuits, rangefinder checks being checked. We tested the TS and each turret was reported correct. We were at 'Action Stations' all through the day and night.
>
> 1st June, we received through the TS voice-pipe, "For information, Zeppelin brought down on the horizon." Shortly afterwards, "Belay last message. *Queen Mary* sunk". The bad news told us that the Fleet was in action with the German High Seas Fleet. Some time later we were informed "*Invincible* and *Indefatigable* lost" We could hear muffled heavy firing through the voice pipes then suddenly our 13.5's opened up with salvo after salvo, and we were in the thick of the battle. Ten guns firing simultaneously, the projectiles each weighing a ton. Ten tons of armour piercing metal being hurled 15 or more miles to the enemy ships. The *Iron Duke* fired 98 salvos.
>
> In the 'Black Hole' we had no communication whatever due to the fact that all was well with the electrical power being stable[11]. To the three of us the hours seemed interminable and none of us had a watch. No food, no sleep and covered in coal-dust which oozed in through the seams of the bulkheads.[12]

The bands played a large part in maintaining and raising morale, overcoming boredom and monotony as well as reducing the effects of fear and concern during the war years. They not only provided the orchestra for ships' concerts but the bandmaster usually produced the whole show. This included pantomimes at Christmas, occasional musical comedies and frequent concerts. BM A C Green achieved such fame with a series of shows that word reached the RNSM Director of Music who wrote to congratulate him. The letter included:

> Such performances do credit to this Institution and do a great deal of good. Given the same numbers our bands can compare favourably with the Divisional Marines Bands, a fact that wants to be known and this is the way to do it.

In 1917, thirty years after he had become a Band Boy in the Royal Navy, H E Lidiard was promoted Captain and appointed Assistant Superintendent, RNSM.

On the 9th January 1917 the battleship HMS *Cornwallis* was torpedoed and sunk by U32 sixty-two miles southeast of Malta. BM Weedon and his band, with the exception of Musn A E Gray who was killed, were all rescued. HMS *Queen*, a veteran of the attempted forcing of the Dardanelles had been sent to Taranto with a Battle Squadron. All were on loan to the Italian Government but gradually all, except *Queen*, withdrew to England. The ship's company, including the band were ordered to make their way back to England overland. The band left *Queen* on the 17th February, did not get a good meal until five days later in France, made contact with the British Army at Boulogne and marched into Eastney Barracks eight days after leaving *Queen* in Taranto.[13]

BM Leeder of the Gold Coast Regiment died of heart failure on January 21st. He had returned home to England in 1915 following his tour of service only to be reappointed to the same position[14].

Recruitment continued throughout the war years with many promising musicians joining as 'Hostilities Only' - although it was hoped that they would adopt the Band Service as a profession. Retired BM T Porteous was one of those who came out of retirement to be a civilian Instructor at the School of Music 1914-1918. (During this period he was co-founder of the Royal Naval Benevolent Trust).[15] The band of HMS *Queen Elizabeth* would frequently land for orchestral practice at the YMCA, Rosyth under the direction of the well-known composer and conductor, Hamilton Harty, who was on the Admiral's Staff at the time. Walking around the orchestra Hamilton Harty made the observation that "I never knew you had such individual talent in the band". Eleven well-known orchestral musicians had found their way to this band.

July 1917 brought another tragedy when HMS *Vanguard* sank following a massive internal explosion. Oil burned on the sea and hot debris falling on the island of Flotta set vegetation alight. The sea was strewn with wreckage, oil and bodies. Over eight hundred men died in this explosion including BM 1st Cl J T Vitou and the entire band.

In July 1918 HMS *Lancaster* accompanied HMS *Orbita* to South America. *Orbita* carried a British Special Mission to South America and BM T R Lowndes and the band of HMS *Lancaster* were much used for entertaining the Mission and, upon arrival in South America, gave concerts in such places as the Exhibition Hall, Lima.

September 1918 saw the arrival of HMS *Achilles* in New York. The ship's band and detachment took part in a "Britain's Day" Parade that was led by Lt John Philip Sousa and his US Marine Corps Band. Sousa's band was 150 strong and had more trombones in the front rank than the *Achilles* band had musicians! Despite that the RM Band, at the rear of the parade, included Sousa marches and were warmly congratulated on their performance.

HMS *Kent* featured in one of the very last actions of the war. Musn R H Stoner joined this ship straight from the RNSM aged 16 years and 6 months. Upon arrival in Devonport the entire crew, including the band, loaded 2,000 tons of coal and 200 tons of upper deck cargo. Within a few hours of completion the ship had been completely washed down and the band was playing for a party. With the slightest sea running the 6" gun casemates on the lower deck allowed the sea in causing the Mess Decks to be perpetually flooded. There were no bathrooms, washing was carried out in tubs and buckets and, when they reached the tropics, there was severe rationing of drinking and washing water as well as of food. It was impossible to keep music stands upright, which made practice a serious problem - especially since much time was spent in the Transmitting Station or with Fire Control duties. The *Kent* arrived in Hong Kong in time for the Armistice celebrations but she then sailed for Vladivostock. Escorted by an icebreaker she made her way further along the coast to bombard the advancing Bolsheviks. Hong Kong was then reached in time for the Peace Celebrations in May 1919 before the band and the crew were sent back to England - the *Kent* remaining in Hong Kong to be broken up.[16]

By the end of 1918 the band of HMS *Glory* had been at Murmansk for two years. The *Glory* was the first ship that Musn Williams served in and he recalled the appalling conditions of the two winters. All the crew were relieved after twelve months but the band had to remain on board. The ship was frozen in for about six months and rations, at the height of the U-boat offensive, became very short. Coaling ship took place in temperatures of - 20 degrees, the Russian Revolution began and there was an epidemic of 'Black Flu'. Early on Christmas Day 1917 BM Woodman vanished from his bed in the sick-bay. This was during the period when the ship was iced-in. He was never seen again and no trace of him was ever found.[17]

Musn J Skuse, a very talented violinist who had been in the Band of HMS *Renown* for the Royal Tour to India in 1905, was the last Musician to die during the First World War. Following the torpedoing and sinking of HMS *Britannia* by a German submarine off Cape Trafalgar on the 9th November he succumbed to his wounds in the Royal Naval Hospital, Gibraltar on the 11th November 1918 - Armistice Day.

Part 3 - The Royal Naval School of Music Between the Two World Wars

The Prince of Wales received the Royal Naval Division, which by then comprised only one Royal Marine Battalion with four Royal Naval Battalions, on Horse Guards Parade on the 6th June 1919. The men of the Division felt that having music provided by a band of the Brigade of Guards instead of a band of the RNSM was an insult to the Senior Service. Just over a month later British troops marched through Paris with the Massed RM Bands of the 2nd Battle Squadron representing the RNSM, led by Drum Major C Hamilton, at their head.

On the 24th August 1920 BM W E Faithfull, veteran of Antwerp and Gallipoli, became the first Band Boy to reach Commissioned rank when he was promoted Lieutenant and Quarter Master.

Royal Marines found themselves supporting White Russian forces after the 1914-1918 war had ended. The Russian (Black Sea) Dreadnought Volya was temporarily taken over by the Royal Navy during 1919. Here the Volya is being coaled by the crew of HMS Agamemnon at Sebastapol whilst the RM Band of the Agamemnon entertain them from the top of one the Volya's 12" gun turrets.

With the RMLI Plymouth Divisional Band accompanying the Prince of Wales to Australia in HMS *Renown* the ship's band was supplemented by Musicians from the RNSM to become a band of thirty-two and sent as duty band to Plymouth Division in their stead. Their services were much appreciated, especially the evening performances on the parade.

In December 1920 Bandmasters were shown in the Navy List as Warrant Officers, as were Royal Marine Gunners, Sergeants-Major, Superintending Clerks and Schoolmasters.[1] The Warrant Officer wore no badge of rank. Warrant rank had been introduced in the Royal Marines in 1881 when thirty-one men received Warrants. Included in this number were four Royal Marine Divisional Bandmasters (Winterbottom, Kappey, Kreyer and Froehnert). In 1904 Warrants were held by the Musical Director and the Bandmaster of the RNSM (Franklin and Lidiard). The Royal Navy had had Warrant Officers since the seventeenth century and because of the close link between the RN and the RNSM it was necessary to ensure parity between Bandmasters serving at sea and their equivalent Royal Navy ranks. In 1916 the rank of Warrant Officer Class II (WO2) was introduced but Bandmasters were always Warrant Officer Class I (WOI). In 1920 it was promulgated that Warrant Officers could be promoted to Commissioned Officers from Warrant Rank under conditions applicable to Naval Warrant Officers except that the condition relating to sea-time would be waived in the case of Sergeants-Major, Superintending Clerks, and Bandmasters. The latter would be called Commissioned Bandmasters[2] and to indicate the rank they wore a single star on their lower arm. After becoming 'a Commissioned Officer from Warrant Rank' - the title Commissioned Warrant Officer having been abolished - their next promotion would be to Lieutenant (Director of Music) or Lieutenant (Quartermaster) depending upon the appointment that they were given. If made Lt(QM) they would remain in the Band Service but in a non-musical capacity - usually as a Company Commander.[3]

Qualifications for attaining the rank of Corporal in the RNSM were laid down. The successful candidate would need to have a minimum of six months' sea service; 2nd Class education certificate; "Very Good" character on his reports; "Very Good" in working of ship's fire control instruments and a certificate for passing the prescribed examination of Band Corporal. At the same time the requirements for Bandmaster 1st and 2nd Class were six months' minimum sea service as confirmed NCO; 2nd Class education certificate; 1st Class Certificate in First Aid; "Very Good" in working of ship's fire control instruments and a certificate having passed prescribed the examination for Bandmaster.

Every member of the RNSM donated one day's pay towards a Memorial to comrades who had died in the 1914-1918 War. The Memorial to the one hundred and forty-three Warrant Officers, Non-Commissioned Officers and men of the Royal Marine Band Service who lost their lives during World War I comprised a set of five silver side drums and a wooden bass drum.The Roll of Honour, also paid for by the men of the RNSM, comprises four massive oak panels richly decorated with the Naval crown surmounted by the Admiralty coronet with carved laurel decorations and a scroll with the carved motto "*Sans peur et sans reproche*". It was originally erected above the drums in the Concert Hall at Eastney Barracks. These drums were dedicated and presented at a parade held on the 5th March 1921 when some four hundred men of the School of Music, under Lt C Maton were present.

During 1921 the practice of having Section Leaders for Band Boys was introduced. They were selected by the Commandant and had to have twelve months' service; a 2nd Class Certificate of Education; 'Very Good' at Infantry Drill, Physical Training and Fire Control as well as having passed their swimming test. Their duties were to cultivate 'Esprit de Corps' and good comradeship amongst Band Boys, set a good example and assist the Non-Commissioned Officers. Privileges awarded to these Section Leaders were a permanent 2130hrs pass, to be excused Barrack Room duties other than supervision, to wear a Section Leader's Badge[4], to have a special lobby set aside as a sitting and reading room and accelerated promotion to Corporal.

In 1920 the ranks of Bandmaster 1st Class and Bandmaster 2nd Class were abolished and the ranks of Band Colour Sergeant (BdCSgt) and Band Sergeant (BdSgt) were to be used in their place[5]. During 1921 this was rescinded and the old ranks of Bandmaster 1st Class and Bandmaster 2nd Class were reinstated[6].

HMS *Ramillies* (BM II F Higgins) was sent to the Dardanelles and the Bosphorous in 1921. At this time Turkey was persecuting the Greeks and the Armenians in the Balkans and causing international tension. *Ramillies* dropped anchor off Constantinople and Great Britain gave Turkey a forty-eight hour ultimatum that must have been effective since the ship left within a few days.

At an RNSM Welfare Committee meeting in 1919 members were unanimous in their desire to sever their connections with the Royal Marines. A new uniform was seen as a good way of announcing this and, as the Royal Marines were quite indifferent, the Clothing Committee recommended the change[7]. As a result the RNSM band formed for HMS *Renown* for the Royal Tour in 1921 (Lt Fairfield and BM Hamilton) was the first to wear the new uniform known as the 'Garter Blue Band Service Ceremonial Uniform' which had a light blue band replacing the scarlet band around the cap; a pale blue collar on the tunic; a girdle with pale blue edging and trousers with a pale blue welt. On the band's return the Superintendent of the RNSM inspected the uniform and in a report to the Colonel Commandant of the RMA stated that the dye had been of a very poor quality with the result that variable fading had resulted in four different shades of pale blue on each uniform. At that time only Mr Fairfield and one musician wanted to return to the uniform with scarlet facings, the rest of the band preferring the pale blue. The AGRM's report had also stated that, by mid July 1922, "Feeling had quite changed and the Band Service is anxious to retain its connection with the Corps and fears that the new uniform may be regarded as a mark of severance". He also made the point that 400 of the 800 uniforms in stock had been issued and some Officers had equipped themselves with new uniforms. In addition, the School had over a thousand items of uniform with the pale blue facings ready for issue. Within a couple of days the First Sea Lord and the First Lord of the Admiralty had agreed that the 'Naval Band' should revert to red facings and that the King had given his approval. This left the tailors with the large task of removing pale blue facings and replacing them with scarlet. The recently purchased Drum Majors' sash with blue cloth would also have to be altered. An RMO was issued on the 21st August 1922[8] stating that uniform facings would be scarlet and that all pale blue faced uniforms should be returned at the earliest opportunity. Part two of the RMRO stated that a return would be made to the use of buff leather waist-belts for ceremonial purposes[9].

During 1922 the Geddes reductions caused some members of the Band Service to leave. Over five hundred Lieutenants left the Royal Navy and the Captains' list was cut by a third. Many others, including men of the Band Service, decided to leave rather than face the threat of further cuts -which did occur in 1926 and 1929.

In 1924 the Band from the RNSM under BMs A C Green and F G Stagg appeared at the Royal Tournament. Stagg was the Drum Major. The same RNSM Band, suitably augmented, also played at the British Empire Exhibition, Wembley, as a result of which it received further praise and thanks. Also in 1924, the march *"Braganza"*[10] was presented to HMS *Excellent* the Royal Navy School of Gunnery on Whale Island. This was the Regimental March of the Queen's Royal Regiment (West Surrey)[11]. The RNSM Band featured with the Divisional Bands from Chatham, Portsmouth, Plymouth and the Depot RM at the Wembley Tattoo in 1924. They were under the direction of Lt J C J Hoby, the Senior Director of Music, RM. This appearance was repeated the following year although on that occasion they were massed with the Chatham Division Band only[12]. At home in Portsmouth the RNSM had opportunities to demonstrate their high standards. They were massed with the Portsmouth Divisional Band and the bands of HMS *Excellent* and the RN Barracks under Lt R P O'Donnell for the King's Birthday Review. They returned to Southsea Common to play for the unveiling of the War Memorial by HRH the Duke of York on October 15th. An innovation was the performance by the RNSM Band Boys' Choir. 1924 ended with the School having 63 Band Corporals and 673 Musicians.

1925 saw the achievement, albeit inadvertent, of a milestone in military music. Whilst in Montreal BM J Allen received an invitation to broadcast on CNRM (Canadian National Railways Montreal) broadcasting station on the 3rd September 1925. Whilst announced as the Royal Marine Band of HMS *Calcutta* it was to perform as an orchestra.

Two or three days after the broadcast a messenger arrived on board HMS *Calcutta* with a package addressed to "Bandmaster Allen, HMS *Calcutta*, Montreal Harbour". The covering letter said:

> In the course of some experimental work the other night, we happened to make some recordings of two of the numbers broadcasted by you from Station CNRM, and thinking that you would like copies of them, we have pleasure in handing you herewith, with our compliments, a copy of each selection.
> Signed H Berliner.

The notepaper was headed "The Compo Company Limited. Canada's Largest Record Manufacturer." Inside the package was a recording of "*Cavalleria Rusticana*" and of "*Bacchus*".[13]

Discussions took place between the RNSM and the Royal Academy of Music in 1925 that appear to have culminated in the adoption of the examination for the Royal Academy Certificate and the Service award that has developed into the LRAM Certificate and the Director of Music qualification.[14]

Whilst the Depot Band was on board HMS *Repulse* for the 1925 Royal Tour of South Africa a duty band, under BM H J T Taylor, was sent from the RNSM to the Depot, Deal.

During the 1920's the band of the RNSM was being mentioned with increasing frequency in England whilst all over the world ships' bands were giving concerts and broadcasts. The Concert Band of the RNSM comprised musicians waiting for ships plus a few of the older boys. To earn such a reputation with a band that had little stability or continuity was testament to the system, to the staff and to the quality of the musicians. During 1926 they were asked to entertain the Lords Commissioners of the Admiralty aboard the Admiralty Yacht 'Enchantress'. Such was the reputation of the School that the Editor of the 'Globe and Laurel' requested that the RNSM "should blow its own trumpets a little louder within the pages of the journal".[15]

1926 also saw the introduction of the RNSM Annual Prize-giving. It was reported that provision had been made for an increase of about three hundred on the establishment of the School that year[16].

Until 1926 the limits to Admiralty expenditure for supplying music for ceremonial bands were included in KR&AI. In that year the KR Committee decided that the limits of value of music supplied should be a matter for Admiralty Fleet Orders (AFO).

1927 was a particularly eventful and busy year for the RNSM with its bands scattered throughout the world. The 12th Bn Royal Marines, a composite Battalion with elements of all three Divisions, departed from Portsmouth in support of the threatened International Legation in Shanghai. They were marched from Eastney to the Dockyard by the Portsmouth Divisional Band and a band from the RNSM, under BM J W Relph, which was placed in the centre of the Battalion. They were met at the top of the High Street by the Bluejacket (Royal Navy Volunteer) Band of C-in-C HMS *Victory*, BM WO T Hawkins, and embarked to the sounds of the massed bands. They sailed to the sounds of the Band of the Portsmouth Division , the Drums and Fifes of the Division and the Band of C-in-C HMS *Victory* all under the direction of Capt. R P O'Donnell. Upon arrival in Shanghai the band of HMS *Hawkins* playing *A Life on the Ocean Wave* greeted them and, later, the 12th Bn took part in the King's Birthday Parade in Hong Kong being led by the massed bands of HMS *Frobisher* and HMS *Hermes* under BM I H Hoyte.

In the same year the Band of the RNSM were given what was believed to be a historically unique invitation. They were asked, as a Service Band, to provide an orchestra for the ceremony of the enthronement of the Bishop of Portsmouth and, the following day, a military band for the Ecclesiastical Procession. BM Papworth and the band received the thanks of the Diocesan Committee who said, "The band played extremely well and just the right kind of music".

During the 1920s new silver instruments were being procured and the bass drum was emblazoned. All made the RNSM Band sound and look much better, although the quality of the Admiralty supplied instruments was always poorer than those used by the Divisional bands. It was announced that qualification upon the piano would become a prerequisite for promotion to Warrant Rank and all boys were urged to commence studies of the instrument.

Standardisation of musical salutes was being considered at this time and the RNSM were asked to make suggestions. The Italian march *Norma* had been used as the Salute for Flag Officers other than Cs-in-C and for Governors but it was felt necessary to change this for something British in origin and more stirring in character. The RNSM were asked to be prepared to play all suggestions for a combined RN and RM Committee to judge. This took place on the 9th June 1926 and the unanimous decision, later confirmed in an AFO, was for *Iolanthe* to be adopted as the General Salute for Flag Officers not entitled to *Rule Britannia*, and for *Garb of Auld Gaul* to be adopted as the General Salute for Governors, High Commissioners, British General Officers and Air Officers; Foreign Officers and Officials. The musical arrangement of *Iolanthe* was made by Lt Fairfield.

RM Band of HMS Hawkins (BM 1st Class S A Howse) leads the 12th RM Battalion along Nathan Road through Shanghai in February 1927.

The major event of 1927 occurred when HMS *Renown* took the Duke and Duchess of York to Australia. A band of thirty-five with BM Martyr as Drum Major, plus sixteen Buglers from Plymouth Division with Sgt Douglas as Bugle Major were aboard. Temp Lt A Pragnell was in command of band and bugles. Eight Silver Bugles, two from each Division and two from the Depot were taken[17]. This was the first time that they had been used afloat and they were kept in a glass cabinet on the aft deck when not required for duties in conjunction with the Guard of Honour. Four buglers would be on watch at all times and bugle calls were played to great effect. One bugler was forward, two amidships and the fourth was on the Quarter Deck. The twelve buglers not on watch sounded *Divisions*, *Evening Quarters*, *Sunset* and some other calls from a platform halfway up the aft funnel. This enabled them to be heard not only throughout the ship but also over the surrounding area when in port. The Drum and Fife Band had to Beat Retreat on the Quarter Deck when in harbour, the band played from Sunset minus ten minutes to Sunset minus two minutes when the massed buglers sounded the *Alert*. A relief of sentries (six men) fired a salvo on the forebridge before the Massed Buglers sounded Sunset accompanied by ruffles of drums followed by the *Carry On*. The Drum and Fife band quickly became very popular with the ship's company and would often perform on the forecastle in the early part of the First Watch. Whilst in New Zealand the Officers gave an 'At Home' to five hundred of Auckland's citizens. The Orchestra played from 3.30pm to 4.15pm when the Drum and Fife Band gave a display on the jetty. Following this the Pipers[18] played from 4.45pm until 5pm. The Jazz band then entertained until the end of the 'At Home'. The Drum and Fife Band attracted a great deal of attention since they were rarely seen on a Foreign Station. This band of sixteen was drawn from the ranks of the Detachment having been especially selected for this purpose. The entry to Sydney was a very complex operation, especially for the Guard and Band. On the day of entering harbour lower deck was cleared at 08.50 am by which time the band had fallen in on the Quarter Deck. The band commenced the musical programme, arrangements having been made so that the band and the Pipers who were on 'B' turret did not play simultaneously. The programme included band and bugles combined for the two bugle marches *Marching Through Georgia* and *Sambre et Meuse*. These two pieces impressed both the crowd and the crew since they were rarely heard on board a man-of-war. An entry in a RM report gives an interesting insight into the way that bands were employed when visiting foreign ports.

> Considerable demands have been made in Sydney for the services of *Renown's* Band. The principle adopted is that a proportion of such demands should be met without charge as a return for the considerable hospitality offered to Officers and Men of *Renown*. Moreover it is felt that it is in the interest of the Royal Marines that the people should hear our Band. The condition for the loan of the Band is that no private person or company should be in the position to benefit financially. The occasions are therefore limited to Government or Charitable ventures. On other occasions a fee is demanded at the local union rates.[19]

One of the Band's principal duties was, with fourteen buglers, to lead a parade of 25,000 ex-servicemen through Melbourne on Anzac Day. The band was followed by part of the Ship's Company and the RM Detachment. Forty-two other bands were in this parade and His Royal Highness took the Salute. It was estimated that 800,000 people watched this parade. Whilst in Melbourne the full military band made five broadcasts. From Australia the Royal Tour progressed via the East Coast of Africa to Mauritius.

As they passed through the Suez Canal troops in the area were paraded as *Renown's* Ship's Company fell in by Divisions with the band playing on the quarterdeck. In Gibraltar the Duke and Duchess gave a dinner party at which the Band of the RNSM provided music. As soon as the dinner was completed the RNSM band ceased playing and the massed bands of the Royal Artillery and the East Surrey Regiment who were in a large tug alongside continued the music. Upon their return to Portsmouth the Band played as the Royal Party left on the Royal Train. Instead of the usual *Auld Lang Syne* they played *Kai Towarie - The Maori Farewell* and then returned to Eastney Barracks[20].

The band from the RN Barracks Portsmouth was sent, with a CplBug and three buglers from Portsmouth Division, to join HMS *Champion* a 3,750 ton Portsmouth based cruiser for passage to Russia during August 1928. The ship's task was to recover the bodies of thirty-eight British crewmen of the submarine L55 lost in 1919 and recently recovered by the Bolshevists. The Guard, Band and Buglers paraded as the coffins were hoisted on board. At 4.30pm HMS *Champion* sailed with the band playing Chopin's *Funeral March* after which the buglers sounded *Last Post*. Four H Class submarines met her as she reached the Nab Tower off Portsmouth and they escorted her into Portsmouth Harbour. Band and buglers were on the aft superstructure. Sentries remained by the coffins until after sunset when the buglers again sounded Last Post.

A similar duty befell the band of HMS *Cumberland* when the hero of Zeebrugge, Major Edward Bamford VC DSO RM, died whilst on board HMS *Cumberland* as the ship approached Shanghai. Six men of the RM Detachment carried his body, draped in the Union flag, on their shoulders from HMS *Cumberland* to a tug alongside. The ship's band, under BM H Kerslake, played Chopin's *Funeral March* and the Guard of Honour remained at the present arms until the tug passed out of sight on its way to Shanghai.

A rather unsavoury event spilled from the first month of 1928 through to April tarnishing the image and the reputation of the Royal Navy. Unfortunately the catalyst was an unsuspecting Royal Marine Bandmaster, Percy Barnacle. The ship was HMS *Royal Oak* and she was the Flagship of the Mediterranean Fleet. At the time of the incident she, and the rest of the Fleet were in Malta. BM Barnacle was conducting his band in some American dance numbers during a ship's dance when Admiral Collard returned to the ship. He was not at all impressed by the lack of dancers, or the playing, and advanced upon the Bandmaster with Commander Daniel, the ship's Executive Officer at his side. Having called the Bandmaster to him in a most unmilitary fashion the Admiral told him that the music was not up to Flagship Band standard and that he had "never heard such a dirge in his life". He passed the opinion that everyone was complaining and that he would have the Bandmaster sent home. As he turned away the Admiral was heard to say, "I won't have a bugger like that in my ship". Next morning BM Barnacle spoke to the Chaplain and told him that he wanted to resign and Maj Attwood, Officer Commanding Royal Marines (OCRM) in HMS *Iron Duke* registered a complaint to the ship's Captain about the "insult to the Corps". The episode gradually settled down but further similar incidents involving ships officers raised the matter once again and a series of inquiries and courts martial saw the guilty parties punished. BM Barnacle, probably as a result of his orphanage upbringing and his brush with death when he was trapped in the transmitting station of the torpedoed HMS *Britannia* during the Great War, found it very difficult to come to terms with the incident and returned to civilian life three years later. [21]

In 1928 two ships, HMAS *Australia* and HMAS *Canberra*, were launched. These were to be the pride of the Royal Australian Navy (RAN) and the RNSM was given the task of training the two bands each of one Bandmaster and fourteen musicians. This situation had also occurred in 1913. The RNSM can be credited with helping to set up the Royal Australian Band Service, especially since a retired Bandmaster, E P Snook, helped to set up the shore-based Musicians at Flinders Naval Depot (now HMAS *Cerberus*). This position was filled by a succession of Royal Marines Band personnel, some retired, and others on loan.

On a warship 'X' turret, which is one of the after turrets, contains the guns that are normally manned by the Royal Marine Detachment. In March of 1929 HMS *Devonshire* re-commissioned and, after working up exercises, the ship sailed to join the Mediterranean Fleet at Malta, arriving there in July. With the rest of the 1st Cruiser Squadron the Devonshire reached the Aegean where the Squadron was to take part in gunnery exercises. Her first salvo was fired at about 10 o'clock. This was accompanied by a violent explosion and a sheet of flame from 'X' turret. The OCRM and two of his detachment were killed outright and a further twelve died either on board *Devonshire* or the hospital ship *Maine*.

Sergeant Snell was missing, presumably blown overboard. All members of the Band (2ndClBM P D Evans) were in the transmitting station. Immediately following the explosion the band was involved in removing the bodies in blankets from the turret to be prepared for burial. The bands of HMS *London* and HMS *Royal Oak* together with the buglers of the Squadron were massed to lead the cortege, which included two hundred men from the Squadron, on the two and a half mile journey to the cemetery at Volo. A Memorial Service was held at sea at the scene of the accident.

A sister ship to the *Devonshire* was HMS *Shropshire* which was commissioned in Chatham in September 1929. The newly commissioned ship's band marched the crew to the ship for the first time by playing the Regimental March of the 2nd Bn, The King's Shropshire Light Infantry, *The Daughter of the Regiment*, which had been presented to the ship by the Battalion's Commanding Officer. A few days later the Shropshire Society went aboard the ship and sang *All Friends Around the Wrekin*[22] accompanied by the RM Band. This was the county's adopted song and was originally set to music by Sir Edward Elgar. Later Sir Edward German, a native of Shropshire, wrote to congratulate the bandmaster on his march and expressed the hope that "…it would be adopted by the ship".

Portsmouth Guildhall on the 16th November 1929 was the scene of the last of a series of RNSM concerts. There was a symphony orchestra of 80 performers and a full military band of 60 performers. All were drawn from the RNSM, the C-in-C's Band, the RN Barracks Band and from HM Ships *Excellent* and *St Vincent*. In addition the RNSM supplied a choir of two hundred Band Boys! Lt S Fairfield and Lt A Pragnell were the conductors.

The Drum and Fife Band of HMS Cornwall play alongside the cruiser probably on the jetty at Wei-Hai-Wei. Note that of the five Royal Marine fifers two are the ship's Buglers whilst the others are probably volunteers from the ship's RM Detachment. It is also worthy of note that some of the seamen carry a bugle as well as the fife whilst one man carries only a bugle.

In 1930 the centenary celebrations of HMS *Excellent*, the Royal Navy Gunnery School at Whale Island, Portsmouth, took place. They began at 9.30pm with a traditional Beating Retreat. A guard from the Queen's Royal Regiment entered and marched to the flagstaff. The buglers of the Royal Marines and the Queen's Regiment sounded the Retreat Call and the Colours were lowered. The Seaman's Band of the RN Barracks, Portsmouth and the Massed Drums of the Royal Marines and the Queen's Royal Regiment then led the guards off parade. The Massed RM Bands of HMS *Excellent*, HMS *Victory*, HMS *Iron Duke*, the RNSM and the 2nd Bn The Queen's Royal Regiment marched into the arena playing George Miller's arrangement of *Marching Through Georgia*. This was followed by Tosselli's *Serenata*, Edward German's Selections from *Merrie England*, both being played at the halt. The bands stepped off to *Braganza* the Regimental march of the Queen's, the using of which is an honour bestowed upon HMS *Excellent* by the Queen's. This was followed by the Troop to *Cavalry Brigade* and the march off in quicktime to *Braganza* again.

The British base at Wei-Hai-Wei was returned to the Chinese with all due ceremony on the 1st October 1930. At the pier a Seaman's Guard of twenty-five and a guard of the same size found from the Argyll and Sutherland Highlanders (Princess Louises') were paraded with the band from HMS *Cumberland* under BM C R M Robinson. Meanwhile, for the Ceremony of Rendition at Government House, twenty seamen, twenty Royal Marines and twenty men from the Argyll and Sutherland Highlanders were on parade with the band of HMS *Kent* under BM (WO) Papworth.

It was announced in early 1930 that the Royal Naval School of Music would move from Eastney to Deal where there would be more room and better facilities.

On the 1st October 1930 at 9am the men of the RNSM paraded at Eastney Barracks. Following an inspection the Royal Marines Portsmouth Division Band and Bugles marched the parade out of the Barracks. Royal Marines lined the drive and the guard turned out. As the parade made its way towards Fratton Station the Divisional Band played *Old Comrades*. At the head of the parade, alongside Capt Faithfull, marched Maj H E Lidiard. Twenty-seven years earlier he led the first band into the new RNSM and now he led the last band out of it. The Royal Naval School of Music at Eastney had closed, having achieved what it had been established to do. The standard of music in the Royal Navy had been raised to that of the Royal Marines; it had provided bands to the ships of the Royal Navy that enhanced the reputation of the service and the country all over the world, and it also provided men who had earned the respect of their comrades in both peace and in war. The loss of the School from the Portsmouth area undoubtedly left a musical void and it was very fortunate for the local population that the young Lt Dunn and the Portsmouth Divisional Band were able to increase their local engagements to compensate.

Upon arrival at Deal they were met by the Drum and Fife Band of the Depot, Deal, under Drum Major W J Small. (The Depot Band, under Lt Ricketts, had been disbanded a few months earlier). The transfer of the RNSM meant that the Chief Schoolmaster and his staff at the Depot RM had to take on the training of Boy Buglers and Boy Musicians in addition to Royal Marine Recruits[23].

A band from the RNSM appeared at the 1931 Royal Tournament in support of a pike drill display team from the RM, Deal, and between the 4th and the 8th August the Depot Annual Tattoo took place. As the Portsmouth Divisional Band was aboard the Royal Yacht, the band for Portsmouth Navy Days was found from HMS *Nelson*, HMS *Warspite* and shore establishments in the area. Twelve Buglers plus Drum Major J Dacombe of the

Guard and Band on HMS Rodney (BM 2ⁿᵈ Class V C Hardy) 1932. Note the rear rank of Buglers.

Portsmouth Division were also used. Those bands serving afloat continued to represent the Royal Navy and to entertain their colleagues and the public generally.

In 1932 the first AFO relating to music costs was issued. Discussion between the RNSM, the Admiralty and the Treasury leading to the issue of the AFO was both meticulous and very investigative. In that year the number of RN ships that were allowed bands was forty-one. Included in this forty-one were the following twenty-two ships that were to re-commission during the 1932 financial year[24].

Aircraft Carriers:	*Courageous* (Flagship), *Glorious, Hermes, Eagle.*
Battleships:	*Queen Elizabeth* (Flagship), *Nelson, Royal Oak, Rodney, Royal Sovereign.*
Cruisers:	*Hawkins* (Flagship), *Berwick, Cumberland, Norfolk, Frobisher, Shropshire, York, Delhi* (Flagship), *Despatch* (Flagship), *Leander,* Dragon,* Dauntless,* Danae.*[25]

The twenty ships that, in 1932, were already at sea and carrying a band were:

Battleships:	*Resolution, Revenge, Warspite, Malaya, Valiant.*
Battle Cruisers:	*Hood, Renown.*
Aircraft Carrier:	*Furious.*
Cruisers:	*Dorsetshire, London, Devonshire, Sussex, Kent, Cornwall, Suffolk, Exeter, Enterprise, Curacoa, Cardiff* and *Durban.*

Other ships that were entitled to bands but were not carrying them because they were undergoing refit or being placed in Reserve included the battleships *Barham, Ramillies* and *Repulse* (all in Reserve) and *Argus* (aircraft-carrier), *Effingham* and *Emerald* (both cruisers).

The wrangling over the cost of music for these ships continued for over six months and again involved not only the RNSM but also the Admiralty and the Treasury. Eventually, all parties involved managed to agree the number of ships requiring music and the way in which distribution and accounting were carried out. In 1933, it was proposed that Massed Bands music should be approved for distribution to the Home and Mediterranean Fleets and the China Station.

Another milestone in Royal Marine Band history occurred in 1932. The massed bands of the Mediterranean Fleet under the Fleet Bandmaster A C Green were due to perform on the Palace Square, Valetta in Malta. The distant beat of drum heralded the approach of the Royal Marines. One hundred and fifty men made up the band that was led by two ranks of drums. They marched and counter marched in both quick and slow time before halting for Sunset. This was the centrepiece of the display and, for the first time, was played not just by massed buglers but also by band and buglers (an arrangement by A C Green) as the flag was lowered from the Palace mast. This has become the acknowledged manner in which the Sunset call is presented by the Royal Marines during this ceremony. As they marched off the band played the very popular bugle march *Marching Through Georgia*.

Capt A C Green later summarised the background to his version of Sunset

Sunset… an original composition by A C Green with an introduction and two fanfares: a military band accompaniment to the Bugle call. First performance 7th December 1932, Palace Square, Malta, by the Massed Bands and Bugles of the Mediterranean Fleet. It was composed aboard HMS *Queen Elizabeth* in response to the late Admiral Sir M Wordsworth Fisher's expressed desire for a 'spectacular show that was different'. The date was also noteworthy for being the first time that the Massed Bands and Bugles of the Royal Marines performed the ceremony of Beating Retreat as we know it today. The ceremony was performed many times during the years 1932-1935 by the massed bands of the Fleet in the Mediterranean countries and at Gibraltar. It was first performed at Deal in 1938, by one hundred Band Boys of the RNSM. As far as I can recall, (going back to 1904) the custom was carried out by Bugles, fifes and drums only. Massed Bands took part in Torchlight Tattoos which consisted primarily of gymnastic displays etc., and Figure Marching by Massed Bands.[26]

In January 1933 the massed bands of the Mediterranean Fleet gave a symphony concert at the Royal Opera House, Malta. The eight bands that took part gave a well-balanced orchestral programme in spite of very few rehearsals and other difficulties. A few months later, again on Malta, the Massed Bands and Drums paraded for the First Lord of the Admiralty and Admiral Sir William Fisher. They trooped to the tune of *Russian Parade March* which became better known as the *Preobrajensky March*[27].

At the 4th Balkan Olympic Games in Athens the massed bands of HM Ships *Queen Elizabeth, Royal Sovereign* and *Glorious* entertained a crowd of 90,000. They stepped off and performed a comprehensive marching display that was much appreciated by the massive crowd. At this time the Royal Navy still maintained its position as the most powerful navy afloat. This was due not merely to the number of vessels that were distributed throughout the world but also to the amount of time spent exercising and training. Whilst the bands of the Mediterranean Fleet were performing so nobly at venues such as Naples and Malta they were also spending much time at sea practising their skills in the Transmitting Stations. Technology was gradually developing to match the progress in gunnery techniques and the commissioning system demanded that the teamwork necessary to achieve efficiency should be constantly honed.

The Massed Bands of the Mediterranean Fleet Beat Retreat on the Marsa, Malta c1932/33.

HMS *York* (BM J H Boyes) was part of the West Indies Fleet in 1934, a commission that was notable for the large distances travelled and the amount of work that the band did. Whilst in Bermuda on this commission the band received the new instruments. The lower pitch pleased the woodwind and bass players but the intonation of the strings suffered until the musicians became familiar with the pitch.

Back at Deal the RNSM continued with the daily toil of clothing parades, coaling fatigues, bed filling, gym at 5.30 on a winter's morning, lighting the fires in the stone gymnasium in South Barracks and what seemed like a never-ending stream of kit and marching order parades. All this was in addition to the musical training. Despite having to endure all of this there was an occasional feeling of loss when the time came to move on to a band. There was a fierce pride in the standards attained and in being an 'RMB'.

1935 was Silver Jubilee Year and RM Bands were involved in celebrations throughout the world. HMS *Sussex* was in Japan with the Duke of Gloucester whilst HMS *Neptune's* band, augmented with six musicians from the RNSM and with two buglers from HMS *Hood*, was with the Prince of Wales in Cardiff. They led the column from the station to the City Hall where a Royal Guard formed up with the Band to receive His Royal Highness. On the 5th July the Prince of Wales visited the Depot and toured the RNSM. He took the salute at the march-past that was led by the Boys' Band. HMS *Devonshire* was in Port Said and, on the 6th October, the King of Egypt's son, Prince Farouk, came on board. As the Devonshire left harbour all ships were dressed overall and paraded Guards and Bands in the Prince's honour. The band of HMS *Kent* (BM WO G L Read) massed with the band of the Royal Inniskilling Fusiliers in Shanghai. The band was much appreciated - especially as they marched back through Shanghai at one o'clock in the morning! HMS *Suffolk* was in Kobe, Japan. HMS *Norfolk* was at Mauritius and HMS *Carlisle* at Capetown. The Massed Bands of the Mediterranean Fleet were joined by the bands of the Royal Artillery (Malta), the 1st Bn The Duke of Wellington's Regiment and the 2nd Bn The Rifle Brigade (Prince Consort's Own) to perform on Palace Square, Malta. Under the leadership of Cd BM A C Green each of the Bandmasters had the opportunity to conduct a part of the programme.

In Portsmouth, for the King's Birthday Parade, the various bands of Portsmouth Port and Garrison massed with the Portsmouth Divisional Band. The C-in-C's band and the bands of HMS *Victory*, HMS *Excellent*, the Royal Artillery (Portsmouth) Band, the 1st Bn

The York and Lancaster Regiment and the 1st Bn The Rifle Brigade (Prince Consort's Own) were under Lt F V Dunn, Director of Music of the Portsmouth Divisional Band.

The Massed Bands of the West Indies Fleet, including HMS York, with RN and RM Detachments march through Hamilton, Bermuda. King's Birthday Review 3rd June 1934.

The First Lord of the Admiralty visited the RNSM in 1935 and saw the Boys' Band carry out a ceremonial troop as well as seeing them under musical instruction. Cd BM A C Green was promoted to Lieutenant and appointed Assistant Musical Director. The duties of the Assistant Musical Director were quite demanding as Capt Green's note reveals:

1) Generally assists the Musical Director in his duties and acts in his stead in his absence.
2) Is responsible to the Musical Director for:
a) Supervising the musical training of all boys.
b) Instructing classes for promotion, [for] Musical Instructor and [for] LRAM[28] (as arranged by the Musical Director)
c) Supervising the training of draft bands.
d) Correcting written work of Theory Classes.
3) Correct Test Papers received from HM Ships
(The number of Band Boys at the School was three hundred and forty at this time.)

Compared to the events of the Silver Jubilee Year, 1936 was much quieter. It was also tinged with foreboding as Mussolini and Hitler began to flex their muscles. In particular Italy had expanded into North Africa and the Red Sea region and had just conquered Abyssinia. In Alexandria the Massed Bands of the Mediterranean Fleet under BM Upsell played for the 2nd Bn Grenadier Guards Trooping the Colour ceremony. With only half-an-hour to rehearse, the Bandmaster and the Grenadiers' Sergeant Major had to resort to 'drilling' pint pots and bottles on the billiard table in Aboukir Barracks in order to prepare.

1936 did have one notable, and peaceful, landmark. The combined bands of Portsmouth Command under BM G C Keen made two commercial recordings on the Columbia label. The first recording was called *Nautical Moments* arranged by Winter, with Part I on one side and Part 2 on the other. The second recording had *Sea Songs Medley Number 3* arranged by Vaughan Williams on one side and *Ship Ahoy March* by Mackenzie on the other.

1937 was Coronation Year. Not only was the Chatham Divisional Band (augmented by the Portsmouth Division) in the parade but a RNSM Band, Nore Command Band supplemented from the RNSM at Deal, were on the route at the Scottish Office in Whitehall. This band was quartered at Olympia and, because of a strike by bus drivers, had to march to the Scottish Office and back. The RNSM Band was selected to play at the Royal Luncheon for the King and Queen at the Guildhall, London a week later. Once again Royal Marine ships' bands were at the forefront of celebrations throughout the world. In Capetown the RN and RM Battalion consisted of two RN companies from *Amphion, Milford, Penzance* and *Rochester* and the RM Detachment from *Amphion*. On the Atlantic and West Indies Station the RM Band of HMS *Apollo* combined with the Drums and Fifes of the Sherwood Foresters (Notts and Derby Regt) and the Jamaica Military Band on Coronation Day. In Nassau HMS *Exeter's* band formed up to lead a parade when torrential rain occurred. After fifteen minutes the parade took place and was as successful as waterlogged instruments and flabby drum-skins would allow. In Shanghai a Naval and Military Tattoo was held on the Race Course to mark the event. For the finale the band of HMS *Cumberland* (BM WO Compton) massed with the 2nd Bn The Loyal Regiment (North Lancashire) whilst a US Marine Corps Band played echo parts "off".

A RN Detachment leads an Army Bugle Band and the massed bands of HMS Arethusa and HMS Despatch at the head of the funeral cortege for the thirty-one German sailors who died on board the Deutschland. The second picture shows the coffins covered with the German Naval flag and the RN pallbearers.

The Spanish Civil War was being fought and ships of the Home and Mediterranean Fleets were embarking refugees from such places as Valencia and Barcelona. 1937 also brought a taste of things to come when the German warship "*Deutschland*" landed her dead and wounded in Gibraltar. She had been attacked by Spanish nationalist aircraft and a direct hit had caused the death of thirty-one and injured almost a hundred. The "*Deutschland*" did not stay in Gibraltar and the British authorities arranged the burials of the twenty-four German dead in North Front Cemetery. Thousands of people watched the massed bands of HMS *Arethusa* (BM I Styles) and HMS *Despatch* (BM II Davis), the firing party from *Despatch* and Royal Marine bearers from both ships. *Deutschland's* Chaplain had been left behind to conduct the service and buglers of the King's Own Yorkshire Light Infantry sounded Last Post and Reveille.

On the 15th November 1937, in Bermuda, the body of the Rt Hon J Ramsey MacDonald, Britain's first Labour Prime Minister, was brought to Hamilton Cathedral for the lying-in-state accompanied by the massed bands of HMS *Apollo* (BM Russell) and HMS *Orion* (BM Tangley) playing Beethoven and Chopin funeral marches. Next morning the body was piped aboard HMS *Apollo* for the journey back to England.

Very few records relating to the training of RNSM ranks for their duties in Fire Control and Transmitting Stations exist; however, in the '*Gunnery Training Manual 1937*' are found details of the courses that they had to pass as part of their training. The 'Other Ranks (RN School of Music) Qualifying in Fire Control' course lasted eighteen days and comprised 'Elementary Principles of Fire Control - Definitions' (one day); 'Control Position of a Battleship, Main and Secondary Armaments, and a Cruiser' (one day); 'Clocks, Dumaresque.[29] Usbourne's Fall of Shot Indicator, Change Over Switches and Telephones' (four days); All other Fire Control Instruments, Rangefinders, Inclinometers and Bearing measuring Instruments. Method of Plotting Time and Range, and Time and Bearing' (one day); 'Use of Fire Control Table supplied to a Modern Ship. Communications. Standard Method of Passing Orders. Communication Drill. Control Procedures. Standard sequence of orders' (four days); 'Use of Director. Personnel stationed in the more important control positions and their duties' (one day); 'General Outline of Concentration procedure. Recording parties. Use of records. Use of Stop Watches' (one day); 'High Angle Control' (two days); 'Lifebuoys, Hammocks, Knotting and Splicing' (two days), all followed by a one day examination. At the end of the course each man had to be capable of carrying out the duties of any person in the control position or transmitting station of a battleship or cruiser.

There was also a course (Number 63) for those needing to requalify in Fire Control. It was carried out at RN Gunnery School, Chatham. The subject was Fire Control lasting eight days (forenoons only) and there was no examination. However, candidates for promotion to Band Corporal or Bandmaster 2nd Class had to have a short practical examination. If they re-qualified successfully the following annotation was made on their individual History Sheet: "*VG in working of fire control instruments.*" There was also a course for formed bands re-qualifying before embarkation. (Course 64). The course, 'Fire Control', lasted four days and would be one of three courses depending upon the ship being drafted to:

(1) Bands designated for HM Ships of earlier than '*Nelson*' and '*Kent*' classes. At RN Gunnery School, Chatham.

(2) Bands designated for HM Ships of '*Nelson*', '*Kent*' and later classes. In HMS *Excellent*.

(3) Bands designated for Cruisers fitted with AFCT Mk V. At their Manning Port.

At the time of the Munich Crisis (1938) the Reserve Fleet was mobilised and all of the musicians in the School went to join them. This meant that the Boys' Band took over the duties of the Depot Band - which they did with very satisfactory results. Statistics regarding the output from the School during the latter part of the decade illustrate what had been accomplished by the School and, due to the tight margins of supply and demand, what a challenge any future mobilisation might place upon it.

	1934-35	1935-36	1936-37	1937-38	1938-39
RNSM total strength (ashore and afloat)		1274	1316	1362	1403
Bands afloat	49	50	50	50	52
Bands disembarked		19	24	27	27
Bands embarked		20	29	27	25
Bands available		8	3	3	4
Band Boys Strength. (Average)		328	359	392	373
Boys promoted to Musician. (Total)		66	63	120	108
Boys afloat		26	33	9	4

The School had been very successful in reducing the number of Band Boys being sent to sea before they had been advanced to Musician by recruiting and training more of them to satisfy the demands of the Royal Navy. Unfortunately the trend had not continued into 1938-1939 and hindsight tells us that this is the very time when a surplus would have been invaluable.

Musical qualifications obtained during the same period also provide interesting information.

	1935-36	1936-37	1937-38	1938-39
LRAM Diploma	4			5
Warrant Officer RM Band	4			
Bandmaster	7	9	10	18
Band Corporal	10	18	13	30
Musical Instructor	13	13	9	10

Educational qualifications obtained by study ashore and afloat also illustrate the size and scale of the RNSM, which had to apply itself to the concept of 'distance-learning'.

In 1938 the RNSM, Deal was staffed by the Superintendent, Maj J E Leech-Porter; the Field Officer General Duties: the Musical Director, Capt A Pragnell: two Assistant Musical Directors, Lt A C Green and Lt Keen; as well as the Adjutant, the Sergeant Major, the Quartermaster, Company Commanders for A, B and C Companies, two Commissioned Bandmasters, or Bandmasters (WO) engaged upon Instructional Duties, a Commissioned Bandmaster or Bandmaster (WO) on General Duties and a Superintendent Clerk. The authorised establishment of the Band Service was one thousand three hundred and forty-seven. The numbers borne were four less but of the total complement three hundred and sixty-two were Band Boys under training. This meant that from nine hundred and eighty one Officers and other ranks about fifty bands had to be provided - a requirement of eight hundred - plus instructional and other staff, promotion classes as well as the limitations imposed through foreign-service leave. Because of this situation almost continuous sea-time was common and was recognised by the AGRM as 'disproportionate'. Even by drafting boys before their training was complete some cruisers could not be provided for. The following facts had to be appreciated. Firstly, conditions of service did not attract the trained civilian musician as did Army Staff or Royal Marine Divisional Bands; secondly, Boys took three and a half to four years to train before their presence was felt, and thirdly, the basis of forming Military and Orchestral Bands is correct instrumentation and, in this respect, promotion to Bandmaster and other 'wastage' are factors affecting any one instrument or combination of instruments.

The average wastage for the years 1938/1939 was 5% and it was deemed necessary to arrive at a datum figure for the establishment size by either estimating the size of the band requirement four years hence or by fixing an arbitrary figure and doing the best with it. The modern RMBS is now able to do the former but in 1939 with about fifty bands all over the world and war on the horizon it would have been utterly impossible. In both 1938 and in 1939 the Reserve Fleet was manned by denuding shore establishments.[30]

The School was run according to 'Superintendents' Instructions' which covered Officers' Leave; Musical Instruments, Drill, Discipline, Requests, Drafting, Company Administration, Private Engagements, Promotion, Equipment, Band Boys and Vocational Training. Maj Leech-Porter's Instructions reveal a well-ordered existence, as did his preparations for the forthcoming war contained in the confidential document 'Orders for Mobilisation - RN School of Music'. These preparations, on receipt of the order 'Prepare to Mobilise' or 'Mobilise', would be initiated by Buglers sounding *RN School of Music* followed by *Assembly* in East Barracks and North Barracks as well as five Buglers sounding the same calls in Deal. It was anticipated that twelve bands would be formed and sent to embark immediately on receipt of the order to mobilise.

During this period of 'phoney war' the Royal Navy continued to patrol the world's seas making sure that it was seen by friend and prospective foe alike.

A RNSM Band was chosen to accompany Their Majesties the King and Queen to Canada and the United States in HMS *Repulse* during 1939. Whilst the School had provided bands for Royal Tours previously this was the first occasion that it had been with the King. Lt A C Green was appointed to the *Repulse* as Director of Music. The ship's band (BM A J Bennett) was retained with the addition of BM I A T Russell and BM G C McLean who would be the Drum Major, and four Musicians who were embarked whilst the ship was at Portsmouth. Preparations were intensive. Ex-Buglers in the RM Detachment joined the marching band that was also heavily rehearsed. Two concerts were to be presented to Their Majesties by the ship's company and, as usual, the band was heavily committed to these. Lt Green wrote a ships' march called *HMS Repulse* that included in the trio the West Country tune *To Be A Farmer's Boy* since *Repulse* was a Plymouth ship. Sadly, thanks to a campaign by the Daily Express the tour of HMS *Repulse* was cancelled just at the last minute. The newspaper campaign was based upon the fact that the *Repulse* was the only ship in commission that would be able to deal with the German pocket battleships. Questions were asked in Parliament and the Prime Minister, Neville Chamberlain, gave in to pressure. Whilst the tour went ahead it was on the especially chartered SS *Empress of Britain*. Disappointment at the cancellation of the participation of HMS *Repulse* in the tour was keenly felt through the Band Service since it was seen as the ultimate recognition of the quality of the bands produced by the Royal Naval School of Music.

There was now talk of mobilisation. Re-enlistment of Pensioners was open to all Band ranks. Those already discharged could return provided that they had not been out of the Band Service for more than 5 years. What would be the impact of this second great conflict of the century upon the country, its services and, in particular, the Royal Marines Band Service?

Part 4 - The Royal Naval School of Music 1939-1945

Upon the outbreak of war the Fleet was mobilised and Pensioners were recalled for duty. Five bands were mobilised in one morning! At this time the disposition of all ranks was 612 at the RNSM, 487 embarked in thirty-one ships of the Home Fleet and 367 embarked in twenty-three ships on foreign service. HMS *Royal Arthur*, the reception camp for naval personnel at Skegness (Butlin's Holiday Camp) had the first Pensioner Band. Their musical comeback was splendid in spite of dental and other difficulties. Soon they were playing orchestral programmes twice a week in the Officers' Mess and twice weekly in the various Dining Halls for the new entries and the ship's company.

In July the Admiralty issued its 'Mobilisation Return - No 1' that detailed the complements for all RN Ships. At this time each of the three Cs-in-C at The Nore (Chatham), Portsmouth and Plymouth (HMS *Pembroke*, *Victory*, and *Drake* respectively) had bands consisting of a Cd BM or BM(WO), a BdCpl and eleven Musicians. This was a peace time complement and these bands could be removed in the event of mobilisation, a situation that would also apply to the bands at HMS *Ganges* (Shotley Barracks), HMS *St Vincent* (Boys' Training Establishment) and HMS *Caledonia* although in this particular case a reserves, or Pensioner, band was to be sent as soon as possible. Mobilisation would also affect the complements of Fleet, and other, Flagships. In such cases a Cd BM or BM(WO) would serve in all Fleet Flagships of the Home, Mediterranean and China Fleets and a BM(1stCl) would serve in other Flagships replacing, where necessary, any BM(2nd Cl). The complement of Musicians would be increased to twenty-one in Fleet Flagships of the Home, Mediterranean and China Fleets; to fifteen in other Flagships over 8,000 tons and in cruisers below 8,000 tons which were Flagships of Cs-in-C on Foreign Stations and to thirteen in Cruisers below 8,000 tons which were Flagships other than Cs-in-C on Foreign Stations. These figures reflect not only the need to retain the ability of a band to provide musical support according to the seniority of the ship's commanding officer but also, since any shortfall had to be made good by an equivalent increase in the size of the RM Detachment, the necessity of the musicians to the fighting capability of the ship through their Fire Control duties and abilities. All cruisers on Foreign Stations that were not allowed an RM Band were entitled to a Ship's Musician. These were usually recruited locally but, if not obtainable in wartime, any additional Able Bodied or Ordinary Seaman would be allowed.

The Mobilisation Return required Royal Marines Bands on ships as follows:

Band Complement:	Ships
1 Commissioned or Warrant Bandmaster 1 Bandmaster 2nd Class 1 Band Corporal 21 Musicians	*Nelson*, *Warspite* and *Kent*. (All as Flagships)
1 Commissioned or Warrant Bandmaster 1 Bandmaster 1st Class 1 Band Corporal 15 Musicians	*Royal Oak* (As Flagship)

1 Bandmaster 1st Class 1 Band Corporal 15 Musicians	*Barham, Hood, York, Norfolk, Shropshire,* *Southampton, Gloucester, Neptune and Ark* *Royal, Arethusa, Galatea.* (All as Flagships)
1 Bandmaster 2nd Class 1 Band Corporal 13 Musicians	*King George V, Prince of Wales, Rodney,* *Royal Sovereign, Revenge, Resolution,* *Ramillies, Queen Elizabeth, Malaya, Valiant,* *Renown, Repulse, Exeter, Dorsetshire, London,* *Devonshire, Sussex, Berwick, Cornwall,* *Cumberland, Suffolk, Hawkins, Effingham,* *Frobisher, Vindictive, Fiji, Bermuda, Gambia,* *Jamaica, Kenya, Mauritius, Nigeria, Newcastle,* *Birmingham, Glasgow, Sheffield, Liverpool,* *Manchester, Belfast, Edinburgh, Indomitable,* *Illustrious, Victorious, Courageous, Glorious,* *Furious, Eagle, Hermes, Argus.*
1 Bandmaster 2nd Class 1 Band Corporal 10 Musicians	*Amphion, Ajax, Orion, Hermione,* *Bonaventure, Dido, Euryalus, Naiad,* *Phoebe, Sirius, Penelope, Aurora, Emerald,* *Enterprise, Danae, Delhi, Despatch,* *Dauntless, Diomede, Dragon, Dunedin,* *Durban.*

At the RNSM, mobilisation would have the effect of the School losing six of its eleven BM (1stCl), five of its eleven BM (2ndCl), fourteen of its eighteen BdCpls and thirty-five of its forty strong band. By comparison the Divisional Bands at Chatham, Portsmouth and Plymouth would not lose any of their strength because of mobilisation.[1]

Lt Kenward, Assistant Director of Music at the RNSM was appointed Director of Music, Mediterranean Fleet. The outbreak of war caused the appointment to be cancelled and Lt Kenward, who had already taken passage on the Depot Ship HMS *Maidstone* found himself a passenger for three months before he could get back to Deal. BM H Wright had spent one year at HMS *Drake*, following many years' service in the Mediterranean Fleet, when he was recalled to the School where he took on the duties of Drafting Officer in November 1939.

Only two weeks after Great Britain declared war on Germany the RM Band Service sustained its first casualty. The bands occupied the same dangerous location and carried out the same duties as their forebears in the First World War. The aircraft-carrier HMS *Courageous*, a veteran of World War I, was patrolling in the South-West Approaches in an area of known U-boat activity without either adequate intelligence or escort. She was spotted, an easy target, by U-29 whose Captain attacked with torpedoes. Musn T Chapman was on board:

I was just under the flight-deck searching for my hammock. A terrific thud, followed by a deathly silence as all machinery suddenly stopped, plunged me into a perfect blackout and a terrible feeling of claustrophobia. Luckily, a distant bulkhead door was open, towards which I staggered along the very steeply sloping deck, then finding myself outside on the flight deck and absolutely alone. Hearing incoherent voices I looked over the side and saw frantic ratings clambering through portholes, splashing into the Atlantic and swimming desperately towards a destroyer waiting to rescue them. Assuming that the order to abandon ship had been given, I slid down an aircraft checking wire secured to the deck and fell only a few feet into the water. The ship was still under way and I grabbed eagerly a passing wooden plank to which another survivor was clinging. We drifted astern a considerable distance, passing many drowning ratings shouting for help, and saw the *Courageous* eventually turn over, with many scared ratings still aboard, and sink immediately. After some time, perhaps an hour, we were picked up by a damaged *Courageous* picket boat with survivors aboard and finally climbed aboard a small merchant ship. At about midnight we were transferred to a destroyer which, after continuing night submarine patrol dropping depth charges, next morning took us to Plymouth. I was taken to Stonehouse Barracks for a medical check-up, reclothed and sent on leave to recuperate. But for that open bulkhead door and the floating wooden plank I doubt that I should be writing this[2].

Two members of the band of HMS *Courageous*, Musns Etridge and Humble were not so lucky and perished.

Further shortcomings became apparent on the 14th October when the inadequacies of the defences of Scapa Flow were demonstrated. The German submarine U-47 managed to penetrate them and sink the veteran battleship HMS *Royal Oak* with the loss of 786 men including BM F C Golding, BdCpl W C Bonner and Musns Treleaven, Webb and Green.

HMS *Revenge* began her new commission in July 1939. Having taken part in the Royal Review of the Reserve Fleet off Portland, war was declared and she went to the North Atlantic on convoy duty between Nova Scotia and Britain. The band spent most of the time 'closed up' in the transmitting station. Despite this they still managed a considerable amount of playing. For Sunday Church one half would play whilst the other half was at Cruising Stations. This allowed for a brass ensemble one Sunday and woodwind the next.[3]

After two and a half years in command of the RNSM Maj Leech-Porter was relieved by Lt Col McCausland who had been recalled from the Retired List. He assumed command on the 8th January 1940. The Musical Director, Capt A Pragnell, and his Assistant Musical Director, Lt A C Green, decided to introduce additional training in order to ensure that musicians being drafted to ships were of the highest possible standard. Warrant Officers were allocated a number of classes to supervise with musical instruction in the evening following the morning's musical instruction or drill and an afternoon's Radio Telephony[4]. This enabled a very comprehensive and easily accessible record of progress of each Band Boy to be maintained. The Concert Hall was requisitioned for accommodation so the Memorial Silver Drums were removed and the plaque taken to East Barracks. In order to give young RM Officers under training an insight into the work of the bands they visited the School and attended a series of lectures by RMB Officers.

All Home shore establishments were supplied with Pensioner Bands during 1940 since a military band for training purposes was considered a necessity at these establishments. Pensioners arrived at the Depot on a Sunday, were kitted out on Monday, drew their instruments on Tuesday and went off to their band as if they had only been on leave. BM F C Frost, a recalled Pensioner, became Drum Major at the Depot thereby releasing an Active Service rank for service afloat.

Permanent Pensioner Bands were allocated to the following establishments during the period September 1939 to April 1942:

Establishment	Date	Establishment	Date
HMS *Royal Arthur*	22 Sept 1939	HMS *St George*	27 Feb 1940
HMS *Raleigh*	22 Sept 1939	HMS *Drake*	27 Feb 1940
HMS *Collingwood*	10 Jan 1940	HMS *Osprey*	23 Mar 1940
HMS *Excellent*	09 Feb 1940	HMS *St Vincent*	31 May 1940
HMS *Ganges*	15 Feb 1940	HMS *Glendower*	17 Aug 1940
HMS *Pembroke*	15 Feb 1940	HMS *Europa*	28 Oct 1940
HMS *Victory*	15 Feb 1940		

Another permanent band was formed from Hostilities Only (HO) recruits and sent to HMS *Proserpine*, a Shore Establishment at Scapa in November 1940.[5]

In February the Band of HMS *Exeter* returned to Deal in triumph following the action off the River Plate. A large band from the School under BM Holt and led by Drum Major Frost was at the head of the procession that marched through cheering crowds along High Street and the Strand to East Barracks. *Exeter* together with *Ajax* and HMNZS *Achilles*, all carrying RM Bands, were damaged as they attacked the German pocket battleship the *Admiral Graf Spee* which fled into Montevideo harbour where she was scuttled. A high price was paid for the victory. Boy Bugler R B Hill was killed on the bridge of *Exeter* when it sustained serious damage and the Captain of Marines, a Corporal and five Marines were killed. The Bandmaster of the *Exeter* was L C Bagley who was Mentioned in Despatches for bravery in the action. The ship's company were landed in her home port of Plymouth and, later, all three ships' companies marched through the City of London to a luncheon at the Guildhall where the Portsmouth Divisional Band provided music.

At sea the band of HMS *Fiji* reported that it was maintaining the School's high musical standard in spite of many duties in the TS, with all its intricacies, as well as the Heavy Armament Control Position (HACP) and their Repel Aircraft Stations (RAS). The band of HMS *Cumberland* found itself washed out of the starboard waist and then blasted out of the recreation space - both in the same morning! HMS *Manchester* was in the Indian Ocean when war was declared and she was immediately recalled to Scapa Flow for Atlantic Convoys and Northern Patrols. During one patrol whilst just north of Iceland a German merchantman, the *Wayhele*, was found. The *Manchester* closed with her and, in response to a shot across her bows, the *Wayhele* stopped. Boats were immediately lowered as the water-cocks had been opened for scuttling. The *Manchester's* Captain, a World War 1 submarine commander, ordered the German crew back into their ship with the threat that he would sink the lifeboats if they did not. When the Germans took no notice the *Manchester* opened fire on one of the boats whereupon the others went back to their ship. At the time this incident had a marked effect upon a young musician on board the *Manchester*. Later he was to see atrocities committed by the Germans that would change his mind and make him realise that he also would have given the order to fire on those lifeboats.[6]

At Deal HO musicians, aged between eighteen and forty-six began arriving in great numbers and by the spring of 1940 there were one hundred and fifty at the School, some of them being outstanding instrumentalists. Unfortunately about half of the applicants were cornet players. The first squad of about fifty had completed preliminary military training and were passed for training in a similar manner to RM recruit squads.

In February or March 1940 some of the large houses on the Walmer seafront were requisitioned by the Admiralty, bands of eleven were formed from the musicians and each band was allocated to a certain house to practise. On the 3rd June about twelve bands from the sea front houses paraded in embarkation order at East Barracks before being sent to various destinations.

During the spring of 1940 the battle of France was raging and the children and people of Deal were being evacuated. The Admiralty decided that the Band Boys would go to the RM Reserve Camp at Exton, Lympstone, which they did on the 30th May with their staff and under the Senior Assistant Musical Director Lt A C Green. Two weeks later, with tons of stores and records, the remainder of the School left East Barracks for Plymouth. All musical practice was carried out in the dungeons of a fort. The Quartermaster's Stores were in the stables and the Staff Officers were in the former Cobbler's Shop. This was not a satisfactory arrangement since everyone was billeted in the town, and gathering them together for practise was very difficult. Eventually they lost the fort and had to practise in a large house in the town. Despite all of this the School's unofficial but much-used motto became "Practice Proceeds Apace". Even with these unsatisfactory arrangements it was felt that the Band Boys took up too much space at Lympstone since it took three years to train a Band Boy whilst it took only six weeks (in wartime) for the Royal Marines to train recruits. In September both wings of the School moved again, this time becoming a single unit once more in a camp at St Andrew's Road, Malvern in Worcestershire. This had been built as an alternative location for the Admiralty, should it be forced to leave London. There were many large underground rooms that could be used for practice. BM WTS Latter LRAM had recently returned from HMS *Fiji* and, as a newly qualified Gunnery Instructor was in charge of Fire Control instruction in a ship's TS[7]. Facilities at Malvern were very good with four blocks A, B, C and G, which were named Auber, Beethoven, Chopin and Gounod, being available to them. Beethoven Block was used for musical practice with a practice room for each class. Gounod Block was the administration building and housed the Quartermaster and his assistants and the Paymaster. The School also had its own Naval Sick Quarters with a Principal Medical Officer, a Surgeon Lieutenant RNVR and also a Dental Surgeon. The School was soon inundated with requests for bands for dances, charity concerts, Church Parades and War Savings Weeks. Two Warrant Officers at the School, C Hamilton and H Wright, were placed on the Retired List and immediately recalled and promoted Lieutenant.

The battle for Norway occupied the months of April, May and early June 1940. Lessons were being learned as the British first attempted to reinforce the Norwegians and then had to extricate its own forces before they were overrun and captured. On June 8th British Forces were being withdrawn from Norway. Having flown on two squadrons of RAF Hurricanes from Norwegian airfields the aircraft carrier HMS *Glorious* was steaming southwards with her escort destroyers HMS *Acasta* and *Ardent* when she was seen by the German *Scharnhorst* and *Gneisnau* on patrol. *Scharnhorst* opened fire at a range of 14 miles and hit the *Glorious*, starting a major fire. The destroyers laid a smoke screen but the *Scharnhorst* continued to hit the carrier and she eventually sank. 1,515 men were lost in this action including Musns Cook, Wybrow and Jones who were killed whilst BM F Woodcock and the rest of the band of HMS *Glorious* were 'Missing, Presumed Dead'.

The 'Globe and Laurel' correspondent on board HMS *King George V* wrote, in 1941:

Whilst the gunnery requirements take a great deal of the bandsmen's time and energy in these days, yet they still have the moral obligation to provide entertainment of all kinds for the ships company - an important psychological consideration just now. And I must say the bands are doing it right well.

Dance bands were a particularly popular form of entertainment and the band on board HMS *King George V* were fortunate in having Tony Moore from Henry Hall's Band, who made his own orchestrations of popular music, and Norman Parker from the Birmingham Hippodrome orchestra amongst their number. One watch of the band was completely HO. HMS *Nelson* also had a very good dance band, BdCpl Seymour's "*Swing Four*", and when weather permitted dances were held on the upper deck when in harbour. HMS *Hermione* had a seven-piece dance band whose popularity was largely due to the efforts of HO Musn L Young who rehearsed and arranged programmes and also organised the "*Hermione Three*" a vocal trio. HMS *Newcastle* staged a weekly show featuring "*Mascagini and his Ambassadors of Rhythm*" with a few novelty numbers thrown in. In between the dance numbers "*Mascagini and his Choir*" were featured! Also, on Sunday evenings, "Music Lovers Half-Hour" was very popular with the ship's company. The band of HMS *Duke of York* under BM W B Willmot gave some lunch-hour concerts whilst in harbour but the work of the 'dockyard mateys' slowed down as they watched so the concerts were stopped and the band made occasional broadcasts over the ship's radio instead. HMS *Victorious* band included eleven HO's, most of whom were well-known musicians in civilian life. The band provided the ship's company with up-to-date dance programmes and were also the backbone of all the impromptu concerts.

HMS *Prince of Wales* carried the Rt. Hon. Winston Churchill, General Sir John Dill and Air Vice-Marshal Sir Wilfred Freeman to meet President Roosevelt who was at sea on board USS *Augusta*. The principles of the Atlantic Charter were set out during this meeting. Sir John Dill and Sir Wilfred Freeman both visited the band at their Action Station. When the two ships met, the Guard and Band fell in on the quarterdeck to salute units of the American Fleet. They paraded many times to play musical salutes during the various arrivals and departures. The band played at Church Service on Sunday 10th August when both leaders and their staff, including several hundred ranks of the United States Navy and Marine Corps attended. Mr Churchill chose the hymns *Eternal Father, Strong*

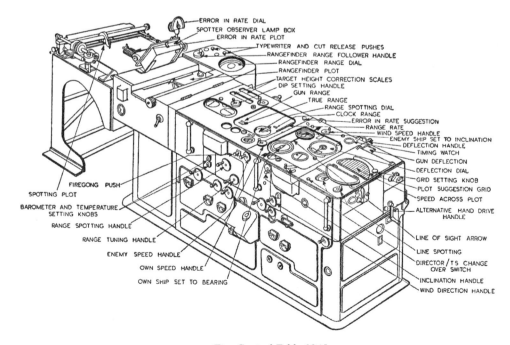

Fire Control Table 1945

to Save, Onward Christian Soldiers and *O God Our Help in Ages Past*. Nearly half of those present were soon to perish.

1941 was the worst year yet for the Band Service. The peak in numbers serving afloat in all theatres of war was reached with 949 at the RNSM and UK shore establishments plus 1,045 embarked in 64 ships. The light cruiser HMS *Bonaventure* was sunk in the Mediterranean with the loss of BM Brain, BdCpl Packer and Musn Goymer. Musn A Howden of HMS *Fiji* went to visit BM Rogers of HMS *Gloucester* when the *Fiji* docked in Alexandria harbour. The Bandmaster and the band had been out in the Mediterranean since 1938 and were feeling pretty low. Musn Bell arrived to relieve BdCpl Burleigh who had been drafted back to the School. *Gloucester* and *Fiji* sailed for Crete together and were together during most of the attacks that followed. German bombers attacked all ships in the area and HMS *Gloucester* was badly hit and sank. Only two of the band survived. They were Musns Brisley and Macdonald. The latter was taken prisoner and formed a band in the New Marlag prisoner-of-war camp. The remainder were posted 'Missing, Presumed Dead'. HMS *Fiji* steamed around the *Gloucester* and dropped most of her own Carley floats to the survivors. Eventually HMS *Fiji* herself ran out of ammunition and was reduced to firing practice and smoke shells in a desperate attempt to keep the bombers away. She received several direct hits after which she sank with the loss of BM Wenham and seven members of the band, all 'Missing, Presumed Dead'. Musn Howden was in the TS:

> It seemed like the end of the world with cork particles showering down from the deckhead. Thankfully, with orders to come up, we scrambled up the sloping ladders (the ship had a 40° list) and lent a hand to get the wounded out of the sickbay and into the sea-boat. As we did so over came another attack and a bomb took us amidships. From the bridge came the order to abandon ship.

He swam around occasionally holding onto a raft. Many men succumbed to the cold water and by the early hours of the morning he too was on the verge of complete exhaustion when he saw destroyers silhouetted against the sky and shouted for help. He then passed out and awoke, after a great deal of artificial respiration, on the deck of HMS *Kandahar* at about 0600. He was the only Musician on board, the other six having been rescued by HMS *Kingston*.[8]

The day before the *Fiji* and the *Gloucester* were sunk HMS *Suffolk* sent a fateful radio signal. She was patrolling the Denmark Strait searching for the German battleship *Bismarck* known to be on the loose in the North Sea. *Suffolk's* signal told HMS *Hood* that she had found, and was shadowing, the *Bismarck* and the *Prinz Eugen*. At 0535 on the 24th May the *Hood* spotted the *Bismarck* and commenced firing at 0553. With only her fifth salvo the *Bismarck's* gunners scored a hit on *Hood's* weakest area - the after deck above the ammunition storage - and at 0600 the *Hood* blew up and sank taking 1,419 men, including BM Herod, a Band Corporal, thirteen Musicians and a Band Boy, with her.

A few days later HMS *Orion* was severely damaged by enemy aircraft south of Crete. Six hundred soldiers rescued from Crete were killed and BdCpl Cole and three Musicians were killed in the TS. The ship went to America for repairs after removal of most of the dead at Alexandria. The musicians' bodies were not recovered until the ship reached America as, during the attacks on the ship, damage had caused the TS to be flooded with fuel oil.[9] In a seven-day period the RM Band Service had lost forty-four men, including two complete bands.

On the 24th November HMS *Dunedin* was torpedoed by U-124 in mid-Atlantic. BM Sargeant, BdCpls West and Jones, seven Musicians and a Band Boy were lost. Next day, off Libya, U-331 torpedoed the battleship HMS *Barham*. BM Chard and twelve Musicians were lost - 'Missing, Presumed Killed'. BdCpl Tobin was on deck at the time. HMS *Queen Elizabeth* was to port and slightly ahead whilst HMS *Valiant* was also to port but slightly astern. A terrific explosion below decks was heard and felt and a submarine periscope was spotted. The submarine was between the three ships, so close that no ship's armament could be depressed enough to engage her. As the *Barham* began to roll Tobin and two others prepared to abandon ship. They ignored the practice of moving to the 'high' side of a rolling ship and leapt into the water just before the deck was vertical.

As I hit the water I glanced over my shoulder, and if you can imagine what it's like to see a 35,000ton[10] battleship tipping over on top of you, you certainly don't linger.

Once he had swum a reasonable distance from the ship Fred Tobin joined his comrades and they turned back to look at the ship.

Barham was right on her side with the funnel almost touching the water. There were hundreds of men on the hull and I said to Frank 'My God, they will never get away'. As I said that - wham - up she went, a 35,000 ton battleship in a million bits and 900 men with her[11]

On the 10th December Japanese torpedo aircraft attacked and sank HMS *Prince of Wales* and HMS *Repulse* off Malaya. Five members of the Band Service were lost. In the Mediterranean, less than three weeks after the loss of the *Barham*, the entire band of HMS *Galatea* was lost on the 15th December when the cruiser was torpedoed and sunk by a German submarine thirty miles from Alexandria. On the 17th December HMS *Neptune* and two destroyer escorts left Malta to meet the fast auxiliary HMS *Breconshire* which, once again, was running the gauntlet with her escort, the ships of Force K, from Alexandria to bring supplies to the island. *Neptune* and her destroyers met the *Breconshire*, escorted her to Malta then immediately left, with the ships of Force K to search for an enemy convoy. Twenty miles east of Tripoli the *Neptune* hit two mines, one of which wrecked her propellers and steering gear. The following ships sheered off immediately but the *Aurora* and *Penelope* also hit mines. *Neptune* drifted onto a third mine and developed a heavy list. The destroyer *Kandahar* went to her rescue but a mine blew her stern off. The *Neptune* then hit a fourth mine and capsized. All but one of her company, including eleven men from the Band Service where lost. BdCpl Gardner was originally posted as missing but was later reported safe. Other individuals were lost as a result of enemy action during the year. Total losses in 1941 were ninety-nine.

In some ships the band managed to get away unscathed, the band of HMS *Ark Royal* being an example of this. On the 16th August 1937 a band left the RNSM to embark in the aircraft carrier HMS *Furious*. In December 1938, whilst *Furious* refitted in Plymouth, the same band was detailed to join HMS *Ark Royal*, commissioning at Portsmouth. The band joined *Ark Royal* on the 8th December 1938. The "Ark" played a large part in the battle of the Mediterranean by sailing towards Malta to fly-off reinforcement aircraft to the beleaguered island. These ferry-trips were known as "club runs". On the 13th November 1941 Ark Royal was on her way towards Malta once more when, at 1541hrs, the German submarine U-81 fired three torpedoes. Only one hit but it was a crucial blow since it detonated near the starboard boiler room. Soon there was a heavy list to starboard and all communications and lighting failed for a few minutes, until emergency power came on and the voice of the Captain could be heard explaining what had occurred and ordering all surplus personnel to be evacuated. Half of the band had been closed-up in the TS, the other half being due to take over at 1600hrs. Those who were preparing to go to the TS followed orders and made for the flight-deck. On the way they stopped to help the Chaplain who was passing a fire-hose down to the boiler-room where a fire had developed. The musicians found that the explosion had damaged one of the two ladders that they needed to use and the other, due to the list of the ship, was at an impossible angle so they made their way aft through the cabins and ward-room and then up to the Pilots' briefing room and onto the flight deck. Two destroyers, HMS *Legion* and HMS *Laforey*, were close alongside to take off the crew. The band used ropes to drop onto the fo'c'sle of the *Legion*. Even tilted as she was nobody thought the *Ark Royal* would sink but, at 0613 next morning, she did. The crew were taken the thirty miles to Gibraltar for passage back to the RNSM. Only one man, a seaman, lost his life in the "Ark".[12]

HMS *Phoebe* was commissioned in Glasgow in September 1940. BM Mortimer and BdCpl Kelly took the band on to the new ship before working up around Scapa Flow and then Gibraltar. *Phoebe* became involved in the evacuation of Greece and then Crete. Escorting small destroyers supplying British troops on the North African coast followed this. It was during one of these trips that, on the 15th August 1941, she was torpedoed. *Phoebe* managed to limp back to Alexandria, with her bows just twelve inches above the water, with nine dead and others wounded. On this occasion the band was unscathed. After temporary repairs the ship steamed to New York's Brooklyn Navy Yard for repairs. The musicians left the ship and were transported to Norfolk where they went aboard HMS *Formidable* for the journey back to the UK.[13]

In an attempt to halt the German invasion and reinforce Norway, HMS *Glasgow* sailed up Trondjen Fjord and landed a detachment of the Green Howards (Alexandra, Princess of Wales's Own Yorkshire Regiment). A week later the ship returned to get what was left of them out. As they sailed up the Fjord they could see that in every village the wooden houses had been burnt and the bodies of women and children left on the ground. As he saw this Musn Penfold was reminded of the incident with the German merchant vessel *Wayhele* a few months earlier.[14]

At Malvern the School's volunteer orchestra had grown to fifty-five performers with CSM McLean and LCpl Annereau as vocalists and Musn W Ivory, a former member of the BBC Scottish Orchestra who had joined as an HO, as solo violinist. The Dance Band, led by BM S C Low, was also making a name for itself. Lt Kenward took a large band on tour to the Clydeside area for "*Music While You Work*" concerts whilst a band of fifty-five under BM W T Lang was touring London for War Savings Weeks. The School contributed a great deal to War Savings, Warships, Wings for Victory and Salute the Soldier weeks. Any bands awaiting draft were sent around the country in support of these. School bands also gave many concerts in factories and in shipyards as well as performances for the Red Cross and other Charities.

One barrack room at the School contained twenty-five NCOs and men with a combined age of 1,197 years; a combined service of 615 years and eighty-eight medals and seventy-one Good Conduct badges between them! They were not all Pensioners since they included a "youngster" with only eleven years' service! (The 'average person' was forty-eight years old with twenty-five years man's service)

By the summer of 1941 the Admiralty had decided that the RNSM must vacate Malvern and, once again, the only option was to split the School. The Band Boys, with

Capt Smith as CO and Lt Green as Musical Director, went to a holiday camp called Howstrake Camp, near Douglas, on the Isle of Man. This was known as Junior Wing and Howstrake would remain its home for the next five years. The Senior Wing moved to Scarborough with the Superintendent, Lt Col H L M McCausland, Capt A Pragnell, Musical Director, and Staff. They were housed in two hotels, the 'Clifton' and the 'Norbreck'. The Malvern Camp became HMS *Duke*, a RN training establishment and in time had a RM Band of its own. The RNSM bands in their new localities continued to give concerts and to tour in aid of money-raising ventures. Lt A C Green had formed a symphony orchestra of 90 players from the Musical Instructors and Senior Band Boys most of whom were under the age of seventeen and, after much practice and hard work, they too performed a concert in aid of Warship Week. This was followed by 'A Grand Orchestral Concert of Russian Music' that was performed in the Villa Marina, Douglas. The programme included *Joan of Arc's Farewell* and *To the Forest* by Tchaikovsky and *Steppes of Central Asia* (Borodin). The concert programme was followed by the *Last Post*, *In Memory of the Fallen*, the Manx National Anthem and *God Save the King*.[15]

A shortage of musical instruments was beginning to cause difficulties for the School. They were not easy to obtain at a time when the demand was increasing and there was a danger that some instruments would disappear for the duration of the war. Cellos and string basses were withdrawn from bands in small ships where suitable storage was not available.

1942 brought even greater demands upon the RM Bands of the RNSM. To promote the war effort further extensive tours of industrial areas and the provinces were made by bands from Scarborough under Lt Kenward, Lt Keen, Lt Papworth and BM(WO) Davis. Several BBC recordings were made whilst touring. From Scarborough, the bands of fifty from Senior Wing became known as Touring Bands. The Boys Band ran Talent Spotting Competitions on the Isle of Man for the troops of all three services with Sub Lt Jon Pertwee RN of HMS *Valkyrie*, a radar-training establishment, as the compere.

As the result of a change in the Regulations governing length of service at their rank Lts Green, Keen and Donne were all promoted to Captain on the 29th May.[16] The Musical Director, Capt A Pragnell, was promoted to Major whilst the Drafting Officer, Lt Kenward, was promoted to Captain.

Members of the Band Service were involved in some of the heaviest fighting, at sea, of 1942. They were in HMS *Penelope* (nicknamed the "Pepperpot" because of the amount of holes in her) undergoing repairs in the most bombed place on earth - Malta. Under almost constant bombing raids from German Stukas and JU 88s that were intended to destroy all the shipping in the harbour, she could not move until her damage repairs were completed. The ship's artificers and shipwrights worked alongside the men of the dockyard in between the air-raids. BM Cooper, at the request of the ship's Captain, wrote a "Shooting Song" intended to inspire the gunners. When all of the band parts were completed the ship's company was piped to "lay aft and sing a song" and with the Captain perched on top of 'Y' turret singing the words through a megaphone and the band playing the entire ship's company joined in.[17] Musn Jemmett died in a Malta hospital of natural causes during this period and BM S C Cooper was Mentioned in Despatches[18]

HMS *Naiad* was sunk by U-565 north of Mersa Matruh on the 11th March 1942 with the loss of Musn Page, 'Missing, Presumed Killed'.

On the 29th of the same month German forces attacked Russian Convoy PQ13 on route to Murmansk. HMS *Trinidad* and HMS *Eclipse* engaged three German heavy destroyers that were threatening the convoy. One of the most bizarre incidents of the war then took place. *Trinidad* engaged the German destroyer Z26 and inflicted serious damage with her opening salvoes. Z26 fired torpedoes and *Trinidad* turned and successfully evaded them. The other two destroyers disappeared into the snow and *Trinidad* pursued Z26, manoeuvring into a position where she could fire her own torpedoes. At 0922hrs the Torpedo Officer fired one torpedo. A few seconds later he fired the other two but they were frozen into the tubes and remained there. A few minutes later a torpedo was seen running towards *Trinidad*. Evasive action was taken but it was too late. The torpedo struck the port side just forward of the bridge and exploded. This torpedo was the one that *Trinidad* herself had fired. As a result of either a malfunction in the gyro-mechanism, possibly freezing, or water turbulence caused by exploding shells the torpedo had run wild. Incredibly it ran in a semi-circle and, within the entire space of the Arctic Ocean, had collided with the *Trinidad* steaming at full speed. The torpedo exploded in the RM Barracks[19], causing the flooding of one of the boiler-rooms and destroying the Damage Control HQ. Many ratings and Officers in these areas were killed. The TS, where the band was closed up at Action Stations, was two decks below. It was plunged into darkness, the ventilation system pulled fumes in from the explosion and the bulkheads between the men and the oil fuel was seriously weakened. The emergency lighting came on and the musicians, regaining their places around the two tables, one large the other small, attempted to re-establish contact with the bridge. The small table had been seriously damaged so its operators moved into the main area. The RN Officer ordered the only seaman in the party to report to Damage Control and seek assistance. When the heavy hatch was opened a mixture of oil fuel and seawater poured into the room. Despite the difficulties caused by the oil the seaman managed to climb the steel ladder and get through the hatch. The Officer then gave the order 'Abandon TS' and ushered the men past him. Three men had escaped through the hatch when, due mainly to the increasing list of the ship, the heavy counterbalanced hatch cover slammed down on the man climbing through it, breaking his back and trapping him there. The hatch could not be opened by either those below or above and, by that time, the fuel oil and sea-water mixture was up to waist-height in the compartment. At that point the weakened TS bulkhead gave way to the pressure of fuel oil behind it and tons of oil burst into the compartment drowning those who were trapped there. Those who had escaped from the TS made their way up oily ladders and through damaged mess decks and the RM Barracks with its huge hole in the side. Eventually they found their way up to the deck, the only three survivors from the RM Band of twelve that had worked together for more than a year. *Trinidad* managed to reach Murmansk where the bodies were recovered from the TS and buried at sea. On the 15th May 1942 it was decided that, following severe damage from German air attacks off North Cape, the Trinidad was too badly damaged to continue and she was sunk by HMS *Matchless*.[20]

The war in the Far East, initiated by the Japanese attack on Pearl Harbour in December 1941, was at its height with the Japanese still on the offensive. HMS *Cornwall* was one of several ships sunk in the Indian Ocean by Japanese carrier-borne aircraft on the 5th April 1942. Nine of *Cornwall's* musicians were 'Missing, Presumed Dead'. One of the ships accompanying Cornwall was the *Dorsetshire*. BM Upstell was in the TS with an RN Sub-Lieutenant and a Petty Officer. All hatches were battened down as an estimated fifty aircraft attacked. Hit by four bombs, all lighting and communication was lost and she began to list heavily. Realising the situation the Bandmaster ordered one of his men to open the hatch. The ladder above the hatch had fallen across the hatch cover and it could only be moved a small amount. In desperation the musician forced his way through the small gap and moved the obstruction. All of the band managed to escape and made their way up to the deck where they were told to leave the ship by the Commander. Approximately half the crew went down with the ship and the remainder were left either in the sea or in boats, awaiting rescue. The sea was covered in fuel oil and heavily infested with sharks. After spending twenty-seven hours in the water they were rescued by British destroyers.[21] Four days later the British aircraft carrier HMS *Hermes*, with two other vessels, was sunk in action off *Trincomalee*, Ceylon. This was the first instance of an aircraft carrier being sunk by carrier-borne aircraft. Hermes had little anti-aircraft armament and her aircraft were operating from a shore base so she was virtually defenceless in this situation. The band was split in two and stationed in the Ward Room First Aid station and in the Sick Bay. BM Roe and nine Musicians were killed, the four survivors having all been stationed in the Sick Bay. Survivors spent four or five hours in the water before being picked up by the Australian Hospital Ship *Vita*. Operations were performed on the survivors during the thirty-six hour passage to Colombo but many died.[22]

Men of the RM Band around the gunnery control equipment in the Transmitting Station in HMS Victorious

© Imperial War Museum

Efforts to relieve the beleaguered island fortress of Malta were stepped up during the summer of 1942. Operation '*Vigorous*', an attempt to force supplies through from the East, was thwarted when the Italian Fleet intercepted the convoy. Both forces turned and made to return from whence they came. German aircraft attacked and bombed the convoy and amongst many other casualties was HMS *Hermione*, the victim of a torpedo attack by U-205 that claimed the life of BdCpl Vincent. Operation '*Pedestal*' proved to be a story of epic proportions as the convoy battled through to the relief of the island. The Axis forces knew about the convoy as soon as it passed through the Straits of Gibraltar and German submarines were positioned to intercept them. The first casualty was HMS *Eagle* that fell prey to U-73 which fired four torpedoes into her. The *Eagle* sank with the loss of more than two hundred of her crew, including nine members of her band. Amongst the escorts was HMS *Manchester* which, whilst passing the Island of Pantelleria, was hit by torpedoes fired from an Italian E-boat. Three of *Manchester's* four propellers were blown off and the fourth was bent. The Captain decided to scuttle the ship rather than let her be captured and ordered the Port Watch of the ship's company to be taken off by the destroyer HMS

Pathfinder. When all arrangements were made for scuttling, the Starboard Watch left the ship and made for the North African shore by either swimming or using Carley floats. Twelve hours after leaving the ship to sink they reached Tunisia. They were taken to Algiers by train and thence through the Atlas Mountains and across the Sahara Desert to an old French Foreign Legion outpost called Laghouat where over a thousand prisoners were held in a compound about 100 yards square with barrack rooms that held forty men each. They remained there until, just prior to the Allied landings in North Africa, they were all transferred to occupied France. Four musicians were amongst the group repatriated in 1943.[23] Five other members of the band were interned but released to return to the UK reporting to the RNSM on 25th November 1942.[24]

A band was in HMS *Nigeria* escorting Russian convoys and then convoys to Malta. *Nigeria's* BM Ridout was a prime example of the calibre of men that the School was producing. During 1940 he had organised many concerts ashore and afloat in the Newcastle and Scapa Flow areas. The ship then spent many months at sea on patrols to Murmansk, went to Spitzbergen and covered Commando raids in Norway. They entertained Russian Army musicians aboard the ship whilst in Murmansk. The Bandmaster was highly regarded by Admiral Burroughs and everyone else on board because of his constant efforts organising concerts and keeping morale high. During 1942 the *Nigeria* was transferred to the Mediterranean to escort the Malta convoys. The band was responsible for manning the HACPs and the TS. On August 12th a torpedo from the Italian submarine *Axum* struck the ship killing all members of the band in the forward HACPs and TS. All were married men, all the single men being in the after HACP. The ship returned to Gibraltar with her fo'c'sle almost awash. The surviving members of the band then had the task of opening the hatches, removing the remains of their Bandmaster and eight members of the band and burying them at sea off Europa Point.[25] On the 29th August Lt Col H L M McCausland, Superintendent of the RNSM, wrote to Gen Bourne:[26].

> I attach an extract from a private letter I have just had from Ellison. It is very nice to get such letters and when one does one can't help feeling that should the RMB turn over to the Navy it would be a loss to the Corps. Unfortunately I cannot promulgate his letter yet as his ship has not so far been mentioned to the public by name. I lost 9 of the Band and a similar number in "*Eagle*". The survivors of "*Eagle*" and "*Manchester*" have arrived back and certainly have not [made] Ellison's statement that it was "exciting". Fifteen "*Manchester*" [word illegible] are unaccounted for but the Bandmaster hopes they got to Tunisia. Yours sincerely H L M McCausland.

This handwritten letter contains both a pride in the RNSM and a sense of personal loss. Major E J O Ellison was the Squadron RM Officer and was on board HMS *Nigeria* and had written, on the 23rd August:

> We have just had Sunday Divisions and Stand-up prayers. A very sad little ceremony as far as the RM Band were concerned. The Band consisted of six musicians only, we actually have seven left on board but Lillford had volunteered to work down below and Wilson is in hospital. You will of course know all about it from the official notification. The Band took a terrible hard knock. The remainder are doing super work and they are the admiration of the whole ship's company. The casualties were all married men which makes it all the harder. I have written to the next of kin. I am most thankful that they recently had a spell of leave to go and see their families. They were all a splendid lot and most efficient both as musicians and at their work owing to the excellent work of Bandmaster Ridout who was ably assisted by BdCpl Powell. They were killed at their action stations after being closed up almost continuously

for three days and nights during which time we were attacked by torpedo and bombing aircraft and submarines. It was certainly a most exciting operation and we are all looking forward to the day when we can take our revenge and blow the accursed enemy out of the sea and the sky.

BM Erridge was killed on board HMS *Phoebe* on 23rd October and the final casualties for 1942 took place on board HMS *Arethusa*. Engaged upon Operation '*Stoneage*', another attempt to re-supply beleagured Malta, HMS *Arethusa* and the rest of the convoy had to fight off continuous air attacks from 0600 on 18th November. Then, at 1800 on the same day, the *Arethusa* was torpedoed. She was towed stern-first back to Alexandria with her crew fighting raging fires and a rising gale and, when she eventually arrived, she carried 155 dead including BM Walker and eight members of the band.

HMS *Exeter*, one of the heroines of the Battle of the River Plate and part of an Allied strike force of five cruisers and nine destroyers encountered a Japanese force of four cruisers and fourteen destroyers. *Exeter*, very early in the battle, received a direct hit that put six of her eight boilers out of action. She slowed down and fell behind in the running battle. Later she was joined by two other ships and had to decide whether to scuttle or make a run for it. Her Captain decided upon the latter. Restricted to a maximum speed of 23 - 26 knots she found herself boxed-in by vastly superior Japanese forces. For two hours she managed to manoeuvre and score hits on the Japanese forces before she received a direct hit that broke her main steam supply pipe and stopped her dead in the water. The order was given to scuttle and then to abandon ship. All members of the band were reported missing but some were later found to be prisoners in Japanese hands. Amongst these was BM Vidler who according to the OCRM, Capt John H McCahon RM

> …was the finest bandmaster I ever had, an excellent NCO and a fine musician. He produced a very fine band on and off parade.

'Bandy' Vidler was taken prisoner and put to work in the prison camp hospital at Macassar where he met a Dutch Medical Officer Dr Adrian Borstlap. They became very firm friends through their work helping the sick in the Camp Hospital and in the Sick Bay. Eventually 'Bandy' himself contracted beri-beri and hunger odema. His own experience told him that he would not survive very long. Dr Borstlap wrote:

> We agreed that when the moment came [to transfer Bandy Vidler to the hospital close to the morgue - the usual practice for those close to death] I would not linger at his side when doing my rounds, telling him the dirty story of the day etc but would pass on without stopping. When that dreaded day came, I could see him staring at me from afar as I entered the ward. He followed my every step. He already knew too, and when I passed him, I did not stop. We just looked each other in the eye, as I said softly 'goodbye Bandy'. Then I had to run out of the ward so that the boys would not see me crying. Later that day, April 24th 1945, in complete peace 'Bandy' Vidler passed away. A Truly Great Man![27]

Four other members of the band of HMS *Exeter* also died in captivity.

The National Press also reported upon a convoy travelling across the Indian Ocean. The Captain of an escorting Royal Navy warship drew alongside a troopship in the convoy and kept his ship in perfect position for forty minutes whilst his RM Band gave a concert to the hundreds of soldiers lining the troopship's rails. At the end of the concert the warship's Captain flashed "Hope you enjoyed it" and resumed his former station in the convoy.

The RNSM Senior Wing Symphony Orchestra, Scarborough 1942.

HMS *Berwick* had a splendid dance band led by Roy Watkinson who became the first HO[28] to be promoted to Corporal. They gave a series of successful stage shows sponsored by Lt V Ellis RNVR, a composer of musical comedies. This culminated in the recording of a dance music programme called *"The Navy's Here"*. This was the first in a series featuring other ships' bands.

HMS *Charybdis* was in Barrow-in-Furness for a refit following the North African landings. Just before sailing Noel Coward came aboard. As they left the dock the band on X Gun Deck played the Coward tune, *I'll See You Again*. Noel Coward was quite touched by this incident and shook hands with the entire band when they had finished. He entertained the ship's company morning and afternoon as it took him to Gibraltar where he was to perform. This allowed both port and starboard watches to see him, an act that was very much appreciated[29].

The Boys of Junior Wing were invited to take part in the annual Manx Music Festival 1943 and they played a very prominent part in it. A band of twelve Instructors took part in a programme of Manx music that was broadcast by BBC Forces Radio. The Junior Wing gave an orchestral concert in the Manx Museum on 20th February 1943. The programme was *La Pere Du Victoire* (Ganne), *Plymouth Ho* (Ansell), *HMS Repulse* (Green), Selection - *The Gondoliers* (Sullivan), *Naila* (Delibes), Incidental Music to *Othello* (Coleridge-Taylor) and *Sunset - Setting for Orchestra* - (Green). Orchestral concerts were also held on a regular, very often weekly, basis at the Villa Marina where the programmes were very testing and provided excellent experience for the young musicians. Soloists were often featured as were guest singers and choirs. A 1943 Christmas Concert was put on at Howstrake Camp. This was produced by CSM K McLean and featured not only the orchestra but also the Boys providing comedy sketches, gymnastic displays, tap dancing and a sketch entitled 'A Band Boy's Dream of Howstrake'. The Schoolmaster and the Chaplain shared the compering of the show.

At Scarborough, during 1941 and 1942 the large Touring Bands were also giving concerts and Albert Marland, a pianist of great renown who, prior to joining the Royal

Navy and transferring to the RNSM, was a member of Henry Hall's Band, played many of his own arrangements. BM Barnes conducted the last in a long series of concerts that had included *Rhapsody in Blue* and Liszt's *Hungarian Rhapsody No 2*. Marland was also a member of the "*Celeste Octet*" a new ensemble from the RNSM that gave concerts in Scarborough. Music featured in these included his arrangement of a concert fantasia of Viennese waltzes, a transcription of *The Donkey Serenade* and the intermezzo from the film *Escape to Happiness*, amongst others. Capt Donne conducted these concerts and they were a great success. Further ventures included a joint RNSM and RAF Concert in front of an audience of over a thousand. BM Barnes again conducted the RM Orchestra playing selections from Elgar, Strauss and Ravel. The RAF Band played modern music using their Dance Band - "*The Red Roses*". Albert Marland gave a performance of *Warsaw Concerto*. Sidney Wright, late of the Halle Orchestra, also played. A joint concert with the Band of the Green Howards also featured Marland.[30] Marland and his arrangements were included in many RNSM concerts before Captain Dunn arranged for him to be drafted to the Portsmouth Divisional Band. BM Pattinson and an eighteen-piece combination made recordings in London for Forces Overseas, being announced as the '*Royal Seafarers Dance Orchestra*'. The Band of HMS *Belfast* was also broadcasting in "*Navy Mixture*".

Boys of the RNSM on the Parade at Howstrake Camp, Isle of Man.

In August 1942 Maj-Gen T L Hunton submitted his report[31] on the Royal Marine Band Service. On the questions of the developing RN Volunteer Bands at the Home Ports and also the desire on the part of several senior RN Officers to have a band of their own, Hunton recommended that if the RN wanted a band then the RNSM and its RM Bands should be transferred to it. He made a strong case for such a transfer but with the caveat that the RNSM was functioning very well as a Royal Marines Department. He did highlight the fact that RM Bandsmen generally felt that whilst they were in the Royal Marines, they were not of them. His major recommendation was that consideration should be given to whether the RNSM should come under the RN or the RM and, if the answer was the latter, then the RM Home Port Bands should be increased in size so that there would be no requirement for the large RN Volunteer Bands. He also recommended a number of detailed improvements to the Band Service many of which, such as an equivalent to the Army psm[32] qualification, were gradually taken up.

Changes at the RNSM in 1943 included the retirement of Capt A C Green after thirty-nine years in the Band Service. Capt L P Donne was also placed on the Retired List. Capt G C Keen was appointed Director of Music, Junior Wing Howstrake Camp, Isle of Man. CdBM Humphery was promoted to Lt (QMI); BM (WO) Barnes promoted to Commissioned Bandmaster and BM I J H Gale to BM (WO). BM J E Marx was promoted to QMS in the Musical Instrument Store. QMS W T Latter was awarded the BEM and BdCpl W F Seymour was awarded the DSM in the King's Birthday Honours whilst BM C G McLean received the DSM for gallantry and outstanding service in the face of the enemy. LtCol H L M McCausland, who had been Superintendent of the RNSM since January 1940, was relieved by Col. H D Weir.

Band Boys in the Isle of Man were issued with forage caps but these were only worn for a short time before being replaced by the beret.

A subtle change in the role of the RNSM took place in 1944 when it was told to supply a band for the RM Infantry Training Centre at Lympstone (later the Commando Training Centre RM). The band found it strange to be living on shore again and marching with morning parades. They were issued with battledress. A band was also supplied for the Royal Marines Depot at Deal. The latter comprised Pensioners with an average age of 49, an average service of 26 years and 79 medals between them. Their main work was on the parade ground.

In order to maximise the numbers available for RM Bands a Circular from the AGRM, on behalf of the Admiralty, was issued. This stated "no discrimination was to be made between Band Ranks and other pensioners as far as liability for service after discharge to pension is concerned. On discharge to pension Band ranks were to be employed on general duties at the Royal Marine Divisions, and for exchange with those at Lympstone when necessary. A record is to be kept of all such ranks so that, if the occasion arises, a band may be formed on similar lines to that now at RM Depot, Lympstone". Band pensioners previously under the 'call-up' age were now to be recalled for service provided they were medically fit. This meant that every potential source of manpower available to the RNSM, apart from the continuing enlistment of young men, had been committed to the war effort.

There were further losses to the Band Service in 1943. Musn Lovick was killed on board HMS *Cleopatra* on 11th July 1943 and six members of the Band, including BM2nd Cl C G McLean, were wounded.

At the time of the ship being damaged the ship was at Defence Stations, or Cruising Watches, so that only about six of the band were actually closed up at the time and I was in fact dozing beside the HA Table with my lifebelt for a pillow and my spectacles beside me. Out went the lights and such was my haste that I left both behind. The main lower TS was quite undamaged and dry while we all made the upper deck without difficulty. The remainder of the band were lying down for a rest after a sleepless night using the after HACP one deck below the upper deck. One of our members, Musn R H Lovick, was preparing to use the bathroom and was almost at the point of impact and was severely injured. He passed away about eight hours later and was buried at sea. Only five of us were uninjured and we made a strange sounding combination on the quarter-deck for entering harbour.[33]

Four musicians were killed in HMS *Uganda* on 13th September and there was only one survivor from the band of HMS *Charybdis* when she was sunk near the Channel Islands on 23rd October. She had left Plymouth with five or six destroyers in company to engage a German convoy on its way to Brittany. When the ship had gone to Action Stations the Gunnery Office piped the plan of attack to the guns and to the fore and aft TSs "We will attack the convoy line-ahead and will go through it, guns blazing, sink what we can then turn through 180° come back and sink the rest". The ship and its crew had been together for two years and, having proved themselves in the Mediterranean and on the Russian convoys, their confidence was such that this seemed perfectly feasible. As they approached the convoy they watched the range getting closer and closer to the point that one wag asked if the next order would be "Out grappling irons"! Soon after the guns began firing and almost immediately a large explosion caused the ship to shudder, the lights to go out and communication between the TS and the guns was lost. Eventually contact was made with a Royal Marine in 'Y' turret who confirmed that the ship had been torpedoed. A few seconds later another explosion rocked the ship which began to heel over and everything went dead. The Petty Officer in charge of the TS gave the order to evacuate. The musicians were relieved to find that their hatch cover had been opened from the outside (a standing procedure for the Helmsman in the event of the ship being abandoned). Musn Penfold saw only one musician from the other TS (aft) before he was told to go over the side. After swimming for what seemed a few hours he found a plank which he used to support himself as he swam from group to group looking for members of the band. Just after dawn they were picked up by a British destroyer and by 0800hrs they were back in Plymouth. Musn Burnage, an outstanding violinist, who had enlisted for HO, had a premonition of impending disaster and was convinced that he would never come back. The sole survivor was Musn Penfold[34].

Musn K R Macdonald, a survivor of HMS *Gloucester*, and the only RM Bandsman Prisoner of War in German hands, wrote to the Musical Director to say that he was now

The RM Band of HMS Charybdis, 1943.

the Bandmaster of the Prison Camp band, that he had eighteen in the orchestra and also had small combinations and a dance orchestra. They had been able to produce comic operas that he had orchestrated for ten performers from the vocal score. They also played for stage shows, accompanied Church Services and organised weekly music classes.

Three days after a band arrived at HMS *Kestrel*, the Royal Naval Air Station (RNAS) on Worthy Down near Winchester, the orchestra made its debut at a ship's concert. They were also co-opted into the BBC ITMA show under the BBC conductor Charles Shadwell and he and Tommy Handley were appreciative of BM Baxter's fine band. They also played in the pit for ENSA and other shows.

Life at sea was not without its moments of humour and incongruity. Musn Nicholls wrote from HMS *Diomede* that the Band whalers crew were away from the ship when they heard Band Call across the water. They pulled quickly to the ship's boom, leapt out of the boat, grabbed their instruments and, still clad in their rowing attire the quintet played for hoisting the cutter - conducted by the coxswain.

It was during 1943 that the Italians surrendered and BM Talling was present at Taranto at the time. He also had to supply and conduct a band during the visit of the King and General de Gaulle to Algiers. Although the Italians had surrendered the Germans still fought in that country. The landings at Anzio (Operation *Shingle*) took place in January 1944 but the Allies found it very difficult to move out of the beachhead towards Rome to the north. On the 17th February HMS *Penelope*, having left Naples, was off Nettuno - which was part of the beachhead. As dawn broke the order "Heavy Armament Fall Out" was given and the men of the RM Band Starboard Watch left the TS and made their way to the Band Mess. Just as they arrived there a torpedo fired by U-410 struck the ship, which stopped dead in the water with a pronounced list to starboard. This was the third hit that *Penelope* had sustained during this commission and the crew reacted to this latest incident in a calm, resolute manner. The crew made their way to the deck to abandon ship. Within one minute and twenty seconds of the torpedo strike the ship had sunk taking well over half of her crew with her. BM Langford and Musns Blandford, Nicholson and Pickett were amongst those that lost their lives when the ship sank[35].

HMS *Asphodel, a* corvette of 1015 tons, was torpedoed and sunk whilst on convoy escort duty off Cape Finisterre on 9th March 1944. The German submarine U-575 scored what was, by this stage in the war, a rare success for the German submarine service. Musn B W K Denness was listed as "Missing in action, presumably killed".[36]

Bands from Scarborough continued with 'Salute the Soldier Week', and other concerts, varying the programmes in order to use both their band and their concert dance orchestra under BM C Hotham as well as their orchestra.

Things were progressing well with newly promoted Maj G C Keen as the Director of Music of the Junior Wing on the Isle of Man. He had inaugurated three boys' orchestras - each graded to suit its members' abilities - plus a Junior Dance Orchestra. The Boys' Ceremonial Band was 70 strong. Maj Keen continued the season of weekly concerts at the Villa Marina and these were very often preceded by a Military Band garden concert in the afternoon. The penultimate concert of the season took place on 24th September 1944 and comprised Suppé's *Poet and Peasant* Overture, Brahms' *Fantasia on Hungarian Dances*, two movements from Mozart's Horn Concerto No1 in D featuring P H Rider from the Liverpool Philharmonic as the soloist, Tchaikovsky's *Capriccio Italienne*, Labitzky's *Idyll* for Two Violins, Friedmann's *Slavonic Rhapsody* and a selection from Sullivan's *The Gondoliers*. There were also several BBC broadcasts in conjunction with the Manx choirs.

Dance Bands also toured the industrial areas. BM C Hotham and his band at Ford's Dagenham plant in 1944. On one occasion this band played to a works audience of 4,000 people.

As D-Day approached ships, crews and bands began, unknowingly, to prepare for the task ahead. The band of HMS *Arethusa* joined her at Chatham in early January 1944 and the ship immediately left to join the Home Fleet at Scapa Flow. Once there the ships routine became a series of exercises of all types. The band would be called on at any time of the night or day to close up in the TS for what was called 'Low Angle firing'[37]. They also practised closing up in the 'CP', which was the control position for the 4" anti-aircraft guns, and for close range LA firing. Damage control routines were also practised over and over again. The band's sleeping accommodation was not the best; some slept in the mess deck whilst others were on the upper deck in the area of the torpedo tubes. Whilst *Arethusa* was at Scapa the King came to inspect the Fleet. He stayed on board the Flagship, HMS *King George V*, and every night throughout his stay he gave a dinner party for various officers from the ships of the Fleet. This meant a lot of work for the Flagship band and, following the King's departure, the C-in-C Home Fleet, Admiral Sir Bruce Fraser handed the Bandmaster, W T Lang, a personal message from the King. It said, "His Majesty wishes to thank the band for their perseverance. As a Sailor he fully realises the inconvenience to which they have been put". A few weeks later HMS *Arethusa* left Scapa and called at Greenock to provision and load ammunition. As the ship cleared the Firth of Clyde the crew was told that they were going to support the Normandy landings. Two days before D-Day the ship arrived off the Lizard and received a signal to say that the operation was cancelled for 24 hours because of the weather. Next morning, in company with other units of the Home Fleet they joined the US Fleet off the Isle of Wight and proceeded to their positions for the landing. They were all to support the 6th Airborne Division and, if required, the landing of two infantry divisions. The nearest large town would be Caen. On the day of the landing HMS *Arethusa* was the first cruiser to move into position and also the first cruiser to open fire. The band were employed in the TS and also as relief telephone operators on the 20mm Oerlikon close-range anti-aircraft guns.

The band of HMS *Frobisher* had worked hard to cheer the troops in the invasion anchorages. The ship took part in the bombardment of the area in front of the Normandy landing sites and managed to hit either an ammunition or fuel dump. Later the band claimed to be the first military band to land in France since Dunkirk. They were certainly the first RM Band ashore.

Meanwhile HMS *Arethusa* had lost contact with their Forward Operational Base (FOB) as he moved out of the range of his radio but by1300hrs he had been picked up again. He called for fire onto a German gun position but at that exact time the TS broke down. Unable to calculate the ranges and bearings for the ship's main armament the band had to use a range clock and a Dumeresque table - both of which were mechanical as opposed to electrical instruments. Each time an air raid materialised guiding of the bombardment stopped as the band went to action stations on the 4" anti-aircraft guns. One member of the band claimed that he had less than an hour's sleep in two days. By the end of D-Day the ship was almost out of all ammunition and so she returned to Portsmouth to re-ammunition, provision and refuel. The ship returned to Normandy on June 10th and was immediately engaged in a bombardment with the band again manning the TS. That night they put to sea in company with HMS *Mauritius* to intercept enemy destroyers. The ships were travelling at 30 knots in line astern with *Mauritius* leading when the oscillator on board the Mauritius detonated a magnetic mine. Because of the speed they were travelling the *Arethusa* took the brunt of the explosion. The after CP[38] was temporarily put out of action by the explosion. The following day the ship went to its normal two-watch sea routine with main armament bombardment during the day and anti-aircraft duties at night. By 1700 the TS was again out of action and the Artificers were working to make it operational. The main armament could not operate without the TS. Musicians were now working twenty-four hours without sleep and then grabbing rest jammed against the TS table and cramped in spare corners. So much firing had taken place since D-Day that the forecastle and upper deck had split in two places. The food was awful as the cooks were also constantly at action stations and the chemical smoke that was put up as a screen made life very uncomfortable. On the 14th the ship went to Portsmouth to replenish stores and the musicians resumed band duties to play as the ship entered harbour and then to entertain the crew as stores were taken aboard. By 0730hrs on the 15th the ship was ready to return to Normandy again. Cars drew up on the jetty and Air Chief Marshal Sir Charles Portal, Chief of the General Staff General Sir Alan F Brooke, Admirals Ramsey and Cunningham, Generals Ismay and Laycock and then Lord Lascelles (the King's Private Secretary) came aboard. At 0800 the King came aboard and HMS *Arethusa* put to sea heading for her usual spot. On arrival the VIPs went ashore to dine with General Montgomery. Returning in the evening the guests were conveyed back to Spithead where the King and the VIPs disembarked. The crew had to wear No 2 uniform (best blues) all the time that the VIPs were aboard.

Next morning the ship left harbour with band playing and sailed to its Normandy anchorage. The shelling by the German guns had not abated and the danger from acoustic mines was still significant. The TS was again damaged and not rectified for 40 minutes. A musician brought a portable gramophone player into the CP and music was relayed via the telephone speakers to the aft plotting office and the bridge. The constant firing of *Arethusa's* guns was causing more vibration damage. Nearly all the lavatory pipe-work had parted company and there were queues to use the few that were still serviceable. The 24th June brought continuous shelling and air attacks from the Germans. Two acoustic mines exploded close by the ship. On the 24th the two radar sets were out of action, the after water storage tank was put out of action and the after gyro-compass, the only one working at the time, was broken. One of the propellers was damaged and out of line; Y turret was out of action; one of the turbines and an oil fuel tank were also damaged. The ship was ordered to Portsmouth and left the Normandy area at two knots to avoid setting off more mines. Once into the open sea speed was increased to 20 knots but the vibration was awful. The ship then received orders to make for Glasgow. As they arrived in the Firth of Clyde the band of a very battered HMS *Arethusa* was playing marches on the after gun deck. Cheering crowds lined the jetties as the ship moored.[39]

At about this time Maj F J Ricketts (Kenneth Alford) retired for medical reasons. The position of Director of Music Plymouth Division was given to Mr R H Stoner, Commissioned Bandmaster. This was the first time that a Director of Music of a Divisional Band was appointed from within the Corps. Eighty-one applications had been received for this position. Ten were short-listed for interview and whilst Mr C Nalden, Bandmaster of the Royal Artillery (Portsmouth) Band, was found to be most suitable and best qualified the Board recognised that Mr Stoner would also make a suitable choice. In 1944 the GOC Royal Marines issued instructions that, in future, preference would be given to RNSM ranks when vacancies occurred in the Divisional bands provided that such ranks had completed nine years' service.

Liberation Parades were taking place throughout Europe as the Allies achieved 'Victory in Europe' and RM Bands featured in many of them. HMS *Orion's* band of twelve marched in the parade through Athens, whilst the band of HMS *Sirius* (formerly the band of HMS *Valkyrie,* a Training Establishment on the Isle of Man) claimed to be "the first band to land in the south of France". The RM Detachment and Band of HMS *Argonaut* landed and marched through the streets of Salonika amidst flag waving, cheering, crowds. The ship moved to Piraeus and the Detachment and Band did the same there.

The Manx Music Festival included winning solos by future Directors of Music, P Neville and P Sumner. When VE Day was announced a scratch band had to be put together at Scarborough for local celebrations as the two bands were on duty away from the town. A big parade was held in Douglas, Isle of Man, with the Boys' Band leading and wearing white helmets - the first time that white helmets had been worn on the Island[40]. A few weeks after VE-Day the phased release of "old and bold" began. The first two Bandmasters to be released from Scarborough were BM Mortimer and Crosby on June 18th. Several were released from Junior Wing to a great send-off as the Boys' Band played *Auld Lang Syne* and *You'd Be Far Better Off in a Home!*

In July the King and Queen visited the Isle of Man and the Boys' Ceremonial Band was kept very busy throughout the week.

Whilst the war was still being fought in the Far East it was decided that a band should be formed from men in the Drafting Pool in Colombo, Ceylon, to tour RN and RM establishments in India. BM C H Brown was in charge of a band of fifteen. At 1730hrs on 1st June 1945 'T' Band, complete with a three-ton lorry full of instruments and equipment, entrained at Fort Station, Colombo for the great adventure. They crossed from Talamar to India by ferry and then, following a two-hour train journey to Manadapan, they re-loaded into lorries for a hot, dusty journey to their first accommodation which turned out to be a hut with three broken camp beds! More bedding was eventually found and the band prepared for their first concert. The piano supplied was totally out of tune and was substituted by the Padre's portable organ. The band then put on a show in the welldeck of an LCT (Landing Craft Tank) that was moored in the middle of the stream. BM Brown later reflected that "the delight of the LCT crews and other personnel repaid the bother entailed". During their stay the band also played for Divisions, Church, Wardroom, and two variety stage shows. Following this the band moved by train to Madras and then Visagapatam. The journey was appalling with temperatures as high as 125°F, with smells to match and water that was almost hot enough for tea. HMS *Amzari*, the RN Landing Craft Base at Visagapatam, was reached after several days travelling. Entertainment was provided in the Officers' Mess as well as two variety shows on stage and a military programme on the parade for the troops. A journey by lorry, ferry and train was necessary to reach Calcutta. On the train for Calcutta the band was expected to occupy a 3rd Class carriage recently vacated. The conditions were absolutely awful and, after a lengthy discussion, the band managed to squeeze into a 2nd Class compartment. The band was billeted in an Army camp in Calcutta but flooding caused an evacuation during the night. Entertainment was provided at various establishments in the Calcutta area including the Allied leave centre camp, various RM Messes and Barracks and the RN Barracks. From Calcutta the band travelled by train to Bombay sharing a carriage with about forty soldiers. Upon arrival a lorry took the band on the drive to Chembur which was a RM camp and a holding depot for both RN and RM personnel. Some of the men were beginning to suffer from the conditions and were feeling unwell but, with such a small band, they had to keep going. Most of the musicians were ill at some time or another as the conditions, the travelling and the changes of food took effect. Despite this, all of the planned jobs went ahead with only one exception. Whilst at Queen's Barracks the band visited, and played at, Sassoon Barracks, Wodehouse Barracks, Minden Fleet Club, the Town Hall and many others. The band arrived at Marve Camp on 3rd of July to find that an ENSA show was scheduled for the evening. This gave the band the opportunity for a rare evening off to watch others entertain them.

Following this they moved overland to Poona but, on arrival, several of the band were feeling very unwell and they all returned to Bombay. It was decided that they should travel by sea to Cochin so lorries took them to the docks where all their instruments and luggage had to be manhandled up the side of RFA *Dewdale* as no cranes were working. On arrival at Cochin the band was allocated to various establishments for a day. These included Anson Camp, Hoste Camp, HMS *Chinkara* (another landing craft base) the RNAS and the Military Hospital at Ernakulum. The band then made its way back to the Fleet Pool in Colombo having completed a very arduous seven-week tour.

Two amenity ships had been commissioned to provide floating entertainment for the men of the Far East Fleet, the SS *Menestheseus* and the SS *Agamemnon*. RNSM bands were sent to each. BM (WO) J E Talling was appointed to the first of these, SS *Menestheseus* a 9,000 ton former Blue Funnel liner, with BM C Hotham as second-in-command. BM (WO) K A MacLean was in charge of the *Agamemnon's* band with BM Hobbs. Members were selected who could show evidence of versatility as they had to be able to play as a first class dance orchestra, a salon orchestra or a grand concert orchestra. Some of the best musicians in the Band Service found themselves on these ships. The London theatrical tailors, Morris Angel Ltd, fitted them with white Tuxedo jackets and dress trousers and this was undoubtedly one of the best engagements for men from the RNSM. A theatre, a cinema and a brewery capable of brewing 1,800 gallons of beer a day were amongst the facilities in these ships. Other duties that fell to the bands included patrolling Hong Kong and Singapore when they were reoccupied, helping at Prisoner of War and Internment Camps and, as always, providing entertainment wherever they could.

SS *Menestheseus* was converted in Vancouver, and sailed for Yokohama, Kure, Shanghai and then back to England.

The musicians of HMS *Exeter* were liberated from a Japanese prison camp but five of their number had died in captivity. They were BM Vidler, BdCpl Buckle and Musns Bance, Harris and Wilkin. Four members of the RNSM had been killed in air raids during the Second World War and a further fifteen died during the same period.

With the war over stock could be taken of the effort given by the Royal Marine Bands from the Royal Naval School of Music. At a peak during the war the total number serving was 1,900 including 280 Pensioners and 300 Hostilities Only. Casualties totalled 225, representing 25% of those serving afloat. Awards totalled two MBEs; three BEMs; nine DSMs and thirty Mentions in Despatches.

Part 5 - The Royal Naval School of Music 1945 to 1950
(The work of the School and its Royal Marine Bands during a period of change)

In 1945 ships of the Royal Navy continued to be on station all over the world and many of them had to remain on duty despite the Second World War being over. At Rosyth King Haakon of Norway and the entire Norwegian Royal Family embarked, with all due ceremony of Guard and Band, on HMS *Norfolk* and were returned to Oslo where they arrived on the 7th June.

HMS *Leander* arrived in the United States shortly after VE-Day. The band under BM W H Cotton played at the Mulberry Exhibition at Philadelphia on ten consecutive days. The band also had several engagements in New York where they were attached to the shore establishment HMS *Saker*. This establishment had been used for personnel standing by ships under construction or refit. The ship then called at Montreal where thirty-five British schoolchildren who had been evacuated from the United Kingdom early in the war were taken aboard. During the passage home the band spent a great deal of time entertaining these children.

HMS *Swiftsure* was one of the first ships to return to Hong Kong following the occupation. The Royal Marine Detachment patrolled the town to round up looters and to help to bring a return to law and order. The band also took part in this work although the thought of "Bandy" with a Tommy gun did cause some misgivings! At Batavia and at Singapore the band of HMS *Sussex* (BM Jackson) worked hard at various Prisoner of War Camps and at Internment Camps.

In December HMS *Sirius* made a goodwill trip to King Ibn Saud of Saudi Arabia and provided a Guard and Band for the Crown Prince at Jeddah. Returning to Malta the band were paid off, some returning to the United Kingdom whilst the rest joined the Band of C-in-C Malta. This band was also known as the RM Central Band, Malta. Under BM WO E H Weller it mainly consisted of men from three ships *Liverpool*, *Sirius* and *Ajax* supplemented with men from the UK. Its temporary headquarters were at RM Training Centre, Mediterranean, which was at Ghain Tuffieha on Malta but it was due to move to a permanent base at HMS *Fareham*, an accommodation ship, at Manoel Island. The band's duties included playing at Service functions and parades in Malta and accompanying the C-in-C when embarked in HM ships for cruises. The band spent ten days in France and carried out many engagements during that period.

Band complements for the Home Fleet had been reduced. The majority of the battleships and cruisers were to be used for training young seamen and therefore only a reduced RM Detachment was required and, in the main, no band. HMS *King George V*'s band had transferred directly from HMS *Nelson* thus ensuring a smooth continuation of its proven musical and ceremonial efficiency. The temporary embarkation of *Birmingham's* band onto HMS *Bellona* for a visit to Jersey for the Liberation Celebrations indicated the flexibility of the RNSM system. A new Fleet Bandmaster of the Home Fleet, Mr J E Talling, was appointed. Massed bands from HM Ships *King George V*, *Implacable* and *Superb* gave a performance aboard the *King George V* and the BBC recorded most of the band's musical duties.

In Melbourne the massed bands of the aircraft carriers of the First Aircraft Carrier Squadron of the British Pacific Fleet Beat Retreat at the Shrine of Remembrance on 27th January 1946. The aircraft carriers were HMS *Indefatigable*, HMS *Implacable* and HMS *Glory*. The seventy-two musicians were massed under the baton of BM (WO) S C Cooper and the Drum Major was BM 2nd Cl A S Pinniger. The massed buglers were commanded by SgtBug Griffin RM of HMS *Indefatigable*. The whole ceremony was broadcast by the Australian Broadcasting Company and short-waved to the BBC in London.

At the RNSM Headquarters at Scarborough the drafting situation was becoming increasingly more difficult as the demobilisation continued. Some of the HO ranks had gone and all of the Pensioners except four bandmasters and ten Musicians who had volunteered to stay on. When the final three hundred HOs were demobbed maintaining the appropriate instrumentation would become a problem that would last until recruitment levels rose. Changes in the hierarchy of the School were also taking place. Maj A Pragnell retired and was replaced as Musical Director by Capt H Kenward. BM B C Barnes was promoted Lieutenant and appointed Assistant Musical Director. Lt H Wright also retired as did Lt Papworth who was replaced by Lt G L Read who was recalled from Junior Wing. D A Jarman was promoted to Commissioned Bandmaster.

BM R H Willmot arrived with a new band at HMS *St Vincent* to find that he had inherited a Corps of Drums and a Drum Major. They were all Wrens and were from all walks of life - including the acting profession. Since they were very popular with the Captain the Bandmaster had to "adopt" them. However he quickly found that they were very efficient and very popular at local functions.

A band from the RNSM under Cd BM K A McLean completed a successful tour of combined operations in the Largs[1] area and a party of RMB ranks augmented the Chatham Divisional Band when it went to Germany.

The January 1946 Accommodation Return for the RNSM indicated that the Senior School, Scarborough, was accommodating one Officer, forty-three SNCOs and two hundred and ninety-nine other ranks in the Norbreck and Clifton Hotels whilst the Junior School at Howstrake Camp on the Isle of Man was accommodating ten Officers, twenty-five SNCOs and two hundred and eighty-eight other ranks. This total included five Wrens and two hundred and thirty-one Band Boys. The need to relocate the two Wings of the School to a common site was paramount and in August 1946 the move was made to a former American Army Camp at Broadwell Grove, Burford in Oxfordshire. A series of Farewell Concerts was given by the Senior Wing at the Opera House, Scarborough, under Musical Director Capt H Kenward with Lt Barnes as the Leader. On 1st August the Junior Wing left the Isle of Man. A letter of appreciation from the Lieutenant Governor of the Isle of Man to the Officer Commanding RNSM was sent on their departure. The CO of the

Junior Wing, Maj G C Keen, retired after thirty-nine years service and was replaced by Maj N U V Roche. On September 10th the Commandant General visited Burford. He stressed the need for recruitment to build up and maintain the "Royal Naval Band Service" and promised that improved conditions for band ranks were on the way.

On 22nd October the RN Medical Officer of Health, The Nore, visited Burford. He described the School as a hutted camp covering nine acres and situated in forty-five acres of Admiralty controlled land. Having been made aware that the total complement in the near future would be between twelve and fourteen hundred the Inspecting Officer felt that this number could not be accommodated without overcrowding and overloading the sanitary facilities. In a response to this report it was stated that Broadwell Grove would not hold the anticipated increased complement without additional buildings but Alonquin Camp at Whitley was being investigated as an alternative site for the School. This would be big enough and the chances of obtaining the site were about even.[2]

Changes to uniforms were made at this time. The famous lyre over globe and laurel cap badge was to be replaced by the globe and laurel with lion and crown cap badge worn by all Royal Marine ranks and the 'RMB' shoulder title was to be replaced by the 'RM'. Musicians would continue to wear the lyre collar badges. Bandmasters 1st Class would wear a lyre encircled by a laurel wreath surmounted by a crown as a badge of rank. They would wear a leather sword belt and carry a sword. The Senior NCOs held "a night of gloom" in the Mess to mourn the loss of the two items that had been worn with great pride and marked them as men of the RNSM and the Royal Marine Band Service - the lyre cap-badge and the "RMB" shoulder-title.

In the 1946 Victory March the RN and the RM led the military section of the parade. Dr Thomas Wood MA MusD(Oxon) Hon ARCM wrote an evocative description of the Parade for the 'Globe and Laurel' which included the following passage.

> And there were the Royal Marines. They marched as they alone can march, twelve abreast, in two columns of six that that divided at the Cenotaph; a detachment drawn from all units, under the command of LtCol F B Pym. Ahead of them were the Massed Bands of the Chatham, Portsmouth and Plymouth Divisions and the Royal Naval School of Music; and if ever a man had a right to be proud it must have been Drum Major Louis Beer, in front. Up swelled a roar of cheering; the men marched by and were gone[3].

In 1946 the whole of the Royal Naval Education Service was reorganised and both the RN and RM Schoolmasters became Instructor Officers with the rank of Instructor Sub Lieutenant etc[4]. At the same time the RM adopted the RN system and their rates of pay. This gave the RM Warrant Officer the same conditions of service as Warrant Officers in the Royal Navy. Other effects were that the maximum age of service for Directors of Music was reduced from sixty to fifty with an option of serving, at Admiralty discretion, to the age of 55; the qualifying period for promotion from Lieutenant to Captain was increased from three to eight years.

The bands of the Home Fleet began to return to their peacetime status during 1947. A tenor drum was obtained and the Fleet, from its own funds, bought a leopard skin for the percussionist and some marches for massed band work. The Fleet visited the Clyde during 1947 and Royal Guards and Bands paraded for Their Majesties. A very high standard was achieved and the Fleet Bandmaster, (Fl BM) Mr Talling, conducted the orchestra of the Fleet Flagship at all of the concert performances in HMS *Illustrious*. At a Naval Display at a stadium ashore CdBM Jarman conducted and Drum Major Wells led the massed bands. For this display Admiral (Air) had lent his Royal Marine Band of HMS *Daedalus* to HMS *Sirius*; Flag Officer Scotland and Northern Ireland (FOSNI) lent his band to HMS *Maidstone* and Commodore RNB Chatham lent his band to HMS *Howe*. These bands together with eighty-five Band Boys, two more Drum Majors and twenty Buglers provided a very impressive performance.

During 1947 Lord Mountbatten, now Viceroy of India, directed that a band should make a tour of the Far East. The band, under BdCpl Thompson, with their instruments, equipment and kit on arrival in Calcutta.

During the same year HMS *Aurora* was in Devonport dockyard undergoing a refit prior to being sold to the Chinese Nationalist Navy. HMS *Renown*, now in the Reserve, was being used as accommodation for the Chinese crew sent to take the *Aurora* back to China. BM R A Hobbs was sent, with a set of military band instruments and drums purchased by the Chinese Naval Authorities, to join the *Renown* with the task of training a band of Chinese in the manner of a Royal Marine Band. A Chinese member of the band took over from Hobbs just before *Aurora* left England. The Royal Navy were responsible for taking the *Aurora* to Hong Kong from where the Chinese crew took her up the Yangtse River where she ran aground and was bombed and sunk by Communist aircraft. BM Hobbs returned to the RNSM in 1948.[5]

Burford was a good location from which the Band Boys went on trips to Cheltenham and Oxford where they were able to attend performances by well-known orchestras. Dr Malcolm Sargent visited the School in January and officiated at the pass-out parade of HMS *Triumph's* Band. He inspected the School, including the Boys' Instruction classes, conducted the Symphony Orchestra and, at the end of the day, was presented with a miniature timpani made by BdCpl McGain-Harding. It was also in 1946 that Sir Felix Cassel began the annual presentation of the Silver and Bronze Medal to Band Boys of the RNSM[6].

The atrocious weather of early 1947 seriously disrupted sport and entertainment at Burford. The C-in-C, The Nore, visited and passed out the band for HMS *Sussex* on parade, as a Military Band, as a String Orchestra and as a Dance Band. He also inspected the School, the Oceanaires Dance Band and the School Staff Symphony Orchestra. Later in the year Sir John Barbirolli, the conductor of the Hallé Orchestra, also visited the School as did Noel Coward.

Col R A R Neville wrote to the Commandant General in June to propose that the 1947 inspection should include a display with four bands. This would provide the opportunity for the Commandant General to see the proposed display for the 1948 Royal Tournament at Olympia. A programme was devised, and notes were provided, that allowed the Commandant General a complete view of the training and the abilities that were within the School whilst also ensuring that he was aware of the concerns of the Staff. These concerns were mainly founded upon the isolation of the camp and the difficulties, and expense, with regard to local accommodation for families as well as the distance to be traversed to 'local' entertainment - even a public house! The programme included being met by a Guard of Honour and Band; Passing Out the band for HMS *Newcastle*; auditioning the Oceanaires Dance Band; watching the display by four bands; attending a Symphony Orchestra Concert and addressing all Officers, Other Ranks and Band Boys. In his address the Commandant General pronounced himself most satisfied with the standard of turn-out, bearing and drill of all those that he saw. His main impressions were of firstly, efficiency of the training, secondly the atmosphere of enthusiasm and pride and thirdly the hard work that had gone into making Burford as comfortable as possible. There was no mention of an alternative site for the School.

The CGRM, LtGen R A Dallas Brooks, visited the RNSM at Burford on the 24th September 1947. He saw the display by four bands of the RNSM that would be performed at the 1948 Royal Tournament at Olympia.

A band of one hundred and twenty Musicians under Capt H Kenward, plus the Oceanaires Dance Band under BM Hotham, appeared at the Royal Albert Hall on Trafalgar Day 1947 for the RN Old Comrades Association. As Musical Director of the RNSM Capt Kenward now had forty bands and approximately twelve hundred musicians under his direction. During this year Lt W T Lang was appointed Assistant Musical Director. The Boys' Company had a Senior and a Junior Orchestra, a Dance Orchestra and a Military Band. As recruits the Boys first passed through 'Churchill' and then 'Battenberg' Rooms before living in rooms named after famous Admirals.

HM the King approved the change of BM1st Cl and BM 2nd Cl to Bandmaster and Band Sergeant. This enhanced the status of Bandmasters by bringing their title into line with their duties and provided bands with Senior NCOs as an instrumentalist and second-in-command. Prospects in the Band Service were now better than ever, their fine work during the War was bearing fruit and, through their own activities, the bands were much more widely known in both Service and civilian circles. Bands continued to represent their country, the Royal Navy and the Royal Marines all over the world. The band from HMS *St George*[7] Gosport, under BM Johnstone went aboard the aircraft carrier HMS *Triumph* and soon after its arrival in Kronstadt where Admiral Tributz, the C-in-C of the Red Banner Baltic Fleet, came aboard. Whilst the Portsmouth Divisional Band were on Royal Duty in HMS *Vanguard* a band from the RNSM, under Lt B C Barnes, covered the musical requirements of the Division. They were hastily sent, with a Royal Guard, to Denmark for the funeral of King Christian X. In this same year the ability of RM Bands was further recognised when the band of the Infantry Training Centre, Lympstone, broadcast a military band programme on BBC West Region network.

November 1947 saw the Royal Wedding of Princess Elizabeth and Prince Philip and a band of sixty from the RNSM under the Musical Director was prominently positioned outside Westminster Abbey.

The Commanding Officer of the new HMS *Royal Arthur*[8] at Corsham, Wiltshire was approached to provide trumpeters to be in attendance on Mr Justice Hillberry, who had served in the RN during World War I, at Wiltshire Assizes. History was made when a Band Corporal and three Musicians from the RNSM escorted the Judge and played a trumpet fanfare composed by BM Whitney.

Also, in 1947 the RNSM was instructed to provide a band for 3 Cdo Bde, Royal Marines, and there was also an increasing demand for bands for Naval shore establishments. In the same year WO K A MacLean was promoted Lieutenant and appointed Assistant Musical Director.

1948 began with the award, announced in the New Years Honours List, of the BEM to CSM Wells who had been Drum Major of the RNSM Headquarters Band and who, during the Second World War, was Bandmaster of HMS *Dido*. Another honour was given later in the year when Dr T Wood, the President of the Royal Philharmonic Society, nominated the Musical Director, Capt H Kenward to be a Member of the Society. His subsequent election represented an honour to the Band Service. In 1941 Dr Wood had turned, on the recommendation of the Admiralty Librarian, to the RNSM for assistance with matters relating to a BBC programme about sea shanties in traditional settings that he was preparing.[9] This led to a strong relationship between Dr Wood and the School.

Meanwhile 3 Cdo Bde was in Malta, having completed training in early 1948. The band, under BM Dixon,[10] became commandos at least in dress since they wore the khaki battledress and green beret of the Brigade. They also wore white belts and anklets. Although part of Brigade HQ the band was responsible for the entertainment of all units. They were sent to Tripoli to entertain 42 Cdo. They also spent time at Castel Benito with the RAF providing concerts and playing at cocktail parties and guest nights. St George's Day was celebrated by Beating Retreat in Malta where the band used the unusual 'lane'[11] formation during the troop. The band returned to Tripoli in June and, as well as playing for Commando units, they entertained the various Army Regiments stationed there with military band programmes, orchestral concerts and dance bands. In July the band took part in the Changing of the Guard at the Palace, Valletta, on Saturday mornings, with units of the Royal Malta Artillery, and then with 40 and 45 Commando who took over the Guard duties for some weeks. They were also involved in the ceremonies for the Shah of Persia during his visit to Malta. Their Drum Major was BdSgt J J Morten.

3 Cdo Bde Band (BM Dixon), attached to 45 Commando, play for Changing the Guard at the Governor's Palace, Valetta, Malta GC in 1948.

Another band formed in 1948 was that for HMS *Devonshire*. This was the Cadets' Training Cruiser that spent the spring on the West Indies Station, the summer in the Baltic and the autumn in the Mediterranean. A band from the RNSM under Capt H Kenward was involved at the unveiling of the Roosevelt Memorial, being positioned close to the American Embassy in Grosvenor Square, London[12].

The paying-off of many ships was, by 1948, starting to create accommodation problems at Burford but five draft bands were under training and their departure was expected to ease the situation. However, at this time the RNSM was probably at its peak. It was certainly an exciting place to be as Maj A H R Buckley discovered:

> As a mere sojourner in their midst, the writer has been struck by two points in connection with this branch of the Corps. First, its outstanding esprit de corps, which yields to none and is an object lesson to many; second, the quite unjustified lack of knowledge and appreciation of its merits and services, not only by our own Corps, but also by many of the Royal Navy which it serves so well, and the general public.

A unique event occurred when Colonel Neville, became the first School Commandant to be promoted Major General. He was replaced by Colonel P R Smith-Hill. Another 'first' for RM Bands occurred when the Musical Director and a military band of fifty-four musicians from the RNSM played at a Royal Garden Party on July 8th. As the RNSM was not allowed a Staff Band, the many commitments for which the School was asked to provide bands or orchestras had therefore to be met by forming combinations for each engagement from the drafting margin available. That these bands compared favourably with other Service bands, which were virtually permanent in composition, was a measure of not only the instrumentalists' ability but also the ability of those directing them, since they only had very short periods for rehearsal. Time and again the School put on a fine show at short notice under these difficult circumstances.

Capt A C Green wrote:

> Recognition had at last come to the Band Service after forty-five years of existence and great service in two World Wars, the great ceremonial occasions in London throughout the year and hundreds of other public engagements at home and abroad and BBC broadcasts. Recruiting was soaring, and an astonishing return to pre-war efficiency in musical standard fostered by an esprit-de-corps second to none in a Corps so justly famed for this quality. 1948 would be regarded as a milestone in progress.

Prospects for promotion within the Service were greater than ever before and arrangements were being made for examinations to be taken abroad so that sea-going musicians were not penalised. The Military Band made a number of recordings of marches to be used as records for instructional purposes on board ships that were not entitled to bands. Two hundred musicians, gathered from many ships and establishments and directed by Capt H Kenward, were at the unveiling of the memorials to Admirals Jellicoe and Beatty.

As far as the RNSM and its Band Service was concerned the major event of 1948 occurred on the 1st June. It had been decided that the example of the Memorial Silver Drums for those of the Band Service who had died in the First World War should be followed to commemorate the dead of World War Two. A Memorial Committee had been appointed to arrange the collection of the money and to select what should be purchased as the Memorial itself. A representative of every rank in the Band Service would sit on the Committee. This included two Band Boys, one of whom was a section leader. There was a suggestion that the Silver Memorial Drums should be replaced as they were very worn and rarely used but there was a keenness to have trumpets and they were duly chosen. The fourteen fanfare trumpets were purchased and 1st of June was the date set for their dedication and their presentation. The rules relating to these trumpets were set down in 'The War Memorial Charter' and the Book of Remembrance became the third part of the Memorial.

Misleading weather forecasts plagued 1st June but by 1550hrs the day was ideal. Firstly, the School Chapel of St Cecilia, the Patron Saint of Musicians, was dedicated by the Chaplain of the Fleet, accompanied by the RNSM Chaplain and Ministers of all denominations and the Commandant. The orchestra (Leader Bd/Sgt Hazle) was conducted by Lt Barnes who had also trained the choir of forty-five Band Boys. The Second Sea Lord, CGRM, Chief of Staff Royal Marines and all three Group Commanders were present. (By this time the three RM Divisions had become Groups) Also present were Gen Weir, Col McCausland, Maj Fairfield and Maj Pragnell (past Commandants and Musical Directors), relatives of those who had lost their lives during the Second World War and past and present members of the Band Service. Also present were Gen Neville, the driving force behind the Memorial, and "The Father of the Band Service" H E Lidiard. Following the Dedication of the Chapel everyone moved outside to the arena. Here the Massed Bands were drawn up before a dais that carried the Book of Remembrance and the stands that carried the Memorial Trumpets. The Dedication Service began with the congregation being led in the singing by the band under the Musical Director. The Commandant General read the lessons and the Book of Remembrance was blessed. All ranks were called to attention and, in the silence, the School Chaplain handed one of the trumpets to the Chaplain of the Fleet for Dedication. "*In memory of those who gave their lives in the service of their country*". The Commandant received the trumpets and, with the Musical Director, handed each of the fourteen to those who had the honour of receiving them on behalf of the Royal Marines Bands. They were BMs Archard and Fitzgerald, BSgts Anderson, Arnold, Saunders and Roper, Cpls Wood, Phasey, Glass and Corben, L/Cpl Dent, Musns Keld and Scott and Band Boy Green. On the command a moving fanfare was sounded. *The Spirit of Joy and Thanksgiving for Victory, and Meditation for those who gave their lives in its cause* composed by Leon Young, a wartime survivor of HMS *Hermione*, and known simply as *To Comrades Sleeping*. After an address by the Chaplain of the Fleet the service concluded with the inspiring words of Sir Francis Drake's prayer and the singing of the Naval Hymn, *Eternal Father*. The Musical Director then passed responsibility for the 'Act of Memorial' by the Massed Bands of the RNSM to Lt Lang. A fanfare by Curzon was played and then the four bands marched on to *Nancy Lee* before performing a complex marching display to Alford's *By Land and Sea* and *HM Jollies* at the end of which they had formed two bands. The drums Beat Retreat and the bands stepped off again to Safroni's *Imperial Echoes* finally halting in front of the dais as one band of two hundred. Led by four Drum Majors and the large Corps of Drums the band played Dr Thomas Wood's *St George's Day* followed by another fanfare by Leon Young then *Rule Britannia* and the Evening Hymn. Capt A C Green's arrangement of *Sunset* was played as the Ensign was lowered, followed by the National Anthem. The Second Sea Lord took the salute and the bands marched off to the Regimental March.

Having provided musicians to augment the Group Bands at the 1947 Royal Tournament it was the turn of the Massed Bands of the RNSM themselves in 1948. Musicians drawn from the Fleet and from RN and RM establishments augmented the School Band to produce a band one hundred strong. Maj Dunn of the Portsmouth Group was asked to rehearse the music for the event. The massed bands under Lt Lang, who had devised the intricate marching display, were called '*The Staff Band of the Royal Naval School of Music*' in the programme. The bands, playing almost the same programme as that performed at the Act of Memorial at Burford a few days earlier and using the Memorial Trumpets for the first time in public, gave a very good musical and marching display in slow and quick time that was based upon Lang's original display at Burford. This was the embryonic beginning of the Beat Retreat performances on Horse Guards Parade. Army and RAF bands later adopted this type of display[13].

Recognition had at last come to the RM Bands, the products of the RNSM, after forty-five years' existence and great service in two World Wars. The great ceremonial occasions in London throughout the year, together with hundreds of other public engagements at home and abroad plus BBC broadcasts, were proof of this. Recruiting was soaring and an astonishing return to pre-war efficiency in musical standard had been achieved.

Another visitor was Sir Malcolm Sargent who had recently been appointed as Honorary Advisor in Music to the Royal Marines. It was hoped that Sir Malcolm would

The RM Band of HMS Norfolk marches the Kenya Police Guard to Government House, Nairobi, to relieve the Guard provided by the ship's RM Detachment.

visit the School annually to witness the musical instruction given to the Boy Musicians and to other instrumentalists.

On the 8th October 1948 The King approved the proposal of the Lords Commissioners of the Admiralty that his own appointment as Colonel in Chief of His Majesty's Royal Marines should be changed to Captain General.

Meanwhile the Band Service maintained its work at sea. By 1949 there were thirty-nine bands spread all over the world. BM Harwood was serving in HMS *London* on the Yangtse River when HMS *Amethyst* was trapped by the Chinese. HMS *London* was also fired upon and the bandmaster was later awarded the DSM for his services in dealing with the wounded men.

> The band had no official Action Stations so they all volunteered for various duties; some went to Damage Control Stations, others to shell handling, cordite rooms, 4" ready use lockers and myself to First Aid. My Action Station was in the Chapel.

BM Harwood found himself administering to the wounded below decks with damage control parties and in the very overcrowded Sick Bay.[14]

3 Cdo Bde Band toured Cyprus for six weeks entertaining troops at various Army camps; Beating Retreat at Nicosia, Larnaca and Limassol and also providing orchestral programmes at the Governor's Palace. The band had been tasked with providing a programme of music on board HMS *Virago* but, upon arriving at the docks, they found that the ship's motorboat had been smashed in a storm the previous night. Undaunted they loaded all of the instruments and gear that a twenty-four piece band needs into a whaler and proceeded to row themselves out to the ship, a task that was accomplished in only two trips! The Brigade Band took part in 'A Ceremonial Parade to Celebrate S[t] George's Day'

at St Patrick's Barracks Malta. The massed bands of the Mediterranean Fleet (HMS *Vanguard*, *Forth*, *Liverpool*, *Ocean* and *Euryalus*) and 3 Cdo Bde were under the direction of CdBM Fitzgerald. The parade itself was an interesting hybrid. It was based upon the ceremony of Trooping the Colour but a *Feu de Joie* was substituted for the Trooping. After that the ceremony became a Beat Retreat. The musical programme had some intriguing items in it. The opening march, *Lilliburlero*, was credited to Thomas Wood because he had arranged it for use as the main theme to his march *St George's Day*. This was followed by Soldier's Chorus from *Faust*, (Gounod),[15] *British Grenadiers* and *Beating of the Assembly* by the Corps of Drums, then 'Scipio (Handel), a Royal Salute, the *Duke of York*'(arr Balfour), two Alford marches *HM Jollies* and *By Land and Sea*, *Sarie Marais* arranged by Dixon,[16] *A Life on the Ocean Wave*,'Early One Morning, *Heart of Oak* (Boyce),'British *Grenadiers* and the *RAF March* (Walford). Following another Royal Salute the Bugles and massed bands played Green's *Sunset*. After the *Hymn of Malta* and the *National Anthem* the bands marched off to *Sarie Marais* and *Eagle Squadron*.

At the end of the year the first issue of the "Blue Band" appeared. This magazine was for the benefit of the men of the RNSM and the RM Bands. It was to appear three times a year and its first editor was Instructor Lieutenant D McLeish and the Commandant, Col P R Smith-Hill, wrote a foreword. It also contained an open letter from Sir Malcolm Sargent, the Honorary Musical Advisor.

In his report issued just prior to Christmas 1949 Maj R G S Lang, the Commandant of the RNSM, gave the following indication of what life for the recruit at Deal[17] would be like:

> With the forthcoming move to Deal, a new system of training was to be adopted which would produce more satisfactory results. There was to be a period of concentrated parade work for newly joined recruits on their arrival. A Draft Squad[18] would be formed each term, with Boy Musicians of seventeen and a half to eighteen years, who were to do revisionary work in all subjects prior to being passed out. Members of the Draft Squad would receive leave privileges, and wear caps and a distinguishing white lanyard. They would still be able to gain accelerated advancement, with the accompanying extra pay, on attaining the age of eighteen. In the educational field, the new scheme of training would enable boys to qualify educationally for promotion before leaving the Boys Wing[19].

A special train took the Boys to Deal on the 6th June 1950 and so the RNSM marched back into what used to be the Depot, Deal, but was now Royal Marines, Deal. The senior officer was now styled "Commanding Officer, Royal Marines Deal" and "Commandant, Royal Naval School of Music".

Boy Musicians were housed in East Barracks, now called the Royal Naval School of Music, whilst trained Musicians and NCOs were accommodated in North Barracks. RM Deal had four Companies. 'M' Company consisted of Musicians; 'B' Company of Boys; 'R' Company of Recruits and staff of the establishment were HQ Company. HQ Company was responsible for the whole establishment. Group Buglers were now sent to the RNSM for all of their training. The Depot Band became the 'Staff Band of the Royal Naval School of Music'. In addition to its parade duties this band was to enable the Bandmasters and other classes to gain experience in conducting. The School continued to deal with the drafting, promotion and records of other ranks of the Band Service.

Capt H Kenward, the Musical Director of the RNSM, retired on the 19th March 1950. The new Musical Director was Lt K A MacLean who had enlisted at Deal as a Royal

RM Detachment and the Massed Bands of the Commander-in-Chief and HMS Triumph on the flight-deck of HMS Triumph in 1950. This ship was the first British aircraft -carrier to arrive off Korea (June 1950).

Marine recruit and was awarded the King's Badge (93rd Squad). He was the only Musical Director ever to wear this badge.[20] Col P R Smith-Hill was appointed "In Continuation" as Commanding Officer, and Commandant, RNSM at Deal. In 1950 the Staff Band at Deal was twenty-five strong; eleven bands were in commission in shore establishments in this country; one band was ashore with 3 Cdo Bde in Hong Kong; eight bands were afloat in Home Waters; thirteen bands were afloat elsewhere including the band attached to the RNZN in HMNZS *Bellona*. The total number of RM Bands was thirty-four, each having a strength of between fifteen and twenty-eight. There were well over 1,000 members of the RM Band Service of whom more than 200 were Boy Musicians.

Following the return to Deal from Burford, and on account of the raising of the school leaving age, it became necessary to completely revise the syllabus of educational training of Boy Musicians in order to ensure that they would receive an education comparable to that given in a civilian secondary modern or technical school. A team of HM Inspectors from the Ministry of Education carried out a detailed inspection of the School working on the new syllabus and approval was given, thus enabling boys below the normal school leaving age to continue to be recruited. This revision meant the introduction of a much wider range of subjects and the fitting up of science laboratories and metal and wood handicraft workshops and led to a much wider interest in education generally.

Boy Musicians and Boy Buglers were reorganised into Houses. Those for Boy Musicians were named after ships in which RM Band ranks suffered heavy casualties during World War II: Gloucester, Neptune, Barham, and Eagle. The first Squad to bear the title 'The Commandant General's Squad' was passed out by him in March. The Squad consisted of Senior Boy Musicians who trained together before being rated Musician 2nd Class. A Commandant General Royal Marines (CGRM) Certificate was introduced and awarded to the best all-round Boy Musician in the Squad. This has since been replaced by the 'The Prince's Badge'.

In March 1950 Maj F V Dunn decided to arrange a Charity Concert that would draw upon not only his own Portsmouth Group Orchestra but also those of the RNSM bands based in the area. These were the bands of the RNB Portsmouth, HMS *Excellent* and HMS *St Vincent*. The concert took place on the 29th March 1950 in the gymnasium of the RNB Portsmouth and was to benefit the Queen of the Hellenes Fund for Greek Refugee Children and the Lord Mayor of Portsmouth's charities. The Portsmouth Bach Society and the Emsworth and District Choral Society were invited to take part. Sir Malcolm Sargent, in his capacity as Honorary Advisor in Music, agreed to conduct at the concert. The programme consisted of *The National Anthem*, *The Walk to the Paradise Garden* (Delius), Symphony No 5 in E minor *From the New World* (Dvorak); *Sea Symphony* (Vaughan Williams); Verdi's aria from *La Traviata*; Handel's *I Rage, I Melt, I Burn* and *O Ruddier Than the Cherry* and finally Sir Malcolm Sargent's own arrangement of Arne's *Rule Britannia* The concert was a great success.

The first Royal Marines Beat Retreat on Horse Guards Parade took place in June 1950. This had not been attempted before and Maj F V Dunn was asked to take responsibility for the musical programme whilst Lt Lang of the RNSM was responsible for devising the display and for all parade work. The Group Bands from Chatham, Portsmouth and Plymouth together with the bands of RNB Chatham; RNB Portsmouth; RNB Plymouth as well as bands from five shore establishments, HMS *Daedalus*, *Excellent*, *Gamecock*, *Ganges* and *Raleigh*, totalling 260 musicians, assembled and rehearsed at Eastney. It was for this display that Lt Lang introduced what was at that time a fairly adventurous and unusual marching display. This display was to set the precedent for all future Beat Retreat performances on Horse Guards Parade and appears to have been based upon his original concept for the presentation of the Memorial Fanfare Trumpets at Burford and later used at the Royal Tournament. When the bands arrived in London very bad weather prevented any rehearsal on the Parade itself. The programme started with a fanfare played upon the fourteen Memorial Fanfare Trumpets of the Royal Naval School of Music and directed by Lt W Lang. On completion the massed bands stepped off to *HM Jollies*. The complete programme was as follows:

Quick March	HM Jollies	Alford
Troop	By Land and Sea	Alford
Bugle March	Mechanised Infantry	McBain
	FANFARE	
	by the Memorial Fanfare Trumpets of the RNSM	
	CEREMONY OF BEAT RETREAT	
	by the Corps of Drums	
Quick March	Imperial Echoes	Safroni
Troop	Tudor Maiden	Trad (arr Dunn)
Quick March	Old Panama	Alford
Quick March	Standard of St George	Alford
Finale:	Trumpet Voluntary	Clarke
	The Day Thou Gavest	Scholefield
	Combined setting for Bugles and Bands of Sunset	Green
	Fanfare for Military Band and Trumpets	Bliss
	Rule Britannia	Arne (arr Wood)
	God Save The King	
	A Life on the Ocean Wave	Russell

The massed bands were led by five Drum Majors, A Woods of Chatham Group Band; Charles Bowden of Portsmouth Group Band (Drum Major L Beer was on leave prior to discharge); R Woodruffe of Plymouth Group Band; and F Tobin and W Spencer from the RNSM[21]. The bands stepped off in quick time and advanced to the Horse Guards Buildings, countermarched and then executed a left wheel at the centre of the parade. After a further counter march the bands halted and ceased playing. The bands advanced across the parade in slow time, countermarched and again halted. The bugle march was then played and the bands marched in quick time. The Corps of Drums moved into position to Beat Retreat which was preceded by a fanfare played on the thirty-two Silver Bugles.[22] It was the first occasion since the presentation that all thirty-two had been sounded together. Drummers from the RNSM were using the World War I Silver Memorial Drums so all three Memorials from the two world wars were on parade. Following this the Corps of Drums rejoined the massed bands as they slow marched across the Parade and, on completion, the bands broke into quick time without halting, marched across the Parade and countermarched. During this phase the band was split into two by Plymouth Group Band and the RNSM Band countermarching whilst the other two bands continued across the Parade. All countermarched and when they met in the centre of the Parade the Chatham and Plymouth Group bands wheeled right and left to join as one band whilst the other two bands carried out a similar manoeuvre to march in the opposite direction. The bands then rejoined to form a massed band as they came to a halt with the Corps of Drums and Memorial Fanfare Trumpets in rear of the bands. Following the finale the bands marched off to *A Life on the Ocean Wave*. The display took place on two evenings and then it was repeated at the White City Stadium before a crowd of 50,000[23].

So, at the close of the half-century the music of the Royal Navy was in a much-improved state. The Royal Marines had in 1903, as the Admiralty had wished, instituted a structure and a discipline that encouraged the Naval or recruit musician to meet new and consistent standards. The bands produced were of a much higher standard than previously - although not as well equipped instrumentally as the Royal Marine Divisional Bands. In their own eyes, and in the eyes of many others, the Royal Marine Bands were every bit as good as the Divisional Bands and they cited the fact that they were, at this time, being invited to play at events that were previously the preserve of Brigade of Guards or Royal Marine Divisional Bands. War service and losses had raised their profile whilst the efficiency with which the provision of bands was carried out endeared them to the Admiralty and to the Royal Navy. 'The British Survey' for April 1950, printed the following:

> The diplomatic and ambassadorial consequences of routine cruises engaged in 'Showing the Flag' are obviously of the highest importance. A first class band of the Royal Marines is probably the best exponent of the art of public relations yet devised by man.

However, the war was four years in the past and, as ever when a war begins to fade in the memory, cuts in manning loomed over the armed forces and the scene was set for not only cuts but also amalgamation. Who would bear the reductions and who would gain the upper hand? Would it be the flexible, adaptable Royal Naval School of Music with its Royal Marine Bands or the, by comparison, insular Group Bands who did their own recruiting and training on an individual basis and whose terms of enlistment prevented them from being drafted to other bands?

Part 6 - The Royal Naval School of Music 1945 to 1950
(The policies and reports behind the changes of 1946 - 1950)

As the Second World War came to a close and both the civil and military population struggled to adapt to peacetime conditions it became apparent to many that radical changes were needed to the musical service that the Royal Marines provided to the Royal Navy and to the Corps itself. Demobilisation was causing manning problems and a new, combined, home urgently needed to be found for the RNSM.

In 1945 the Superintendent of the RNSM had submitted his draft 'Instructions for the RN School of Music' to the CGRM. This document not only described the organisational, administrative and educational systems that were in place but also clearly demonstrated that everything was in place for the RNSM of the future. The wind of change was blowing and the School was clearly prepared. The Instruction began with a description of the function of the School and introduced a subtle change of emphasis when it stated that:

> The functions of the RM Band Service as part of the Corps of Royal Marines, is the provision of bands for the Fleet, Royal Naval and certain Royal Marines Shore Establishments. Personnel are trained at the Royal Naval School of Music for this Service and at Royal Naval Gunnery Schools for Fire Control duties in the gunnery organisation of HM Ships.

The staffing of the School was described in detail and showed that it was run on the lines of a RM Division with the Superintendent, who was responsible for discipline, training and administration, reporting directly to the CGRM on all matters relating to the School whilst communicating directly with Naval Authorities on all matters relating to the RM Band Service. The School was organised into Headquarters, Senior Wing (Trained Soldiers) and a Junior Wing (Band Boys under training). The Superintendent had a Second-in-Command who, as well as commanding the RNSM in the absence of the Superintendent, was Field Officer General Duties; Examiner of Accounts; President of the Officers' Mess and of the Institute Fund; Supervisor of the SNCO's Mess and also responsible for welfare. A Company Commander was appointed for each of the Companies. Other staff were the Adjutant, Superintending Clerk, Drafting Officer, Paymaster, Quartermaster (V), Quartermaster (M)[1] and the Musical Director and Assistant Musical Director.

In 1946 the Lamplough Committee, chaired by Col CRW Lamplough had been formed to propose detailed arrangements for the 'Re-organisation of the Royal Marine Establishments in the United Kingdom'. One of the recommendations made was that the RM establishments should be formed into three Groups: Chatham, Portsmouth and Plymouth[2]. When issued in 1946 the report noted: "The future status of the Royal Naval School of Music, as an integral part of the Royal Marines, is at present under consideration by an Admiralty Committee. It is not therefore possible to forecast the way in which this establishment will ultimately fit into the new organisation"

The Director of Manning reviewed the allocation of bands during 1947 and 1948.[3] This was a matter that was under constant review not only by the manning department but also by CGRM and other Departments. Ships and Shore Establishments were being scrapped or closed, retention of RNSM Musicians completing their first enlistment period was very difficult (due mainly to the location of Burford and its effect upon married life and entertainment) and requests for new bands in various parts of the world made balancing supply to demand a very difficult task. At the time of the review the following sea-going ships had RM Bands:

Home Fleet:	HMS *Duke of York* (C-in-C)
	HMS *Anson* (Flag Officer Training Squadron)
	HMS *Superb* (Flag Officer 2nd Cruiser Squadron)
	HMS *Implacable*
Mediterranean Fleet:	HMS *Newcastle* (C-in-C)
	HMS *Mauritius* (Flag Officer 1st Cruiser Squadron)
	HMS *Triumph* (Flag Officer 2nd in Command)
	HMS *Forth* (Flag Officer Destroyers), HMS *Ocean*
	HMS *Ajax* or HMS *Euryalus*, HMS *Phoebe*
British Pacific Fleet:	HMS *London* (C-in-C)
	HMS *Sussex* (Flag Officer 5th Cruiser Squadron)
East Indies Fleet:	HMS *Norfolk* (C-in-C), HMS *Birmingham*
South Atlantic Fleet:	HMS *Nigeria* (C-in-C)
American & West Indies Fleet:	HMS *Sheffield* (C-in-C)
Cadet Training Cruiser:	HMS *Devonshire*
New Zealand Navy:	HMNZS *Bellona*

This review allowed four further bands for HMS *Vanguard*, HMS *Vengeance*, HMS *Theseus* and a third cruiser in the British Pacific Fleet and also made the point that if another cruiser went to the American & West Indies Fleet she would only have a band at the expense of HMS *Phoebe* of the Mediterranean Fleet. No changes were made, other than updating, to the bands allocated to ships but the review also looked at Shore Establishments. HMS *Excalibur*, *Raleigh* and *St George* were all paying off and their bands were available for elsewhere. At the time bids had been received for bands for HMS *Bruce*, RNAS Yeovilton, RNAS Bramcote and HMS *Collingwood*. It was agreed to send the newly available bands to HMS *Bruce*, RNAS Yeovilton and RNAS Bramcote. Shore Establishments bands were thereby allocated as follows:

Depots:	HMS *Victory* (Portsmouth), HMS *Drake* (Plymouth)
	HMS *Pembroke* (Chatham)
Boys' Training Establishments:	HMS *Ganges* (Shotley), HMS *Bruce* (Fife)
	HMS *St Vincent* (Gosport)
Mens' Training Establishments:	HMS *Excellent* (Portsmouth)
	HMS *Royal Arthur* (Corsham)
	HMS *Imperieuse* (Devonport)
Royal Marines Establishments:	RM Depot RM (Deal)
	Infantry Training Centre RM (Lympstone)
Royal Naval Air Stations:	RNAS Yeovilton, RNAS Bramcote
General:	HMS *Cochrane* (Rosyth), 3 Cdo Bde (Malta)

Other establishments that requested a band but could not be allocated one were: HMS *Dolphin*, *Ceres*, *Impregnable*, *Mercury* and one or two Royal Naval Air Stations.

The Lords of the Admiralty transmitted details of band allocations to all officers commanding ships and establishments on the 17th December 1947.

RM Band of HMS Sheffield in New York 20th September 1947.

During 1947 Maj F V Dunn, Director of Music of the Portsmouth Group Band, proposed that the Group Bands, the RNSM and their RM Bands be amalgamated. This was most appropriate timing for such a suggestion since the Lamplough Committee had recently reported to the CGRM, the Newman Report was commissioned, there was a definite need for cutbacks and amalgamations and anything that had a hint of reduction and savings had a very good chance of gaining an interested audience. However, in this case the other Group Bands and the RNSM opposed the proposal.[4]

The CGRM initiated a Conference of Directors of Music and Port Bandmasters and Fleet Bandmasters in January 1948. Agenda items that were raised give an indication of what topics were uppermost in the minds of those responsible for music in the Royal Navy and the Royal Marines at the time[5]. The topics were:

1	Proposal that Admiralty Grant for maintenance of RM Group Bands should be increased and that provision, maintenance and repair of instruments should be at Admiralty expense.[6]
2	Make recommendations for producing a standard drill for Group and RNSM Bands.[7]
3	Clarify recent Admiralty Fleet Order (AFO) on private engagement fees.[8]
4	Draft an AFO concerning payments for charity engagements.
5	Make recommendations for uniform method of making and fitting drums.
6	Band Fees in relation to Musicians' Union Rates.
7	Formulate recommendations for maintenance of Band Funds on board ships and in Shore Establishments.
8	Recommendations for preservation of symphony orchestra music libraries.
9	Recommendations for improved training of Drum Majors.

It is curious to note that amongst the flurry of reports issued in the post-war years was one called the "Report of the RN School of Music Conference" chaired by the CGRM and having members from various Royal Navy and Royal Marines branches as well as the Superintendent of the RNSM. The main thrust of this Report was directed towards the rapid expansion of the RNSM and the bands. The reasons for this were three-fold. Firstly the need to make good the losses incurred during the war and in the period following it. Secondly to increase the numbers in ships bands to make them effective and thirdly, to create a Band Service that was capable of supplying the needs of the Royal Navy and the Royal Marines without the need for Volunteer Bands.[9] However the members were aware that if such expansion was approved the need for the Volunteer Bands would remain for a while and so they offered to train them to a required standard. Members were also very aware of the differences in pay and conditions between the RM Bands and the bands of the Army and the Royal Marine Group Bands. Amongst their recommendations were improvements to practice space and instrument storage on board ship as well as a small office for the bandmaster; the proportion of sea service to land service to be reduced to come in line with other branches of the Navy; bandsmen not to be employed on ship's duties. (The report did note that it was aware that the Admiralty had just issued an instruction to this effect since they had noted that Musicians were being used in this way). Other recommendations were that the School had to remain an independent establishment but that it had to move from Burford as a matter of priority. A new location close to one of the three Home Ports was recommended. Professorial staff needed to be recruited; the minimum band size to be seventeen; large 'Command Bands' to be created instead of the two smaller C-in-C and Barrack Band at each Port or Command and a band of twenty-six to be formed as Admiral (Air)'s Band. They also asked for authority to continue investigations and discussions on the assumption that the increase to numbers would be approved in principle. Whilst many of the recommendations were acted upon the main recommendation of overall enlargement was not acceptable. The report also stressed that in the past it had "been the practice for a Royal Marine Divisional Staff Band, which does not serve the Navy afloat, to lead Navy personnel on ceremonial occasions. We consider that it is appropriate that the band should lead the Navy on such occasions and consider that such a practice would be beneficial to the morale of the RM Band Service".[10]

In June 1948 the "2nd Interim Report of the RNSM Conference" was issued. This discussed the Director of Manning proposal that two classes of band should be formed and allocated on a ships' complement basis. The DofM sought a reduction by putting bands of twenty-two on ships having a complement of more than one thousand with smaller complemented ships having bands of seventeen. In neither case would the band size be increased if they were on board a Flagship. The RNSM did not support this, preferring the system of larger bands for C-in-C, Home Ports, etc. They also stipulated that twenty-four instrumentalists plus the bandmaster was the minimum to produce a satisfactory orchestra and military band. They did accept that accommodation on smaller ships only allowed a band of seventeen but stressed that seventeen plus a bandmaster was much better than sixteen plus a bandmaster since it allowed them a French horn which could be used in both orchestra and military band. Another point made was that some ships had a Warrant Officer Bandmaster who also acted as Fleet Bandmaster. These were on the ships of the C's-in-C of the Home, Mediterranean and British Pacific Fleets. Bandmasters were with the bands of HMS *Victory*, *Drake* and *Pembroke* whilst the C's-in-C of these Naval Depots also had a Bandmaster Warrant Officer on their staff whose role was that of Port Bandmasters. In addition to the six Bandmaster Warrant Officers mentioned above the Treasury had approved an establishment of one Bandmaster Warrant Officer with 3 Cdo Bde Band and five as Instructors at the RNSM. The report went on to seek approval for two classes of band.

RM Band of HMS Victory (The Portsmouth Royal Naval Barracks later renamed HMS Nelson) with the Volunteer (Bluejacket) Band of the Royal Naval Barracks marches an RN Detachment into the Barracks.

Class A Band:

Would comprise one Commissioned or WO BM, a BdSgt, three BdCpls and twenty musicians. To be supplied to C's-in-C of the Home, Mediterranean, and British Pacific (also known as Far East Fleet), the three Home Ports and the Band of the 3 Cdo Bde.

Class B Band:

Would comprise one BM, one BdSgt, two BdCpls and fourteen Musicians. To be supplied to all other bands.

The Conference also recommended that Musicians should no longer undertake Fire Control Duties because it entailed Watch-keeping duties whilst in harbour which meant that the band could neither practise nor play and therefore this duty prejudiced the proper use of the band in harbour - which was to maintain morale. Alternative duty was Damage Control which meant standing watch at sea but not in harbour. Following careful study this was accepted and on the 19th December 1949 the Secretary of the Admiralty informed all C's-in-C and Flag Officers of the changes to complement necessary for the bands to relinquish their traditional role of Fire Control.

Staff of the Director of Manning and CGRM[11] agreed the recommendations for 'A' Bands and 'B' Bands in June 1949. However, it was pointed out that *Dido* Class cruisers could only physically accommodate a band of fifteen so it was decided not to allocate bands to them. The pre-war scheme of complement for HMS *St Angelo* allowed a Maltese Band of one BM, one BdCpl and thirteen Musicians. Approval had been given for replacing this Maltese Band with a RM Band after the war but with the difficulties of recruitment it was decided to retain the Maltese band. The C-in-C was quite happy with this arrangement and was allowed a Senior Commissioned Bandmaster or Command Bandmaster and sufficient Musicians (ie six) to enable him to augment, to Class A strength, a Class B Band from whichever ship on the Station that he chose.

[12]As far as education was concerned the School recruited youngsters of 14 and 15 because it was recognised by the Board of Education as providing full-time education. A recruit would be given a general education for two years beyond the school leaving age, would receive full board and lodging and uniform and would be paid each week. In addition he would be musically trained in the three musical disciplines of orchestral, military band and dance band work. During the three to four years of training the proportion of musical training would be gradually increased. A mixture of civilian professors and Non-Commissioned Officers were used for musical training whilst RN Instructor Officers were used for other subjects. As they progressed boys took their place in the Junior Orchestra, the Senior Orchestra, the Military Band of the Junior Wing and perhaps the Boys' Dance Orchestra. Each year the Worshipful Company of Musicians awarded two Cassel Prizes for the best students on a string and a wind instrument. Once a qualified Musician, preparation would commence for promotion. The Fleet Bandmasters had an important part to play since it was their responsibility to train and prepare those individuals serving on ships so that they could make maximum use of their time when they returned to the Senior Wing at the School.

Following promotion to Bandmaster he would serve a period at sea in charge of a band and would then serve further commissions afloat alternating with being a Bandmaster at a Royal Navy or Royal Marine Shore Establishment or with Instructional Duties at the School.

Bandmasters selected for the Warrant Bandmasters Course were given a further twelve months' advanced instruction during which time they would be expected to pass the examination for Licentiate of the Royal Academy of Music (LRAM) in Military Bandmastership. They must also hold a First Class Certificate of Education. Warrant Bandmasters were employed as Senior Instructors or as Fleet or Port Bandmasters where they would have about six bands under their command.

At any one time at the School there would be two or three Corporal's courses, one or two Band Sergeants' courses, one Bandmasters' course and one Warrant Bandmasters' course being run. Officers' Courses were run as required.

In addition to the individual training courses there would be the training of draft bands. This usually covered about two months during which time the musicians detailed for the band of a newly commissioning or recommissioning ship were welded into an efficient combination. These bands had to practise in dance, military and orchestral work as well as a parade Band. Before embarkation they had to be passed by the Musical Director as proficient and a full report written on them.

In support of all this training and commitment the School's Drafting Officer had a very complex task to manage the drafting of individuals to suit the commissioning and recommissioning of ships; the training of individuals as well as the men who were passing out of the School or retiring from the Band Service.

The Quartermaster (Musical) had a music store and workshops which, at that time, were probably unique for a musical establishment. The store carried enough stocks of instruments and parts to maintain all of the RM Bands in commission plus those about to be commissioned and the instruments for two hundred and fifty Boy Musicians under training. Big reserves had to be kept to meet such things as the fluctuations in the number of Boys under training, which could rise to four hundred, and the damage to stringed instruments caused by tropical climates. The workshops were started during the War when it was extremely difficult to maintain the numbers of instruments necessary for all of the ships' bands. All repairs to instruments could be carried out other than major re-conditioning.

The Library was required to supply music for the students at the School and for all of the bands at sea and in Naval Establishments all over the world. Dance Band music was bought by the individual bands themselves since the popularity of such music was deemed to be very short-lived. Forty compositions for symphony orchestra were despatched in 1948 to the Commando Brigade Band touring North Africa. Over six thousand compositions were held in the library and some dated back to the formation of the RNSM in 1903. The School also had a reference library of eight hundred books of musical reference.

The title of Band Boy became Boy Musician on the 28th January 1949; the training of all Buglers at the School commenced this year and civilian Professors were re-introduced for the first time since 1920. Three Professors were allowed but only in lieu of one BM, one BdSgt and one BdCpl.

The Newman Committee reported on the re-organisation 'on a functional basis' of the Royal Marines in the UK. This report stated that the RNSM was not within the terms of reference of the Newman Report since another Committee was considering it[13]. This would be the Leech-Porter Committee

It was during 1949 that the winds of change began to blow. Consideration was being given to moving the School back to the Depot, Deal since Burford was isolated from all other RM establishments and married accommodation was very difficult to find. The re-building of the Depot, currently in progress, would allow space for the School to return to its old home[14]. In August 1949, RMRO 384/49 relating to the re-location to Deal, was promulgated and arrangements began to be made for the move.

The terms of reference given to the Leech-Porter Committee were:

> You will enquire into the existing organisation and administration of Royal Naval School of Music and Group Bands, and make recommendations regarding the formation of a Royal Marine Band Service catering for both Naval and Royal Marine requirements. In your enquiries you will consider in particular the following:
>
> 1 The whole question of recruitment for bands,
> 2 The future of the personnel of Group Bands including the welfare aspect
> 3 The responsibilities of the Admiralty, Officers messes, etc. for the upkeep of bands,
> 4 The disposal of musical libraries and instruments belonging to Group Bands,
> 5 The musical and other training of band ranks,
> 6 The functions of the Group Bands vis-à-vis Royal Naval School of Music Bands.
> 7 The effect on the Corps of such an amalgamation.

The Committee itself consisted of Maj-Gen J E Leech-Porter as Chairman with Colonel P R Smith-Hill, Maj J Lampen, Capt P L Mackay, Capt I F Wray as Members and Capt J A Bamford as secretary.

Three meetings were held. The first, at Portsmouth, was used to interview Maj F V Dunn, Director of Music, Portsmouth Group. This was followed by two presentations, the first by Col Smith-Hill about the Administration and Organisation of the RNSM. The Secretary collated and presented the second paper which was about the Organisation, Administration and Function of the Portsmouth Group Band. It was decided not to visit either Kneller Hall or RAF Uxbridge since they had the evidence taken by the Newman Committee when they had visited those organisations.

The second meeting was held at Burford and evidence was taken from the Directors of Music of Chatham and Plymouth Groups - Capt T Francis and Capt R Stoner - and from the Musical Director RNSM, Capt H Kenward. They were followed by nine other ranks from the RNSM and then Lt Lang (Assistant Musical Director) and Capt Davis QM(M). At the final meeting at Portsmouth evidence was taken from four ranks of the Plymouth Group Band and seven ranks from the Portsmouth Group Band. The data concerning functions, recruiting and training, control, instruments and music, musical proficiency, Officers, advantages and disadvantages of the two organisations were carefully compared. The advantages and disadvantages provide a good summary.

RNSM Bands - Advantages were that bands embarked in HM Ships had operational duties and were unique in this respect; their opportunity for service all over the world has a high recruiting appeal. On the other hand, when men marry they preferred service in a static band and, finally, men of the RNSM bands, as members of a large organisation, had good chances of promotion. Disadvantages included the lack of a Staff Band at RNSM making it impossible to give prospective bandmasters requisite experience in conducting, this also deprived promising students (eg members of a Staff Band) of advanced musical training, and prevented the School from parading a band under Admiralty directions without disrupting training. The location of the School was deemed unsuitable.

Group Bands - Advantages included high musical proficiency since band remains together; bands are large so can perform music of high quality; individual instrumentalists are able to take more pride in their musical standard; opportunities for earning extra pay from private engagement's and bands are static which allows members to settle down in one of the Home Ports. The disadvantages were slow rate of promotion, which is however largely balanced by chances of earning extra pay from private engagements. General Duties Officers had to subscribe to the band, even though they could be serving at sea, in order to keep the Group Bands in being. This survival from ancient times was resented by a number of officers, particularly as they seldom heard the music played by these bands. The Committee decided that three possible courses of action could be adopted:

a) To continue with the present two separate organisations.

b) To form one large central staff band at Portsmouth under the same terms of service as for the present Group Bands, all other bands being provided by the RNSM.

c) To place all bands under the same terms as those which now apply to RNSM bands.

The first two were considered impractical and it was decided to recommend the third option. The Summary of Recommendations included the following points:

a) Merge two organisations into one to be known as the Royal Marines Band Service.

b) The RNSM should be known as the School of Music, Royal Marines.

c) No alteration of service should be made to those currently serving in Group bands.

d) No action should be taken that lowers the reputation of the Group Bands.

e) The Admiralty should accept responsibility for all instruments, appurtenances and music used in orchestras, military bands and dance combinations of all bands in the RMBS.

f) Group music libraries and instruments should remain with Groups but be presented to Admiralty.

g) Officers' subscriptions to Group Bands to cease. Admiralty to take responsibility.

h) Civilian instructors should be maintained at the School of Music, Royal Marines.

i) The School should be moved close to London or the Home Ports as soon as possible.

j) Staff Bands should be located at Chatham, Portsmouth, Plymouth and School of Music Royal Marines. Temporary strength of Staff Bands to be thirty-eight in all cases. Group Bands to be run down to this number. When manpower situation permits consideration should be given to raising the number to fifty - a number recently approved by the Admiralty.

k) Group Staff Bands should remain under MGRM[15] for the time being.

l) Musical proficiency of Port Bands to be responsibility of Director of Music of Group concerned.

m) Appointments of principal musical Officers to be as follows. School of Music Royal Marines: Director of Music to be Lieutenant Colonel, Assistant Director of Music to be Captain or Major. Group Staff Bands: Director of Music to be Lieutenant, Captain or Major.

BANDSMAN-R.N.
1880.

Watercolour by Richard Simkin, courtesy of Royal Naval Museum, Portsmouth

ROYAL MARINE LIGHT INFANTRY
1858.

Watercolour by Richard Simkin, courtesy of Royal Naval Museum, Portsmouth

ROYAL MARINE LIGHT INFANTRY.
1913.

Watercolour by Richard Simkin, courtesy of Royal Naval Museum, Portsmouth

ROYAL MARINE ARTILLERY.
1913.

Watercolour by Richard Simkin, courtesy of Royal Naval Museum, Portsmouth

ROYAL MARINE LIGHT INFANTRY.
1875.

Watercolour by Richard Simkin, courtesy of Royal Naval Museum, Portsmouth

Royal Marine Light Infantry Band of the Depot Royal Marines, Deal 1907 (BM Nicholson)

A typical scene at Stonehouse Barracks in the early part of the 20th Century with the Band of the Plymouth Divisional RMLI playing on the parade ground - probably after Church Parade

Boy Bugler (1935) painted by Victor R Bees, a tailor at Deal Barracks who provided occasional illustrations for 'The Globe and Laurel'. The Boy Bugler is wearing a peaked version of the unpopular Broderick cap that also has a leather support to the cap. When the Broderick was replaced by a peaked cap the Corps tried several ways of modifying their stocks.

An after I met 'im all over the world
Adoin' all kinds of things,
Like landin isself with a
Gatlin Gun,
To talk to them 'eathen kings
E sleeps in an ammick
instead of a cot,
An e' drills with the
deck on a slew,
Es one of the Jollies,
Er Majestys Jollies
Soldier an' Sailor too!.
KIPLING.

BM II R W Wenham photographed on the 18th September 1932. He carries a Divisional pattern Drum Major's staff with buff grip, as opposed to an RNSM one, and is wearing a standard Drum Major's Dress Belt. Lyre collar badges can be seen. Bandmasters often did Drum Major's duties. BM Wenham was embarked upon HMS Fiji when she was sunk off Crete 23rd May 1941. He and seven members of his band died in the Transmitting Station.

(Photograph courtesy of John Rawlinson)

The Tynwald Ceremony. Every law that has been passed by the Manx Parliament during the previous year has to be promulgated from Tynwald Hill on the 5th July each year. In 1985 A Coy 40 Cdo and the Band of Flag Officer Scotland and Northern Ireland (FOSNI) were part of the proceedings.

40 Cdo Trooped their Colours on the 19th August 1967 at Dieppe Barracks, Singapore to commemorate the 25th Anniversary of the Dieppe Raid. 3 Cdo Bde Band massed with the Band of Commander, Far East Fleet.

n) Only one source of recruitment to RMBS through the School of Music Royal Marines, once established.

o) NCOs in band service to be styled Staff Bandmaster (equivalent to Staff Sergeant[16] RM); Bandmaster (equivalent to Colour Sergeant RM); Band Sergeant (equivalent to Sergeant RM) and Band Corporal (equivalent to Corporal RM). Promotion and qualifications for promotion to be standard throughout Band Service. If promotion is declined the rank should permanently forfeit the chance of any further promotion.

p) The School should draft suitable Musicians to Group Bands as soon as possible.

q) Every effort should be made to convince the right type of musician to re-engage.

r) All RMBS ranks should wear Corps uniform but with the substitution of a broad red stripe on the trousers. Group Staff Bands should continue to wear the special cap badges and Portsmouth Band to wear the 'Royal Yacht' flash.

s) All instruments should be silver-plated.

t) A grant of £56 per annum to be made by the Admiralty for each of the staff bands to replace Officer's subscriptions. The Admiralty also to become responsible for supply and maintenance of instruments, music and appurtenances for which a further grant of £22 per annum per staff band should be allowed.

The Committee felt that the public and the Royal Navy would be in favour of amalgamation and that:

If the foregoing scheme of amalgamation be adopted and put into effect with vigour, the foundations will have been laid for a Band Service of the highest repute and efficiency - having no equal of its kind in the world.

The Committee were also very firm on the fact that the leader of the amalgamated Band Service should be a Lieutenant Colonel. They also strongly proposed that Capt H Kenward should be promoted to that rank and given the senior position since he was "the only person in either the Group Bands or the Royal Naval School of Music with the necessary experience, musical proficiency and personality to assume this role". Since he was due to retire in 1950 the Committee proposed that he should be given a three-year extension. They did not consider that any other present officer of the RNSM had the qualities required for such a post and that it would be most unwise to give the post to anyone who had not graduated through the ranks of the RNSM.[17] In the event, Capt Kenward did not assume this role - possibly because of illness and a need to retire.

Whilst, officially, none of the Group Band Directors of Music nor the Musical Director of the RNSM had been allowed to sit on the Leech-Porter Committee, Maj F V Dunn, the Director of Music of the Portsmouth Group, was asked by Leech-Porter to write a 'blue-print' and was frequently called into Leech-Porter's office (he was Commanding Officer at Eastney at the time) to discuss the merits of such a plan.[18]

In 1949, following a series of conferences, discussions and reports, the CGRM, Lt Gen Sir Leslie Hollis, decided that the amalgamation of the two organisations should take place. Having made the decision the General then had to qualify it. The Admiralty had taken the decision the previous year to scrap the RM Commando role. Although he was able to reverse this decision Hollis had to make cuts elsewhere to compensate. Amongst these cuts was the closure of the Chatham Group, including its fine band. At that time (April 1950) it had to be assumed that the recommendations of the Leech-Porter Group would be approved and it was therefore proposed to plan for the disbandment of the Chatham Band.

When Maj-Gen J E Leech-Porter died in 1979 Sir Vivian Dunn contributed to his obituary in the Globe and Laurel and wrote:

> He was far from easy to know, for beneath a somewhat forbidding exterior and an unerring instinct for detecting what was wrong, lay unsuspected kindly and generous qualities. As Superintendent of the RN School of Music, where his strong views had made him more feared than loved, he had gained an insight into the workings and the attitude of the RMB of those days. This was invaluable when in 1948 he headed the Leech-Porter Committee. Although it was opposed by elements on both sides, the Committee steered by Leech-Porter, backed my proposals of 1947 for the amalgamation of the Group Bands and the RN School of Music. Implemented on 1st September 1950, its report brought lasting benefits, for which Leech-Porter should be remembered with gratitude today[19].

Other reductions were taking place during 1949. As a result of manpower problems RNAS Yeovilton lost its band on 1st January 1949. The band of HMS *Euryalus* went on 1st March, HMS *Phoebe* on 1st June and the Training Squadron Band on 1st July. In October the Flag Officer of the Reserve Fleet sought a band but was refused since it would have to be at the expense of a ship or Shore Establishment already in possession of a band. Bands serving at this time were:

Home Fleet:	HMS *Duke of York* (C-in-C *[20] - to transfer to HMS *Implacable* with Flag)
	HMS *Anson* (Flag Officer Training Squadron - to transfer to HMS *Howe* with Flag)
	HMS *Superb* (Flag Officer 2nd Cruiser Squadron)
	HMS *King George V* (Until 1st July 1949)
	HMS *Illustrious* (As Trials and Training Carrier)
	HMS *Vengeance* (Flag Officer Air, Home Fleet)
	HMS *Theseus*
Mediterranean Fleet:	HMS *Liverpool* (C-in-C *)
	HMS *Newcastle* (Flag Officer 1st Cruiser Squadron)
	HMS *Triumph* (Flag Officer Air (Med))
	HMS *Forth* - Destroyer and Submarine Depot Ship (Flag Officer Destroyers (Med)
	HMS *Ocean*, HMS *Euryalus* (Until 1st March 1949)
	HMS *Phoebe* (Until 1st May 1949)
Far East Fleet:	HMS *London* - Part of band ashore on HMS *Terror*, Singapore (C-in-C *)
	HMS *Belfast* (Flag Officer 5th Cruiser Squadron)
	HMS *Mauritius*
East Indies Fleet:	HMS *Norfolk* (C-in-C), HMS *Birmingham*
South Atlantic Fleet:	HMS *Nigeria* (C-in-C)
American & West Indies Fleet:	HMS *Glasgow* (C-in-C), HMS *Jamaica*
Cadets Training Cruisers:	HMS *Devonshire*
Special Service:	HMS *Vanguard* (As a Training Ship)
New Zealand Navy:	HMNZS *Bellona*

Bands at Shore Establishments were now as follows:

Depots:	HMS *Victory** (Portsmouth), HMS *Drake**(Plymouth)
	HMS *Pembroke** (Chatham)
	HMS *Daedalus* (Lee-on-Solent)
Training Establishments:	HMS *Ganges* (Shotley),HMS *St Vincent* (Gosport)
	HMS *Bruce* (Fife -Closing down 1949)
	HMS *Excellent* (Portsmouth)
	HMS *Royal Arthur* (Corsham)
	HMS *Imperieuse* (Devonport)
RM Establishments:	Depot, RM (Deal), Infantry Training Centre, RM (Lympstone)
RNAS:	RNAS Bramcote
General:	HMS *Cochrane* (Rosyth), 3 Cdo Bde *

During the period between the CGRM's recommendations and the Lords of the Admiralty giving their approval, an Admiralty Order-in-Council (28th October 1949) abolished the 'Warrant List' and substituted it with a 'Branch List'. All officers on the Branch List were to be appointed by Commission. This meant that Bandmaster Warrant Officers became Commissioned Bandmasters and Commissioned Bandmasters became Senior Commissioned Bandmasters. This became effective for all generic titles within the Royal Navy and the Royal Marines. 'Commissioned…' wore a small star on their shoulder 'Senior Commissioned…' wore a large star on their shoulder.

The Director of Manning warned that the number of bands in 1950 would need to be considerably reduced to complement the restricted fleet. The Band Committee would be meeting soon to discuss which ships or establishments would lose their bands.[21] It was at this time that Major F V Dunn organised his Charity Concert in Portsmouth that involved both his own Group Band and the local RM Bands and this was followed by the combined Beat Retreat on Horse Guards Parade.

Direct entry into the Group Bands ceased and all recruits had to enter the Band Service via the School of Music. The Musical Director of the School of Music became the first "Director of Music, Royal Marines" and the Directors of Music of the Group Bands at Portsmouth and Plymouth became "Director of Music, Portsmouth" and "Director of Music, Plymouth" respectively. Both of these bands retained their special cap badges and the Portsmouth Band also retained its Royal Yacht shoulder flash.

During this period bands were allocated to HMS *Belfast*, HMS *Kenya* and HMS *Jamaica* all of which were on the Far East Station. *Jamaica* was due to be withdrawn but CGRM decided that she would retain a band until early 1951. He also made the point that the RM Band Service would be overborne by 100 men in 1951 and 1952 and this would allow a number of additional bands. On the 1st June 1950 the band of HMS *Cochrane* was withdrawn.

As a result of the amalgamation further changes were approved. All other ranks in the Royal Marines Band Service, except for Boy Musicians, would wear the Globe and Laurel on the collar and not the Lyre of the RNSM. Also, all trained personnel would wear the broad red stripe on the trousers, not just the Group Bands, whilst boys under training would continue to wear the lyre collar badge and the narrow trouser welt in order to distinguish them from Royal Marine recruits under training. The King approved these changes on the 2nd of November 1950.

Coincidentally it was in this year, the year that the title 'Royal Naval School of Music' ceased to exist, that Major H E Lidiard, the 'Father of the Band Service' died.

It is important to note how much the RNSM and its RM Bands brought to both the amalgamation and the current Royal Marines Band Service. The Massed Bands Beating Retreat display; marching routines; predecessor of the Prince's Badge; the Memorial Silver Trumpets; the War Memorial Silver Drums; the setting of Sunset; the Medal of the Worshipful Company of Musicians (begun in 1910) and therefore the relationship between the two organisations; the Cassel prize; Band Conferences that were started in 1948: the framework of instruction and training with civilian professors and Service instructors that is still relevant in, and applicable to, the current Royal Marines School of Music. The idea of the Winter Concert season, so important to the Bandmasters' Course, was created for that very purpose by the RNSM. The philosophy of promotion through the ranks to Officer level came from the Royal Naval School of Music. The Group Bands brought their distinctive headdress badges and the Silver Bugles that had been paid for by the Officers of the Corps but, probably most significantly, the changes they had to make in order to become fully integrated resulted in them becoming as flexible as the Royal Marine Bands.

Guard and Band on HMS Glory as she leaves Malta for Korea 1950

CHAPTER THREE

Royal Marine Divisional Bands and Corps of Drums at the Turn of the Twentieth Century

At the very beginning of the twentieth century, the Royal Marine Light Infantry had three Divisions. One, previously known as the First Grand Division, was at Chatham; another, once known as the Second Grand Division, was at Portsmouth[1]; whilst the third, once known as the Third Grand Division, was at Plymouth. Also at Portsmouth was the Division of the Royal Marine Artillery. There was also the Depot at Deal.[2] A General Order, Royal Marines[3] (GORM) fixed the numbers for the Divisional bands as one Bandmaster, two Sergeants, two Corporals, twenty-five Musicians and ten supernumeraries.[4]

The Band of the Depot Deal, play for a ceremonial parade on the sports field. The Barracks Church, St Michael's and All Saints, can be seen in the background.

The band at the Depot, Deal comprised one Sergeant for duty as Bandmaster, one Sergeant, one Corporal, seventeen Musicians and five supernumeraries:

The Supernumeraries are allowed for training to fill vacancies with a view to ensuring, as far as possible, that efficient Musicians may be available to take the place of men becoming non-effective by length of Service or other causes. In cases, however, where exceptional fitness or aptitude as a Musician render it desirable, a man may be specially enlisted to fill a vacancy in a Marine Band. [5]

The Band of the Depot Deal, was unofficially formed in 1890. This 1898 photograph shows Bandmaster J S Nicholson with the band.

This Order left the bandmaster with the option of either training members of the Corps or recruiting from outside the Corps. Another GORM[6] states: "Bandmasters will, invariably, be in uniform when leading their bands". This was to end the practice of the time of bandmasters leading and conducting their bands wearing civilian clothes.

The Corps also had the oldest specialist branch. When the six Companies of Marines were raised in 1664 each had to have on its strength a drummer. These six drummers were later increased to twelve and each had to learn fife as well as drum. In 1693 the Drum Major General issued a Warrant to raise a band for each Regiment. This applied to the entire Army, not just the Marines. Recruiters were expressly forbidden to recruit the listed drums (those on the Company strength). Since the Marines had no wind bands in the 17th century we can contend that the Corps of Drums were the earliest form of band.

Part 1 - Royal Marine Artillery Band up to 1900

The Band of the Royal Marine Artillery (RMA) was established in 1823. A year previously three of the four companies in the RMA Division had been moved from Portsmouth to Chatham on account of the unsanitary conditions that existed at Fort Monkton, Gosport. In that year the Division's Major Commandant[7], Lt Col Sir Richard Williams, asked the Admiralty for a similar band allowance to that which was available to the RMLI Divisions, the Royal Artillery and other Regiments. After due consideration the Colonel Commandant, Royal Marines, at Chatham was authorised to enlist fourteen boys as private marines, to be transferred to the RMA and formed into a band. This was at an expenditure of five shillings a day. Mr Thompson, a clarinettist, was appointed Master of the Band and James Gunnis is believed to have been the band's bassoonist. During 1832 the RMA were reduced in strength and the band was disestablished. Whilst most of the musicians joined the Royal Navy, Gunnis and two others joined the RMLI Band, Portsmouth Division.

On the 2nd January 1861 Colonel J Fraser applied to form a band such as that which the RMA once had. The application was approved for a band of the same strength as that of the RMLI Divisions to be established. Thomas Smyth, brother of the Royal Artillery Bandmaster James Smyth, was appointed as the band's first leader. (Thomas had previously succeeded Mr Henry Winterbottom as bandmaster of the RMLI Woolwich Division and had been followed by another member of the Winterbottom family, William). An official march past, or quick-step, was selected, Gounod's recently written The Soldiers' Chorus from *Faust*, and this was used by the RMA until 1883 when *A Life on the Ocean Wave* became the march past of the whole Corps. By 1865 the Division had moved to its new barracks at Eastney, Portsmouth, the band having marched in with a combined detachment from Chatham and Woolwich on the 1st April that year. By this time Smyth had enlarged the band to forty-six musicians and eight boy musicians. Yet another member of the Winterbottom family, John, became the bandmaster in 1870 when Smyth left. He continued to develop the band and, in 1881, he was made a Warrant Officer. In 1892 John Winterbottom left to take charge of the band of the Artists' Rifles and was succeeded by an Army bandmaster, Albert Williams of the 10th Royal Hussars, who remained with the band for five years. He left to become Bandmaster of the Grenadier Guards and, later, Senior Director of Music of the Brigade of Guards. In 1897 the band welcomed someone who would become one of its most famous Bandmasters, B S Green who had been Albert William's predecessor as Bandmaster of the 10th Hussars![8] So at the turn of the century the Band of the RMA, unlike the bands of the Royal Navy, found itself on a well-established firm footing, in a large well equipped barracks, with a very competent Bandmaster to lead it.

The Band of the Royal Marine Artillery, Eastney 1884. Bandmaster, standing on right, is Warrant Officer John Winterbottom.

Part 2 - 1st Grand Division Royal Marine Light Infantry - Chatham Band up to 1900

The first mention of a Marine Band occurs in 1693 in a Royal Warrant. It is highly likely that this would not have been a military band but a fife and drum band. Eighty years later, in 1773, the band of the First Division under Acting Sgt Maj Clements was ordered to go aboard HMS *Orpheus* at Sheerness.[9]

The Chatham Division Order Book for the 8th October 1781 sets out the band's working arrangements in no uncertain manner:

> In order that the Marine Musical Band may not hereafter be looked upon in the light of common Fidlers(sic), and permitted at the desire of indifferent persons to play in that capacity at ordinary and common Balls and Concerts, it is directed that in future, the Band or any part of them, shall not have liberty to play anywhere out of Barracks, but where the Divisions Business calls upon them, or where Government may take any concern.[10]

In 1797 the six Drummers and the band of the First Division marched a Captain's Guard of one hundred and forty other ranks from Chatham to London to accompany the King to St Paul's Cathedral. No doubt they exercised their privilege of marching through the City "with bayonets fixed, Colours flying and band playing". The band at this time probably numbered eight. In 1802 an order was issued that increased the size of the band to fourteen. However, with the introduction of instruments such as clarinets, bassoon, flutes, horn, trumpets, key bugles, trombones and serpents the size of the band again increased. The size and shape of the present military band can be seen starting to appear at this time. The influence of 'Turkish Music' also increased the number and variety of instruments as drums, cymbal and other percussion instruments began to appear in British military bands. In 1826 history was made when the Chatham Band accompanied the British Ambassador to Russia for the Coronation of Tsar Nicholas I - the first occasion a British band had left Great Britain to attend a foreign ceremony. By 1830 the band numbered about sixty. Chatham's first known Bandmaster, W Rogers, served between 1836 and 1857[11] and was a civilian conductor who drew his income from the Band Fund and from private sources. He laid the foundation for what became a very fine band and being asked to take the band to London for Queen Victoria's Coronation and other State ceremonial in London rewarded his efficiency and thoroughness. His successor was Herr J A Kappey, a German who had been serving as civilian bandmaster to the 89th Regiment of Foot, later 2nd Bn The Royal Irish Fusiliers. In the early 1860's Herr Kappey established a first-class string band. Whilst he composed many pieces of music he will be mainly remembered as the arranger of *A Life on the Ocean Wave*. In 1874 the War Office ended the practice of employing civilian bandmasters and then, in 1881, instructed that all Kneller Hall qualified Bandmasters were to be given the rank of Warrant Officer. Between 1889 and his retirement in 1897 when he was succeeded by John Wright, Bandmaster to the 40th (South Lancashire) Regiment, Kappey also filled the post of official examiner of Student Bandmasters at Kneller Hall. Within the first year of his appointment Mr Wright had taken his musicians, as a string band, to play at such events as an important reception at the Foreign Office and, as a military band, to the opening of the Imperial Institute by Queen Victoria and to the opening ceremony of Tower Bridge. Also in 1893 "Ten of the most accomplished performers of the band under Bandmaster Wright made several visits to the establishment of Mr Edison in London in order to make phonographic recordings of martial airs"[12]. If this did happen, and even though no recordings are known to have survived there is no reason to doubt the report, then this would be the first instance of a military band making a recording other than those made in the United States.

Once again we see a contrast to the RN Bands as the dawn of the twentieth century takes place for, like the RMA, the year 1900 saw the Chatham Band with a very high reputation both as a military band and as an orchestra and, also like the RMA, with a very good Bandmaster appointed.

Part 3 - 2nd Grand Division Royal Marine Light Infantry - Portsmouth Band up to 1900

It is believed that this is the oldest of the full Divisional bands, as opposed to a drum and fife band, being formed in 1765. The oldest documentary evidence of a band is dated 1776 when the Colonel Commandant wrote to the Admiralty asking for funds to "buy a pair of French Horns, ours being worn out". It could be that the instruments that needed replacing were the original instruments and this, allowing a serviceable life of ten years, would corroborate the suggested date of origin as 1765.[13]

On Tuesday 23rd June 1773 the King came to Portsmouth to review the Fleet and Establishments. Prior to his arrival the Plymouth Band was ordered to Portsmouth to assist in covering the number of dinners, salutes and Guards and Bands that would be required.[14] In December 1797 the Portsmouth Division band marched from Portsmouth to London to accompany the King to St Paul's Cathedral. At the beginning of 1815 the Master and principal performers of the Band of the Oxfordshire Militia (presumably being disestablished) volunteered for, and were accepted by, the Portsmouth Band.[15] In August of 1821 the band under John Smalley became the first band to sail on a Royal cruise, embarking in HMS *Action* to accompany the Royal Squadron to Ireland. The band was constantly in attendance when the Queen was on board the Royal Yacht. In 1824 Mr Arroll, who served as bandmaster until 1847, replaced Smalley. During this period the band began presenting regular concerts at the Portsmouth Assembly Rooms.

The next Bandmaster was James Gunnis who had been the bassoon player in the original RMA Band under 'Master of the Band' Thompson. In 1848, soon after Gullis had taken over, the Division moved from Clarence Barracks, Portsmouth to Forton Barracks at Gosport on the other side of Portsmouth Harbour and, the following year, Mr A Earle arrived as bandmaster and stayed for the next sixteen years. He formed the Division's orchestra in 1853 and, as a result of a number of successful visits to Osborne House to perform for Queen Victoria and the Prince Consort, the band accompanied the Royal couple on board the Royal Yacht for a visit to Cherbourg in 1858. The Divisional Officers appointed a German to replace Mr Earle. German civilian bandmasters were very much in vogue, possibly because of the closeness of the Royal Families at that period, and, as a result, Mr W Kreyer served with the band for nearly twenty years. He took the band of thirty on board HMS *Serapis* to accompany HRH The Prince of Wales on his 1875/1876 visit to India and Ceylon. As a result of this the band was awarded the Prince of Wales Plumes as an addition to the cap badge and helmet plate.

In January 1885 George Miller, bandmaster of the Royal Military College[16] Sandhurst Band was one of one hundred and fifteen applicants for the post vacated by Kreyer. He was the only Englishman on the short-list of six bandmasters for interview. As a result of his training, experience and immaculate references he was appointed to lead the Portsmouth Division Band, which he did for the next thirty-two years. He was the son of

George Miller who had been Bandmaster of the 63rd Foot, later the 1st Bn. The Manchester Regt, before his retirement, and the father of another George Miller who eventually became Director of Music, Grenadier Guards. Miller continued to develop the special relationship that existed between the band and the Royal Family, the band crossing the Solent to play at Osborne House sixty-six times between 1890 and 1897.

At this time the orchestra consisted of five first violins; four second violins; three violas; two violincellos; two double basses; two flutes; one oboe; two clarionets; two bassoons; two horns; one euphonium; two cornets; one trombone; one kettle drummer and one bass drum. The 'double-handed' musicians would convert to the following military band instrumentation: one piccolo; one flute, one oboe; two Eb clarinets; nine Bb cornets; one tenor clarinet; one bass clarinet; two bassoons; four horns; one baritone; one euphonium; five basses; four cornets; two trumpets; three trombones and two drums. It is interesting to note that amongst the list of soloists appears "Piccolo: Drum Major Shadwick"[17].

In 1896 the Plymouth Band was at Forton en route to Aldershot and the opportunity was taken to stage a Tattoo. Bugle Major Bryan, Drum Major Keen and the Drums and Fifes were very involved. This was repeated in 1897. Bugle Major Bryan retired in 1900 after twenty-five years with the Band and Drums.

In 1887 Queen Victoria commissioned Dan Godfrey of the Grenadier Guards. He was the only bandmaster to be commissioned[18] until, in 1898, the Queen conferred the same honour upon George Miller of the Portsmouth Division, RMLI, Ladislao Zavertal of the Royal Artillery and Charles Godfrey of the Royal Horse Guards.

So another Division of Royal Marines approached the new century with a strong, capable orchestra and military band and with a very able officer to lead it.

Part 4 - 3rd Grand Division Royal Marine Light Infantry - Plymouth Band from 1900

The Officers of the Division decided to form a band in 1766 and, the following year, eight musicians were engaged as the 'Band of Musick'. The first mention of them occurs in Plymouth Orders 12th January 1767 and refers to the payment of subscriptions by the Officers to purchase instruments. Amongst the musicians was Antonio Rocca who was paid 2/6d a week to teach the others. Four years later the newly-formed Royal Artillery Band at Woolwich enticed Rocca from Plymouth by offering him 1/6d a day. In 1768 the band wore white stockings and breeches with black buckled gaiters at roll call and at guard mounting. William Gilbourn succeeded Rocca but he was sacked for "being incapable of teaching a martial band and not able to teach the softer musick". He was replaced in 1783, the same year as the band moved into the newly erected Stonehouse Barracks, by 'Master of the Band' James Parsons who was promoted from within the band. Parsons was told to instruct the fifers in martial music whilst Lieutenants Gibson and Gordon had volunteered to make the band 'capable of the softer musick'. Parsons was succeeded by Mr Ashweek in 1796 and then Thomas Stockham from 1822 until 1845. It is not known who succeeded Stockham but, in 1851, Thomas Winterbottom, a civilian, was appointed as 'Master of the Band'[19]. During this period the 'Master of the Band' continued to play his own instrument and did not conduct in the manner of today. Thomas's instrument was the flageolet, a cross between a flute and a recorder. Thomas died whilst serving (1869) and was succeeded by his younger brother William, who was the first to be referred to as Band Master. At about this time the bandsmen's uniform was white tunics with scarlet collars and cuffs, and scarlet trousers with white braided stripes[20]. William had already served with the RMLI Woolwich Division Band as did another family member, Henry. Four years later William exchanged positions with the Bandmaster of the 2nd Life Guards, Carl F H Froehnert - a native of Saxony who had been sponsored by the Prince Consort. Froehnert served with the band until his death in 1890. Neither he nor his fellow countryman Jacob Kappey of the Chatham Division wore uniform until 1883 when their bands were massed for a special occasion. Froehnert would return from visits to Germany with new band music including '*Turkish Patrol*' which the Plymouth Band claim to be the first band to play in this country. He became a naturalised British subject, was made a Corps Warrant Officer in 1881 (when the Warrant rank was first introduced into the Royal Marines) and, in 1875, became Inspecting Bandmaster of HM Training Ships in Devonport, which as described earlier, were HMS *Lion*, *Impregnable* and *Implacable*. Since the practice of Royal Marines inspecting the Bands of the Training Ships only began in 1874 Froehnert must have been one of the first to perform this duty.

In 1880 when playing at the ceremony for the laying of the foundation stone of Truro Cathedral the band attracted the attention of the Prince and Princess of Wales who asked them to play, as an orchestra, for various social functions. A new Troop, composed by Edwin Binding, a musician, was played on this occasion. In 1875 Binding, who had served as a Musician through his career, received his Naval Long Service and Good Conduct Medal, was promoted Sergeant "and was appointed Bugle Major".[21] A few years later the band returned to play at the Dedication of Truro Cathedral. On this occasion they performed as a military brass band but, for an unknown reason, wore choristers' surplices over their full dress uniform!

Prince Alfred, Duke of Edinburgh (and Saxe-Coburg and Gotha) presents new Colours to Plymouth Division RMLI on 3rd July 1896 on Brickfields. The Divisional Band is at the centre of the ceremony.

Upon Froehnert's death in 1890 another Winterbottom, Frank the nephew of William, succeeded him. Frank was the first to join as a Warrant Officer Bandmaster. William had taught Frank the techniques of military band scoring and Frank was able to develop this skill to such a high degree that many of his military band arrangements of the classics remain in use. When the Division received new Colours in 1896 Winterbottom directed both the Divisional band and the drum and fife band.

Yet again, at the beginning of the twentieth century an RM Divisional Band, in this case the Plymouth Division, was held in high regard with a very fine musician to lead it.

Part 5 - Drummers, Buglers, Fifers and Corps of Drums

In charge of the Corps of Drums would be a Drum Major. Drummers, Drum Major, Fife Major,[22] Band and Bandmaster would be responsible to either the Field Adjutant or the Band and Drums Company Officer. An 'Order of Plymouth Division' dated 1784 directs the Field Adjutant to take 'Band, Drums and Fifes under his entire care as to dress and interior economy and the beating of the drummers.' Drummers, because of their specialist role as signallers both on land and at sea, were paid as Corporals. A 1799 'General Weekly Return' indicates that the Portsmouth Division was complemented for three hundred drummers of whom one hundred and thirty were at sea.[23] On the 7th June 1832 orders were given that all Drummers were to be instructed in the Fife and none embarked until

The Drum Major of the Royal Marine Artillery c1896. He wears the RMA tunic that was worn by the band and is now worn by all Royal Marines Drum Majors. He also wears the blue cloth helmet and carries the staff, which was of a completely different design to other RM bands.

© Victoria and Albert Museum

competent and, in 1835, it was ordered that Drummers were to be designated Fifers when embarked but this idea did not last long.[24]

The bugle was adopted as the signalling instrument of the RMA and the RMLI in the mid-19th century. In 1850 the RMA appointment of Trumpet Major had been dropped and Bugle Major took its place. Sgt G Coney was Fife Major[25] of the Chatham Division RMLI until his retirement in 1856 but it is not known when this appointment ceased. In 1855, the Drummers became known by the clumsy title of 'Drummers and Buglers' but this was changed to 'Buglers' after twelve years. Drummers, being on the Company strength and not a separate entity in the same way as the band, found themselves being used for various other tasks including, up to 1868 when the practices ceased, that of flogging and 'drumming out'. They were also very involved in recruiting 'by beat of drum'. The Bugle Major and the Bandmaster at the Divisions trained all Buglers but since not all had the same method of tuition standardisation was necessary so that Band and Drums could be massed. This did not apply to the bugle calls themselves, which were very explicit and completely standardised.

It is known that in 1867 the Chatham Division had 'a particularly fine drum and fife band that was second to none, Guards not excepted, under that splendid Drum Major Charles Duncan, a handsome fellow, six feet two inch in height'.[26]

The Bugler's ability was periodically tested by a Board comprising a Lieutenant Colonel, a Senior Major, an Instructor of Naval Gunnery (for the signalling) the Field Adjutant and, if required, the Bandmaster. No Bugler was allowed to go to sea unless he had been passed 'Very Good' for bugle and 'Good' for drum and fife. He was re-assessed whenever he disembarked or embarked and if his assessments were too low he would be sent for further revision instruction.

So, at the end of the nineteenth century the Royal Marines had Divisional Corps of Drums capable of not only carrying out their primary task of signalling by beat of drum or by bugle call but also performing in whatever combination of bugle, drum and fife instrumentation might be required.

The Drum Major and the Bugle Major can be seen seated on either side of the RM Officer. Fifers can be seen quite distinctly, as can the Buglers and bass drummer. This photograph shows the Drums of the RMLI Portsmouth Division 1898.

CHAPTER FOUR

The Development of the Royal Marines Divisional Bands and Corps of Drums from 1900 until 1950

Anumber of official decisions and documents influenced the development of the Corps, its bands and its Bandmasters during this period. Recruitment to the Divisional and Depot Bands was tightened in 1910 when a General Order was issued which stated that all future vacancies for Musicians must be filled by the absorption of the Gunner, Private or Bugler who had been attached to the Band as a Supernumerary for the longest period. In 1914 an Order-in-Council allowed two Musical Directors, and the two senior Bandmasters were to receive the appointments automatically. They were Honorary[1] Major G J Miller of the Portsmouth Division RMLI and Honorary Lieutenant B S Green of the RMA. From this date Musical Directors were to be eligible for promotion to Captain after ten years' commissioned service and to Major after fifteen years commissioned service. Retirement at sixty-five years of age was compulsory. The word 'Honorary' was removed by a further OIC of 1918[2].

In 1921 another OIC allowed five Directors of Music to the Corps, one at each of the HQ RMLI Divisions (Lt C J Hoby at Chatham, Lt B N O'Donnell at Portsmouth and Lt P S G O'Donnell at Plymouth), one for the RMA (Lt R P O'Donnell) and one for the Depot, Deal (Lt S J Nicholson). This OIC also indicated that they were to be known as 'Directors of Music' and not 'Musical Directors'. It is to be noted that at this time three of the five RM Directors of Music were brothers.

1923 saw the amalgamation of the RMA and the RMLI to form, once again, the Royal Marines. This obviously had an effect on some of the bands.

A composite band was formed in 1935 to support the London Duties Battalion that, similarly, was drawn from all three Divisions as well as from the Depot[3].

With effect from 1st January 1947 instructions were issued that covered the subscriptions payable by both permanent and temporary officers of the Corps together with those officers on detachment plus additional charges for those at Divisional Headquarters[4].

Part 1 - 1st Grand Division Royal Marine Light Infantry - Chatham Band

In January 1901 the Chatham Divisional Band was on parade in London for the funeral of Queen Victoria[5]. 1901 also saw the Band accompany the Duke and Duchess of York on board the *Ophir*, an Orient Line ship, for a tour of the colonies (The Duke was the Colonel in Chief of the Royal Marines at the time). The Royal Party arrived in Portsmouth to the sounds of the bands of the Royal Artillery and RMA playing at the Harbour Station and the old viaduct whilst the *Ophir* (Chatham) Guard and Band was on deck. The band played at the Royal Review saluting battery in Gibraltar as 6000 men of the Army and Navy marched past. As a result of the band's performance during this 45,000 miles tour Mr Wright was commissioned and the badge of the White Rose of York was conferred upon

The Band of Chatham RMLI march out of the Chatham Dockyard after Church Parade. They are wearing the blue cloth helmet. This was before the Corps of Drums paraded in front of Royal Marines Bands.

the thirty-four strong band in March 1902[6]. This was to become part of their cap badge and helmet plate.

In 1905 a Torchlight Tattoo and Pageant was performed in the RM Barracks, Chatham by the Divisional Band, Divisional Corps of Drums and the RM Band of the Port Admiral. The programme began with a trumpet fanfare followed by *Under Seigers Banner* the Troop in Quick time performed by the Corps of Drums. The Grand Troop in Slow Time, *In Cawsand Bay*, was played by the Divisional Band followed by the RM Band playing *The Staffords* for the Troop in Quick Time. After the pageant was completed the Band performed Lantern Marches the music being *Toledo* (RM Band); *Salute the Russian Eagle* (the Drums) and *Old English Airs* (the Divisional Band). The band played *Boys of the Old Brigade* and *Shoulder to Shoulder* and then, as the Guards saluted, *Sons of the Sea* and, as the Guards marched off, *Soldiers of the King*. The Drums beat First Post and the Troop *Under the Double Eagle* and the Divisional Band played the overture *1812*. The band and drums provided the music for an illuminated cycle ride before Last Post was sounded by the band and the Troop *Navahoe* by the drums. The March Past took place to 'Red, White and Blue, The Englishman* and *The White Squall*.

Lt Wright died in 1907 and a highly qualified and skilled musician, Lt C J Hoby, a military musician before joining the Musical Department of the London School Board, took his place.

1910 saw another Torchlight Tattoo and Pageant at Chatham Barracks but on this occasion only the Divisional Band and Drums took part[7]. From the programme it is apparent that the Bugle Major was heavily involved since he wrote a bugle march, arranged the Sunset call and also arranged the marches *Along with the Soldiers* and *Red*

Wing. All of these were for the drums of the Division. Lt Hoby wrote *Echo Fanfare* and the march *Colonel Commandant* as well as arranging a chorale for trumpet and trombones.

One of the Matinee Musicales held at the RM Barracks, Chatham featured an orchestral programme consisting of *Tristan and Isolde* and *Siegfried Idyll* (Wagner); Symphony in D (Op 4) - the Finale (Svendsen); *Serenade Badine* (Maries) and *Petite Suite de Concert* (Coleridge-Taylor). The second half consisted of *Suite* (Chopin); the *Serenata* from Hoby's own Suite - *Scenes from Venice*; *Slavonic Dance Op 46, No 4* (Dvorak) and the waltz, *Artist's Life* (Strauss).

During the First World War the band raised money for War Funds and, in 1917, they went to France and were attached to 63rd (RN) Division on the Arras Front, relieving the Portsmouth RMLI Divisional Band. After the war, in 1919, they played a significant part in the RN Memorial Service held at S[t] Paul's Cathedral. Several members of the Royal Family attended this Service.

The Chatham Divisional Band played at the Funeral Service for Admiral of the Fleet, the Marquess of Milford Haven, at Westminster in 1921[8]. In 1924 the bands of the Royal Marines (Chatham, Portsmouth, Plymouth and the Depot) were massed with the Band of the RNSM under Lt Hoby for the second week of the first Wembley Torchlight and Searchlight Tattoo[9]. In 1925 Lt Hoby again conducted the Wembley Tattoo and, on this occasion, the bands of the RNSM and Plymouth Division also played a major part[10]. This was the first occasion that the Chatham Band had worn its new, blue, RM tunics instead of their traditional RMLI scarlet. Three years later Maj Hoby retired after an illustrious career spanning twenty-one years with the Royal Marines at Chatham. Lt P S G O'Donnell, who transferred to Chatham from the position of Director of Music, Plymouth Division, succeeded him.

One of the high points of O'Donnell's leadership of the Chatham Band came when a composite band of sixty-five was responsible, with the RM composite Battalion, for Public Duties in London during 1935, the Jubilee Year of the reign of King George V. The Drums of the Battalion numbered forty and the Colours for the Battalion were furnished by Portsmouth Division. Rehearsals were carried out at Eastney and blue uniform was worn to accustom the Battalion to the expected heat in London[11]. The Band marched the Battalion to Portsmouth Station to board a special train to London and, on arrival at Waterloo, they all marched to Chelsea Barracks where an advance party had prepared for their arrival. On 1st September the Battalion attended Divine Service at the Guards Chapel, Wellington Barracks. Every third day they mounted guard on the two Palaces, the Magazine in Hyde Park, the Bank of England and the Central London Recruiting Depot. At that time the ceremony of changing the guard took place daily at S[t] James' instead of Buckingham Palace owing to the absence of Their Majesties from London. Greatcoats were worn on the first day owing to the heavy rain but the weather was fine after that. The band shared the playing of music in the forecourt with the Coldstream Guards whilst the ceremony took place. A Band Sergeant and two men detailed by the Company finding the King's Guard paraded in Church Order at 09.45am to take band music by march route to Friary Court and to return on completion. The band played standing in the traditional circular formation. Normally the Guards Band plays throughout the ceremony but this arrangement was ordered in view of the special circumstances of the visit of a RM Battalion. For part of this period the Officers of the Battalion wore mourning bands for the late Queen Astrid of the Belgians who had been killed in a car crash on 25th August. During this tour of duty the Royal Marines exercised their ancient right to march through the City of London with drums beating, Colours flying and bayonets fixed, this being the first time that it had occurred for over two centuries[12]. Band preparations for this event had been complex and largely fell upon the shoulders of Capt O'Donnell as Senior Director of Music. In December 1934 he had decided not to take a RM Drum and Fife Band but additions to the duties of the Royal Marines meant that he needed them after all[13]. It was also decided that a new Slow Troop was required.[14]

Rehearsal for the 1935 London Duties on the parade at Eastney Barracks. Band and Drums are followed by the Drum and Fife Band. The Buglers wear Dress Cords Royal for the first time. The Colours and their Escort can also be seen.

Other major events during Maj[15] O'Donnell's period included a visit to Brussels in 1934 for the funeral of King Albert of the Belgians; being present at the Jubilee of King George V; the musical part of the celebrated Greenwich Pageant and playing in the procession of the Coronation of King George VI and Queen Elizabeth. O'Donnell was also responsible for the music at the funeral of Admiral of the Fleet Earl Jellicoe at St Paul's Cathedral in 1935 where he used his own band and also Lt Dunn and his Portsmouth Band. Buglers from Chatham, Portsmouth and the Depot were used and sounded Last Post and Reveille particularly well. O'Donnell wrote to Dunn in February 1936 with preparatory instructions, in case they were called upon to perform similar duties as a result of the death of Admiral of the Fleet Earl Beatty[17]. In 1937 Maj P S G O'Donnell retired to become the conductor of the BBC Wireless Military Band but not without a very busy period beforehand. The Chatham and Portsmouth Bands had to combine for the Coronation[16] and O'Donnell had to organise this. He told Lt Dunn that a band of sixty would be required and that the front rank of eight would be drummers. He also told Dunn that he wanted his best players - no seconds! O'Donnell was balancing this duty with that of organising the musical display in support of the King's Squad for the Royal Tournament at Olympia. He needed to take twenty from Portsmouth Band plus a further twenty for the last four days of the show to replace the Chatham contingent when the Chatham Band had another commitment. The Plymouth Band also needed to send twenty performers to

O'Donnell. Dunn's itinerary for the period was checked by O'Donnell to ensure that all commitments, including a Portsmouth Band requirement on board the Royal Yacht, could be met.

Although it was not realised at the time Capt T Francis, by succeeding Maj O'Donnell, was to become the last Director of Music of the Chatham Band. He had previously served with various Army bands before becoming Director of the Chatham Band.

During the Second World War the Band raised money through 'War Savings Week' concerts throughout the United Kingdom, including London and Windsor - where they played for Their Majesties at Windsor Castle.

In December 1943 RM Administrative Instruction No 10 was issued on the subject of 'Visits by RM Divisional Bands' As from 1st January 1944 the Divisional Bands were ordered to make quarterly visits to a number of RM Establishments, formations and units in the United Kingdom. These visits would be at public expense and would last about three days. The Chatham Band was given HMS *Westcliff* - a Combined Operations base at Southend, HMS *Helder* - a Combined Operations base at Brightlingsea, HMS *St Matthew* a Combined Operations Training base at Burnham-on-Crouch and the 4th Special Service Brigade.

The band went on morale boosting tours and made numerous broadcasts at home and abroad. They played at Antwerp and in the gunsites of the 5th RM AA Brigade (responsible for the defence of Antwerp) in the Scheldt defences, also Walcheren and Brussels. This tour was repeated in April and May 1945 when Nijmegan and Paris were also included. By coincidence they were at Nijmegan, Holland the night that Holland was liberated and in Paris on VE Day. In July the band, augmented by members of the Portsmouth Band, embarked in the destroyer HMS *Garth* at Sheerness to play at Hamburg, Kiel, Bremen and Cuxhaven. It was then flown to Berlin to lead the Victory Parades. On the 14th July it took part in the British March Past in the Charlotten Burger. On the 15th the Band, together with a RN Guard, were part of the Guards of Honour for the Chiefs of the General Staff who were on their way to Potsdam for the meeting of Churchill, Truman and Stalin. The band was present for a Guard of Honour at Winston Churchill's residence in Potsdam when Harry Truman, the President of the United States, arrived. The Prime Minister presented Capt Francis to the US President during this ceremony. Next day the band performed the ceremony of Sunset in Berlin's Kurfurstendamm and, on the 21st the band led the RN Guard at the head of the official march past of British troops before Winston Churchill. They were the only band in the procession. This was the end of the tour and the next day they travelled back to Hamburg where they went on board the destroyer HMS *Cottesmore* and played themselves into Sheerness at the end of a rather choppy voyage.

1947 brought the restart of the Royal Tournament; the Chatham Group Band appeared with musicians from Plymouth and Portsmouth Groups and the RNSM. In 1948 the band, together with the Portsmouth Group Band and the St Paul's Cathedral Choir played at the unveiling of the Franklin D Roosevelt statue in Grosvenor Square. Also present were Buglers of Chatham Group and the band of the RNSM.

1949 saw what was to be the last involvement of the Chatham Group Band during the Remembrance weekend. They were massed with the Portsmouth Band for the Festival at the Royal Albert Hall where their Director of Music Capt T Francis conducted both the Royal Marines and the Brigade of Guards playing Handel's *Largo*. The Silver Memorial Fanfare Trumpeters of the RNSM were used to great effect during this piece of music.

On the 8th December 1949 the Royal Marines received the Freedom of the Borough of Chatham in the RM Barracks. The Companies and the Band marched onto the Parade at

1040hrs and awaited the arrival of the Colours and the guests. Then, at 1123hrs, the Group Drum and Fife Band led the Mayor and the Corporation from the Town Hall. At the end of the ceremony the Group Band led No's 1 and 2 Companies through Chatham with the salute being taken at the Town Hall.

The Final Parade of the Colours of the Old Chatham Division, which took place on the 27th June 1950, was a poignant, but proud, affair. The Battalion, having formed up, marched on to the parade ground and formed line in open order whilst the Group Band under Capt T Francis played *Hoch Hapsburg* an early quick march of the Chatham Division. The MGRM[18], Chatham Group, arrived at the saluting base and was received with a General Salute *Garb of Auld Gaul*. No 1 Guard moved across the front of the Battalion to draw the Colours as the band played *HM Jollies* and the National Anthem. The Colours were trooped along the line in slow time with the parade at the 'Present' thus ensuring that every man had a close view of the Colours whilst according them the highest honour. The band played *The Grenadiers' March* for the slow troop. The Band and Drums then trooped in slow and quick time in front of the Battalion whilst playing *By Land and Sea* and the old RMA quick march Soldier's Chorus from *Faust*. Following the Drum Beatings the Battalion formed close column and then marched past in columns to the music *Dashing White Sergeant*, another traditional march of Chatham Division, and *A Life on the Ocean Wave*. The Battalion then reformed line, the Colours were marched out of the Escort, and were saluted before passing in slow time in front of the Battalion to be lodged in the Officers' Mess. After the National Anthem the band played *The Admiral's Regiment* and *Auld Lang Syne*. The Sunset ceremony then took place and the Union Flag was hauled down from the staff as the band played *Abide With Me*, *Sunset* and the National Anthem. The Battalion then marched from the Parade to *Sambre et Meuse*.

Next day, Whit Sunday, the Colours were laid up in Rochester Cathedral. The band marched the parade to the Cathedral and then the Congregation assembled whilst the Orchestra of RM Chatham under Capt Francis played Beethoven's Symphony No.5 in C Minor (First Movement). As the Colour Party advanced from the West Door the orchestra played the slow march *The Trumpet Voluntary*. During the Service the National Anthem was played and then, as the Colours were borne through the Quire to be placed upon the High Altar, the slow march *Scipio* was played followed by a fanfare. At the conclusion of the service the orchestra played the finale of Beethoven's Symphony No 5 in C Minor. The music used during the Final Parade was later recorded and broadcast, with appropriate commands, on the radio.

As has been described, on 14th August 1950, the RM Barracks at Chatham closed and therefore the First Division, Chatham, ceased to exist.

Part 2 - 2nd Grand Division Royal Marine Light Infantry - Portsmouth Band[19] 1900 - 1923

After a fine record of service to Queen Victoria one of the first Royal Duties of the 20th century for 2nd Lt G Miller and his Portsmouth RMLI Band was, massed with the Band of the RMA, at her funeral. They played the procession from Osborne House to the East Cowes Pier and during the embarkation onto the Royal Yacht, *Victoria and Albert*. The Band played the Beethoven and Chopin funeral marches and was relieved by the massed drums of the RMA and RMLI (without bugles or fifes) playing Miller's *Solemn March*. This had been originally written for the funeral of Prince Henry of Battenburg in 1896. The playing of this march was reported as being one of the outstanding features of the day[20]. As the Royal Yacht *Alberta*[21] moved away from the quay the band played *The Saints of God, Their Conflict Past*. The Band of the RMLI was also in attendance the next day when, at Gosport Station, the coffin was transferred to the train for London. In the funeral procession through London the band of the Chatham Division was selected to play[22] and the Corps took its precedence with the Royal Navy.[23] Later, the King personally presented the Victorian Order to Miller in recognition of his services at the funeral. The following year the band attended King Edward during his convalescence cruise and then Queen Alexandra joined the King and travelled with them to Portugal, Malta, Italy and Denmark.

Under Miller's directorship the band was noted for its depth of tone, due to the excellent euphoniums and the old circular basses.

At the Coronation Review, Aldershot, in 1902 an event took place that was to have a far-reaching effect for RM Bands. The massed bands of the four RM Divisions, under the Senior Bandmaster 2nd Lt Miller, were to accompany the RM Brigade. Knowing the importance of drums in playing a march past on a large scale, Miller had ordered the bands to bring as many drummers from the Divisional Corps of Drums as they could manage. Three of the Bands ignored this and brought only one or two percussionist side drummers. Portsmouth Band had brought a Corps of Drums that numbered between thirty and forty and so 2nd Lt Miller decided to prove a point. At the church parade before the review he massed all of his drums and the sound of them with the massed bands as they played the hymns, particularly *Onward Christian Soldiers* was said to have equalled the effect of any cathedral organ. It would appear that it is with this event that the tradition of the bands of the Royal Marines always marching with a large Corps of Drums to the front of their bands began.

This band often went to Glasgow to take part in the Glasgow Trades Exhibition and 1903 was no exception. Permission was given for the band to remain for an additional week after completion of their engagement and this allowed the band to earn enough money to pay for a cor anglais and another violin. These instruments could not have been afforded any other way.

During October 1903 Lt Miller was forced to bring to the attention of his Band President the serious manpower losses that the band was experiencing. He made the point that this was a direct result of Royal Yacht duty. These duties prevented the bandsmen from taking part in band and orchestral engagements, as well as private tuition, which severely reduced the extra earnings that they took home. Whilst on board the Yacht bandsmen could not make reduced rate purchases from the barracks for their families. The third reason was that the Bandsmen had not enlisted to go to sea. After asking Lt Miller to provide figures, which he did and at the same time mentioned that the band had received a gift of £60 from the Queen, the Band President wrote to the Commandant with regard to how serious the situation was. As a result of these sea duties the band had lost its solo violinist, solo flute, solo cello, principal oboe, principal bassoon and first clarinet - a high proportion of the band. This was in addition to the loss of four musicians for reasons unconnected with the Royal Yacht duty. He recommended that if Royal Yacht duties were to be a regular part of a bandsman's duty then special duty pay should be organised to make good the losses that were being incurred. Capt Blumberg, the Adjutant added weight to the argument by stating that under the Army Act the bandsman would be entitled to separation allowance for his wife and children.[24] The situation was resolved during the month of November 1903 but probably not to Lt Miller's satisfaction. Commodore Sir A Berkeley Milne[25] forwarded a copy of his report to the King to the Colonel Commandant, RMA. It said:

I now have the honour to submit the scheme for the supply of a band to His Majesty's Yacht "*Victoria and Albert*" when required by His Majesty the King at any time, and which has been approved by the Admiralty.

As the bands of the Royal Marine Artillery and the Royal Marine Light Infantry (Portsmouth Division) had alternately sailed in the various cruises of His Majesty in the "*Victoria and Albert*", my proposition to the Admiralty was that each of these bands should be increased by ten men, in order to make it quite fair between them; however the Admiralty did not consider it feasible to increase both bands but decided as follows:-

(1) The Royal Marine Artillery band to be increased by ten Privates or Gunners, which will raise the number of the band to fifty.

(2) Whenever His Majesty requires a band for H M Yacht "*Victoria and Albert*", a band of twenty men, including Bandmaster, will be provided.

(3) While the band is embarked, one shilling per diem to be paid by the Admiralty to each man for expenses.

When this scheme was proposed it was under the understanding that no extra expense was to fall on the Officers of the Corps, and that His Majesty should bear the initial expense, and this will be as follows:-

> Costs of instruments for the ten men,
> Military and string (See Sheet 'A') £160.0.0
> Paid annually to the Band Fund of the Royal Marine Artillery,
> in half yearly instalments (See sheet 'B') £45.0.0

I have drawn up an agreement with the Colonel Commandant, Royal Marine Artillery, (see sheet 'C') and he is to provide a band of twenty musicians (including Bandmaster) whenever His Majesty requires it.

In submitting this scheme to His Majesty, I would point out that His Majesty will now get the services of a first rate band; also, from a business point of view, there will be great economy, for, up to the present time, His Majesty has given upwards of £300 per annum in gratuities, which will in the future be quite unnecessary, for the reason that the band of thirty who are left at Headquarters are sufficient to perform all private engagements, and the amount they receive is pooled for the good of the whole band. Again, at the outside the band would probably be only embarked for four months in the year, thus for the remaining eight months leaving a fine band of fifty performers, which should obtain far more lucrative engagements.

You will notice in the agreement (sheet 'C') that I propose that His Majesty's instruments should be turned over to the Officers of the Royal Marine Artillery, for the reason that during the time the band is embarked, His Majesty has the use of ten instruments belonging to the Officers of the Corps, and I consider the wisest course is the one that I have proposed, as it will save complication.

It would much add to the prestige of the band if His Majesty would be pleased to confer upon it some special title and a badge, and thus mark the distinguished nature of their employment[26]

Sheet 'A' lists the military band and orchestral instruments and cases, and their costs, that the King would supply whilst 'B' detailed the annual payment of £45 per annum to be paid by the King for the ten men, the repair and upkeep of instruments and music. 'C' was the agreement between the King and the Colonel Commandant for the use of the band.

This document appears to dispel the story that the RMLI Band fell from grace on account of Lt Miller's blunder in offering the King a cigar, and indicates instead that the decision was based upon fiscal and business reasoning.

It is interesting to note that in 1905 Sir Berkeley Milne, by then a Rear-Admiral, and whilst on the '*Victoria and Albert*' at Cowes, wrote the following:

Up to the end of 1903, the Bands of the RMLI (Po[27]) and RMA embarked alternately, whether for a long or short cruise, but the cruise to Copenhagen in September and October 1903 was the last time the RMLI Band came[28]

In December 1905 Lt Miller wrote a letter to the Colonel Commandant, Portsmouth Division RMLI, the content of which would probably be echoed by the Directors of Music serving almost a century later.

Sir,

1. I have the honour to allude to the present regulations whereby we lose our Bandsmen at the early age of 40, when after years of steady training a bandsman is at the very height of his powers; and some other band and some other Service derives the benefit of our training.

2. The advisability of retaining the services of experts trained in the Division was recognised long ago in the case of Tailors and Shoemakers.

3. I have the honour now to allude to GSO (Supply) Para III which if applied to all RM Band Ranks would necessarily result in the higher efficiency of the Divisional Bands and at the same time effect a considerable saving to the State by getting a much better man at a much smaller price - since a re-enlisted pensioner may be said to involve no pension whatsoever.[29]

It is not known what response this letter received.

The Band of Portsmouth Division RMLI for the tour of the Western Front 1916-1917. Notice the two sets of pipes in the foreground.

The Portsmouth Band was the first of the Divisional bands to be sent to France during World War I. They went there in 1916, playing not only for the RMLI Battalions of the 63rd (RN) Division but also for the RMA howitzers in that sector. They met the 2nd Bn at Abbeville and played them to rest billets at Rue, after the battle of the Ancre. Maj Miller was taken ill and had to return to England a few weeks in advance of his band which returned in January 1917. As a result of his illness Maj Miller was invalided from the Royal Marines after thirty-two years' service. During the period that Maj Miller was Bandmaster the band were honoured with more commissions from Royalty than any other band. It is authoritively stated that no Bandmaster in any service has received so many Royal acknowledgements for duty done, for pleasure given, or for the band's worth.[30]

Lt B W O'Donnell, who came from the Band of the 7th Hussars in India, succeeded Maj Miller. In 1918 the band was in frequent attendance at the Royal Pavilion during the King's visits to Aldershot. In the spring of 1919 the band went on a tour of Belgium where they found very appreciative audiences amongst the keen musicians of the mining towns and villages. At this time the official complement of the band was forty. The cost of railway travel at that time was restricting the band to giving concerts only along the south coast with occasional visits to Cardiff, Leeds and Birmingham. Lt O'Donnell, during an interview[31] and in response to criticism that Service bands were too quick to perform programmes made up of musical comedy selections and other 'trivial' music, described the types of musical programme that his military band and the orchestra were performing. Typical orchestral and military concert programmes, recently performed on South Coast piers, included Smetana's overture *The Bartered Bride, Scotch Rhapsody No 1* (Mackenzie), *Capriccio Italienne* (Tchaikovsky) and Svendsen's *Norwegian Rhapsody* played by the orchestra and Wagner's *Entry of the Gods into Valhalla*, Grieg's *Solveg's Song*, the suite *Pantomime* by Lacombe and Liszt's *Rhapsody Number 1* played by the military band.

In 1922 the bands of the RMA and of the Portsmouth and Plymouth Divisions RMLI gave a massed concert in Glasgow - the Musical Directors being the three brothers, Lieutenants PS, BW and RP O'Donnell respectively.

When the RMA and the RMLI were amalgamated in 1923 the members of the Portsmouth RMLI band became the Band of the Depot RM, still led by Lt B W O'Donnell, and retaining the famous Prince of Wales Plumes in addition to its cap badge. This had been awarded to the band in 1876 for its service to the Prince of Wales during the voyage to India on HMS *Serapis*.

Part 3 - 3rd Grand Division Royal Marine Light Infantry - Plymouth Divisional Band

Mr F Winterbottom continued to lead the Plymouth Band until 1910. In 1900 the Divisional Band joined a Battalion of RMLI under the Colonel Commandant for the opening of the new wing of College Green Hospital, Bristol, by Queen Victoria. Upon arrival in the city the band led the Battalion through the streets to the hospital where they lined the route. They arrived back at Plymouth Station at midnight and the band played the Battalion back to barracks with a memorised march. In 1902 the band had the honour of playing on board the HM Yacht *Victoria and Albert* for the King who ordered them to return to play during the following evening. On this occasion he presented BM Winterbottom with the Medal of the Royal Victorian Order[32].

One of his greatest achievements was the success of his fortnightly symphony concerts that were held during the winter. They began in the Assembly Rooms of the Royal Hotel, Plymouth but were soon moved to the Town Hall at Stonehouse because of the huge demand for seats. Even then the concerts soon became season-ticket holders only - such was the demand. His final concert proved to be a surprise to Mr Winterbottom because the Chairman of the Stonehouse District Council presented him with the proceeds! It was a joint orchestral concert featuring the Plymouth Division RMLI Band and the Band of the Royal Garrison Artillery under Winterbottom's friend, BM Evans. The "orchestral *piece de resistance*" according to the Western Weekly Mercury was Winterbottom's own composition, the overture *Jorinda*.[33]

In 1910 Mr J Newton became Bandmaster. In 1894 he had been Trumpet Major, Prince of Wales Own Norfolk Artillery. Newton was well respected by his band and received the congratulations of many including King George V. He may well have carved out an excellent career but, sadly, he was taken ill and died in June 1916.

The band then passed into the very capable hands of Mr Percy O'Donnell who had served with 2nd Bn. The Black Watch (Royal Highlanders) and the Royal Artillery Staff Band in Gibraltar. He served with the Plymouth Band from 1916 to 1928, being commissioned in 1921. The band embarked upon a concert tour of the Western Front in 1917 winning great acclaim from the Staff Officers and from the troops, particularly for the impromptu performances that the band provided anywhere and at any time. The following year the band returned to France for a further extensive tour of the front line areas. Because of its high standard of playing it was selected to be resident band at the first post-war Royal Tournament and then, as a tribute to its dedication to duty during the war years, it was invited to accompany the Prince of Wales (later King Edward VIII) on a post World War I morale-raising tour to Canada in the battle-cruiser HMS *Renown*. They returned four months later and the Prince was so impressed with the band that he asked them to accompany him to Australia, once again in HMS *Renown*. The two successful tours, and in particular the bands part in them, were acknowledged by the presentation, in 1920, of the Prince of Wales plumes to be worn as part of the cap-badge.[34] The amalgamation of the RMLI and the RMA had little effect upon this band apart from the change of title and the change to a blue uniform.

In 1928 Lt O'Donnell transferred, as has already been noted, to the Chatham Division where he became Senior Director of Music of the Corps. Lt G W E Grayson replaced O'Donnell, joining from the 1st Bn. The Seaforth Highlanders but he retired two years later.

Probably the best known of all British military bandsmen, Lt F J Ricketts, who was equally well known as the composer Kenneth Alford, joined from the Depot, RM in September 1930. He took the Plymouth Band to Kelvin Hall, Glasgow for almost two weeks in September and October. An Engagement Form exists for this engagement that shows that the percentage system was in operation with the Band Fund receiving 10%, the Director of Music receiving 20% and the remaining 70% being distributed amongst the musicians.

For the Coronation of HM King George VI in 1937 the band, with a Royal Guard of Honour found by the Corps, was positioned outside Westminster Abbey[35].

Ricketts took the Plymouth Band to Paris for the 150th Anniversary of the fall of the Bastille in 1939 before boarding the RMS *Empress of Australia* to visit the Canadian National Exhibition at Toronto. He was a great believer in the necessity of rehearsal and he used the journey to full effect. Glowing press notices regarding the tour performances were received by the band. 1939 was an exceptionally busy year as Major Ricketts also found time to make ten records for HMV.

As has been described, from 1st January 1944 the Divisional Bands were ordered to make quarterly visits to a number of RM Establishments, formations and Units in the United Kingdom. Plymouth Band was given the School of Signalling RM, the Signal Holding Company, the Royal Marines Military School, the Home Based Ledger Office and the RM Support Craft Regiment[36] at Wimborne. In 1940 Maj Ricketts went back to the recording studio to make a further five recordings.

Maj Ricketts was due to retire in 1940 but, in view of the war situation, his Service was extended. However, in 1944 he was forced to retire due to ill health. During the period 1940-1944 Ricketts and his band toured extensively and broadcast on many occasions. As if in anticipation of Ricketts' eventual retirement the Adjutant General, in November 1943, issued a Circular giving details of a change to the Regulations governing the promotion of Directors of Music, RM:

> Officers entering direct from Civil life will be promoted to Captain after 8 years commissioned service, and officers promoted to Lieutenant from Warrant Officer in the RM, or in the Army, will, as a wartime measure, be eligible for promotion to Captain on completion of three years commissioned service.

Necessary amendments to regulations would take place and the change was retrospective, taking effect as from November 1942.

In March 1944 the General Officer Commanding informed the Under Secretary of State, War Office, Whitehall and the Air Ministry that a vacancy would be occurring for the post of Director of Music at the Plymouth Division, RM. This was promulgated throughout the RN and the RM as well as the Army. However, it later transpired that the Air Ministry had two Director of Music vacancies themselves and decided not to advise their Service. Candidates for the Plymouth Band vacancy had to have experience as a Director of Music, or Conductor of Military Bands or Orchestra of standing. Eighty-one applications were received and ten were selected for interview. Of the seventy-one applications that were rejected fifty-one were from the Army, seven were civilians, six were from the RNSM, one each were from the RN and the RM. One application came from New Zealand and two from Canada. Despite the Air Ministry's decision not to advertise, two enterprising men from the RAF applied.

A Board comprising Maj-Gen H W Simpson, Brigadier T H Jameson and Major Ricketts assembled to interview the candidates on 25th April. The Board unanimously decided that the best candidate and the most suitable for the appointment was BM G Nalden of the Royal Artillery (Portsmouth) Band. Second choice was Cd BM R H Stoner the Port Bandmaster, Staff of C-in-C Portsmouth.

According to Paragraph (3) of the report Stoner was quite outstanding and "should, for any reason Mr Nalden not be appointed, the Board wish to place on record that they were unanimously of the opinion that he be a most suitable selection for the appointment". The next three candidates were BM J L Judd (Royal Signals Band), BM D McBain (Royal Artillery Mounted Band) and BM F L Statham (Manchester Regt). The GOCRM, Maj Gen T L Hunton, decided that Lt Stoner should be appointed and wrote to the First Sea Lord to seek final approval. He said:

> GOCRM is strongly of the opinion that, in view of the recommendation in paragraph (3) of the report, Commissioned Bandmaster R H Stoner LRAM, RNS of Music, should be appointed, in spite of the

recommendation for Bandmaster C Nalden Mus Bac, LRAM ARCM psm RA. It will be seen that the Board were unanimous that Mr Nalden was considered best qualified and most suitable for the appointment, but that Mr Stoner was quite outstanding and would be most suitable. GOCRM would very much like, therefore, to recognise the fine work done by the Royal Naval School of Music and in particular the outstanding capabilities of Mr Stoner, to which attention has been drawn by Admiral of the Fleet Sir John C Tovey GCB KBE DSO in the recommendation enclosed. GOCRM feels that the appointment of Mr Stoner would be greatly appreciated, not only by the Royal Naval School of Music, but by the Corps as a whole .

The recommendation was approved by the First Sea Lord.[37]

During the remaining war years the band, as part of a large composite band, under their new Director of Music, toured Holland and Normandy and led British troops through Paris from the Arc de Triomphe immediately following the liberation of that city. On the previous evening the band had played in the Champs Elysees until dusk. An extensive tour of Ceylon, India, Burma and Siam took place in 1946 during which they participated in the Peace Celebrations in Bangkok, the Victory Parade in Delhi and many important functions for His Excellency the Viceroy of India and the Supreme Commander, South East Asia. On 9th January 1946 the band, comprising elements of the three Divisional bands at Chatham, Portsmouth and Plymouth and the RNSM (and bearing the name HM RM Far East Band), performed a Ceremonial Beat Retreat on the Padang, Singapore. It is interesting to note that the musical programme contains five of Kenneth Alford's marches - perhaps Capt Stoner used it as a tribute to his predecessor who had died eight months earlier[38]. The same band but without the RNSM component also performed a Beat Retreat in Bombay on 19th March.

A slight oddity in the programme was the use of Bugles and Band for Last Post. The programme describes this as follows: "The Last Post is sounded by the Buglers to a hymn-like accompaniment from the band".

Tragically Major Ricketts' death occurred only a year after his enforced retirement at the age of sixty-five, but he left a legacy of recorded and written music the quality of which will probably never be equalled. He had contributed a total of fifty years' service to military music in the Army and the Royal Marines. Stoner had been promoted to Captain in 1945 and, in 1947, the title of the band was changed to the Band of HM Royal Marines (Plymouth Group). In 1949 the band led the Ship's Company of HMS *Amethyst*, of 'Yangtse Incident' fame, on a march through Plymouth. In August the Plymouth Group Band gave a combined concert and Beat Retreat in the Royal Marine Barracks, Plymouth.

Part 4 - Royal Marine Artillery Band 1900-1923 and Royal Marines Portsmouth Division Band 1923 - 1950

The RMA began the new century by taking part in the prestigious Glasgow International Exhibition in 1901. The beginning of the new century also brought a continuation of the Band's service to the Monarchy. Numerous visits to Osborne House as well as aboard the Royal Yacht *Victoria and Albert* included attendance upon the new King, Edward VII, in 1902 when he took a trip in the Royal Yacht to help restore his health. In Coronation Year BM B S Green and the Drum Major CSgt E S Keen were awarded the Bronze Coronation Medal, whilst BdSgt T Holding was awarded the Royal Victorian Medal. Mr Green was presented with a baton mounted with a gold and emerald crown for his service. In early November 1903 the King gazetted the RMA Band as the permanent Royal Yacht Band but, in 1904, the Lords of the Admiralty made it clear that the Bandsmen embarked in HM Yacht were not necessarily to be members of the RMA Band[39]. In 1909 the band had to write to the Commodore of HM Yachts to remind him that the King's annual payment, which was paid in two half-yearly instalments, was overdue.[40] This was at the same time that they approved an allowance of a shilling a day for each Band NCO and Musician, up to a maximum of twenty, for service in HM Yacht[41]. During 1911 King George V and Queen Mary travelled to India for the Delhi Durbar on board the P&O liner *Medina* with the RMA Band in attendance. As a result of this the band was awarded a special cap badge consisting of a gilt grenade on which was mounted the Royal Cypher 'GRV' and Crown in silver all surrounded by a gilt laurel wreath. The Durbar itself was a magnificent occasion. Following the official proclamation a battalion of soldiers fired a *feu-de-joie* and then a thirty-three gun salute was given by a battery of Artillery. Then the Massed Bands of the RMA and the RM Bands of HMS *Defence*, HMS *Cochrane* and HMS *Argyle* played the first four bars of the National Anthem. This was all repeated and then the battery completed the one hundred and one gun salute before the Massed Bands played the first verse of the National Anthem. After various introductions and presentations the bands struck up with *A Life on the Ocean Wave* and the Naval Brigade led the massive march-past. As the battalions of infantry marched past the bands played the appropriate regimental marches.[42]

In 1917 Lt B S Green retired and was succeeded by Lt R P O'Donnell who had just completed ten years as Bandmaster 21st Lancers. In 1923, because of the amalgamation of the RMA and the RMLI, the Portsmouth Division RMLI ceased to exist and the band was integrated into the Depot Band. As a result the Band of the RMA became the Band of the Portsmouth Division, RM, with Lt R P O'Donnell as its first Director of Music.

In 1925 Rear Admiral Buller, Commanding Officer Royal Yachts, (CORY) wrote to the Adjutant General on behalf of the King who wished the Portsmouth Division Royal Yacht Band to wear the letters 'RY' as an emblem of the service provided by themselves and their predecessors the RMA. The Regulations for the wearing of a badge had been promulgated in AFO 2522 in 1922 but with the changes to organisation and to uniform brought about by the amalgamation the idea had not been progressed. A few days later the Rear Admiral wrote to the Adjutant General with further information. The King wanted the badge to be worn on both arms and to consist of the words 'Royal Yacht' surmounted by a crown. Although the King had only the band in mind the alterations would also apply to the RM Detachment serving on the Royal Yacht. Sample badges were quickly produced since the King wished the Band to be wearing their new badge for Cowes Week. It was to be in gold for wear on the blue cloth tunic and in scarlet worsted for wear on the blue serge tunic. Rear Admiral Buller concurred, with slight alteration to the size of the lettering, to the design and suggested that the badge should be worn on the right arm only. It was stressed that the band should wear such a badge on all occasions not just when embarked. The Adjutant General then wrote to the Admiralty stating that the King wished the RM Detachment embarked upon the Royal Yacht to wear a special badge. He then remarked that the King also wished the band to wear the badge, as if it were an afterthought and not the King's original intention. He made the point that the band already wore a special cap badge and that he felt that the proposed badge should only be worn when embarked. This letter was forwarded to Buckingham Palace and then, with an accompanying letter from Clive Wigram,[43] to Rear Admiral Buller. Wigram's letter confirmed that the King wanted the whole of the Band of the Portsmouth Division to wear the new badge. The King also wanted Buller to speak to Capt O'Donnell to find out if there was any reason why this should not be done. O'Donnell informed the Rear Admiral that he felt it highly desirable that the entire band should wear the badge at all times and not only when embarked. The Rear Admiral endorsed this view adding the point that wearing the badge only when embarked was impractical and that continual sewing on and removing of the badge would damage the tunic itself. He also repeated his view that the wearing of the badge on both shoulders as advocated by the Adjutant General was too showy and that O'Donnell agreed with this view. The Rear Admiral also pointed out that the King would no doubt be aware that the special cap badge worn by the band had been specifically awarded for the 1911 trip to India in the 'Medina' and therefore had no bearing on the current proposals that were designed to signify the association of the Band with the Royal Yacht. The final riposte to the Adjutant General's letter was a remark to clarify that the award to the Detachment was as a result of the award to the Band and not the other way around. On the bottom of the letter Rear Admiral Buller added a hand-written note dated 20th October 1925:[44]

> No further correspondence took place, but the badge was issued to the whole band and to the Marine
> Detachment and was worn for the first time at Cowes - 1925.
> It is worn on the right sleeve only.
> On the cloth tunic it is worked in gold.
> On the serge tunic it is worked in red worsted.
> In the case of the band it is worn by all members and alway.

In 1931 Capt R O'Donnell left the Royal Marines to become the Director of Music of the Royal Air Force Band and was succeeded by F Vivian Dunn, the last civilian to be appointed to lead a Royal Marines Band. He was granted the rank of Lieutenant.[45] Within four months of first wearing a RM uniform Lt Dunn found himself directing the

The Band of the Portsmouth Division, Royal Marines (Capt F V Dunn) take part in raising money for the war effort through a 'Warship Week' during World War 2.

Portsmouth Division Band when the Division was presented with new Colours by HRH Prince George, with the King watching, on Eastney Parade.

On the 25th November 1935 the Band joined the Chatham Band and attended the funeral of the late Admiral of the Fleet, Earl Jellicoe. They played both the Beethoven and the Chopin funeral marches. In 1935 the band was in attendance for the funeral of King George V and also the Jubilee Fleet Review and, in 1937, the Coronation Fleet Review. In the same year the Band accompanied King George VI and Queen Elizabeth to Ireland. A further Fleet Review took place in Weymouth in 1938. War was now on the horizon and, to quote Captain Derek Oakley, the author of 'Fiddler on the March':

> The outbreak of war heralded a new era for the band… the Divisional bands remained based in their respective barracks. However they travelled the length and breadth of the country, playing concerts in canteens, naval and military establishments, broadcasting and performing on many ceremonial occasions. They helped to give the people of Great Britain a much-needed boost to their morale and in many ways it was a busier time than ever.

During 1940 Capt F V Dunn made a number of recordings for Columbia but, unlike Ricketts three years earlier, he elected to use the orchestra of Portsmouth Division rather than the military band. Further recordings were made by the orchestra in 1941.

Capt Dunn always maintained that the recording studio was the ultimate expression of music and it seems as if he was smitten with the medium almost as soon as he became familiar with it. A year later he returned to make three more recordings.

Between 1942 and 1948 the Overseas Recorded Broadcasting Service (ORBS) made many recordings that were distributed overseas for the entertainment of troops anywhere in the world. They were very often in the form of a variety programme recorded onto both sides of a set of three records. Capt Dunn became involved with this movement in 1943. Stars of radio, stage and film gave their services and the recordings were distributed through ENSA, Air Ministry Movements and NAAFI export. The Orchestra of the Portsmouth Division was featured in a great many of these programme recordings. So also were many RM dance bands, military bands and choirs.[46]

In December 1943 Portsmouth Band was also told to visit specific RM units and were given HQ Special Service Group, the Special Service Group Holding Commando, HQ RM Engineers and HMS *Northney*, previously the Sunshine Holiday Camp on Hayling Island that was being used as a Landing Craft base.

Just before the end of the war, April 1945, a pageant was staged at the Royal Albert Hall. This featured a symphony orchestra from the three Divisional Bands and the RNSM, RN Chorus of Wrens and Ratings from HMS Collingwood, the RM Band from the RNSM, under BM (WO) K A MacLean, as well as singers and actors including Lt Alec Guinness RNVR who played Nelson[47].

In 1945 the band went to Holland to play for the RM Commandos and the Royal Netherlands Navy. The band was also on parade for, and presented to, Prince Bernhard.

It was intended that the Director of Music would take a composite band on tour to the Far East during 1945 but the Admiralty decided that as the King paid an annual subscription to the Band Fund from the Privy Purse, a small band and the Director of Music should remain behind. This was because the Portsmouth Band was the Royal Band set apart for attendance on Their Majesties and it might be required by Royal Command at any time.[48]

The first post-war Eastney Tattoo took place in 1947 featuring the recently re-named Portsmouth Group Band. During 1947 a Guard and Band from Portsmouth Group went to Paris to take part in the ceremonies at the Embassy when French men and women received British decorations for gallantry and service in the Allied cause. The Guard and Band also paid tribute at the Tomb of the French Unknown Warrior. This was one of the rare occasions when a stand of Colours was taken out of the country.

HMS *Vanguard* took the Royal Family on a tour to South Africa in 1947 and this provided the Band of the RM Portsmouth with a unique opportunity to show the world what a RM Group Band was capable of. Maj Dunn took a band of forty plus fourteen buglers. This provided the capability of a full orchestra of forty, a military band of forty or a marching band of fifty-four. It also gave the facility of splitting into smaller groups to enable the large number of rehearsals and performances to be covered. Concerts were given twice daily, at lunch and at dinner, and in addition to these there would often be a need for music for ballroom and for Highland dancing, the latter requiring a special ensemble. Smaller combinations would play on the forecastle from 1000 - 1030, the upper deck or cinema from 1230 - 1315 as well as from 1730 - 1830 for the ship's company. A small band was used for occasional concerts in the Officers' Wardroom, or the Gunroom for the Midshipmen as well as elsewhere for the Warrant Officers and ship's company. Concert Party rehearsals were also necessary. Whilst in South Africa the Band played for Receptions, Royal Garden Parties, State Banquets, Beat Retreats and other ceremonial. In addition the Band undertook tours of the mining areas and visited and played in many of the country's cities and towns. After re-joining the ship they continued their work as the ship visited various ports. This included many radio broadcasts. When HMS *Vanguard* came back to Portsmouth the band settled back into life in its barracks at Eastney.

During 1947 and 1948 various town and city Parks Departments and Horticultural Societies began to return to the normal pre-war practice of inviting tenders from various military bands for bandstand and park entertainment. At that time there were enough bands, and enough demand, for such tendering processes to be competitive. Alterations to Musicians' Rates, as applied to Military Bands, made this quite a complex task. Horticultural Societies and others also expected to be able to approve the musical programme in advance.

In 1948 the band of the Depot, Deal and the bands of HMS *Pembroke, Excellent, Victory* and *Daedalus* augmented Portsmouth Group Band for the Eastney Tattoo. In the same year the band, augmented from Plymouth Band, visited France with a Guard of Honour and the Regimental Colour of RMB, Eastney[49]. They also took part in the unveiling of the Roosevelt Memorial in London on the 12th April[50], a few days earlier.

1948 was the first year that the 23rd April, St George's Day, was commemorated as 'Corps Remembrance Day'. The band took part in a ceremonial parade at Eastney that included a march past and a Drumhead Service. Later they gave a concert and then, with the buglers, played during the interval of the evening's ball. A week later the band were on parade in London for the 25th Wedding Anniversary of the King and Queen and the State Drive to St Paul's Cathedral. Later that day, augmented by members of the Chatham Band, they gave a concert at the foot of Nelson's Column to raise funds for King George's Fund for Sailors.

April 1948 was also the time when a rather embarrassing situation occurred. The band had been asked to furnish a Dance Band for a dance to be held in the Officers' Mess at Eastney. Following the event the Mess President was asked to write to the Commanding Officer of the Barracks regarding the Band's performance. It was criticised for being too large and thereby too noisy; the Band Sergeant was criticised for his announcements and it was generally felt that the standard of the Band would be improved by asking the leader of the RNSM Dance Band "The Oceanaires" for some tuition in modern dance band technique. The letter was passed to the Director of Music for comment.

The Band was invited to play at the Staff College, Camberley in August on the occasion of the Camberley Cocktail Party. Band and Corps of Drums attended and Beat Retreat.

Part 5 - The Depot Band of the Royal Marines

The Band was officially formed at Deal in April 1900 from the small band of seventeen that had been at the Depot since 1890 under BdSgt Batson of the Portsmouth RMLI Band. BM J S Nicholson, formerly 15th Kings Hussars, succeeded Batson in 1897. Although never a Divisional Band it had, from 1900, a similar structure to them. During 1901 it officially stood in for the Chatham Band which was on Royal duties. In 1902, at the Coronation of King Edward VII whilst the four Divisional bands had static positions lining the route, the Depot Band had the distinction of marching with the RMLI in the procession. By 1905 BM Nicholson had brought the orchestra to such a standard that it played at the Trafalgar Centenary Banquet. During the First World War the band was kept busy marching drafts of marines from the Depot to the railway station, en route to various parts of the world, including those who embarked upon the Zeebrugge raid. The band also visited the Western Front on at least one occasion.[51] When the King of the Belgians made a State visit to England the band played at Dover for his arrival and departure. Massed with the band of the Portsmouth RMLI they took part in the funeral of the Marquess of Milford Haven, father of Earl Mountbatten of Burma and, at one time, First Sea Lord. Lt Nicholson retired in 1924 leaving a band of a very high standard to be amalgamated with the Portsmouth RMLI Band and inherited by Lt B Walton O'Donnell who moved from Portsmouth Division RMLI to Deal upon the amalgamation of the RMLI and the RMA. A year later O'Donnell was given an extraneous appointment as Professor of Military Music at the Royal Academy of Music. In the same year he and his band were selected to accompany the Prince of Wales to the West African colonies, South Africa and South America on board HMS *Repulse*. The new, post amalgamation, blue divisional band pattern uniform was worn on this tour for the first time.

In 1928 Drum Major W A Gouge of the Depot band died at the age of thirty-four. He was a remarkable figure and his loss was reflected in the funeral arrangements that were made for him. Gouge joined the Portsmouth Division of the RMLI in 1908 at the age of 14 years. Whilst a Lance-Sergeant he was appointed Drum Major at the Depot, his first duty being the Armistice Parade. He had just been promoted CSgt when he died. Following the Catholic Service the coffin, draped in the Union flag with his helmet and sword on top, was carried to the waiting gun-carriage. The escort presented arms and, led by the firing party furnished by 156 Squad marching with arms reversed, the cortege stepped off as the band played Chopin's *Marche Funebre*. Drums were muffled and the Bugle Major's staff was draped. The gun-carriage was pulled by a team from 160 Squad. Amongst the mourners were the Officers and NCOs of the Depot in full dress uniform, Drum Major Wilson and QMS Peasnell from Portsmouth Division, representatives of the Artists' Rifles and many clubs and associations as well as his family. As the procession drew near to the cemetery the band played the Dead March in *Saul* and then the band took its position, as did the firing party, at the graveside. After the Catholic rites the customary volleys were fired and, between each volley, the band played a verse of *Peace, Perfect Peace*. Then came the Last Post and Sunset and the troops then marched back to barracks[52].

When Walton O'Donnell accepted the position of Director of Music to the BBC Wireless Military Band in 1928 he was replaced by Lt F J Ricketts, late of the 2nd Bn The Argyll and Sutherland Highlanders. Ricketts remained in post until 25th August 1930 when he was moved to the Plymouth Band since the Depot Band was to be disbanded as a result of the move of the RNSM to Deal. To mark the event Ricketts and his men played seven consecutive military band concerts in the mornings during the week leading up to the closure and seven orchestral concerts in the evenings. Fifty pieces of music were played by the band and fifty-seven pieces by the orchestra. Not one item of music was repeated and the last piece to be played was *A Life on the Ocean Wave*.

Lt F J Ricketts and the Band of the Depot RM, Deal. This was taken in 1930 shortly before the band was disestablished.

Part 6 - Buglers and Corps of Drums

Torchlight Tattoos continued to be popular entertainment for those close to Barracks. One took place in August 1901 at the Depot and the Drum and Fife Band were featured playing alternately with the band during the various displays. Following the sounding of First Post the drums and fifes then played Tattoo and, after Last Post, band and bugles played a bugle march prior to the march-off. Another was held a month later at Forton Barracks when the Drum and Fife Band led by Drum Major Keen was considerably augmented. This was repeated the following year when sixty Buglers led by the same Drum Major sounded an opening fanfare before he led the Drum and Fife Band out from the colonnades. Drum Major Keen left the Corps in 1903 after twenty-five years' service, fifteen as Drum-Major, having instructed a total of four hundred and fifty-six boys at Forton Barracks. Of the two hundred and seventy-eight who transferred to the ranks when eligible almost two hundred became NCOs and the Drum Majors of The Manchester Regt, The Northumberland Fusiliers, and The Lancashire Fusiliers, as well as his successor, Drum Major Burns[53], were trained by him. Keen arranged many of the displays at Forton and he was at the head of the RM Massed Bands at the 1902 Coronation. The following year Drum Major Burns not only led the Drum and Fife Band but also the Drum and Fife Band of the Divisional boys' school. The Torchlight Tattoos and Pageants continued, with occasional breaks, at the Divisions and at the Depot until the Second World War.

The Drum and Fife Band of the Portsmouth Division, Royal Marine Light Infantry.

In 1905 the Band of the Royal Garrison Artillery, who had asked to take part, and the Drum and Fife Band led the funeral procession of a Portsmouth RMLI musician. The Drum and Fife band played the *Sicilian Mariners Hymn*, used throughout the Royal Navy as the funeral march. Twenty-four buglers sounded Last Post. The buglers were always heavily committed as drummers with the Band and Drums, as the Drum and Fife Band and as Buglers.

In 1909 Bugle Major Bunting, Chatham Division, made a special arrangement of Sunset for their Tattoo. This was also played in 1911 when the report states, "Then came the sounding of Sunset by the drums, to music arranged by Bugle Major Bunting".

In 1915 Boy Bugler S C Reed drowned when HMS *Formidable* was torpedoed and sunk by U-24 in the English Channel. Politicians in the House of Commons were told that when Reed was advised to use his drum to keep him afloat he replied that he had thought of that and had given it to a blue-jacket boy who could not swim. Others who died in WW1 include Bugler A E Flory, HMS *Castor*, at Jutland and Boy Bugler Timmins, age fourteen, who was killed on the bridge of HMS *Cardiff* shortly after sounding *To Quarters* at Heligoland. Boy Bugler A Morgan was, at the age of fourteen, the youngest combatant at the defence of Antwerp where he was wounded in the leg. He also saw action, aged eighteen, at Zeebrugge. He died of anaemia in 1927 aged only twenty-seven. A total of fifty-three buglers lost their lives, on land and on sea, during the First World War.[54]

Seven buglers supported the King's Squad at the 1919 Royal Naval, Military and Air Force Tournament when the resident band was Plymouth Division. Eight buglers under Bugle Major C E Lidiard[55] (Plymouth Division) were used the following year.

Bugler 'Sticks' Burnett wearing World War 1 fighting order. Burnett was on board HMS Suffolk in 1918 at Vladivostock when Allied war materials were waiting to be shipped on the Trans-Siberian railway. One of Suffolk's six-inch guns and four 12pdr guns were mounted on the train which, with the RM Detachment, travelled over 6,000 miles and was in action supporting Czech forces fighting the Russians. The unit spent six winter months in Russia.

In 1920 thirty-two Silver Bugles were purchased by private subscription as a Memorial to RMLI officers who were killed during the First World War. The bugles were the standard Service pattern but in sterling silver with the Corps crest embossed upon them and an engraved inscription. They were issued, in groups of eight, to the RMLI Divisions at Chatham, Portsmouth and Plymouth as well as to the Depot, Deal. They were not played together until the first massed bands Beat Retreat on Horse Guards Parade in 1950, and then were only played together at two more Beating Retreat ceremonies.[56] Although not a Band Service Memorial they are an inherent part of Band Service history.

When the amalgamation of the RMA and the RMLI took place the Colours of the Portsmouth RMLI were taken from Forton Barracks to Eastney Barracks. Drum Major Wilson marched the band and colours to the floating bridge and from Portsmouth Point to Eastney. They were preceded by the band of The Prince of Wales Volunteers (South Lancashire Regt) and an RNSM Band under Lt S Fairfield from Portsmouth Point.

Buglers were also very busy at sea. Bugler Brand was responsible for training the volunteer band of HMS *Revenge* in 1925. He had brought the playing of drum, bugle and fife to a very high standard thanks to having a number of ex-Buglers in the RM

The Corps of Drums of the Plymouth Division RMLI. Many are wearing the 1902 pattern Drummers Scarlet Tunic. This would only be worn until amalgamation in 1923. Bugles and fifes can be clearly seen. Prior to the issue of Dress Cords Royal in 1935 the bugle cord was attached to the bugle so that the tassles were high on the left shoulder when the bugle was at the bugler's side. The bass drummer can be identified as can the Drum Major and the Bugle Major (probably C E Lidiard).

Detachment. A report in a 1927 issue of G&L describes what was probably a fairly typical scene on board ships of the Royal Navy. "HMS *Nelson*: The band, augmented by ex-Buglers from the Detachment with Cpl Heaton as Drum Major complete with staff and gauntlets, were very conspicuous. On Sunday mornings at 0900 there is a voluntary 'clear lower deck' to witness 'the troop'. The band presents a fine spectacle marching the length of the top deck to the strains of "*Sambre et Meuse*" and the Buglers, who have been organised by Cpl Desmond render a good account of themselves." Buglers were an important link between the band and the detachment on the ship as well as between the marines and the ship's company. Having joined the Corps as Boy Buglers they later had the choice of whether to remain a Bugler or transfer to General Service. If they chose the latter they would invariably find themselves as part of a ship's detachment. Many would take the opportunity of using their musical skills on drum, fife and bugle by working with the band or, if in existence, the drum and fife, drum and bugle or any other volunteer group that could make use of them. Their experience also made many of them very able, and willing, Drum Majors. HMS *Queen Elizabeth* had a bugle band, trained by Bugler Elliott, that was the envy of the Fleet. It consisted of four side drums, one bass drum, cymbals, twelve buglers and Sgt Spanson as Drum Major. There are many instances of ships' bands being able to improve their ceremonial displays by utilising ex-buglers from the detachment. Buglers also had to be resourceful and independent since smaller ships also required buglers but did not have bands.

The story of BM J Allen's band of HMS *Calcutta* broadcasting on Montreal Radio in 1927 has already been described. Included in the broadcast was Bugler R Newman sounding various bugle calls used in HM ships. A GORM[57] of 1929 set out the drill to be adopted by all buglers at RM Establishments. It included the method of raising and lowering the bugle for playing, marching with the bugle held (not carrying a drum) and the flourish.

In 1929 Drum Major Wilson of the Portsmouth Division retired after eleven and a half years in the appointment. On 14th April, on parade after Church, he formally handed his staff to his successor BdCpl J Dacombe who would in turn hold the appointment until 1941. Drum Major Dacombe was not only a fine athlete and a very good Drum Major but was also considered by Boy Buglers as a mentor[58].

The 1931 Royal Tournament again saw Buglers in support of a King's Squad display but this time it was expanded to Band and Buglers with drums played by LCplBug Elliot, three Buglers and four ex-Buglers whilst fifes were played by Cpl Astle and five buglers. The 1st Flutes were played by an RNSM Bandmaster and a Band Corporal with eight Musicians and Band Boys. Four of the buglers were from General Service and each Division had provided two buglers. Portsmouth Divisional band was supporting a Royal Tour at this time so Drum Major Dacombe and twelve buglers led bands found from warships and local establishments.

In 1935 a Drum and Fife band consisting of forty buglers and ex-buglers was formed for London Duties. Dress Cords Royal were issued to buglers for the first time on this occasion and they have been worn by them ever since. This tended to give the front rank of a ship's band an unbalanced look since the difference between the Buglers and the percussionist drummers was immediately obvious.

HMS *Caledonia*, the Training Establishment at Rosyth, was able to produce a display by massed bands consisting of a Boys' Bugle and Pipe Band and an Artificers' Fife and Drum Band for the Rear-Admiral's Inspection. CplBug Dowdell of Plymouth Division appears to have had a great deal to do with the training of these.

The Second World War claimed its first casualties in the Buglers Branch when HMS *Royal Oak* was torpedoed at Scapa Flow with the loss of Bugler Mountford and Boy Bugler Priestley. The next occurred when Bugler Owens was killed on HMS *Ajax* and Boy Bugler Hill was killed on HMS *Exeter* at the Battle of the River Plate. The second Bugler of HMS *Exeter* LCplBug Kent was presented to the Duke of Kent when he visited Divisions at Plymouth. A further eighteen Buglers, eleven of them Boy Buglers, were killed at sea or in Shore Establishments during the Second World War.

In 1941 Drum Major J Dacombe of the Portsmouth Division retired, his place being taken by Drum Major L Beer who had enlisted as a Boy Bugler, transferred to the ranks and served on various ships including HMS *Hood* where he became Drum Major of the Home Fleet. He later became Drum Major Mediterranean Fleet and then a Drill Instructor at RM Depot, Deal before being appointed as Drum Major, Portsmouth Division. In 1941 Plymouth was blitzed and the room where the unit bagpipes were stored was hit. The bagpipes were destroyed but, in 1944, it was announced that they would be replaced and that they would carry the tartan of the Argyll and Sutherland Highlanders to commemorate the association between the two Regiments.

8th RM Battalion, later to become 41 Cdo, was being formed during 1942 and one of the Unit Buglers, LCplBug Rayfield, was very involved in running the 8th Bn Band that consisted of eight bugles, six drums and three bagpipes and which practised three times a day. They later paraded with the Guard when the Adjutant-General visited the Battalion.

The youngest member of the Corps afloat, Boy Bugler Wills, had his 15th birthday on 7th July 1943 on board HMS *Kent*.

In 1945 the ancient ceremony of Drumming the Vicar to Church was revived when the Rector of Chatham arrived at his church to conduct the annual parade service of the Chatham Division escorted by two Marines and preceded by Boy Bugler D Hawdon. This custom began in the late 17th Century when the Clergy, carrying the Sacramental Silver to

Church, were often set upon by hooligans, and had continued into the 18th Century before lapsing.

Some Drum Majors had got into the habit of using their staff to put on a bit of a show whilst on the march or on parade but an RMRO in 1946 stated "throwing their maces [sic] in the air will only be carried out at the discretion of the Major-General, RM, on the parade ground of a RM Establishment"[59].

In 1946 an extension to the training of Boy Buglers was introduced; lasting a week it covered Basic Naval Training, Royal Marine Duties and General Seamanship. Shortly after this, in December 1947, an RMRO[60] was issued that stated that training in the fife was no longer a requirement of Boy Buglers unless they specifically wanted to learn in which case, at the discretion of the relevant Commander, it might be possible for Buglers having completed their first commission at sea. The following year training of Boy Buglers was taken away from the Groups and made the responsibility of the RNSM at Burford. The three Group Bugle Majors, Baker, Brown and Goddard with SgtBug Daley met with other instructors and Cd BM McLean and BM Thundercliffe at the RNSM in connection with this.

By 1948 the Plymouth pipes had indeed been replaced because, at the RMA Bristol Annual Ball on 12th December the Pipes and Drums from Plymouth Group, led by Drum Major Woodruffe, gave a display.

Drum Major R Woodruffe with the Pipes and Drums of Plymouth Division at the Royal Marines Association Ball - Bristol, 1948.

CHAPTER FIVE

A Leaner Royal Navy

Part 1 - The Formative Period 1950 - 1953

Capt K McLean had the distinction of being the only Director of Music to wear the King's Badge on his sleeve. Having enlisted in the Royal Marines in 1924 he was made a King's Badgeman when his Squad, 93 King's Squad, passed for duty in 1926. He then transferred to the RNSM and only a year later passed out as a Musician (Flute and Piano) and went to the band of the C-in-C Portsmouth. In 1949 he was appointed Deputy Director of Music and then, upon the retirement of Capt H Kenward in 1950, he was promoted Captain and appointed Musical Director of the RNSM at Deal.

In September 1950 he was placed at the focal point of the new Royal Marines Band Service. From being the last Musical Director of the RNSM he became the first Director of Music of the RMSM with, alongside him, Maj F V Dunn, Director of Music of the Portsmouth Group and Capt R Stoner, Director of Music of the Plymouth Group. Two of them were products of the RNSM whilst Maj Dunn was the last serving Director of Music to have been appointed as a civilian.

As has already been noted the Leech-Porter Committee had discovered that only Maj Dunn was in favour of amalgamation. Dunn's counterpart, Capt Stoner, was very much against it. Various options had been studied and discussed with, it can be assumed, the RNSM and the Group Bands each trying to ensure that their own organisation remained as intact as possible. Options had included the possibility of the Groups losing all of their bands in favour of a single, large, staff band.

This situation was obviously very difficult for McLean. In September 1950 he found himself carrying the responsibility for the School, for all bands in commission at Shore Establishments and the band ashore with 3 Cdo Bde in Hong Kong. He had approximately eight bands afloat in Home Waters and thirteen afloat elsewhere including the RM Band attached to the Royal New Zealand Navy in HMNZS *Bellona*. He also had the new Royal Marines School of Music Staff Band. There were well over one thousand members of the RMBS, including more than two hundred Boy Musicians. By comparison, Dunn and Stoner each had only one band and, whilst Dunn was a Major and therefore outranked both McLean and Stoner, none was more senior than the others.

Derek Oakley wrote of the period:

One of the conditions imposed upon the Divisional Bands which Vivian initially opposed was the relinquishment of the truly valuable music libraries to a central music library at the new Royal Marines School of Music at Deal. However, he could clearly see the way ahead and his next probable appointment. He therefore recommended that this might be done but only if the RNSM bands were provided with silvered instruments. This went through unopposed.[1]

This was certainly part of the Leech-Porter Committee recommendation that covered uniformity of clothing and instruments. He also wrote:

It is abundantly clear that Vivian Dunn had not only looked carefully at the future of music within the Royal Marines, but had established his own future. He had been promoted to Major in 1946 and now became the longest-serving Director of Music in the Corps. He foresaw his future clearly as a supremo of the whole Band Service, and from that moment on, he directed all his thoughts and efforts towards it.[2]

John Trendell wrote:

Major Vivian Dunn's visionary encouragement of the amalgamation of the two Royal Marines musical organisations did not cease once the policy decision had been taken to follow this course of action, in fact this was almost a signal for such activity to be stepped up. With six months still to go to 'amalgamation day' he arranged a grand charity concert to be presented in a 'make-shift' concert hall in the Royal Naval Barracks at Portsmouth by an orchestra of eighty-five performers drawn from his own band (Portsmouth Group RM) and RN School of Music bands based in the area[3].

Against this background Capt McLean had inherited a very large, and a very tough, job and the retirement of the Commandant, Col P R Smith-Hill, who could have given McLean the benefit of his experience and maintained a continuity, would not have helped. It also has to be remembered that the Staff Band of the RNSM had only been formed in February of the same year and that the School had also taken on the training of Boy Buglers of each of the Divisional Headquarters in 1948. All of these would have had to be integrated into the already complex training schedules of the school. As if this difficult situation was not enough McLean had four bands at sea in a war situation. The Korean War had started a few months earlier and the bands aboard the Light Fleet Carrier HMS *Triumph*, and the cruisers HMS *Ceylon*, *Jamaica* and *Kenya* were all in action off the coast of Korea as part of the Fleet on the Far East Station.

The key personnel at the School during the embryonic period of the restructured Band Service were:

Royal Marines School of Music Staff.	
Director of Music (Staff Band)	Capt K A McLean
Bandmaster (Staff Band)	Cd BM C W Hotham
Director of Music Training	Lt J E Talling
Asst. Musical Director (Theory)	Capt W Lang
Director of Music 'M' Company	Lt J H Gale
Assistant Director of Music	Cd BM E S Ough
Staff Bandmaster or Chief Instructor	QMS E R Jackson
Company Sergeant Major	BM Wells
Supply Officer (Music)	Capt B C Barnes
Drafting Officer (Non musical)	Capt W D Gregory
Drafting Officer & 'M' Company Commander	Sen Cd BM D A Jarman
Company Sergeant Major	BM Pinnigar
Director of Music's Secretary	BM T C Merrett

One of the last events to take place at the RNSM was a music festival. This was such a success that the public hoped that it would become an annual event. Two Symphony Concerts by the 75-piece orchestra attracted full houses but the two military band concerts and the concert with the Deal and Walmer Handelian Society were not as successful. The local press said "Quite apart from the standard of playing, this is the largest festival ever staged by the School, and it is the biggest and most momentous musical event in the history of Deal" The playing received great critical acclaim and Capt McLean must have felt well satisfied.

Royal Marines School of Music c1950. Ranks of the Band Service showing, from the right, Boy Musician, Musician, Band Corporal, Band Sergeant, Bandmaster and Staff Bandmaster

The orchestral programme included Beethoven's *Concerto No 3 in C Minor* for Piano and Orchestra and Mozart's *Eine Kleine Nachtmusik*, whilst amongst the military band programme were *Spirit of Pageantry* (Fletcher), *Die Fledermaus* (Strauss) and Svendsen's *Norwegian Rhapsody No 1*.

It was in this year, at the same time as the other changes, that the rank of Staff Sergeant in the Band Service was changed to Staff Bandmaster to avoid misunderstanding of their status in relation to Bandmasters and Band Sergeants.[4]

The Band of the Flag Officer Scotland and Northern Ireland (FOSNI) at HMS *Cochrane* (BM 1st Cl Margetts[5]) was withdrawn after ten years. Another loss was to be the very busy band at the Infantry Training Centre RM. One of their last tasks was to travel to France to take part in the D-Day celebrations. They left Portsmouth in HMS *Suvla*, a Landing Ship Tank, and arrived off Arromanches at 0930hrs. Having waded ashore they quickly began a very full programme being joined by the Drums of the 5th Bn The Bedfordshire and Hertfordshire Regiment. Their programme included Beating Retreat and playing for luncheons and dances. They re-embarked at 0200hrs on the 7th June, three days after their arrival.

At the end of 1950 the CGRM requested Board of Admiralty approval for the re-issue of Full Dress uniform to RMBS other ranks. At that time there were about 8,000 in store in the UK, about 87% of them being part worn and handed in at the beginning of the war. Although deterioration was occurring there were enough to clothe the entire RMBS indefinitely at the rate of one per man. It was intended that Band Sergeants would wear the same as other musicians[6]. He made the point that the improved appearance would match the Foot Guards - who were wearing full dress. This request was granted and yellow braided tunics were issued in accordance with an AFO[7].

Part 2 - Korea.

In the Far East, just prior to the outbreak of the Korean War, the combined bands of HMS *Triumph, Kenya* and *Jamaica* Beat Retreat following exercises with the US Navy[8]. The band of the Argyll and Sutherland Highlanders also performed. This was *Triumph's* last day before sailing for Hong Kong and then the UK. In view of the war, *Triumph* was ordered to Korea instead where she remained until September when HMS *Theseus* relieved her. When HMS *Ceylon* commissioned at Portsmouth the detachment were met at the Harbour Station and marched to the ship by the ship's band. Also aboard were the Argyll and Sutherland Highlanders with their pipe band. The ship's Globe & Laurel correspondent later wrote, "At Pusan we were met by two American bands and a girls choir. These the pipe band of the Argylls soon silenced!" The ship then began the routine of patrolling and bombardments. Six months later, at the end of February 1951, HMS *Ceylon* returned to Hong Kong and then to Singapore for refit.

The band of HMS *Kenya* (BSgt Wilson) Beat Retreat on the jetty before leaving Japan for Korean waters where the ship took part in the bombardment of Inchon. A few months later the band left the ship being replaced by another under BM P Taylor. The ship then covered the evacuation of Inchon and returned to Hong Kong in late January 1951 for three weeks' leave. By the first anniversary of the beginning of the Korean War HMS *Kenya* had covered 63,000 miles and been in the operational area longer than any other United Nations vessel. BM Taylor and his band broadcast "Kenya Bandbox" over the ship's system. This was considered quite a feat since heavy watch-keeping duties prevented any serious practice by the band.

In October 1950 HMS *Belfast* with her RM Band under BM R A Martin left Chatham for the Far East. After working up she arrived off Korea and commenced the bombardment of targets ashore. The weather was, by now, much colder with great slabs of ice covering the sea. HMS *Belfast* left the area at the end of January 1951 for a short period. BM D Woods relieved her Bandmaster upon Martin's promotion to Cd BM. Whilst in Singapore the band combined with the Band of C-in-C Far East Fleet and under the direction of Cd BM Long, led the King's Birthday Parade. The ship's detachment was also involved and many rehearsals were needed to get them back to their former standard of drill. Cpl L C Pauly, the detachment PTI performed, at very short notice, as Acting Drum Major of the combined bands and as Senior Drum Major of the massed bands.

Belfast's band gave at least one concert each week in the ship's cinema and these were broadcast throughout the ship. Weekly Church Services, playing to the replenishment vessel when it came alongside and morning prayers were all part of the band's duties. They also went ashore to entertain troops. On one occasion the dance band went to a UN held island that had been under fire for several days. They later claimed:

The Dance Band sallied forth in a landing craft, dressed in jungle green, did the equivalent of a Bickleigh assault course in scaling a cliff with string bass and drum kit and gave forth on an hillside for an hour. The enemy co-operated by keeping quiet. The troops, mostly American, were astonished and extremely enthusiastic.

Guard and Band on the flight deck of HMS Theseus entering Sasebo Harbour, 1950. Aircraft are Sea Furies.

When in Hong Kong several of the band's string players would play with the Hong Kong Concert Orchestra, an organisation that received the regular support of RM Bands on the Far East Station. On June 4th the band arrived in Kure and took part in the King's Birthday Parade. There were many units of Commonwealth Forces on parade and, being the only band, they had to play Inspection Music for all of them - the Inspection lasted thirty minutes! Since Army units going to Korea left their bands in Hong Kong the two RM Bands in the area were in great demand.

HMS *Glory*, Light Fleet Carrier, arrived in April 1951, replacing *Theseus*. She carried four Fleet Air Arm Squadrons and an average of fifty sorties a day were flown. The band under BM Spencer became very proficient in re-arming aircraft with rockets, bombs and cannon shells. The sheer number of aircraft carried meant that the servicing had to be carefully organised and efficiently carried out. The carriers had to return to harbour for replenishment of ammunition and *Glory* alternated with the USS *Sicily* to maintain air cover and capability in the area. In September the *Glory* sailed for Australia for a refit and, whilst there, the ship's band played for the opening of the Davis Cup.

By early May HMS *Ceylon* was back in Korean waters once more and she remained until early September when she returned to Hong Kong. *Ceylon's* band changed places with the band from HMS *Kenya*, which was now in Singapore. The band's war role on the cruiser during its time in the Korean campaign was in the aft Fire Control Position. As the ship left for Korea the Pipes and Drums of the Argyll and Sutherland Highlanders were on the jetty to play them out.

In April 1952 HMS *Belfast* was flying the flag of Flag Officer 2, Far East Station, and was once again patrolling and bombarding enemy positions. She called at the new Korean Navy Base at Chinhae, the first British cruiser to visit. The band marched the Detachment Drill Squad onto a local football pitch and then, following a display that was well received by the Korean Naval and Marine cadets, the band Beat Retreat. *Belfast* relieved HMS *Ceylon* in July 1952 and was, in turn, relieved by HMS *Birmingham*, returning to the UK in September.

In 1952 BM E W Buckingham was Mentioned in Despatches for distinguished service whilst serving as Bandmaster in the Fleet Carrier HMS *Theseus*.

HMS *Ocean* was commissioned in June 1951 and, since she did not have her own band at the time, she had to borrow a band to march the detachment to the ship. She arrived in Hong Kong to relieve HMS *Glory* in September 1952.[9] During the patrols off Korea the detachment spent many hours closed up at the guns whilst BM Williams and his band worked on the flight deck providing rocket and bomb supply parties. Despite this work, which often went on until late hours, they still provided impromptu concerts on the fo'c'sle. After three months on station BM Shipway brought a band from the UK to relieve them. On arrival the new band added a touch of colour by parading in Number Ones. These were soon stowed away as the band continued the fine work carried out by its predecessors. During this commission HMS *Ocean* broke every known record for Light Fleet Carriers and was awarded the Boyd Trophy for the most outstanding feat in naval aviation during the year, for which the band must take some of the praise.

The newly commissioned cruiser HMS *Newcastle* arrived on the Station in the middle of the year. Her band was under BM L Arnold and their first appearance was for C-in-C Plymouth's inspection just before they left. Passage was via Malta where they massed with the Mediterranean Fleet Bands for the Queen's Birthday Parade. On arrival at Singapore they were met by the Fleet Bandmaster Mr R Long, who explained what their future might hold. From Singapore they went to Hong Kong and then to Korea for patrol duties. Their twelve-piece Dance Band was extremely popular and 'Band Show' was put on whilst on patrol. However, the opportunities for playing on patrol were very limited but when in ports such as Sasebo, duties included ceremonial and canteen programmes. American troops were entertained both at their front-line camps and in Services Clubs, Depot Ships and Replacement Depots.

As HMS *Glory* made her way back from Australia to the Korean theatre she paused to allow her aircraft to launch a strike against the terrorists in Malaya, of which more will be described later. Having left Australia and crossed the equator she relieved HMS *Ocean* in November 1952, the ships crew then having to face the Korean winter. Replenishment periods continued to be taken at Sasebo and Kure in Japan. In May 1953 *Glory* was withdrawn and made her way to Singapore where, on 3rd June, her band massed with the band of the C-in-C to Beat Retreat in Singapore in celebration of the Coronation.

When HMS *Ceylon* was withdrawn from the fleet in 1953 HMS *Newfoundland* became the Flagship. At this time *Ceylon's* band was transferred to *Newfoundland* to complete their commission. HMS *Newcastle* had returned to Korean waters in time to suffer some of the worst weather of the campaign. The band's duties were much restricted because of this but they managed to provide Concert Parties and broadcast over the ship's internal system instead of playing on the upper deck. Part way through the commission a large number of members of the band were returned to Deal on completion of their service.

Although the Armistice had been signed in July 1953 vigilance was still exercised and HMS *Unicorn*, *Ocean*, *Birmingham* and *Newcastle* continued patrols and surveillance. The bands of the Far East Fleet gradually returned to normality after three years of what became known as "The Forgotten War". During this period they once again earned the respect of the Royal Navy, the detachments and many others for their ability to take on any task given them whilst maintaining, at every opportunity, their own musical skills and the morale of those amongst whom they worked.

A few of these bands had also been involved in another campaign that had been waged in conditions far different to those of Korea.

Part 3 - Terrorists in Malaya

The Band of 3 Cdo Bde, consisting of twenty-three musicians plus a number of buglers, was formed in 1948[10]. The Brigade had served in the Middle East and in Hong Kong but, in June 1950, it was moved to Malaya to combat the growing threat from terrorists and bandits. 40 Cdo was the first unit of 3 Cdo Bde[11] to leave Hong Kong. The Brigade Band played at the last Morning Service at the barrack church, Lyemun, Hong Kong before they embarked in HMS *Jamaica* on 23rd May 1950. The massed bands of the Brigade and the Argyll and Sutherland Highlanders played the ship out. Upon arrival at Penang the band of the 1st Bn. The King's Own Yorkshire Light Infantry were on the jetty to play during the disembarkation.

When the band arrived in Malaya, following their voyage on the troopship, they were each given a rifle and fifty rounds of ammunition. This was followed by a talk about possible bandit attacks on their train prior to the journey itself, which lasted an uncomfortable twenty-five hours. There was little to eat and all had to take turns as sentry. On arrival at the station they were put into three-ton lorries for the sixty-five mile journey, in darkness and torrential rain, to Brigade HQ at Ipoh. This training and experience enabled the band to move through the country without an escort. Once established the band began a tour of all of the Commando and Troop localities, staying a night at each place. Bedding often had to be taken as well as the instruments required to perform as a Dance Band and Military Band. They also led part of 40 Cdo on a march through Kuala Kangsar and played for a Trafalgar Night Dinner in Kuala Lumpur. This was disrupted, as were many engagements, by bandits blowing up the railway lines and causing transport difficulties. The band formed their own defence when making journeys, a Bren gun being manned on each vehicle with every member of the band armed.

The band massed with the band of the 4th Queen's Own Hussars, whose HQ was only two miles away, for ceremonial and military band performances, sometimes wearing full ceremonial uniform. Later in the campaign the Hussar's band went on jungle patrol with 40 Cdo.

Within a few months of their arrival BM Reynolds had formed a symphony orchestra from amateur musicians supported by men of the band. This was fifty-seven strong and soon, as the Perak State Philharmonic Orchestra, was able to perform two concerts, conducted by Reynolds, at the Celestial Cabaret Hall. These amateur musicians were a mixture of Chinese, Indians, Goanese and European.

In August BM F P Rees assumed command of the band, two days before a tour of 40 Cdo. Orchestral instruments were left behind and, since the road they were taking was notorious for ambushes, a convoy was formed. Armoured vehicles of the 4th Hussars led the two three-tonners and a half-tonner carrying the band armed with their Bren and small arms. A Hussars armoured car with a two-pounder gun that the band rudely referred to as a 'mobile saluting gun' followed them. When they arrived at Grik, having got very wet on the journey, the band settled in and then the dance band played in the Canteen. Next day the band played whilst the Troop had 'tiffin' and in the evening supplied music at a football match and then gave a military band concert. On Trafalgar Day 1951 45 Cdo paraded with the Brigade Band. After inspection the band marched the Commando to Church and, after the Service, they marched to the golf course for a presentation. The band trooped and then presentations were made between the unit, the local Police and local planters. After the presentations the Commando formed line, the buglers sounded a fanfare, the band played the Police March and the National Anthem and then they all marched off to the Regimental March.

In 1952 the band had a rare opportunity to perform as an orchestra when, augmented with woodwind and brass players from the 12th Royal Lancers (Prince of Wales's) Band,[12] they performed *Messiah* with a choir of sixty drawn from the European, Chinese and Tamil communities. During this period the majority of Brigade HQ were out on exercise so the band was given the task of guarding the main gate, as well as normal band duties.

45 Cdo left Malaya on the 12th March and the band played for their Memorial Service, March Past and Cocktail Party. They also played the Commando away from the station to the strains of *Auld Lang Syne*. 40 Cdo held their Memorial Service and March Past on the 16th April which was attended by the GOC. Following the March Past the band had to attempt to get back to Ipoh before the General arrived there. Unfortunately of the two lorries carrying the band, the one carrying the instruments broke down so when the General drove past escorted by a scout car the band sang the salute! Next day Brigade HQ held their Memorial Service, a plaque bearing the names of those members of the Brigade who had died in Malaya being unveiled. Following the Service the Guard of Honour from 40 Cdo was marched to the Saluting Base where they were inspected by the Sultan of Perak. That evening the band played for the farewell dinner to the Brigadier and then hastily packed instruments ready to go on the stores train at 0800 next day.

Next morning the band loaded all their personal kit, including their rifle and bayonet, onto the train for the journey to Singapore. At one of the stops members of the band got a bass, accordion and side drum from the band van and put on an impromptu show that was much appreciated by the members of the Commando who were within earshot and able to join in the singing. Arriving in Singapore they were sent to a transit camp where they lived in tents. Their instruments were available and they played almost continuously throughout the fourteen days that they were there. They played at a concert in the Chiefs' Mess in Singapore and gave an orchestral concert massed with HMS *Terror's* Band under Cd BM R Long. Next day the band went to Radio Malaya to make a recording for future broadcast. The Assistant Director of Broadcasting was thrilled to have an orchestra instead of the usual military or dance bands. The following day required a Dance Band at one of the major hotels and this was followed, on the next day, by an orchestral concert at Raffles Hotel that was broadcast on the radio. In three days the band had earned three hundred dollars. Reference to the Engagement Book showed that it had taken them nine months to earn the same amount whilst in the Perak area. They then realised why Army bands made the trek to Singapore every three months!

Brigade HQ, with the band and 42 Cdo, embarked on the HMT *Empire Halladale* next morning and found that No 4 Regional Band RAF under F/O R E C Davies was already aboard. The two bands were employed throughout the trip performing for the troops or for the cabin passengers. In addition an orchestra of fourteen from the Commando Band played each night for the Officers in the Dining Saloon. When the band arrived at Malta it transferred to St Patrick's Barracks where the emphasis became ceremonial.

Part 4 - The Home, and other, Fleets

Despite the reductions that had taken place since the end of the Second World War Britain was still able to maintain, albeit reduced, Fleets around the world. Whilst the Far East Fleet was engaged in support of operations in Korea and Malaya the Home Fleet, the Mediterranean Fleet and others tried to maintain the prestige and repute of Great Britain. Inevitably, as the Empire began to decrease in size so did the need to maintain such a presence throughout the world. The Mediterranean Fleet had ended the year of 1949 with a visit by HRH Princess Elizabeth to the Fleet in Malta. The massed bands of HMS *Glory*, *Liverpool* and *Kenya* were on the flight deck of *Glory* when the Princess came aboard to inspect the Royal Guard and the Officers and men of the Fleet. During the visit the bands of the Mediterranean Fleet (*Liverpool*, *Gambia*, *Ceylon*, *Euryalus*, *Glory* and *Forth*) combined with the band based at St Angelo, Malta, to Beat Retreat. On conclusion the band played '*Hymn of Malta*' and the National Anthem before marching off. The Maltese Parliament adjourned for one hour to allow its members to watch the ceremony.

The early months of 1950 saw the ships of the Home Fleet preparing for the Spring Cruise whilst HMS *Liverpool* and *Euryalus* left Malta to show the flag in the Adriatic. *Liverpool* carried out all of the usual ceremonial duties, including Beating Retreat whilst in Piraeus. Following this the ship went to Alexandria where King Farouk of Egypt came aboard to witness a Beating Retreat that had to be abandoned because of torrential rain. The ships of the Mediterranean Fleet also began their Spring Cruise. The culmination of these cruises was the combined exercises of the Mediterranean and Home Fleets. When these ended the ships of both Fleets entered Gibraltar. The ships carrying bands were *Implacable*, *Glory*, *Liverpool*, *Vengeance*, *Superb*, *Phoebe*, *Cleopatra* and *Forth*. The Bands and Drums of all of these ships except *Phoebe* and *Cleopatra* assembled to Beat Retreat in front of the Governor of Gibraltar on the 24th March. Cd BM E Ough was in command. Only at the end of the Combined Fleet exercises could such a display be seen at Gibraltar. About one hundred men were in the massed band. Shortly after this the band of HMS *Phoebe* was withdrawn although it was not long before a volunteer band began to flourish. When the Home Fleet completed its Spring Cruise[13] its ships made their way to their Home Ports to take part in the Easter Navy Days, the bands playing alongside or in the vicinity of their own ship.

Following the Spring Cruise of 1950 the bands of the Mediterranean Fleet began rehearsals for the King's Birthday Parade ceremony. The massed band appeared, for the first time in Malta, wearing trousers with the wide red stripe.

Ships of the West Indies Fleet also carried out exercises and cruises. Whilst at Bermuda, the band of HMS *Glasgow* went ashore to carry out military training. Then, in Hamilton, the band continued, albeit on its own, the ceremony begun the year before by the band of *Jamaica*. A military parade such as Beating Retreat was a rarity for the inhabitants, and the American tourists, of Hamilton.

Beating Retreat was not the only ceremony performed by bands in the various Fleets. Guards and Bands, Divisions and Colours were frequently carried out. As well as ceremonial the bands played for receptions and concerts as well as the entertainment of officers and crew. Ships completed their commissions and returned to Great Britain for refit with their bands returning to the RMSM as previously happened with the RNSM. This cycle continued through the early nineteen fifties.

In Great Britain the amalgamation was still a fairly contentious issue. A confidential appreciation of it was written and submitted five months later.[14] In this appreciation the author discusses various problems arising from amalgamation. He contends that the Committee did not avail itself of sufficient representation from the bands and that only layman's questions were asked of those that were interviewed, thereby missing a more professional level of input. He maintained that conditions of service offered to the men of the Group Bands were not equitable with those of similar Army and RAF bands; that the new titles of the bands at Portsmouth and Plymouth, as well as the titles of their Directors, did not have the same dignity and tradition as the old ones. Both of these points were now being looked into. Whilst he felt it correct that, as the general feeling indicated, the Group Bands had been absorbed into the system he did not feel that enough had been done to ensure that the standards of the Group Bands were upheld as the level of attainment required of all of the RNSM bands. Allied to this it was not felt that enough effort had been made to take the best from each organisation and apply it to the other. A marked and rapid increase in the number of civilian instructors and professors was called for. He also strongly hinted that new blood was needed and that a new standard of musical guidance was needed at the top of the organisation. He stressed that whilst the Group Bands did not go to sea and were regarded as being 'kept in cotton wool'; it was that very circumstance that allowed them to attain the very high standards that made them the best of the Service bands. It was suggested by the author that the planned conference in January 1952 should include long and detailed discussion of the problems and the way ahead.

Junior Wing Symphony Orchestra under the baton of the Director of Music, Musical Training, Capt Talling. Average age of Boy Musicians is sixteen and a half.

Meanwhile the Staff Band at Deal and the Group Bands under Dunn and Stoner were just as busy. The Staff Band played for the WRNS Association reunion at the Royal Albert Hall, the Memorial Silver Trumpets appeared with the Band of C-in-C The Nore at the opening ceremony of the Sailor's Chapel in Lincoln Cathedral and the band, under Capt W Lang, took part in the 1951 Royal Tournament with the RM Drill Squad. The Staff

Symphony Orchestra, under Capt McLean, gave a Matinee Musicale on two consecutive nights to a large and appreciative audience. The Boys' Military Band took the place of the Staff Band for the King's Birthday Parade at Deal. In June the Boys' Symphony Orchestra gave a Festival Concert. Maj F V Dunn conducted the final rehearsal and acknowledged the high standard of their performance.

Drum Major F Tobin leads Junior Wing Military Band through South Barracks, Depot Deal. Six of the Boy Buglers and the bass drummer carry the Memorial Drums. The other three Boy Buglers carry standard service pattern drums.

1952 saw the death of the Captain General, Royal Marines, HM King George VI, with the funeral taking place on the 15th of February. The Plymouth Group Band augmented by twenty-three musicians from the RMSM, Deal, and under the command of Capt R H Stoner were in the procession, leading representative detachments of the RN and RM. Bands took it in turn to play and the Royal Marines played Panne's *Regrets* between the east end of the Mall and Marlborough Gate and then Beethoven was played as they marched from the corner of Oxford and Cambridge Terrace to Radnor Place.

Many of the events of the next sixteen months were subsumed by the preparations for the Coronation of HM Queen Elizabeth II. However, during that period a number of important events did occur.

November 1952 saw the Presentation of Colours to 40, 42 and 45 Commando, RM at Floriana, Malta GC. This triple presentation would not occur again for forty-nine years. The bands and drums of HMS *Glasgow* (Cd BM E S Ough),[15] HMS *Ocean* (BM G G Shipway), HMS *Tyne* (BM L R Lorentsen) and 3 Cdo Bde (Cd BM J M Jemmett) were under the direction of Maj F V Dunn and Drum Major R G Knox, both from Portsmouth Group RM. Also on parade were the Pipes and Drums of 42 Cdo. As a mark of respect to Malta's strict Roman Catholic beliefs the Colours had been consecrated in St Paul's Anglican Cathedral before the parade and so, on this occasion, there was no need for piled drums.

Three months later, following the presentation of new Colours to the Plymouth Division, it was decided that the old Colours should be laid up in the King's Chapel, Gibraltar.[16] On this occasion the Massed Bands of the Home Fleet were under the command of Cd BM A White.

At the School the number of recruits was increasing so alterations were made to the structure of the Boys' Wing. RM subalterns became housemasters and the Boy NCO system replaced the Section Leaders.

RMRO 340 of 1952 confirmed that the correct pace for Royal Marines marching in quick time was 116 paces to the minute and that rifle movements were to conform to that speed.

The following bands were serving at sea and in shore establishments during 1952[17]:

HMS *Indomitable*	Cd BM S C Cooper	HMS *Glasgow*	Cd BM E S Ough
HMS *Implacable*	BM J H Reynolds	HMS *Tyne*	BM L R Lorentsen
HMS *Eagle*	BM J J Martin	HMS *Terror*	Cd BM R G Long
HMS *Devonshire*	BM J Wilks	HMNZS *Bellona*	Cd BM C D R Duncan
HMS *Superb*	BM W H Newcombe	RNB Chatham	Cd BM A E J Stagg
HMS *Belfast*	BM D R Woods	RNB Portsmouth	Cd BM A O White
HMS *Glory*	BM W Spencer	RNB Devonport	Cd BM W Fitzgerald
HMS *Ceylon*	BM P L Taylor	RNB Lee-on-Solent	BM P C Thorn
HMS *Ocean*	BM O R Williams	RNAS Bramcote	BM W Saunders
HMS *Liverpool*	BM D C Hartley	HMS *Raleigh*	BM F G Harwood
HMS *Theseus*	BM W J H Machon	HMS *Excellent*	BM R A Hobbs
HMS *Bermuda*	BM W C Greasley	HMS *Ganges*	BM A K Butler
HMS *Kenya*	BM D Guthrie	HMS *St Vincent*	BM R G Fairall
HMS *Sheffield*	BM H E Attfield	3 Cdo Bde	BM F P Rees

In the Editorial of the April 1953 issue of Globe and Laurel appeared the following: "Major F Vivian Dunn MVO ARAM, Director of Music at Eastney since September 1931 has left the Barracks to take up his appointment as Director of Music at Deal. He will be remembered for his musical contribution, both by members of the Corps and the city music lovers. We wish Major Dunn all good fortune and welcome in his stead, Captain K A McLean LRAM" In the same journal, the Corps Gazette records: "Major F Vivian Dunn MVO ARAM to Deal as Corps Director of Music. 1.3.53: Captain K A McLean LRAM to Portsmouth as Director of Music, vice Major F V Dunn 1.3.53." Some time before this occurred Major Dunn appears to have written an appreciation of his own circumstances and the effect that such an exchange would have upon them.[18] The appreciation began, "Consequent upon the decision of the Commandant General, Royal Marines that the Directors of Music, Royal Marines, Portsmouth and Deal shall exchange appointments…". He then went on to outline the losses that he and his family would suffer through such a move. These include the loss of contact with the Royal Family and loss of earnings due to his moving from an area where he had built-up a strong association with local musicians and other groups. He also wrote the following. "It is considered that with the expansion of the Royal Marines Band Service and the circumstances which have been brought to light necessitating the transferring of the Director of Music, Royal Marines, Portsmouth to Deal to solve the problem, a new conception should be brought to bear on the appointment of the musical head of the Royal Marines Band Service". He then went on to outline his concept of the post. Amongst his strong suggestions were that the title should become 'Principal Director of Music, Royal Marines' and that the rank should be Lieutenant Colonel. He also stressed that his own terms of appointment in 1931 guaranteed service until the age of 60. Whilst he did not elaborate on what the problem at Deal might be it was obviously neither recruitment nor, from what has been covered elsewhere in this book, the quality of the School's bands, orchestras or staff.

The Royal Marines Band Service representation at the Coronation was to consist of the Royal Marines Portsmouth Group Band under their new Director of Music, Captain K A McLean, with the Royal Guard of Honour and the Queen's Colour of the Royal Marines Barracks[19], Eastney, at Westminster Abbey. With the Naval Processional Contingent were to be the bands of the Plymouth Group, and the RMSM. With one of the two street lining battalions would be a RM Band formed from the bands of the C-in-C, Portsmouth and HMS *Excellent* under the direction of a Commissioned Bandmaster.[20]

Overnight the Bands had been accommodated in Chatham Deep Shelters, not a particularly attractive place within RN Barracks, Chatham. On the morning of the Coronation the RM Band marched, playing, down the Embankment, Bridge Street and into Parliament Square (North Side) at the head of its street lining battalion. When it cleared Bridge Street it countermarched, halted and ceased playing. It remained there until directed by the Brigade RM Staff Officer to move into position at the east end of Horse Guards Avenue, which was carried out with band playing. A Bluejacket Band (BM E P Harrison) marched, playing, up Northumberland Avenue, across Trafalgar Square (South Side) through Admiralty Arch and up the Mall. At a predetermined point the band countermarched, halted in the centre of the roadway and ceased playing. On the order the band marched, playing, to its position in Trafalgar Square.

HM The Queen's Coronation, 1953. The RN Bluejacket Band plays from its position at the bottom of the Mall as the State Coach passes by.

By 0800hrs the street lining battalions and Bands had taken position. They would remain there until approximately 1530hrs. Bands were formed in eight ranks of four with the Corps of Drums in two additional ranks in front of the band. When taking position the Corps of Drums marched to left and right and took position with four on either side of the front rank of instrumentalists. The Drum Major remained one pace in front of the front rank of the band. The combined bands from the RMSM (Maj F V Dunn) and Plymouth Group (Capt R H Stoner) under the control of Drum Majors Charles Bowden and L Keefe led the Naval contingents. The RMSM band included some boys from the Boys' Wing.

On Coronation Day, June 2nd 1953, HM The Queen appointed HRH The Duke of Edinburgh to be Captain General, Royal Marines. The appointment, originally known as Honorary Colonel, had first been given to Queen Victoria's second son, Alfred who was also Duke of Edinburgh, on the 9th December 1882[21]. Two weeks after her Coronation HM The Queen reviewed the Fleet at Spithead. HMS *Surprise* (frigate) acted as Royal Yacht and had a detachment of Royal Marines from 45 Commando embarked as well as Maj F V Dunn and the Royal Yacht Band drawn from the Portsmouth Group Band. The C-in-C's orchestra under the Fleet Bandmaster, Senior Cd BM A O White, provided music for the dinner for HM the Queen on board HMS *Vanguard*. HMS *Eagle* (aircraft-carrier) and HMS *Swiftsure* had bands whilst the aircraft carrier HMS *Illustrious* had a Sea Cadet Band.

The RMSM was the venue for the 50th Anniversary Celebrations of the Band Service in September 1953. The programme of events included an Orchestral and Military Band concert by the Boys' Wing, a Symphony Concert by the Combined Orchestras and a Jubilee Massed Bands Concert, both with the Portsmouth and Plymouth Group bands joining the band of the RMSM. During the re union that preceded the Golden Jubilee Dinner the Band Boys gave a ceremonial display that was, once again, prepared by Capt W Lang. The band used the Silver Memorial Drums and the Memorial Silver Trumpets. BM D Guthrie was Drum Major. The Military Band Concert featured eight conductors: Capt W Lang, Capt H Kenward, Lt J E Talling, Maj A Pragnell, Maj S Fairfield, Capt K A McLean, Capt R H Stoner and Maj F V Dunn.

On the 27th October 1953 Maj F V Dunn was promoted Local Lieutenant-Colonel. Despite having been appointed Principal Director of Music at the RMSM on the 1st October 1953 he did not relinquish the Directorship of the Royal Yacht Band to its rightful holder, the Director of Music Portsmouth, for the Royal Commonwealth Tour of 1953/4.[22] Colin Bowden was a Lance-Corporal Bugler on the tour and described the tour in an article from which the following extracts are taken:

November saw the sailing of the SS *Gothic* on the first Royal Commonwealth Tour of the reign of HM the Queen. *Gothic* was a Shaw Saville vessel chartered by the Royal Navy to be used as a Royal Yacht - the new Royal Yacht *Britannia* had been launched but was not fitted out and commissioned. The *Gothic* was crewed by Merchant Navy officers and men with the addition of some RN Communicators and a Royal Barge crew. The Flag Officer Royal Yachts was in command with a Merchant Navy Captain as master. A thirty piece Royal Marines Band drawn from the Portsmouth Group Band with the inclusion of two players from the Royal Marines School of Music and one from the Plymouth Group Band, under the direction of Lt-Col Vivian Dunn, the Principal Director of Music, completed the complement. The Royal Tour in *Gothic* lasted six months and places visited included Jamaica, Panama, Fiji, Tonga, New Zealand, Australia, Ceylon and Aden, ending when the Royal Party, accompanied by the Band, transferred to *Britannia* on arrival in the Mediterranean.

During the tour the band provided music on board for various occasions - lunch and dinner in the Royal Apartments, church services, receptions, concerts, entering and leaving harbour and other ceremonial duties. Ashore the band was in great demand and fulfilled numerous engagements as a concert and marching band. Many of the performances were for national and local charities and the band were often feted by local dignitaries of the towns and cities in which they played.

Of all the many engagements, two of the most memorable were at Tonga where the band was entertained to a feast by Queen Salote and later, towards the end of the tour whilst in Ceylon, the band travelled from Colombo to the ancient city of Kandy for a Royal Perahera, a spectacular procession of one hundred and twenty-five magnificently decorated elephants accompanied by over a thousand drummers and dancers.

The 50th Anniversary of the Portsmouth Band being confirmed as the permanent Royal Yacht Band by King Edward VII occurred during the voyage and to mark the jubilee year HM The Queen and HRH The Duke of Edinburgh graciously consented to being photographed with the band, possibly the only formal photograph of a reigning sovereign with a military band. Further recognition for the band came at the end of the tour when Colonel Dunn was awarded a CVO and Bandmaster Horsley the RVM. All members of the band received a commemorative medallion which had been struck by the Royal Mint[23].

The arrival of the new Royal Yacht *Britannia* in London on the 15th May 1954 with the Queen and her family on board marked the end of a year of ceremonial on a scale that could never be repeated again.

Not only was life busy, possibly exciting, for the band of the Royal Yacht but for the librarian it was a major logistical exercise. The librarian was usually an experienced Band NCO or Musician. The band always had to take a large amount of music on a tour and, when the SS *Gothic* sailed she carried nearly a thousand different orchestral pieces and over five hundred different military band pieces. Categories were overtures, suites, symphonies, symphonic poems, ballet music, incidental music, rhapsodies, grand marches, marches, selections, waltzes and 'miscellaneous' which included music for small ensembles and dance music.

Meanwhile RM Bands around the world had also been celebrating the Coronation through Beating Retreat and other ceremonies, displays and concerts. For the RMSM 1953 had also been a very important year. Apart from the new Principal Director of Music other changes had taken place. By the end of 1953 the School structure had changed again. Lt E Ough had replaced Capt W Lang as Director of Music (Boys' Wing), and Senior Cd BM Weller had been made Assistant Drafting Officer. Capt W Lang had been awarded the MBE in the Coronation Honours List. The professorial staff had been increased to twelve during Capt McLean's tenure and in July 1953 the Admiralty approved the proposed Fleet Band Scheme.

Part 5 -The Effects of the 1953 Fleet Band Scheme and Developments to 1960

At the end of 1952 a scheme for coping with the shortage of manpower together with improvements to the conditions of the RMBS was submitted to the CGRM. This was eventually approved and took effect in 1953[24].

As from July 1953 the Home, Mediterranean and Far East Fleets would each have one large band of forty-five under the control of the C-in-C. This meant that certain Class 'B' bands were withdrawn. Each of the Fleet Bands would be under a Staff Bandmaster. It was anticipated that by September 1957 natural wastage would reduce the size of these bands to about thirty-seven all ranks and then, as a result of high recruitment during 1951/1952, the numbers in each band would increase. The Fleet Bands were expected to be able to produce a military band, a dance band and a small orchestra all at the same time and it was also expected that other combinations could be satisfied. Bands appointed to other ships and shore establishments would be unaffected. As a result of the introduction of the Fleet Band Scheme the following bands became, or continued to be, effective: C-in-C Home Fleet; C-in-C Mediterranean Fleet (Cd BM A E Pottle); C-in-C Far East Fleet (Cd BM T C Merrett) based in HMS Terror and 3 Cdo Bde (Cd BM J H Jemmett).

In July the Combined Orchestras of the Mediterranean Fleet, which included those of the C-in-C and Flag Officer, Flotillas, and 3 Cdo Bde gave two Coronation Concerts on successive evenings under the baton of Sir Malcolm Sargent, the Honorary Musical Advisor. Amongst the invited audience on the first night were Lord and Lady Mountbatten. The programme included Elgar's *Pomp and Circumstance* No 1, Handel's *Water Music*, Walton's *Crown Imperial*, Edward German's *Henry VIII* dances and the overture from Wagner's *Tannhäuser*. The total number of men in the orchestras and the male voice choir was about one hundred and forty. The choir, whose members all had singing experience, was drawn from the three services. Cd BM E S Ough, the Fleet Bandmaster, later wrote to Maj F V Dunn to confirm that the concerts were as successful as they were claimed to be. He commented upon the difficulties of getting all members of the choir together for rehearsal. He also included the following paragraph:

> I must mention here that Sir Malcolm found fault with one of the 'clarinets' from HQ, on asking how much playing he had done lately the musician replied that he 'had been working in the galley for three months'. This did not please Sir Malcolm..

The Fleet Bandmaster also mentioned that special recordings were made of *Hymn of Malta* and the National Anthem for Malta Rediffusion as master tapes for use in cinemas and elsewhere.

The 1st Bn The Argyll and Sutherland Highlanders were due to be transported by HMS *Implacable* to British Guiana. They arrived at RN Barracks and were escorted to the Parade where they formed up and called the roll. The Battalion marched through the Dockyard headed by their Pipes and Drums and led by the RM Band. A few hundred yards from the ship the Band wheeled away and allowed the Pipes and Drums to play the Battalion alongside. As the ship slipped her moorings and proceeded down harbour the Pipes and Drums of the Argyll and Sutherland Highlanders and the RM Band played alternately. As they passed Eastern Kings a lone piper from the RM Barracks could be heard.[25] On arrival at Port of Spain the troops, equipment and vehicles were transferred to transport vessels and as the transports sailed they were played away by the RM Band with the Pipes and Drums responding. During a short period in Barbados, the band Beat Retreat in tremendous heat, played for a cocktail party on the quarterdeck and for lunch in the Wardroom. HMS *Implacable* then returned to Port of Spain to collect the Royal Welch Fusiliers. The ship then sailed for Kingston and, as they entered the harbour, the troops manned ship whilst the RM Band and the Band of the Royal Welch Fusiliers were massed on the flight deck playing marches that were common to both. The Fusiliers' pioneers, with white aprons and burnished axes, lined the for'ard end of the flight deck.

During this period the bands of HMS *Glory* (BM Pearce), HMS *Tyne* (BM Peters), HMS *Eagle* (BM Mr Diamond), HMS *Excellent* (BM Hemingway) and HMS *St Vincent* (BM Martin) returned to the School of Music. Only one band departed from the School and that went to the America & West Indies Fleet (BM Jefferson) but, in order to bring the Fleet Bands up to their new strength, large drafts were sent to Malta (BM Diamond), and to the Home Fleet (BM Stratford).

The Officers and crew of HMS *Vanguard* soon benefited from the upgrading of their band from twenty-five to forty-five as the Home Fleet Band. Even though they had to draft bands to other ships in the Fleet as required they still found that "if we are crafty we save enough minstrels to have two bands for Sunday dinner - one for'ard and one aft - which is perfectly splendid".

During the spring of 1954 it was being reported that the Home Fleet Band commitments had been very heavy and the demands upon them seemed to be on the increase. Music of all types was in great demand both aboard ship and ashore. Although most members of the band remained with the C-in-C, one military band was tending to remain with HMS *Eagle* whilst HMS *Superb* was enjoying the more informal services of a trio. The entire band was involved in the Ceremony of the Keys at Gibraltar. At the end of the Spring Cruises the bands of the Home Fleet and the Mediterranean Fleet massed to Beat Retreat. The Pipes and Drums of the Royal Scots Greys (2nd Dragoons) joined with the Royal Marines for the ceremony.

The Queen and the Duke of Edinburgh visited Malta in the Royal Yacht *Britannia* and, on the second day of the visit, a Combined Services parade was held at Floriana. The Royal Marines of the Fleet and of 3 Cdo Bde were formed up around the three stands of Colours (40, 42 and 45 Commandos). The music was provided by the bands of the Mediterranean Fleet and 3 Cdo Bde massed under the command of Cd BM Pottle. During the parade they trooped, quick marched, slow marched and then played a bugle march. Amongst the bugles were seven of the Silver Bugles held by the Commando Brigade including one that was sounded when HRH the Duke of York opened the new Parliament House, Australia in 1927 and one that was sounded in St Paul's Cathedral in 1945 at the Memorial Service for President Roosevelt. The parade consisted of an Inspection, a March Past, a Feu-de-Joie and Three Cheers. When 40 Cdo returned to El Ballah they took with them "that happy band of brothers, the Brigade Band".

In Great Britain the responsibility for RM participation in the Remembrance Ceremony at Whitehall, the Festival of Remembrance at the Royal Albert Hall and the Lord Mayor's Parade all fell to the Band and Drums of Portsmouth Group under Capt K McLean. At the Alamein Reunion at Wembley the combined Bands of Portsmouth and Plymouth gave a stirring display under the direction of Capt W Lang, Plymouth Band's new Director of Music who, a few months earlier, had once again directed the Massed Bands at the 1954 Royal Tournament.

The Royal Yacht Band was twice on Royal Duties during the second half of 1954. On the first occasion it provided music for the Duke of Edinburgh's visit to Cowes Week and to Britannia Royal Naval College, Dartmouth, (BRNC). The second occasion was to bring the Duke of Edinburgh back from Canada after his tour. During the visits to Canadian ports the band was kept very busy with the ceremony of Colours and Beating Retreat as well as providing concerts ashore and entertainment aboard the Royal Yacht.

Other important events of 1954 included the recruitment of two more stringed instrument professors and the reinstatement of the orchestral concerts, previously run by the RNSM, to raise the standard of the orchestral performance. During the year the number of boys under training had increased from three hundred and thirty the previous year to three hundred and seventy, although this was still thirty below the Admiralty anticipation. New music practice huts were brought into use at this time.

HMS *Bulwark* sailed to Oslo with the combined bands of HMS *Theseus* and HMS *Daedalus* and twenty Musicians from the RMSM under BM E Ough. They Beat Retreat, played in the bandstand and took part in all ceremonial ashore and aboard. In Stockholm the massed bands of the Fleet and the Highland Light Infantry (City of Glasgow Regiment) Beat Retreat and then, when the RM Bands departed, the band of the HLI went aboard HMS *Bulwark* to provide musical support.

During 1955 the Royal Marines Bands in service consisted of the following:

Band	Director or Bandmaster
C-in-C, the Nore	Sen Cd BM McLean
C-in-C, Portsmouth	Sen Cd BM White
C-in-C, Plymouth	Cd BM Jemmett
C-in-C, Mediterranean Fleet	Cd BM Pottle
C-in-C, Far East Fleet	Sen Cd BM Cooper
C-in-C, Home Fleet	Cd BM Long
3 Cdo Bde	Cd BM Weller
RMSM	Lt Col Dunn
Portsmouth Group	Capt McLean
Plymouth Group	Capt Lang
Royal New Zealand Navy	Cd BM Medcalf
Royal Australian Navy	Cd BM Arnold
Royal Ceylon Navy	Cd BM Reynolds

Having slipped from South Railway Jetty, Portsmouth, in the middle of January 1955 HMS *Tyne* made her way to Gibraltar where her Guard and Band undertook the Ceremony of the Keys[26]. The parade was carried out each month by the various Regiments of Gibraltar Garrison and about once a year by Royal Marines of the Home Fleet. The next ceremony was Beating Retreat carried out by the combined bands of the Home Fleet and the Duke of Wellington's Regiment. Lt E Ough, the Director of Music, Boys' Wing at Deal took the band and orchestra to HMS *St Vincent* where their sixty-piece orchestra gave a magnificent performance in the Drill Shed to an audience of over a thousand. A few days later the Boys' Band with the Volunteer Band of HMS *St Vincent* and the RM Volunteer Cadet Corps under BugMaj Weight Beat Retreat on the Parade Ground. The Ceremony concluded with the Sunset by the massed bands and bugles (one hundred and eighty strong) whilst the Boys of HMS *St Vincent* manned the mast.

On Saturday 7th May 1955 the City of Plymouth presented the Freedom of the City to the Royal Marines. Although only the City of London has the authority to question the right of a military unit to enter its precincts with '*Drums beating, bayonets fixed and Colours flying*' many cities, towns and even villages make this symbolic gesture of respect and honour. The Hoe was used for the ceremony and the buglers who beat *Markers* and *Fall In* were dressed as Drummers of 1755 - the date when fifty companies of Marines were raised for service in Plymouth. As the Casket containing the Certificate of Freedom was passed to the Corps representative the fanfare *Gibraltar* was sounded on fourteen silver bugles. Following the speeches the Battalion presented arms and, led by the Band and Drums of the Plymouth Group, they marched through the city.

At Eastney the ceremony of Trooping the Colour took place at the Barracks on St George's Day. This celebrated two events, the Corps Day of Reunion and Remembrance and the two hundredth anniversary of the Corps becoming established under the Admiralty as a permanent part of the Royal Navy.

HMS *Superb* was at Hamilton, Bermuda, at the time of the Queen's Birthday Parade. Her RM Band was the only band in the parade and, during the march past, had to play ten marches including a 'gallop at 140 to the minute' for the Duke of Cornwall's Light Infantry.

During 1955 the Admiralty approved the new development of sending two Bandmasters to study at the Royal Academy of Music each year for the Conductors' Course. Mr Maurice Miles was to supervise the course that included conducting, choir training, harmony, counterpoint, musical composition and individual lessons on orchestral instruments and pianoforte. Many opportunities were provided for playing in the senior orchestra as well as attending opera and chamber music classes. The objectives of this arrangement were to raise the standard of the selected Bandmasters and to enable them to gain knowledge that could be distributed throughout the Band Service when they returned. The first Bandmasters to be selected were Staff BM D Guthrie and BM A D Haigh. Another development that occurred at about the same time was the institution of the Band Corporals' Course. Commonwealth Students from Canada and Burma were at the School and BM Reynolds was sent to Ceylon to form a band for the Royal Ceylon Navy. This continued a tradition of RM Bandmasters forming and teaching Commonwealth bands, particularly in Australia and New Zealand.

The Home Fleet visited Leningrad in 1955 and its band was strengthened by the band of the accompanying HMS *Triumph*. HMS *Albion* was also part of the Fleet for the purpose of this visit. The Home Fleet Band had transferred, with the Flag, from HMS *Tyne* to HMS *Apollo* whilst in Oslo. On its way to Leningrad they called at Copenhagen where the Home Fleet Band marched through the city, with the Argyll and Sutherland's Pipe Band, to the British Trade Fair in the Tivoli Gardens. Two days before reaching Leningrad the Bandmaster and seven musicians were transferred from *Apollo* to *Triumph* at sea by jackstay[27] to augment *Triumph's* band. The ships arrived with Guard and Band paraded as thousands lined the banks of the River Neva. Next evening a small orchestra was left in HMS *Triumph* for the C-in-C's dinner party and the remainder of both bands, forty musicians, gave a concert in Tavritchesky Park that was attended by a crowd of 7,000, press and radio, and the whole concert was broadcast throughout Russia.

The Band of the Mediterranean Fleet was under the command of the Fleet BM, Cd BM Pottle who had a Bandmaster, two Band Sergeants and approximately thirty-six musicians as the Cs-in-C band. It was centralised at HMS *Phoenicia*, Manoel Island Malta. Its role was to supply music for the entire Fleet including shore establishments and embarked programmes for the C-in-C and his Second-in-Command. For these the band was split in two but was massed at various ports of call to Beat Retreat and for other ceremonies. The band was also called upon to supply music for other ships of the Fleet and had done so for HM Ships *Eagle, Forth, Gambia, Jamaica, Cumberland, Glasgow, Sheffield, Birmingham, Surprise, Roebuck, Peacock, Duchess, Wakeful* and *Diana*. On average each member of the band did five months at sea each year. During a trip with C-in-C to Istanbul the band massed with the 14th/20th King's Hussars Band, which was embarked in HMS *Duchess* en route to the UK and, together, they Beat Retreat.

1955 also saw the world premiere of the film *Cockleshell Heroes* which was based upon Operation *Frankton*, the raid upon German shipping at Bordeaux in December 1942. It was filmed at RM Barracks Eastney and on the adjacent Southsea beach. The PDM, Lt Col F V Dunn, composed the march for the film. At the premiere the Captain General was welcomed by a fanfare from the buglers under Bug Maj Wagstaffe. This was followed by BM Woods conducting the orchestra of the RMSM and then a fanfare played by the Silver Memorial Trumpets, Silver Bugles and Drums of the Corps. The Band of the RMSM with

Drum Majors Bowden and Knox then gave a display that culminated with the Sunset ceremony.

The CGRM visited the Mediterranean Fleet and went aboard HMS *Ark Royal* and saw the Mediterranean Fleet Band under Cd BM Pottle. The band was later inspected at its barracks in HMS *Phoenicia*. Band and Drums then went to Gibraltar to take part in the Ceremony of the Keys but they were back in Malta in time for the arrival of the old heavy cruiser HMS *Cumberland*. The C-in-C's Band played on the quayside as the ship came alongside and, for a short time, "a fierce, if brief, cacophonic competition"[28] took place - the *Cumberland* was carrying 42 Cdo, en route to the Port Said operation, whose Pipe Band were playing on deck! It is not recorded who gave in first! In the East Indies the C-in-C's band was on board HMS *Superb*. The band, under BM Shipway, Beat Retreat for the last time before leaving for the UK, the performance being very good in spite of the fact that a bus had run over one of their side drums ten minutes earlier. The replacement band, under BM Spencer visited Trincomalee where they performed as a Massed Band with the bands of the Indian and Pakistan Navies. Despite lack of time for practice they put up a very creditable performance.

It was during 1956 that the titles 'Junior Bugler' and 'Junior Musician' replaced those of 'Boy Bugler' and 'Boy Musician'. This was necessary because the Royal Navy had removed all reference to 'Boy' ratings. It was also during 1956 that the Queen Mother visited Deal to open the new accommodation blocks. The massed bands of the RMSM marched on Parade to *HM Jollies* leading the Recruits Squads of the Depot and the Junior Wing RMSM. They then played the bugle march *Mechanised Infantry* before the Royal Guard of Honour marched on to *Imperial Echoes*. As she entered the North Barracks a fanfare *Royal Flourish* written by Lt Col F V Dunn was played on the Silver Memorial

Funeral of Lt PM McCarthy, one of the officers of 40 Cdo killed at Suez 1956. The Portsmouth Group Band under the direction of Captain K A McLean lead the cortege.

Fanfare Trumpets. This was the first time that they were played with the new RMSM banners, instead of those of the RNSM. The Royal Salute and the Inspection Music, *The Globe and Laurel* followed the fanfare. Following the religious service the Royal Guard of Honour and the Companies marched off parade to *The Standard of St George*.

The major military event of 1956 was the landing at Port Said, Suez, by 3 Cdo Bde. During this very brief operation two Officers and nine other ranks were killed. Their bodies were brought back to England and some were reinterred at the RN Cemetery, Gosport on 17th December 1956. The Bands of C-in-C Portsmouth, the Home Fleet and the Portsmouth Group Band itself under the direction of Captain K A McLean, led the cortege on its journey from the RN Hospital to the cemetery. HMS *Newfoundland* had been at the southern end of the Canal and engaged the Egyptian frigate *Domiat*. After a short battle the Egyptian ship was sunk by *Newfoundland's* gunfire. The only Band Service casualty, BSgt Evans, had been wounded by shrapnel and was sent home.

In 1956 the Band of HMS *Triumph*, the ship that for several years had been engaged upon RN Officer Cadet training, marched into Dartmouth, to become the College band with a new title, the Band of HM RM Britannia Royal Naval College.

January 1st 1957 heralded changes to Officer rank structures. Commissioned Bandmasters became Second Lieutenants SD(B) and Senior Commissioned Bandmasters became Lieutenants SD(B). This, combined with other changes, gave the following Officer structure to the Band Service:

RMSM & Staff Bands		Ship & Establishment Bands	
PDM	LtCol F V Dunn	Far East Fleet	Lt Cooper
DoM Junior Wing	Capt E Ough	3 Cdo Bde	Lt Weller
DoM Musical Training	Capt Talling	RNZN	Lt G C McLean
OC 'M' Company	Capt White	RAN	2 Lt Arnold
Supply Officer (Music)	Capt Fitzgerald	RCN[29]	2 Lt Reynolds
Asst Drafting Officer	Lt Stagg	C-in-C Portsmouth	2 Lt Butler
Portsmouth Group	Capt McLean	C-in-C Plymouth	2 Lt Jemmett
Plymouth Group	Capt Lang	RNZRMBS[30]	2 Lt Medcalf
RMSM	2 Lt E Barnes	C-in-C Med. Fleet	2 Lt Newcombe
RMSM	2 Lt Pottle	C-in-C The Nore	2 Lt Merrett
RMSM Boys' Wing	2 Lt Long	C-in-C Home Fleet	2 Lt Greasley

On 26th January 1957 the 50th Anniversary of the Garrison Church at Deal (St Michael's and All Angels') was celebrated. Lt Col F V Dunn conducted the orchestra and after the service the CGRM presented the British Empire Medal to Senior Drum Major C H Bowden[31].

On 17th May 1957 Capt J E Talling took a Band and Corps of Drums of fifty-one onto HMS *Ark Royal* which was moored at Rosyth in preparation for a visit to the United States. The band was a composite one made up of the band of HMS *Eagle*[32] and Home Fleet as well as ranks from the School of Music. Staff BM Martin was Drum Major. Next day the Guard and Band practised a drill display in readiness for the visit and then, on the 21st HMS *Ark Royal* and the other ships of the Home Fleet assembled at Cromarty to practise the manoeuvres that they would make when they met the Queen returning from Copenhagen in the Royal Yacht. The Fleet's capital ships, the three aircraft carriers HMS *Ark Royal*, *Albion* and *Ocean* steamed out to meet the Royal Yacht and her escort of three destroyers. Following the steam past, during which the crew manned ship and the Guard and Band were paraded, the *Ark Royal* turned away to fly off her aircraft for a fly-past. The Queen and the Duke of Edinburgh went on board HMS *Ocean*, anchored in Cromarty Firth, for a banquet that evening, Capt Talling conducting HMS *Ocean's* band that was augmented by selected members of the band of *Ark Royal*. Capt Talling had the honour of drinking the traditional glass of port with the Queen at the end of the dinner. Guard and Band were paraded the following day as the Royal Barge sailed past and then, in the evening, *Ark Royal's* Corps of Drums went to *Albion* to welcome the Queen aboard for a reception. The day after was *Ark Royal's* big day. The Queen and the Duke of Edinburgh came aboard and were received by the RM Guard of Honour. After the Inspection the band played appropriate music whilst the Queen was driven around 'Divisions' in a Land Rover. Following flying demonstrations the Guard and Band paraded for the Queen's departure. As soon as the Royal Barge left the *Ark Royal* preparations were made for the visit to the United States. During the voyage the band practised as often as possible and gave a number of concerts for the crew. The ship spent fifteen days at various cities on the eastern seaboard. During that time the Guard and Band paraded on twenty-six occasions (four of them being Royal) and gave one drill display, Beat Retreat six times and gave five other public performances.

In September 1956 HM Yacht *Britannia* sailed from Portsmouth on a world tour carrying Princess Margaret as far as Kenya. The Duke of Edinburgh then joined the ship at Mombasa. The usual custom was followed with the band of fourteen under the direction of the Yacht Bandmaster (BM Morgan) from leaving Portsmouth until, on the return leg, the Director of Music, Capt McLean, went aboard prior to the Queen joining the ship for a State visit to Portugal.

The Far East Fleet Band was involved in the celebrations to mark the Independence of Malaya within the Commonwealth. They represented the Corps and were given the privilege of marching immediately behind the Naval Contingent at the head of the parade.

In 1957 HMS *Excellent* at Whale Island and HMS *St Vincent* at Gosport were both given bands, having lost theirs in 1954.

HMS *Ocean* was involved in exercises in the English Channel when she received a signal to return to Portsmouth "with despatch". King Haakon VII of Norway had died and the ship had been selected to carry the UK representatives to Oslo. The Portsmouth Group Band under Capt McLean was the first to go aboard followed by three Officers and eighteen other ranks of the Green Howards (Alexandra, Princess of Wales's Own Yorkshire Regiment) - the late King was their Colonel-in-Chief. Then came a Naval contingent from HMS *Victory* and HMS *Excellent* who would combine with men from HMS *Ocean* to form a Royal Guard. During the voyage to Oslo, Asian flu broke out amongst the band and this was a great concern for the Director of Music. Fortunately he was able to form a band from those who had not succumbed or who had recovered. With muffled drums the band led the British contingents through the streets towards the Akerhus, the Royal Fortress. Having taken position the British contingent remained there for an hour and a half. The cortege led by the band of HM the King's Guard was then seen making its way towards the Akerhus and the crowd fell silent. As the Norwegian band came abreast of the British contingent they ceased playing and the RM Band played Chopin's Funeral March. It was later learnt that King Olaf, on being told that a RM Band would be present particularly asked that this should be done. An hour later the Royal Family returned and, during this period, the King's Guard had fired two Royal Salutes and had fixed bayonets. The Royal Marines played solemn music for the first quarter of a mile and then played "lively airs".

HMS *Maidstone*, the veteran Submarine Depot Ship, embarked the Pipe Band and Military Band of the Argyll and Sutherland Highlanders for passage to Helsinki. A hundred submariners were moved out of their mess, hammocks were made up and mess equipment drawn for the Army to use. Spare submarine ratings were detailed to act as 'sea-fathers' and shepherded their charges around when they arrived on board. They were amazed at how much ceremonial gear a Highlander manages to amass! The Argyll and Sutherland Highlanders spent the next two hours having supper and learning about shipboard life and the intricacies of sleeping in a hammock. Next day when HMS *Maidstone* sailed it was to the stirring sound of the Pipes alternating with the ship's RM Band. After landing the Highlanders ashore at Helsinki the ship prepared to sail. As the ship slipped from the jetty the Pipe and Military Bands of the 'Argyll and Submarine Highlanders", as they had become known, gave a colourful marching display on the quay and then marched along the flight deck of HMS *Ocean* to play the *Maidstone* out of harbour.

In July 1957 CGRM decided to regularise the wearing of miniature medals by Drum Majors. The four Drum Majors at Portsmouth, Plymouth, Mediterranean Fleet and the RMSM all had at least six medals and it had been shown that a bar holding four or more medals damaged the tunic collar and could easily cut the bare neck when swinging the arm. This problem did not apply with the other services due to the design of the sash and the positioning of medals. It was decided that this regularisation should apply to all future Drum Majors irrespective of the number of medals held. CGRM promulgated this instruction and by October 1957 the matter was settled and Dress Regulations were amended[33].

Exercise *Strike Back* - the biggest Naval exercise since the war - took place in the autumn of 1957 and HMS *Eagle* was given the job of sorting and delivering mail. A ton of mail was delivered and found to be unsorted and containing mail bound for other parts of the world and to ships not in company. The massive task of sorting and distribution was given to the two Royal Marines Butchers and the band. On arrival in Vigo, Spain, members of the Spanish Forces were welcomed aboard. After watching the band, under BM Macdonald, Beat Retreat in the hangar "evoking cheers from the Spaniards and emotional satisfaction from British residents". A Lt Cdr pilot turned to the Officer Commanding Royal Marines (OCRM) and said, "Well Major, now I know that the aviators are not the only worthwhile men on board"!

1957 was not only a particularly busy year but it was also the year when the Band Service was expected to have recovered from the cutbacks of 1949 and the changes of 1953. It was also the year in which the first major Defence Review was promulgated. Designed to reduce the size of the Services, National Service was to be phased out and the Royal Navy was to be reduced from 121,000 to between 90,000 and 100,000 by 1962. This included the loss of 2,000 serving RN and RM Officers. In a speech to a Royal Marines Association Branch General Sir Campbell Hardy made it known that in the forthcoming Services reshuffle the Royal Marines would not suffer as badly as most and that detachments would still be sent to sea, albeit on a reduced footing[34].

During 1958 much thought was given to the scale of the cuts and their effect. The Royal Navy once again cast covetous eyes towards the RM Bands serving on board ships and by July the CGRM had been tasked by the Admiralty Board to look at the use of bands within the ships' Action Information Organisation (AIO) which was the current term for the technically more advanced procedures that replaced the use of such things as Transmitting Stations. This request was passed to the Commandant of the RMSM who discussed it with Lt Col F V Dunn. They were told to assume that the duties would not involve harbour watch-keeping, although some harbour drills would be inevitable, and that training in the duties involved would take place after embarkation. The RMSM responded that duties should be well defined and a reply was formulated which made the following points: Firstly, bands should be closed up to Action Stations only during exercises and in action and that "these duties would not involve any more time to be spent away from musical duties than when the band manned the Transmitting Stations". Secondly, duties would not risk damage to lips or fingers. Thirdly, RN and RM Officers must realise that being a member of a RM Band is a full time employment the same as being a writer, a shipwright or any other 'dayman'.[35] Finally, no specialist qualifications would need to be gained to do these additional duties.

It was felt that if these conditions were met then employment of bands on such duties would be acceptable. Capt J M Halford RM serving on board HMS *Victorious* wrote a letter in August 1959 on returning from a commission that included a visit to the United States. He referred to the trials that the ship's band had taken part in. The band had been enthusiastic to learn the AIO and, over the length of the commission, the interest had been maintained. After the two-week training period that was carried out on board the band had been split into three watches so that they each spent one or two afternoons a week building their experience. This routine allowed the Bandmaster the entire band each morning for practice and rehearsal whilst at sea. Most of the band would be available in the afternoons enabling section practice, instructional work and other musical duties to be carried out. The routine was likened to the bands working in the Transmitting Stations ten years earlier. Capt Halford also remarked that ships' Officers had begun to feel that, under the Fleet Band System, the bands were merely passengers in between the periods when they flitted from one ship to another.

In October 1959 the OCRM in HMS *Tiger* wrote to RMSM to seek guidance in employing the band in the modern cruisers that were then entering service. He explained that, upon commissioning, he realised that Naval officers had forgotten what it was like to have a ship's band as opposed to having a C-in-C's Band embarked for a cruise. The band had been blamed for taking billets in the Seaman complement, an area that had already been reduced since, in the cruisers entering service at that time, large numbers of Technicians were necessary. Modern cruisers also had no recreational space so band practice was carried out in the Senior Rates' Dining Hall in between clearing and setting up meals. The OCRM was acting incorrectly by keeping the band together instead of blending them with the crew in various parts of the ship but he wanted to prevent them being involved in communal duties that would reduce the practice opportunities even further. Individual practice and other instruction was taking place in the RM Barracks or the small schoolroom on board. The duties carried out by the band included playing for entering and leaving harbour, gun salutes, guards of honour, concerts ashore, dance band concerts for the ship's company, Church, children's parties ashore, Wardroom Guest Nights, Wardroom Cocktail Parties, Captain's Dinner and Lunch Parties, Seamen's evolutions (fuelling ship, towing, weighing anchor by hand, etc) and Beat Retreats. The Action Station for the band was to provide Damage Control Patrols.

Later that month CGRM instructed the RMSM that the bands due to commission with HMS *Ark Royal* and *Hermes* would report to HMS *Dryad* for AIO training prior to sailing. A period of five days' training at *Dryad* was required for HMS *Ark Royal* but only two days' preparatory training was necessary for the HMS *Hermes* band. This placed an additional strain on the training and drafting system since bands also had to join with the ship's detachment prior to joining their ship as well as undergo basic firefighting and damage control training prior to embarkation. A few months later the Admiralty issued instructions that as a result of successful trials in HMS *Victorious* the band were to be used in time of war and on major exercises to supplement staff working in the AIO. The document went on to confirm the pre-embarkation training routines and that further trials would take place in HMS *Ark Royal* and *Lion*. It was emphasised that the use of the band for this type of work should not interfere with the musical efficiency of the band.

A few months later it was proposed by CGRM's staff that the Band ranks should have training in Nuclear, Biological and Chemical Warfare, known in the Royal Navy at that time as ABCD Training, with a view to this becoming their operational commitment. Commandant RMSM agreed that Junior Musicians could have an 'acquaint' with NBCW training during their final term as Commandant General's Squad and that two days of a band's pre-embarkation training should be spent on NBCW training.

The Juniors' acquaint consisted of six lectures on alternate Saturday mornings with the subjects being respirator drill and gas chambers; war gases; radiac instruments; effects of radiation and defence against radiation.

The Massed Bands rehearse at Deal for the 1960 Beating Retreat on Horse Guards Parade. Captain W Lang can be seen keeping an eye on his developing parade from the middle of the band that is probably playing Sambre et Meuse at this point. The Fanfare team are in the background and there are six Drum Majors, one of whom is the spare, and two of whom are from the Buglers Branch.

CHAPTER SIX

Reductions and Rationalisation
Commandant General's proposal for Band Reductions (1958)

This report[1] was based upon the forecast of employment of ships within the Royal Navy and was duly approved by the Admiralty[2]. The aim was to reduce the trained adult strength of the RMBS to five hundred and sixty by 1965. This equated to a full strength of eight hundred including those under training, a reduction of one hundred and thirty overall. To achieve this would require the reduction of Class A and Fleet Bands with an increase in the number of Class B bands. Since certain instrumentalists would not be required in the reduced A Bands a certain amount of retraining would be required, especially those Junior Musicians currently under training in those particular instrumental categories. The withdrawal of the C-in-C Home Fleet's Band, and that of HMS *Excellent*, was critical as this would provide a pool of musicians necessary to implement the first stages of the plan. However, if the New Zealand Government no longer required the band on loan to that country after 1960 then that band could be sent to HMS *Excellent*. Another option was to place a spare band in the Home Counties once the Nore Command was abolished. CGRM also proposed that when Fleet Bands were abolished the Fleet Bandmasters should be retained on the strength of the staffs of the C-in-C Mediterranean and the C-in-C Far East in order to advise on matters of music, band, ceremonial and other special occasions. The retention of these appointments would also be essential for Band Service career structure. Bands formed at this time were:

Foreign Service	Type	Commands	Type
C-in-C Mediterranean (2Lt Newcombe)	Fleet	**Portsmouth:**	
C-in-C Far East (2Lt A K Butler)	Fleet	C-in-C Portsmouth (2Lt A E Pottle)	Class A
3 Cdo Bde (Lt W C Greasley)	Class A	HMS *Excellent* (BM R H Nash)	Class B
C-in-C South America & South Africa	Class B	HMS *St Vincent* (BM S Rose)	Class B
RNZN Loan (Lt C G McLean)	Class B	**Plymouth:**	
Ships in Commission		C-in-C Plymouth (2Lt R G Long)	Class A
HMS *Gambia* (BM D Haigh)	Class B	HMS *Raleigh*	Class B
HMS *Eagle* (BM J D Place)	Class B	BRNC Dartmouth (BM D Johnson)	Class B
Home		**The Nore:**	
C-in-C Home Fleet (2Lt B Medcalf)	Class A	C-in-C Nore (Lt T C Merrett)	Class A
RMSM (LtCol F V Dunn)	Class A	HMS *Ganges* (BM M G Pearce)	Class B
Portsmouth Group (Capt K McLean)	Staff	**Air:**	
Plymouth Group (Capt W Lang)	Staff	FO Air (Home) (BM J West)	Class B
		HMS *Gamecock*	Class B

Whilst HMS *Gambia* and *Eagle* were the only sea-going ships with a band at this time it was intended that other ships would have bands when in commission. They would be HMS *Victorious*, *Ark Royal*, *Hermes*, *Lion*, *Tiger* and *Blake*. The plan called for the band at HMS *Gamecock* to be withdrawn during 1958 and the bands of C-in-C Home Fleet and HMS *Excellent* to be withdrawn during 1959. However a band would be required for HMS *Condor* at Arbroath during 1959. 1960 would see the demise of the bands serving C-in-C Far East and C-in-C South Africa and South America, whilst C-in-C The Nore's band would not be required after mid-1961. So it was anticipated that by 1962 there would be thirteen bands at Foreign, Home or Command locations plus a further number, up to a maximum of six, with ships in commission. It was later agreed to maintain the Far East Fleet Band.

The "General Halliday VC" Searchlight Tattoo at the Infantry Training Centre Lympstone.

This report was to be the first of many reviews of the Band Service that would litter the next fifteen years with huge amounts of paperwork requiring much staff-work and causing much concern for those who were part of the Service. Reaction to the CGRM's report was quick, and expected, coming as it did from senior RN Officers anxious to retain their 'own' bands. Despite the assurance that the Far East Fleet Band would be retained and would increase in strength after a short period as a Class B band the Vice Admiral made the point that the Far East had been served by the C-in-C's band based ashore but supplemented, as required, by a sea-going section that had recently been withdrawn. It was suggested that HMS *Belfast*, shortly to arrive, should be given a band so that the old system could be re-introduced and the problems associated with sending the C-in-C's band to sea eliminated. These problems included difficulties with accommodation on some of the serving ships and separation from their families in Singapore. (Several wives sent complaints to their MP). CGRM had already allocated a young band to HMS *St Vincent* and moved *St Vincent's* experienced band to RNAS Arbroath. It was decided that, by careful drafting, the additional band for the Far East could be commissioned earlier than forecast. However it would be embarked in HMS *Centaur*, not HMS *Belfast*. It was firmly stated that any other requests for bands could only be met by the removal of a band from a Training Establishment. All of these arrangements would need to be reviewed in 1962.

Partly as a result of these recommendations the Commandant RMSM wrote to the CGRM to suggest that the nomenclature concerning bands be altered. Apparently officers from other services were of the opinion that a Class B band was of a lower standard than a Class A band. His suggestion was that a Group Band of thirty-eight ranks should retain its name but Class A Bands with twenty-four ranks should be called 'Command Bands'. The Class B Bands of eighteen ranks including the Bandmaster or Band Officer should be called a 'Ship's Band'. This was approved and issued as AFO 676/62.[3]

In due course the C-in-C Mediterranean Fleet Band became a Flag Officer's Band whilst the bands of C-in-C South America and South Africa, C-in-C The Nore and HMS *Gamecock* were withdrawn in 1960, 1962 and 1959 respectively. The loan of the band to New Zealand ceased in 1960 and the bands of HMS *Gambia* and HMS *Centaur* were withdrawn. The band of C-in-C Home Fleet survived well beyond its planned closure date and the RMSM band was reclassified as a full Staff Band since its projected size as a Command Band would have made it impossible to carry out its training role. The band for Arbroath was commissioned as the band of HMRM Flag Officer Scotland and Northern Ireland.

During 1961 The Nore Command itself closed and its C-in-C's Band was disbanded so that, by 1962, the Band Service consisted of the following bands:

C-in-C Portsmouth (HMS *Excellent*)	2Lt W W Shillito
C-in-C Plymouth (HMS *Drake*)	Lt A D Haigh
C-in-C Far East Fleet (HMS *Terror*)	2Lt J R Mason
C-in-C Home Fleet.	BM H C Farlow
C-in-C Med Fleet (HMS *Phoenicia*)	2Lt C Taylor
Portsmouth Group, RM	Capt P J Neville
Plymouth Group, RM	Capt L H A Arnold
Flag Officer, Naval Air Command	BM G S Brown
Flag Officer, Scotland and Northern Ireland	BM G F Collins
HMS *St Vincent*	BM A O'Donnell
HMS *Raleigh*	BM P W Plock
HMS *Ganges*	BM D Carpenter
HMS *Ark Royal*	BM J F Browning
HMS *Hermes*	BM D O'Donnell
HMS *Eagle*[4]	
HMS *Victorious*	BM D P Lawrence
BRNC, Dartmouth	BM R S J Sharpe
3 Cdo Bde	BM J D Place
Royal Marines School of Music	Lt Col F V Dunn
Royal Australian Navy (*Cerberus II*)	Lt L T Lambert
HMS *Tiger*	BM R Banning
HMS *Lion*	BM P D A Toms
HMS *Blake*	BM V J Harris
HMS *Centaur*	BM D Hall

Review of the RMBS Rank Structure(1960)[5]

This review was carried out by CGRM as a result of the introduction of the Royal Marines Special Duties List. At that time there was an approved over-bearing due to the provision of four Officers on loan to Australia, New Zealand and Ceylon. Since the last of these loan arrangements was due to end in 1962, and as a result of the redeployment of the

Corps, five officers were selected for compulsory retirement. In addition, rank titles were reviewed. The Noble Committee had been formed (1946) to look at the effects of the adoption of RN rates of pay and pension and had made recommendations. So had the Cost Committee (1956). All had been accepted and the changes, as far as the Band Service was concerned, can be summarised as follows:

Pre-1946	1946-1955	Post -1956
Bandmaster (Warrant Officer)	Commissioned Bandmaster	2nd Lieutenant
Commissioned Warrant Officer	Senior Commissioned Bandmaster	Lieutenant
Lieutenant	Lieutenant	Captain[6]
Captain	Captain	Captain
Major	Major	Major

RM Band of HMS Ark Royal Beating Retreat for the United States Marine Corps at Subic Bay, 1962. The front rank consists of two ship's Buglers and a Band percussionist - note the wide red trouser stripe, the lyre on the sleeve rather than a drum, no Dress Cords Royal and no bugle.

Future requirements for the Band Service had been calculated as one Major, four Captains, two Captain/Lieutenants and eight Lieutenant/2nd Lieutenants. It had already been agreed that all Captains within the RMBS would be styled Director of Music and would be appointed to both administrative and band appointments with this title. The point was also made that the Principal Director of Music and two of the five Directors of Music had been granted extensions of service owing to the lack of qualified officers in the Band Service. This would be unlikely to happen in the future since Directors of Music would be highly qualified. Final conclusions were that direct promotion from Lieutenant to Captain would cease, it was unwise to promote young and outstanding musicians to Director of Music too early and exceptional circumstances would be necessary to retain a Director of Music beyond the age of fifty.

As a result an AFO was issued in 1961 stating that promotion from 2nd Lt to Lt would be by selection from 2nd Lts having four to eight years' seniority. Promotion to Captain would also be by selection from Lts and, for a short time, 2nd Lts who had passed the examination for Director of Music. The appointment of Principal Director of Music and promotion to Major would be made from Royal Marines Band Service Captains provided a suitable candidate was available. The Admiralty reserved the right to appoint the PDM from outside the RMBS if a suitable candidate could not be found from within.[7]

Organisation, Drafting and Promotion within the RMBS (1961-1966)[8]

In 1962 an attempt was made to introduce a Regimental Bandmaster as a Regimental Sergeant Major of the RMBS. Employment as the Principal Musical Instructor of Junior Wing was felt to be commensurate with the status of the rank. Following discussion and debate this proposal was not accepted by CGRM. In 1964 the matter was resurrected but, once again, it was turned down by the CGRM on the grounds that, amongst other things, the proposed duties could be carried out by a serving Band Officer or a Staff Bandmaster.

Band Service instrumental categories were reviewed in 1963/4 and certain problems, mainly associated with the quality of music provision in ships' bands, were identified. As a result the Flute and Piano category was changed to Flute/Tenor Saxophone and Piano/Cornet; Solo Cornet and Solo Clarinet were to be taught the violin; Bassoon and Oboe were also to be taught the guitar or piano-accordion.

During 1968/69 the RN was due to centralise their Pay, Records and Drafting functions and CGRM directed that RMBS drafting, promotion and records be transferred from the Band Service[9] to the new organisation. After a number of meetings it was agreed that because of the specialist knowledge required for the drafting of RMBS other ranks to the various types of bands a Band Officer would be appointed as Assistant Drafting Officer (Band). In addition, a Band Sergeant would support him and a Bandmaster would be responsible for promotions. As a result of this, and the fact that the Major General, Royal Marines Portsmouth, would assume responsibility for the drafting and welfare function of the RMBS, it was deemed necessary to confirm the remaining responsibilities of the Commandant of the RMSM. These responsibilities were the musical training of all Band ranks serving at RMSM; the musical instruction of all classes of candidates for promotion and arrangements for marking certain theoretical examination papers and the musical training and initial administration prior to embarkation of all RM Bands newly formed for service. In addition he had responsibility for the correct accounting and returns relating to the receipt, custody and issue of musical instruments on charge to the School and those obtained for the use of RN[10] and RM Bands as well as maintaining liaison with RN and RM formations, units, establishments or ships to which a RM Band was allocated. He also needed to liaise with the appropriate schools of the Army and RAF on training or technical music matters. Queen's Regulations and Admiralty Instructions were altered accordingly. By implication it can be seen that, at this time, the duties of the Principal Director of Music were almost totally concentrated upon the musical performance of the RM Bands and not their administration.

Costs of Service Bands[11]

During May 1967 a Parliamentary discussion, based upon a Defence White Paper, regarding the policy for maintaining Service Bands took place. As the result of a question asked by a Member of Parliament the Ministry of Defence had to provide statistics and information regarding the cost of, and income from, the bands of all three Services. By

July 1967 the MoD had provided a summary that showed the strength of all Service Bands including those of the RM. The bands of the C's-in-C Portsmouth, Plymouth and Far East Fleet each had a Band Officer and twenty-four men; C-in-C Fleet had a Bandmaster and seventeen men as did HMS *Daedalus* (FONAC), HMS *Condor* at Arbroath (FOSNI), HMS *St Vincent, Raleigh, Ganges, Ark Royal, Hermes, Eagle, Victorious,* BRNC and 3 Cdo Bde. The Flag Officer Mediterranean had a Band Officer and seventeen men whilst the Portsmouth and Plymouth Group Bands had one Band Officer and fifty men and one Band Officer and thirty-nine men respectively. The RMSM had a Band Officer and twenty-four men in the Staff Band, six Band Officers and seventy-six men as Instructors and Administrative staff with one Band Officer and two men in the Drafting Office. In addition there were one hundred and fifty New Entry Trainees and thirty men undertaking Higher Training. This gave a total, with the drafting margin, of fifteen Band Officers and seven hundred and sixty men.

The orchestra of HMS Ark Royal practise on the ship's quarter-deck, 1962. (BM J F Browning)

The Naval Personnel Division (NPD) felt that the Parliamentary Question raised three different points: the manpower employed in bands or the amount of music provided; the kind of music provided; and the receipts from private engagements. They also made the point that other studies were in hand. This whole issue became more and more complex as members of the general public, representatives of the Arts Council and many others also questioned the costs of Service Bands. Treasury asked for more and more detail and, as time passed, the strengths and locations of bands altered and changed. Much of the responsibility for coordinating the response had been given to the Army as they had the largest number of bands. Gradually the Treasury turned the search for the answer to the Parliamentary Question into a cost-cutting exercise and subjects such as instrument use and cost began to be examined. Two years later the Treasury were still awaiting a reply to the original request for information relating to the Parliamentary Question. The MP eventually gained access to the papers and decided that they presented a very confused picture. The result of this was that he asked for further, and more detailed, information. The MoD then felt that the Treasury were trying to gather information that would allow them to decide what was the proper scale of military bands - which was a matter for the MoD to decide.

By October 1969 a draft response to the Treasury had been compiled by the Admiralty on behalf of the RMBS. This showed that the time spent on military duties associated with music was 58% of the total whilst quasi-military musical duties[12] accounted for 7.5%, as did private engagements. Other duties such as military training, company administration, recreational training, leave, etc, accounted for 27%. In 1970 the Treasury fired another broadside. Having read the mass of information supplied to them they made several points. Firstly, they felt that expenditure on military music was excessive and were particularly critical of the Army generally, and also the RAF Bands at Cranwell and the WRAF. Secondly they felt that training should be rationalised and criticised the RMSM at Deal in particular. (The Corps was caught in a crossfire since the Treasury wanted Deal to close, some politicians wanted Service music to be rationalised to the point of suppression whilst other politicians wanted Deal kept open for the sake of the local community). Thirdly, they felt that financing of bands should be reconsidered, especially private engagements. Another Parliamentary Question, on the same subject, was raised in March 1971 and this served to keep the pot boiling but, by the end of 1971, the subject was becoming confused as the Services were embroiled with redeployment and rationalisation brought on by the latest round of Defence cuts.

Enlistment of Junior Musicians [13]

During 1964 and 1965 the training of Junior Musicians was considered. This was mainly as a result of the news that the school-leaving age would be raised to sixteen in 1970. The Corps enjoyed a special dispensation that allowed them to recruit and enlist from schools at any time after the age of fourteen. Junior Musicians were currently recruited at that age with the RN Instructor Officers at the Depot taking responsibility for the provision of the final year of school education rather than the State. This meant that the final year had a distinctly military and disciplined bias which, combined with the teaching of basic school subjects, allowed the Depot to concentrate not only upon musical training but also what was referred to as 'citizenship'. It was felt that the time was opportune for consideration of whether to continue the practice of enlistment of Junior Musicians one year before the school leaving age, or retain the enlistment age at fourteen and provide two years education at the Depot, or simply change the age of enlistment to school leaving age. Either of the first two options would have entailed serious alterations to the syllabus taught at the School and would probably, certainly in the case of the second option, require expanded and upgraded facilities. The Commandant of the Depot recommended that the recruitment age should be raised to fifteen, the same as the recruitment age of Junior Buglers, and that no Junior should be enlisted below the statutory school-leaving age in the future. Upon examination it was decided that with the recruitment level being high a phased introduction to the target of an enlistment age of sixteen by August 1970 would not cause any difficulties with RMBS manning levels. On the 1st October 1965 a RMRO was published stating that the minimum age of recruitment of Junior Musicians would be raised to fifteen on the 1st April 1966. The intention was then to fall in line with the raising of the school-leaving age when it occurred in 1970.

Royal Marines Band Service Redeployment 1967-1973[14]

In 1967 RN planning required that the strength of the RMBS be cut to three hundred and fifty by 1975/6. CGRM requested a minimum Band Service of five hundred and the point was made that a Band Service of three hundred and fifty could only provide for the RMSM and bands for the Groups and Portsmouth, Plymouth, Scotland and Naval Air Command; it could not provide a band for HMS *Raleigh*, or any other training establishment. A cut of 53% would also ruin morale. Using figures already provided by the Treasury, for the reasons discussed earlier, it could be shown that the RMBS with a strength of five hundred would be 0.6% of the total RN strength. The RAF bands were 0.4% of the total RAF strength whilst the Army bands were 2% of the total.

The Admiralty approved CGRM's recommendation that the RMBS be cut to five hundred but the cuts had to be made by 1973. CGRM was able to show that the reductions would come by removing bands from HMS *St Vincent*, HMS *Ganges*, BRNC, all ships, Malta and the Far East Fleet. Volunteer Band Instructors would also be removed. Plymouth Group Band would reduce in size whilst the bands at HMS *Daedalus*, FOSNI, *Raleigh* and Western Fleet would increase. The MoD quickly agreed with this planned deployment but the Director General of Naval Training was disturbed to note that bands were to be withdrawn from *Ganges* and *St Vincent* earlier than anticipated and was shocked to see that the band was to be withdrawn from BRNC. He asked if alterations to timings and to band strengths could be made to accommodate the proposed phased reductions in training establishments. The Commandant of the RMSM also had comments. He suggested that Portsmouth Group Band should decrease to its 1955-1960 strength of thirty-nine and that the RMSM needed a band of thirty-nine in order to be an effective training unit. Others made recommendations and gradually the CGRM's plan was revised. In March 1968 the CGRM visited the RMSM and informed them that the Admiralty had approved the strength of five hundred and that the detailed plan of deployment was still being prepared. Major factors in this preparation were the reduction of ships requiring bands and the streamlining of shore support.

In July 1968 the Naval Personnel Division (NPD) informed the Royal Navy of the provisional plan for the reduction of the RMBS. By 1973 the remaining bands were to be:

Band	Complement[15]
Royal Marines School of Music (RMB Deal)	39
Portsmouth Group (RMB Eastney)	43
Plymouth Group (ITCRM)	24
C-in-C Western Fleet (HMS *Pembroke*)	43
C-in-C Portsmouth (HMS *Excellent*)	24
C-in-C Plymouth (HMS *Drake*/HMS *Raleigh*)	24
Flag Officer Scotland and Northern Ireland (HMS *Condor*)	24
HMS *Ganges*	25
Britannia Royal Naval College, Dartmouth	25
HQ 3 Cdo Bde	24

The bands of Portsmouth Group and C-in-C Western Fleet would have bands of forty-three to enable them to provide a sea-going band as well as a standard band. This would enable the Portsmouth Group to fulfil its Royal Yacht commitment and Western Fleet Band to send a small band to sea when required. C-in-C Plymouth's Band would be accommodated in HMS *Raleigh* after 1971 to provide a band for that establishment and

BRNC would have to be prepared to make its band available for other tasks. The decision not to provide Volunteer Band Instructors was reversed and requests for VBIs were sought. The Admiralty Board made the CGRM responsible for the co-ordination of band engagements for all RM Bands including those in RN ships and establishments. A repercussion of these cuts was that the training of Junior Musicians had to be assessed in the light of a smaller throughput and a required reduction in the length of training from three to two years. The School of Music examined the problem and looked for reductions in the non-musical subjects taught at the school. These were: Parade Work, Drill, Instructors Disposal (used by instructors for whatever purpose they deemed suitable), House Disposal (used for personal hygiene and administration), Physical Training, recreational training, Swimming, Clubs, Education, Handicrafts, Current Affairs and Religious Instruction. The recommendations were that Handicraft Training should be removed and Parade Work and House Disposal be reduced. An increase in the tempo of musical training was also advocated. A warning that these reductions would result in the demise of the Junior Wing Band and Orchestra was reluctantly accepted by the CGRM as were the recommendations.

In October 1970 the Commandant of the RMSM informed HQ Training Group that, after five terms of the new syllabus, it was the professional opinion of the Directors of Music and the Music Professors that the two-year training period would not produce adult musicians of a sufficiently high calibre to maintain present standards. Neither would the syllabus allow sufficient time for the teaching of general citizenship responsibilities. It was then decided that manning levels would allow the reinstatement of the eight-term programme from 1972 so CGRM sought, and received, the approval of the Admiralty in April 1971 to reinstate the eight-term syllabus from 1972.

During the review period the investigation into a Joint Services Musical Training Establishment, (JSMTE) which could affect the future of the RMSM at Deal, was progressing. CGRM requested a delay in the review of redeployment until the future of the School was decided. This was agreed and the review was scheduled for October 1969. When it was discovered that the JSMTE was unlikely to progress, the future of the RMSM at Deal was called into question. By that time all other Departments and Units had left Deal and it was felt that the RMSM should be located at Eastney once again. A Working Party was convened to assess the situation. The provisional proposal then had to be altered to take account of this situation before the review could take place. It was suggested that, in order to overcome the fact that two Staff Bands would be co-located at Eastney if the School moved there, a Corps Staff band should be created. This would comprise the Portsmouth Group Band and sufficient musicians to cover the Higher Training requirement of the RMSM. It was felt that the Royal Yacht commitment, with additional musicians, should be transferred to the band of C-in-C Portsmouth (now renamed as C-in-C Naval Home Command). This Band could be located in HMS *Excellent* adjacent to the Royal Yacht's permanent berth. Such an arrangement would also allow better coverage of public engagements in London and the southern half of the country. This plan raised the question of which band should inherit the special headdress badges worn by the Portsmouth (Royal Yacht) Band. Despite the Corps Historian's recommendation that the Corps Staff band should inherit these, CGRM's Department decided that they should be transferred to the C-in-C Naval Home Command Band. The Major General, Plymouth Group, did not accept the plan and further discussions took place leading to an alternative that was accepted by the Admiralty in July 1970.

Under this accepted proposal the Band Service would become:

Band	Complement	Notes
RMSM (Eastney)	24	To Eastney in 1973. Increase to 50 by 1974
Portsmouth Group (Eastney)	49	Close in 1973, become RMSM
CTCRM	40	Reduce to 25 by 1972[16]
3 Cdo Bde/Plymouth Group	18	Increase to 43 by 1974[17]
C-in-C Naval Home Command	24	Increase to 43 by 1974
C-in-C Western Fleet	43	
Far East Fleet	24	Close in 1970
FONAC (HMS *Daedalus*)	18	Increase to 24 on closure of *Ganges*
FOSNI	24	
FO Plymouth	24	Transfer to HMS *Raleigh* on 3 Jan 1972
HMS *Raleigh*	18	Retained until end of 1971
HMS *Collingwood* (ex- *St Vincent*)	18	Close in 1972
HMS *Ganges*	18	Close in1974
BRNC Dartmouth	18	Increase to 25 on closure of *Ganges*
Ships (Aircraft carriers)	54	None after 1972

All of the reductions were linked to the closures and withdrawals of the Royal Navy. It was also decided that, after 1973, there would only be two types of band, Staff Bands commanded by a Band Officer with forty-three musicians and twelve buglers; and a Standard Band commanded by either an officer or a Staff Bandmaster with twenty-four musicians and seven buglers. The C-in-C Naval Home Command was consulted about the plan to transfer responsibility for providing a Royal Yacht Band to his own band - a prospect to which he readily agreed. The Flag Officer Royal Yachts (FORY) was also consulted and he confirmed that it would be appropriate for the C-in-C Naval Home Command Band to wear the Royal Yacht shoulder flash and the special headdress badges. The Admiralty wrote to Buckingham Palace to explain that the Portsmouth Band would be merged with the RMSM Band and how it was proposed to supply a band for the Royal Yacht. It was then pointed out that the demise of the Portsmouth Band raised the question of insignia and asked for the agreement of HM The Queen and the Duke of Edinburgh to transfer them to the Band of C-in-C Naval Home Command. Both proposals were approved on 9th November 1970. With everything apparently in place, detailed complements for the redeployed bands were constructed and published. Indecision continued until late 1972 when it was decided to retain both the RMSM and the Portsmouth Band but to disband the band at Whale Island and transfer its name to the Portsmouth Band. So, the Portsmouth Band lost its famous name and became the Band of the Commander-in-Chief Naval Home Command which allowed the band to keep its Royal Yacht flash and special headdress badge[18].

HMS *Eagle*'s band was paid off in early 1972 and Flag Officer Carriers then expressed concern that HMS *Ark Royal* would not have a band between 1972 and the end of her career - which had just been extended. This was brought to the attention of both the First and Second Sea Lords. Adjustments were made that allowed HMS *Ark Royal* to retain her band until she was decommissioned in 1978.

In February 1968 the Plymouth Group Band left Stonehouse Barracks and moved into a brand new band complex at the Infantry Training Centre at Lympstone. Included within this complex was 'Ricketts Hall' named after the Plymouth Divisional Band's most famous Director of Music. As part of the general restructuring of the Services several of the 'parent' organisations had their titles changed on 31st October 1969. Portsmouth Group RM and Plymouth Group RM ceased to exist and were replaced by Training Group Royal Marines and Commando Forces, Royal Marines respectively; as seen earlier C-in-C Portsmouth became C-in-C Naval Home Command and, due to cuts to the Royal Navy as well as rationalisations, C-in-C Plymouth became Flag Officer, Plymouth. The C-in-C Home Fleet became C-in-C Western Fleet with the band, under Capt P Sumner, increasing in size from eighteen to forty-three. On 24th August 1970 the Infantry Training Centre became the Commando Training Centre RM with a consequent name change for the band. Band of 3 Cdo Bde returned to England and was disbanded. Members of the band joined with the part of the Plymouth Group band that returned to Stonehouse Barracks in 1972 as the RM Commando Forces Band and which retained the Prince of Wales Plumes in the cap badge. The other part of the band remained at CTC being augmented by musicians from the bands at HMS *Drake*, HMS *Raleigh* and the RMSM. BM Rawson from HMS *Drake* took charge of this band that was also renamed as the Band of HMRM Commando Training Centre[19].

Joint Service Training of Musicians, 1969 [20]

This subject had been discussed before but little enthusiasm for it had been shown[21]. When the subject was raised by the Army Department in 1968 it was felt that, with reductions in the numbers of bands in Service, it would be worth re-evaluating. However, CGRM's Department made it clear that with the RMSM at Deal having plenty of spare capacity it would have many advantages over Kneller Hall from both a national and a service point of view. The Office of the Director General (Naval Manpower) felt that with the reduction of RMBS complement to five hundred there could be a strong case for the closure of Deal and the rationalisation of Service band training at Kneller Hall. This was quickly followed by the Army taking the initiative and inviting the other Services to discuss a concentration of training at Kneller Hall which, as a result of cuts, now had adequate room. CGRM was quick to point out that, in the Army, basic training of all musicians was carried out at the various regimental or Corps Depots. Only Higher Training was centralised at Kneller Hall whereas all basic and Higher Training of RM Musicians and Buglers was carried out at the RMSM, Deal. Therefore Army proposals to concentrate on Kneller Hall could only affect Higher Training which made it more appropriate to relocate Army training to Deal, and possibly RAF training as well. At a preparatory meeting it was decided that this would form the RN proposal. The first meeting took place in the MoD on 1st April 1968 and the Commandant, Kneller Hall identified that a major problem in rationalising training was the Army's lack of a career structure. Conclusions were that the rationalisation of training was desirable; the possibility of sharing tri-service training between Deal and Kneller Hall should be examined, the alternative would be to concentrate at Deal; possibly all Junior Training at Deal[22] and intermediate grades and Student Bandmasters at Kneller Hall.

The other pressure upon the Royal Marines was that the local population of Deal were aware of the plan to move all units away from Deal and concentrate the Corps in the West Country - a policy that was causing them great concern[23].

A Working Party and two Sub-Working Parties were formed. The PDM, Major P Neville, was asked, at a very early stage, to sit on all three whilst the Organising Director of Music (RAF) was asked to sit on two and the Army chose to be represented by the

Commandant, Kneller Hall who also sat on two of the Working Parties. The career structure of the RMBS at that time was:

Junior Musician 2nd Class.	Achieved through entry by Careers Office recommendation and an audition at RMSM.
Junior Musician 1st Class.	Pass musical efficiency test. Must have served a minimum of twelve months if under sixteen on enlistment.
Musician 2nd Class.	This was rank on entry for adults. Automatic advancement at age of seventeen years for Junior entry.
Musician 1st Class.	(M3 qualification) Junior entry: Minimum of fifteen months' service as Musician 2nd Class and to be rated as a satisfactory instrumentalist in Orchestra, Military and Ceremonial Bands. Adult entry: Minimum age of eighteen years and nine months. Minimum of six months' service as Musician 2nd Class and to be rated as a satisfactory instrumentalist in Orchestra, Military and Ceremonial Bands. Must have attained Naval mathematics and English Test with a grade of 8/7 or above.
Band Corporal (M2 Qualification)	Pass the Junior Command Course (Band) of five weeks' duration and a 2nd Class (Musician 2) Upgrading Examination (or gain the LRAM or ARCM Performers Diploma). Pass Naval Mathematics and English Test grade 5/5. There was, on average, a period of five years and two months spent as Musician Candidate for Promotion.
Band Sergeant (M1 Qualification)	Pass the Senior Command Course (Band) of five weeks and a 1st Class (Musician 1) Upgrading Course of nineteen weeks' duration (or gain the LRAM or ARCM Military Band Conducting Diploma). Average time of five years and seven months as Bd Cpl.
Band Colour Sergeant.	A minimum mark of 40% required to pass Bandmasters' Course of eleven months' duration (or LRAM or ARCM Military Band Conducting Diploma). Average five years and one month as BdSgt.
Staff Bandmaster.	Any two HET[24] subjects (or equivalent) plus a pass in the Bandmasters' Course required. Average seven years as BdCSgt before promotion.
Lieutenant (Special Duties)(Band).	By SD(B) Selection Board to fill vacancy after qualifying in professional examination. Must pass LRAM or ARCM Military Band Conductor's Diploma.
Captain (SD)(B).	Complete and pass Royal Academy of Music Course. Pass examination for Director of Music (pdm)[25]. Average of eight years from date of commissioning to promotion to Captain.
Major (SD)(B).	By Selection Board.

Qualifications and ranks for buglers were similar but known as B3, B2, and B1 for Bugler, Corporal Bugler and Sergeant Bugler. It was quickly accepted by the Committee that Junior Training could be integrated without difficulty and that the Army Bandmasters' course could be cut to two years to conform to the other services. It was also accepted that training for promotion purposes and preparation for the Bandmasters' Course should follow the RM system since it was closer to what was needed for the future than the other two. It was also agreed that Command Courses would need to be undertaken at separate locations because of the differences between the Services. Maj P Neville, PDM RM, made a strong case for the RM Instrument Workshops by showing that instrument repair costs were only two thirds of the cost that a contractor would apply, with the additional benefit of having an instant reaction to major and minor repairs. By January 1969 the Working Groups were being pressurised by Ministers who were anxious for an outcome. Shortly afterwards it appeared that the Household Division and the Royal Artillery Bands might exclude themselves from the rationalisation exercise. Other major points highlighted by Maj Neville were that the Royal Marines had a Staff Band upon which Student Bandmasters and Directors of Music could practise. Since the Students themselves did not have to spend time playing in the band or orchestra the total length of the course was shorter. He also reinforced the fact that all RM Students had to be as familiar with the conducting of an orchestra as they were with a band. The Chairman noted that: "…rationalisation with the Royal Marines presents formidable difficulties. The Royal Marine system would appear to be economically geared to their particular requirements".

During the course of these deliberations Lt Col Jaeger, who had joined the Working Party when he was appointed the Director of Music at Kneller Hall, visited the RMSM at Deal. He was most impressed by the Bugle and Drum Section and commented that, if rationalisation went ahead, he would be keen to adopt the RM method for the proposed Army Corps of Drums. All were agreed that alternative locations needed to be examined and Old Park Barracks, Dover and RAF Hemswell were added to the list. By March 1969 the Working Party were in a position to ask the Army Department to co-ordinate the preparation of an establishment report for a JSMTE incorporating a RMSM and an Army School of Music for Junior Bandsmen. Whilst no definite recommendation for location had been made it was felt that the report could be based upon Deal. At this time the Working Party were assuming that a logical timescale for setting up the Junior School would be 1972/3 but they now found themselves in a very confusing situation. Details of the Defence Review had been promulgated and all three Services were each now deeply involved with planning for cuts within their own areas of responsibility. The alterations to the training of Junior Musicians described earlier (reduction from eight to six terms) were now brought into effect. The Working Party report, which was intended as a feasibility study, was issued in June. The Chairman went to great pains to describe the systems used by the three Services and to indicate the differences and the difficulties. The report's recommendations were that a Joint Service School for the training of Junior Musicians was practical and desirable and the location should be either at Deal or Old Park Barracks, Dover. Integration of part of the higher training was feasible but would give no advantages. The Army should remain at Kneller Hall but the RM should be located alongside the Junior Musicians' School whilst the RAF should remain at Uxbridge. "Given these arrangements, there will be no degradation of musical standards. On the contrary, on the Army side, there should be a significant improvement in due course". It was also recommended that storage and issue of instruments should be centralised at the

Junior School location as should the RM instrument workshop facilities which should be expanded to meet all requirements.

The RM and the RN considered the recommendations of the report with the knowledge that it was very likely that the Army Council would turn down the concept on the grounds that running costs would be far higher than their alternative which was to concentrate the training of Army Junior Musicians (Cavalry and Infantry Line Regiments) at Shorncliffe. The CGRM was very concerned at the possible lowering of standards if RM Junior Musicians were in a Joint Services environment and preferred the option of closing Deal and relocating the RMSM elsewhere. The expectation was correct and, on the 30th July 1969 the Army Board announced that they had decided against the Joint Services concept, partly because of extra costs and partly because of objections from the various Corps. In September 1969 the Second Sea Lord proposed that in view of the Army stance and because of RM/RN reservations no further action should be taken with regard to the recommendations of the report. A few days later the Admiralty told CGRM that a study commission to appraise the transfer of the RMSM to Eastney would begin.

Band Engagement Policy[26]

During 1971 the MoD were attempting to move all non-policy making functions away from Whitehall. The CGRM therefore decided to give the responsibility for the co-ordination of RM Band engagements to the RMSM itself. His office would retain responsibility for 'Special Ceremonies', production of annual band engagements programme and policy issues. On the 12th May 1972 a Defence Council Instruction (DCI) appeared giving the details of how the proposal would work. As far as Deal was concerned bands would continue to carry out their own local engagements programme and respond to requests from ships, establishments and RM units for the service of a band. If requests could not be met they would be forwarded to the Commandant RMSM who, if a band could be made available, would categorise the engagement in accordance with QRRN (Queen's Regulations for the Royal Navy) Chapter 39 Section IV and any other applicable instruction.

Categories were as follows:

Category I - Duty Engagement. Ceremonial, training parades, displays, Officers' Messes, ship or unit concerts, official ceremonies, entertainments for public in interest of RN, Army or Air Force or general official functions where no profit is made by anyone through band's appearance. No fees to be accepted, all expenses covered by public funds and ranks are on duty.

Category II - Public Engagement. When ordered by appropriate RN or RM authority to attend a function, organised by non-service organisations, is in interest of service or is entirely in aid of officially sponsored RN, Army or RAF charity. No fees to be accepted, all expenses to be charged to organisers and ranks are on duty.

Category III - Service Engagements. Solely for entertainment of Officers or ships/units company including personal friends. Mess or unit to contribute to Band fund. Expenses to be borne by public funds. Ranks are on duty.

Category IV - Private Engagement. At request of a civilian organisation subject to exigencies of the service. Fees to be charged to organisation or person requesting band's service. All costs are borne by requesting organisation or person. Ranks not on duty except for disciplinary purposes. (Fees must not be lower than comparable civilian band would charge).

Three years later the Band engagements procedure was reviewed and it was found that some weaknesses were inherent in the system. Responsibility split was causing communication problems; the system was confusing to event sponsors and varied interpretations of the band categories were causing anomalies. Improvements were suggested following a check of the systems used by other Services and the Band Engagements Office was once again centralised at CGRM's office and a priority listing was produced. However, it was emphasised that this listing should be used flexibly and not dogmatically.

By September 1975 this priority list had been circulated for comment and was then issued as the definitive, but flexible guide:

Engagement	Remarks
1 State and Royal occasions at home and abroad	Includes visits to ships and establishments by members of the Royal Family
2 Major national ceremonial events	Including Royal Tournament, Edinburgh Tattoo, Beat Retreat on Horse Guards, November ceremonies in London and others ordered by MoD (eg: Guards of Honour)
3 Events abroad strongly supported by the FCO and the MoD Committee on Special Ceremonies	
4 Major Command/ship/unit ceremonial events	Including freedom ceremonies, Navy and Open Days, King's Squad Pass Outs (and RN equivalents) and visits to ships/units overseas
5 Category IV recruiting and public relations engagements	Generally those that the public pays to attend. Of higher priority than Category I recruiting events because they incur no extra cost to the Crown
6 Category I recruiting and public relations engagements	Including civilian shows and exhibitions
7 Ship/Unit Category I events	Including Divisions, unit parades etc
8 Ship/Unit Category III events	Including mess functions
9 Category II engagements	Including those for RBL, RNA etc
10 Category IV events	Other than Priority 5 above

Considerations Regarding Relocation to Eastney and Joint Training... again[27]

In 1970 it was decided that the RM adult training carried out at Deal was to be transferred to Lympstone whilst the Sea-Service training at Eastney (Fort Cumberland) would go to Poole. CGRM needed to decide upon the future of RMSM and this was inextricably linked to the future of the Deal and Eastney Barracks. There was no space, without major financial input, for them anywhere else. One option was to use North and South Barracks at Deal, disposing of East Barracks, the other option being the move to Eastney with the advantages of closeness to the RN and all its facilities. It was decided to recommend that the RMSM should relocate to Eastney. Cost estimates were made and a case made for the Second Sea Lord to decide upon whether Eastney or Deal should be retained as the home of the Band Service. With Parliamentary Questions about Deal being asked and the Army making decisions about which of their establishments to close or retain there was a feeling that the best course would be to defer any decision for a while. This was achieved by asking for yet more financial appraisals to be carried out. Costs began to escalate, as did the power of the politicians who were anxious that Deal should not close. The CGRM visited the Under Secretary of State (Navy) who was dissatisfied with the reports and cost proposals. He obviously wanted Deal retained and Eastney closed.

By May the issue had become further clouded and other units, formations and locations were sucked into the debate. As all investigations were being carried out in a covert manner it was almost impossible to get detail from those 'on the ground'. Later that month the Under Secretary of State (Navy), Roy Hattersley, wrote to say that he supported the MoD argument for retaining Deal, especially since other politicians were advocating its retention and he was prepared to state, if asked, that the RMSM would remain at Deal. Further studies were called for by the MoD but the terms of reference were very much based on the fact that Eastney would close. Later, the First Sea Lord announced that he favoured the retention of Deal.

By the end of June 1970 the CGRM had decided that it would no longer be right to press for the retention of Eastney and that the emphasis should be on reducing the Deal Barracks to an economic size for the RMSM. A submission went to the Admiralty seeking the closure of Eastney but carrying the caveat that the loss of either Barracks would not necessarily guarantee the long-term survival of the other.

CGRM visited the Secretary of State for Defence, Lord Carrington, and found him in agreement with the policy of arms being more important than bandsmen. A few weeks later, on the 30th July 1970, CGRM visited the Under Secretary of State (Naval) and they discussed the recently completed estimate of more than £1,000,000 for refurbishing Eastney. They also agreed that the proper answer would be to leave both Eastney and Deal and build a new establishment for the RMBS - but that would be some time in the future. August found the announcement to close Eastney and maintain Deal still unmade when the Treasury stepped in with the comment that they were not convinced that a separate RMSM was required at any location. Once again the shadow of joint training was raising its head and the result was that Eastney would close, leaving Deal with a Sword of Damocles hanging over it.

It took a little while but, in early 1975, it was announced that an enquiry, conducted by someone from outside the MoD, would be made into the extent to which the MoD made use of joint training. Sure enough, after Chefs and Dog Handlers had been examined it was to be the turn of Service Police, Telephonists, Telegraphists, Musicians and Marine Craft Trades. A Defence Training Committee Standing Working Party on Rationalisation of Training was formed and CGRM's Department immediately wrote to them. They explained that CGRM was keen to relocate the RMSM closer to the new centre of RM activity in the West Country and that a study (The Way-Ahead Committee) into relocation was about to begin. CGRM had to report to the Admiralty on this matter by the end of 1975 and, whilst CGRM had no objection to the RMSM being on the list for examination for joint training, he asked that the start of any such examination be postponed until after his report was made to Admiralty. The Way-Ahead Committee directed the Way-Ahead Executive Sub-Committee to examine the possibility of making 10%-20% cuts in various support organisations. One of these was the RMSM. Alternative locations were the Commando Training Centre RM, Royal Marines Poole or Royal Marines Eastney. It was quickly apparent that Eastney had great advantages over the other options. A preliminary costing exercise quickly confirmed that the Eastney option would be by far the cheapest of the three - which conflicted with the hopes of CGRM to close both RM Deal and RM Eastney. Despite the request by CGRM the MoD Working Party wrote an interim report in December 1975 that summarised the previous investigations into joint training of musicians. It went on to make the point that the Army had never implemented the plans that were accepted as a cheaper option following the 1969 dicussions and proposals. It also made the point that the RMSM would be relocated by 1980. The report concluded that further investigation into joint training would be worthwhile and that cost reductions could be made, particularly by rationalising Army bands. It was therefore decided that the Royal Marines would support the Report's suggestion that the Army should undertake a study of the work of its bands with the aim of reductions and centralising its own organisation and training. Furthermore it would also insist that any involvement of the Royal Marines in a joint school would require the inclusion of all Army Staff Bands including those of the Household Division.

The Way-Ahead Committee then began to wonder if Eastney would be considered as a suitable site for joint training and then, as matters became more urgent and more complex the PDM assigned Lt Hoskins to the Committee. Two of his early observations were that the C-in-C Naval Home Command band, now established at Eastney, should be able to maintain a separate identity to the RMSM band and that the new accommodation should include a rehearsal room and facilities for massed band events.

By now both the MoD Working Party and the Way-Ahead Committee were working in parallel and during May the former produced an Interim Report. Its recommendation was that "unless or until a major reduction in the number of Bands occur, and this in turn reduces the training task, further rationalisation of Junior Musicians' training should not be pursued". Shortly after this the decision was taken not to pursue the joint training concept and the Royal Marines filed a Position Paper on their views of the inquiry. Their conclusion was that the line to be taken should be that "…forming a joint musical establishment would be an extravagant sop to the protagonists of rationalisation for its own sake, which the Navy cannot afford".

The Way-Ahead Committee made its recommendations to the Naval Personnel Division who recommended that the Admiralty relocate the RMSM to RMB Eastney subject to a detailed feasibility study to be carried out by the Public Service Agency (PSA) and a validation survey by C-in-C Naval Home Command and CGRM and this recommendation was supported by the Admiralty. During November 1976 preliminary, and covert, financial investigations were carried out. These confirmed the viability of a move to Eastney and it was decided that the subject and intentions should be made public. The Department of the Environment (DoE) became involved and asked that the PSA costing exercise should embrace the opposite possibility, that of moving everything remaining at Eastney to Deal. Since C-in-C Naval Home Command Band had to remain in the Portsmouth area and the HQ Training Group were more suited to being relocated to the West Country this only left the RM Printers to move to Deal should this alternative be followed. All would now depend on the detailed costings for the project and, in October

1977, it was announced that the RMSM would move from Deal to Eastney in 1981[28]. This announcement followed a strange twist to the story of Deal. In March 1977 41 Cdo was disbanded in Malta, this being the result of a Government decision. A few months later the Government reversed its own decision and decided to retain 41 Cdo and to base it at Deal. So, on the 30th September 1977 the Depot Royal Marines ceased to exist and the Barracks became Royal Marines, Deal. At the same time the CO of the Depot, who was also Commandant of the RMSM, handed over command to the CO of 41 Cdo while Lt Col P Neville became Commandant of the RMSM as well as its Principal Director of Music. The Final Pass-Out Parade at Depot RM Deal had taken place the day before[29].

Costs and Size of Service Bands Re-examined [30]

Further Parliamentary Questions that were aimed at a Guards Band appearing at a well-known London nightspot reopened this subject in 1975. The band in question was able to show that it was not breaching Musicians' Union Rules. Very quickly the questioning involved, once again, all three Services and, as before, the main target was private engagements carried out by Service musicians. Variations between the three Services confused the issue greatly. By 1976 the redeployment programme described earlier, apart from the relocation of the RMSM, had been put in place and the Corps Working Group were able to report that the RMBS undertook twice as many Category I engagements (Non-paying - Official) as Categories II, III and IV. The reduction from eight hundred to five hundred personnel five years earlier counted in the favour of the RMBS as did their significant military role. This did not prevent them again coming under scrutiny during 1976. A report by the Assistant Adjutant General 'The Shape and Size of the RM Band Service' described the current functions of the Band Service as "...the projection of the National and Naval image in UK and abroad and the infusion of 'colour' and ceremony into the traditional pageantry of the Country and the Royal Navy". He went on to describe how the Band Service, with a strength of five hundred, was just able to fulfil those functions but made the point that the number of engagements upon which CG's Office had to adjudicate was increasing. Forty-five engagements had been turned down in the past twelve months plus a further five that the Army had covered because no RM Band was available. These five engagements were the deployments of HMS *Bulwark*, HMS *Intrepid* and HMS *Fearless*, the commissioning of HMS *Arrow* and Divisions at HQ Fleet. Further Parliamentary Questions were tabled in 1977 the subject being, once again, the cost of military bands.

The Walden Report of 1977[31]

The aim of this report was "To define the organisation, deployment and conditions of service of the Royal Marines Band Service and the bugle section of the technical branch to meet the requirements of the Naval Service into the 1980's".

At the time the bands in commission were as follows:

Band of HM Royal Marines Commander-in-Chief Fleet. (CINCFLEET). A Staff Band comprising forty-three musicians and thirteen buglers and based at HMS *Pembroke*.

Band of HM Royal Marines Commander-in-Chief. Naval Home Command (CINCNAVHOM). A Staff Band of the same size as CINCFLEET and based at Eastney.

Band of HM Royal Marines School of Music. (RMSM) A Staff Band of fifty musicians and thirteen buglers based at Deal.

Band of HM Royal Marines Commando Forces. A Staff band as CINCFLEET based at Stonehouse Barracks.

Band of HM Royal Marines Flag Officer Naval Air Command (FONAC) A Standard band of twenty-four musicians and seven buglers based at HMS *Heron*[32].

Band of HM Royal Marines Flag Officer Scotland and Northern Ireland (FOSNI) Standard Band as FONAC based HMS *Cochrane*.

Band of HM Royal Marines Flag Officer Plymouth (FOP) Standard Band as FONAC based at HMS *Raleigh*.

Band of HM Royal Marines Britannia Royal Naval College, Dartmouth. (BRNC) Standard Band as FONAC based at Dartmouth.

Band of HM Royal Marines Commando Training Centre, Royal Marines (CTCRM) Standard Band as FONAC based at Lympstone

Band of HM Royal Marines HMS *Ark Royal*. (*Ark Royal* Band) Ship's Band of eighteen musicians and two buglers.

Junior Band of the Royal Marines (Junior Band) Complement varied with intake. Based at Deal.

The general recommendations of the comprehensive Walden Report (Lt Col I M Walden) were very much inclined to maintaining the status quo in overall terms but took notice of the fact that the RMSM should be at Eastney by 1981. There were many detailed recommendations, many of which were put into practice. Whilst all of these discussions and debates were taking place the bands themselves carried out their duties, sometimes aware of the discussions taking place whilst at other times being deliberately kept in ignorance of them. In June 1978 the Under-Secretary of State (Royal Navy) confirmed that the move of the RMSM from Deal to Eastney could take place in 1981.

Band of the Royal Marines School of Music, Deal led by the Senior Drum Major, Royal Marines, Charles Bowden and with the Principal Director of Music, LtCol F V Dunn, marching on the left of the Band. Photograph taken in Toronto in 1959 when the band were at the Canadian National Exhibition.

CHAPTER SEVEN

The Work of the Bands 1957-1980

At the end of 1957 Prince Philip, the Captain General, had visited the Depot Deal where he saw all the various stages of the training of recruits and musicians. He was particularly interested in the range of handicrafts that the Junior Musicians undertook. He officially opened the Grandstand on the Drill Field during this visit. In the same year it was announced that the RMSM Band would be making a recording for the HMV record company in the New Year. At the time it was considered to be an honour to be selected to record with this company.

At sea in the Mediterranean the band and crew of HMS *Eagle* paid tribute at the retirement of BM K Macdonald who was completing twenty-five years of service. He left to take up a post as BM to the Rhodesian Forces. HMS *Gambia* recorded that her band had returned and that this time it was 'for keeps' as the Fleet Band Scheme began to be dismantled. The RM Detachment, but not the band, for HMS *Victorious* was formed at Eastney in late 1957. It 'passed out' in January 1958 and commissioned the ship on the 14th January. The detachment was marched from Eastney to the Guildhall by the Portsmouth Group Band and from there to the RN Barracks where they were joined by the bulk of the ship's company prior to the march through the Dockyard and onto the ship. The local press commented, "A pity this sort of thing is not done more often".

The band of HMS *Excellent* was reformed under BM Pollard. At Dover, the Boys' Band played out the 1st Bn, The Buffs (Royal East Kent Regiment), who were on their way to Aden.

During 1958 BM Reynolds returned to England having established a Band and Corps of Drums for the Royal Ceylon Navy. He had been loaned to them in 1955 and on arrival had to advertise, interview, audition and select the men; indent for instruments and frame Band Regulations and Examinations for Advancement and Specialist Pay. He received over five hundred written applications, mostly in Tamil or Sinhalese, and unfortunately none of them were from experienced musicians; indeed, only two of the applicants could even play an instrument. Despite this, Reynolds, was able to establish a musical training school at HMCyS *Rangalla* at Diyatalawa. A Chief Petty Officer was sent to the RMSM and, after a year's work, he returned to Ceylon with a 'distinguished' Certificate. Bugle Major Close also went to Ceylon with the responsibility for band training as well as his usual duties. After eight months' tuition they were able to parade a ceremonial band of forty when the Royal Ceylon Navy provided a Guard and Band for the opening of the Ceylon Parliament. By 1958 Reynolds was able to leave the band in the charge of the Chief Petty Officer.

Following the 1958 Beating Retreat by the Massed Bands on Horse Guards Parade, a band of sixty under Lt Col Dunn flew to Canada for the British Columbia Centennial Tattoo. The first Eastney Exhibition took place and over 10,000 people attended during the seven-day event. Massed Bands were one of the major attractions. In Gibraltar the Massed Bands from HMS *Birmingham* and *Tyne* supported the Ceremony of the Keys, with the Outpost Platoon and the Escort being provided by the RM Detachments of HMS *Eagle* and *Birmingham* respectively. Later, the bands from *Birmingham* and *Tyne* massed with the band of the Royal Sussex Regiment to Beat Retreat. The RM Gunnery Instructor from HMS *Birmingham* was the Drum Major.

Back at Deal the Junior Wing preparations for Christmas included the first issue of the Wing's own magazine "Piccolo".

In 1959, after a year of HMS *Victorious*' commission, during which time a Volunteer Band had provided musical support, a band of eighteen joined the ship. During the first two weeks on board the band spent a great deal of time getting lost. As well as performing as a band they also carried out watchkeeping duties in the Aircraft Direction Room during flying stations.

Thirty years after the "*Devonshire* explosion", HMS *Gambia* visited Volos and a commemorative ceremony was held in the cemetery. Headed by the Pipes and Drums of the Black Watch the Royal Marines Guard of Honour together with three Royal Navy Platoons marched to the cemetery where, in 1929, the bands of HMS *London* and *Royal Oak* had led the way.

During 1960 one of the major events was the Beating Retreat by the Massed Bands on Horse Guards Parade. The previous year Prince Philip had told the First Sea Lord (Admiral Mountbatten) that he would welcome the ceremony on his birthday (10th June) about three or four years out of seven - the years when his birthday fell on a weekend should be avoided.[1] The bands taking part were C-in-C The Nore; Flag Officer Air (Home); HMS *Raleigh*; HMS *St Vincent*; Portsmouth Group; Plymouth Group; RMSM and BRNC. Before moving to London the Massed Bands carried out the customary rehearsal on the South Field at Deal. The date was the 30th May and a special event was added to the rehearsal. Each year on the 1st June a simple act of remembrance takes place but, because the bands would be preparing to move to London, it was brought forward one day. In 1948 the Memorial Silver Trumpets had been dedicated at Burford and the

On the 14th March 1960 HMS Bulwark embarked 42 Commando following the aircraft carrier's conversion to a Commando Carrier and the Band of Royal Marines Plymouth Group provided musical support.

'Dedication Fanfare' was sounded. The conductor had been Senior Cd BM W Lang and, in 1960, as a Captain and in his retirement year, Capt Lang once again conducted Leon Young's fanfare.

During the same year, at sunset on the 23rd February the last RM Band on the South Africa Station, based on Simonstown, marched on to the Grand Parade at Capetown to end a tradition of a hundred and fifty years of imperial regimental music being played there. The organisers of the special event to say farewell to British military music, the 'Young South Africa League', would be the providers of the music in the future. Meanwhile in New Zealand Lt C G McLean was preparing to end what was, at the time, the longest commission in the Royal Navy. Three years for an Officer, a Band Sergeant, three Band Corporals and thirteen Musicians as the RM Band of the Royal New Zealand Navy would end in March 1960 when they would leave HMNZS *Philomel*, the home of the Royal New Zealand Navy at Auckland. The New Zealand Naval Force was a part of the Royal Navy until 1942 when the Royal New Zealand Navy was established. Gradually the Royal Navy Officers and ratings were replaced by men of New Zealand and then, in 1951, the last RM Detachment left. Finally, with all due dignity and ceremony, the last RM Band was withdrawn.[2] 2Lt Reynolds, who had been responsible for organising the Band of the Royal Ceylon Navy, found himself drafted to Australia on loan to the Royal Australian Naval Band Service.

The Band of Plymouth Group supports the ceremony of Laying Up the Colours of RM Barracks Plymouth in 1960

3 Cdo Bde Band continued to be employed in support of the Brigade and its individual Commando units as needed. In 1963 the band found itself committed to adapting to the problems of guerilla warfare in Borneo. Prior to this the band had been with the Brigade in Aden, where they combined with the bands of the 9/12th Royal Lancers (Prince of Wales's) and the King's Own Scottish Borderers on the Queen's Birthday Parade and other occasions. In Borneo the band went on a tour of the troubled areas and, as always, the transportation of the instruments became a major headache. One of the trips was to a Royal Artillery position very close to the Indonesian border. The position could only be approached on foot and the rugged route included traversing a river by using a slippery tree that had been placed there by the local tribesmen. The RA had organised a party for

the local tribesmen's children and it was all a great success. Radio Sarawak later asked the band to broadcast, which it did, both as a dance band and as a military band. By the time that it left the region the band had travelled further than all the other emergency troops put together.

23rd April 1961, St George's Day. The Portsmouth Group Band leads the Parade past the Officers' Mess. Bugle Major C H Weight leads the Band because Drum Major Colin Bowden was embarked in the Royal Yacht. This was a regular duty for the Bugle Major because Portsmouth Band was not allocated a second Drum Major until much later.

The Royal Marines Tercentenary Year of 1964 was a year of celebration that began with the Beat Retreat on Horse Guards Parade on the 10th June. The bands involved were from C's-in-C Portsmouth, Plymouth and Home Fleet; FONAC; Portsmouth and Plymouth Groups; the RMSM; BRNC; HMS *St Vincent*; *Raleigh* and *Thunderer*. The ceremony included the new march *The Admiral's Regiment* written by Lt Col F V Dunn, the new bugle march *Silver Bugles* written by Capt P Neville and the first public performance of the new Regimental Slow March *The Preobrajensky March*. At a planning meeting Capt Neville produced a routine for the Ceremonial Parade that was accepted by the Committee but with the proviso that three further ideas be investigated. These were a bomb-burst formation, a Union Flag formation and thirdly, a 'Spin Wheel', but none of them were introduced. After the Captain General had left the parade the Massed Bands marched off to the Regimental March and instead of turning left towards Wellington Barracks they reformed with a frontage of fourteen file and marched down the Mall towards Buckingham Palace before dismissing in the Barracks. On the 22nd July a Review Unit together with the Band of the RM Portsmouth Group and the Colours of the RM Barracks Eastney, 41 Cdo and 45 Cdo were paraded on the Artillery Ground for an inspection by, and an address from, the Lord Mayor of London. After giving the Lord Mayor three cheers the Unit left the Artillery Ground and marched through the City of

London with bayonets fixed, drums beating and Colours flying led by the Band of Portsmouth Group. A luncheon at Armourers Hall, at which official guests from the United States Marine Corps and the Royal Netherlands Marine Corps were present, followed the Parade. In the early evening members of the Corps were the guests at a Lord Mayor's Reception in the Guildhall at which an orchestra from the RMSM, under Capt Guthrie, provided background music. The following day a Royal Review was held in the garden of Buckingham Palace.

The Captain General had directed that the Queen should be shown the modern Corps and so the Review Unit paraded in ceremonial uniform, Lovat dress and combat dress. This took place at Buckingham Palace. A display party demonstrated the various weapons and equipment used by the modern Corps and was dressed appropriately. The Band of Portsmouth Group, augmented by buglers and musicians from the bands of the Commander-in-Chief Portsmouth and HMS St Vincent, was under the direction of Captain Paul Neville. 23rd July 1964, Royal Marines Tercentenary Year.

Following the inspection the Royal Guard and Band stood fast whilst the rest of the Parade marched past. As the Royal Marines Association and the Old Comrades, who were bringing up the rear, disappeared from sight the Royal Guard gave the Queen a final salute and, followed by the Band, marched past. That evening the Corps held a dinner at the Royal Naval College, Greenwich, at which the Captain General presided and the Queen was the guest of honour. Following presentations the Queen, followed by the other guests, made her way to the top of the steps to watch the Corps of Drums of Portsmouth Group perform the Mess Beating[3]. Following the Dinner, during which the Queen, at Earl Mountbatten's suggestion, granted the Corps the privilege of drinking the Loyal Toast seated when in their own messes, a group of musicians moved into the Painted Hall to play the 'Extras'. At 1130 the Queen and the Captain General made their way to the steps facing the Grand Square for a fireworks display to Handel's *Music for the Royal Firework*.

The afternoon of July 24th was devoted to Thanksgiving Services at St Paul's Cathedral and at the Roman Catholic Church of St Etheldreda. At ten past two the Memorial Silver

Bugles of the Royal Marines sounded a fanfare from the steps of the Cathedral to herald the arrival of the Captain General. During the Service the Orchestra of the RMSM combined with the organ and choir for the hymns and also played voluntaries before and after the service. These included *Judex* from *Mors et Vita*, *Jesu, Joy of Man's Desiring*, *Solemn Melody* and *Nimrod*. As the Captain General left the Cathedral the Memorial Silver Trumpets sounded a fanfare. That evening was Corps Night at the Royal Tournament and although it was not an official event it certainly dovetailed in well with all the other events. Because of the significance of the occasion it was decided that the Captain General should take the salute instead of the Commandant General and that the Queen would also attend. As a double honour for the Corps Her Majesty invited four senior Royal Marines Officers and their wives to join her in the Royal Box. The bands taking part were those of the RMSM, Plymouth Group, Cs-in-C Portsmouth, Plymouth and Home Fleet; Flag Officer Naval Air Command, HMS *Condor*, *Raleigh* and *Thunderer*[4]. The Captain General dined with the Senior Non-Commissioned Officers at the Banquet held at the Guildhall, London on the 30th July. Before the top table was the orchestra of the Portsmouth Group under the direction of Capt P J Neville. Many other events involving the bands took place around the country to mark the Tercentenary Year[5].

In December 1963 Lt Col (local) Dunn was placed on the retired list, promoted Lt Col and then re-employed whilst on the Retired List to continue as Principal Director of Music.

At the end of 1964 the CGRM was asked to authorise the purchase of a set of fanfare trumpets to replace the original Memorial Silver Fanfare Trumpets[6]. This request was sanctioned and new fanfare trumpets purchased.

1965 was marked by the death of one of Britain's greatest leaders, Sir Winston Churchill. Documents[7] indicate that, although not mentioned by name but as 'a personage', preparations for Churchill's funeral began in 1959 when the Principal Director of Music met with Lt Cdr Cardale RN and a representative of London District HQ. At that time it was decided that the Royal Marines would be required to supply two bands of sixty, one from Portsmouth Group and HMS *St Vincent* and the second from Plymouth Group and HMS *Raleigh*, to march in the procession. In addition the band of the RMSM would parade with the RN Guard of Honour. A minimum of forty buglers, excluding those with the aforementioned bands, would be required for the ceremony. Contingency plans allowing for the absence of bands or Directors of Music abroad were put into place. Salutes and related music were carefully considered and the expected First General Salute of *Garb of Auld Gaul* (for an Air Commodore) was replaced with "*Dover Castle*"[8]. The Second General Salute was to be *Rule Britannia* (for a First Lord of the Admiralty) which would be followed by *Sunset* and *Tom Bowling*. During late 1963 the procedures for recalling men from leave were checked and the availability and efficient utilisation of bands were scrutinised. June 1964 brought forth the Draft Orders for a State Funeral naming Sir Winston Churchill but stressed that the orders could not be transmitted since the Queen still had to sanction a State Funeral. The scale of the ceremony was to be "a little less than that for HM King George VI." Band requirements had been changed to one officer and fifty ranks from Plymouth Band augmented from HMS *Drake* or HMS *Raleigh* for the RN Guard of Honour and a massed band of two Officers and sixty ranks from FONAC, Portsmouth Group, RMSM augmented from *St Vincent* and/or HMS *Excellent*. When he died, on the 23rd January 1965, orders for the rehearsal and for accommodation arrangements were swiftly issued. The final requirement for RM Bands was set at four Officers and one hundred and twenty ranks from Portsmouth Group and the RMSM as part of the Armed Escort plus the augmented Plymouth Group Band with the Guard of Honour. This was all based upon the assumption that the Queen would wish a State Funeral to be accorded to Churchill. On the 25th January this wish was announced, the Government endorsed it, and the funeral went ahead as planned on the 30th January.

1966 was the year of the World Cup being played in England and, as well as involving the RM Bands in performances at various football venues - including the World Cup Final at Wembley - the event also put considerable pressure on another aspect of the facilities provided by the RMSM. For a number of years they had been responsible for the upkeep of the twenty-two volume BR12 "National Anthems, Salutes and Official Marches". This publication was first issued in 1964. The procedure was that Embassies obtained details of changes to Anthems and passed details to the Foreign Office who subsequently sent them to NP2.[9] From there the details would pass to the RMSM via the CGRM. Piano scores of the anthems for all participating countries were obtained through the Foreign Office to check the accuracy of BR12. Following the World Cup, Major P Whitehead of CGRM's Department wrote to Lt Col Brinkley at the Army Band Office suggesting that it would make sense for the Army to take on the job of amendments to the now well-established BR12. Whilst the Army Band Office was keen, this situation did not develop, and the RMSM continued to be responsible for what was now almost a national reference work.[10] Increasing changes to anthems brought about by the radical restructuring of post Communist and Third World countries, coupled with the reluctance of any Government Department to sponsor the BR12, has resulted in anthems now being checked individually when required for use.

The 1960's saw a radical change in the way that the Royal Marines could be deployed. The Commando Carriers, HMS *Bulwark* and HMS *Albion* were commissioned in 1960 and 1962 respectively[11], followed by the Amphibious/Assault Ships HMS *Fearless* in 1965 and HMS *Intrepid* in 1967. In 1962 it was decided that RM Detachments would no longer be provided for fixed wing aircraft carriers; however, buglers and bands would continue to be embarked on this type of ship. As has already been described the period 1967-1973 saw drastic cuts and changes to the Band Service[12].

In 1967, HMS *Victorious* paid off, her band going to Eastney on a temporary basis. Also in 1967, as a result of changes to the Mediterranean Fleet and the move of HQ to the NATO base at Naples, the C-in-C, Mediterranean became Flag Officer, Malta. Then, with all other military units based in Malta, the band of the Flag Officer, Malta, under Lt Shillito, returned to the United Kingdom. On the 5th February 1968 the Plymouth Group Band had moved to their new facility, 'Ricketts Hall', at the Infantry Training Centre at Lympstone.

Lt Col F V Dunn retired shortly after what could be described as his swan-song - the 1968 Royal Tournament. It was during this Tournament that he was able to use the ideas that he had hoped to use in 1964. The Massed Bands consisted of Plymouth Group, Portsmouth Group and the RMSM. The display began with a fanfare, *The Royal Tournament*, played on the Fanfare Trumpets of the RMSM. Then, eighty buglers marched in to give a three-minute display comprising two drum and bugle marches and drum beatings. The ninety-piece RM Symphony Orchestra played for five minutes before handing over to the Oceanaires Dance Orchestra for a selection of music prior to the Massed Bands marching on to present a traditional display based upon *Sunset*. A week after his official retirement date, his 60th birthday, Lt Col F V Dunn was honoured in the 1969 New Years Honours List with a Knighthood in the Royal Victorian Order - the only military musician to be so honoured.

The man who had been chosen as his successor was Maj P Neville and he found himself inheriting a prize jewel in terms of the worldwide respect that the Royal Marines Band Service had earned. However he was inheriting it at a time when radical change was being discussed and implemented and a time when cuts were necessary. He must also have felt that he had a 'hard act to follow'. He would not have the benefit of his predecessor's hard won connections and neither could he expect to be able to shake off the mantle left by Sir Vivian Dunn very easily. Maj Neville, who had enjoyed the benefit of a year's Sabbatical with Sir Malcolm Sargent and Gordon Jacob prior to becoming Principal Director of Music, immediately became involved with the work of the bands as well as continuing his involvement at various meetings and committees involved with rationalisation. It will be remembered that, at this time, the Band Service had to be cut from seven hundred and fifty to five hundred by 1973.

In June 1968 42 Cdo were presented with new Colours by the Captain General at Dieppe Barracks, Singapore. Since this was an operational unit the Assistant Adjutant General had asked the Commanding Officer at the Depot, Deal to devise a shortened version of the traditional ceremony that still had dignity and solemnity without requiring the usual lengthy preparation. As a result, and with the agreement of the Captain General, a number of stages were eliminated including the March Past. On this occasion the Massed Bands of the RM Far East, comprising the Band of C-in-C, Far East Fleet; Band of Flag Officer Second-in-Command, Far East Fleet; and the band of the 3 Cdo Bde, under Lt R Woodfield were joined by 42 Cdo Pipe Band.

One of Maj Neville's first innovations as Principal Director of Music was to improve the setting in which the RMSM Winter Concerts took place. By extending the concert hall stage he was able to increase the size of the orchestra. Removal of unnecessary soft furnishings improved the acoustics and ordering that the dress for orchestral concerts should be No 2 blues with cloth belt gave the string players much better arm movement due to the looser sleeves.[13] Maj Neville was a great supporter of the orchestra and throughout his career he believed that extensive experience of the orchestral repertoire produced a more mature and capable musician in the band. The recordings of this period are felt to reflect this belief and the performances by the orchestra of the RMSM both at Deal and in London during his period as PDM were of an exceptionally high standard.

During 1968 preparations for the Investiture of Prince Charles as the Prince of Wales on the 1st July 1969 were begun. Lord Snowdon was Chairman of the Organising Committee and a sub-Committee dealing with music was formed. It was decided that the Director of the Army School of Music[14] would represent the Services on this Committee despite the attempts of the Services Co-ordinator Capt R G Lewis-Jones RN to have the PDM, RM included. The MGRM Plymouth wrote to the CGRM requesting that the Band of the Plymouth Group, who carry the Prince of Wales plumes as part of their badge, be included in the arrangements being made for the Investiture. At a later briefing meeting Capt Lewis-Jones reported that the Organising Committee had decided that only one military band would be required inside the castle and that would be the band of the Royal Welch Fusiliers. CGRM's Department and the RAF representative argued against the decision not to include RM and RAF bands, pointing out that under normal ceremonial procedure Service contingents were marched to their route lining stations by their own bands. The Army representative said that it was quite ridiculous for them to provide a band for another service on this sort of occasion and that had they been in a similar situation they would have resented it very strongly. This discussion was reported as "a remarkable degree of tri-service unanimity"! This situation was confirmed in February by the Earl

Marshal via the CGRM, when it was also stated that the Plymouth Group Band would participate in associated events. One of these was a wreath-laying Ceremony at the National War Memorial in Cardiff and, as a result of this event and another in Swansea, it was decided to arrange a band tour of North Wales with the band being based at RAF Sealand. Over nine days the band visited Colwyn Bay, Wrexham, Llandudno, Prestatyn, Rhyl and Conway performing concerts each afternoon and a Beating Retreat in the evening. Capt Pottle, the Director of Music later reported to the MGRM, Plymouth Group, that the tour was well organised with good liaison and was well received by the public. The only major problem was the usual one of finding food on return to RAF Sealand late at night. He made the point that a band cannot be expected to survive totally on sandwiches but, with the RAF victualling being almost entirely civilianised, food had been a problem.

Lt Col C H 'Jiggs' Jaeger, Chief Instructor and Director of Music at The Royal Military School of Music Kneller Hall, died in 1970 and his widow duly presented his large and very comprehensive library of music scores and textbooks to the RMSM at Deal for use by its students. The School was proud to accept it as a tribute to his memory.

During 1970 the Band of the C-in-C, Far East Fleet, at HMS *Terror*, Singapore was withdrawn. The very last ship-borne band was commissioned to join HMS *Eagle* in June of the same year. Although other bands would embark for specific tours of duty they would be permanently borne by shore establishments. In 1971 the Navy left the RNAS at HMS *Condor* and 45 Cdo moved in which made the FOSNI Band 'visitors' whilst they remained there. A couple of months later the band, still bearing the same name, moved to HMS *Cochrane* at Rosyth.

Band of Commando Forces leads a parade through the City of London from the Church of St Lawrence Jewry. 10th May 1974

In November 1971 the Commandant of the Depot presented a case for the bands to be furnished with a concert uniform based upon the need for a more comfortable set of clothing for small ensemble and dance band work. It was proposed that the tunic should be similar to the scarlet mess jacket worn by SNCOs. The SNCOs had indicated that they would have no objection to Band Service junior ranks wearing such an item of clothing provided that it was restricted to service and private engagements of the concert military band, the orchestra and the dance band. It was proposed that Corporals and Musicians would wear a black cummerbund instead of the scarlet one worn by SNCOs. It was also suggested that the lyre should be worn on the lapels of the jacket by all ranks. The recommendation was completed by the suggestion that 50% of the cost should be borne by Band Funds whilst the individual paid the other 50%. The design was slightly modified, approved by the RM Dress Committee and CGRM. The Royal Yacht Band would not use such a uniform since it traditionally wore a pre-war Divisional Band full dress tunic. Problems arose when the responses from some of the bands in support of the introduction of this uniform on a cost sharing basis were not supportive. The subject dragged on and, by 1973, photographs were taken for the Queen to approve. As time went by so the implications of cost of replacement and a growing objection on the part of the Corps WOs and SNCOs that others would be wearing the scarlet mess dress jacket, of which they were very proud - became apparent. The CGRM then decided that the project could not be allowed to fester any longer and the matter was discontinued. At the same time a stiff reminder regarding the unofficial wearing of uniform or civilian dress was given.

Maj P Neville was elected a Fellow of the Royal Academy of Music in 1972. The high regard in which the Academy held the Corps was very apparent. It was therefore appropriate that the RAM turned to the RMBS to help them celebrate their 150th Anniversary. Commando Forces Band went to Northern Ireland in September 1972 in support of 40 Cdo. The band played at all of 40 Cdo's tactical locations and their tactical HQ. They also supported community relations by playing for the Belfast community in areas deemed by their hosts to be safe.

In 1973 the band of the RMSM, led by the Principal Director of Music, journeyed to Toronto for the Canadian National Exhibition, the largest of its kind in the world. They played as a concert band during the day and with other service bands during the evenings.

In 1972 the RAM had invited the RMSM to send a suitable Junior Musician to the European Summer School for Young Musicians at Montreux, Switzerland for two weeks. The RMSM considered this a great honour and Musn H Mills was selected to attend. The following year Jnr Musn Gilmore attended and, in 1974, it was Jnr Musn J Zawada.[15] During 1975 and 1976 correspondence took place between the CGRM's office and the RMSM regarding the use of the word 'orchestra' in the title of a Royal Marines 'Band'. Whilst CGRMs representatives wanted strict adherence to the official titles set down as a DCI(RN) in September 1974 the RMSM found that promoters, and no doubt audiences were confused when they went to a concert "by the Band of HM Royal Marines" only to discover that it was an orchestra. Lt Col P Neville wrote a paper explaining the situation in detail and arguing that he did not anticipate any problems over the use of the word orchestra either from the Musicians' Union or the public. He highlighted the fact that the Orchestras of the Royal Artillery and Royal Engineers advertised themselves as such and went on to recommend that the word 'Band' should, when appropriate, be substituted by 'Orchestra'. This was accepted by the CGRM's office although it was decided not to make a formal alteration to the DCI at that time[16].

Combined Bands of Commando Forces and the Black Watch in Philadelphia, 1976, for the United States Bicentennial celebrations.

"The British are Coming!" was the name given to the tour by the Band of Commando Forces (band of 60) and the Band, Pipes and Drums of the 1st Battalion The Black Watch (band of 69 including dancers) to mark the USA bicentennial anniversary. The Tour Director of Music was Capt W W Shillito and Lt J Roberts RM was the Tour Administrative Officer. The Black Watch furnished a Bandmaster, Pipe Major and the Tour Commander. Advance publicity had been carried out by Bugle Major Woods RM and a representative from the Black Watch, both of whom spent a great deal of time in old style uniforms. On completion both were congratulated for conducting themselves in an exemplary manner during this period. The pace of the tour was intense with sixty-three performances being given in ten weeks. This required travelling sixteen thousand miles of which fourteen thousand were by Greyhound type coaches. The Director of Music felt that the tour was a great success but strongly recommended that for any future tours command should be in the hands of Royal Marines.

Lt Col Neville took the Massed Bands of the Royal Marines to the Canadian National Exhibition, Toronto in August 1976. This was the first occasion that a Service Massed Bands from within the UK had carried out such a commitment. This was to be repeated two years later.

The year of 1977 was particularly notable for a number of major events that affected the Corps. The entire country celebrated the Silver Jubilee of the Queen's accession to the throne whilst, in Malta, 41 Cdo were Trooping the Colour to mark their disbandment and the start of the British withdrawal from its famous island base. March 16th saw the Band of Commando Forces (Capt W W Shillito) providing musical support for the the last parade to be held in Malta after one hundred and seventy-five years of close military links. The Life Colonel Commandant of the Royal Marines, Admiral of the Fleet The Earl Mountbatten of Burma, took the salute as 41 Cdo, which had been reformed in 1960, once again passed into history[17].

The Queen's Jubilee was celebrated with a series of events that featured RM Bands. On Silver Jubilee Day, June 7th, the Massed Bands of FONAC and the BRNC (Lt J M Ware) led 40 Cdo at the Silver Jubilee Thanksgiving Service where they also exercised their right to march through the City of London with Colours flying, bayonets fixed and bands playing. The Massed Bands of Commando Forces and Commando Training Centre RM paraded with a Tri-Service Guard of Honour at Buckingham Palace. The same two bands supported a pageant on the Thames that featured RM Rigid Raiding Craft and Landing Craft whilst the Band of BRNC provided music ashore.

The next major Silver Jubilee event was the Fleet Review. The aircraft carrier HMS *Ark Royal* was the flagship and this meant that the ship's band under WOII (BM) J Whelton played a major role in the ceremonial. The ship herself was responsible for the returning of salutes from foreign warships joining the review and for the co-ordinating and firing of Royal Salutes, all of which required the Royal Navy Guard and the band to be paraded on the flight deck. Guard and Band were paraded each morning for Colours. Rehearsal of the Royal Salute and the Review rehearsal on the afternoon of the 27th also required them to be paraded. When guests arrived by sea the Guard and Band paraded on the quarterdeck. They fell in on the flight deck itself when guests were flown in. During this arrival period a second RM Band was on board but was later transferred to undertake Review duties elsewhere.

The Band of Commando Forces (Captain W W Shillito) parade for the last time on Malta as 41 Commando withdraws from the Island for disbandment, a Government decision later to be reversed.

During the Review itself HMS *Ark Royal's* Guard and Band paraded for the 21-gun Royal Salute. As the sound of gunfire died away the Royal Yacht approached the Fleet. *Ark Royal's* crew were manning ship and the ship herself was dressed overall. Guard and band were drawn up on the after end of the flight deck. As the Royal Yacht came abeam, prior to making a turn to starboard to cross the bows of *Ark Royal* and enter the Review Lanes, the *Alert* was sounded and the Guard and Band stepped off and marched forward to arrive with customary precision. They ceased playing after the National Anthem, in time for the ship's company to respond to the orders 'Off Caps' and 'Three cheers for HM The Queen' as the Royal Yacht crossed ahead of the *Ark Royal*. Guard and Band were also paraded for the firing of the Royal Salute as the Royal Yacht *Britannia* weighed anchor and returned to Portsmouth Harbour. The Queen's Colour of the Fleet with a Royal Guard of Honour was paraded during the rehearsal and the Review. On the evening of the 28th the Queen dined on board HMS *Ark Royal* and the RM Band performed as a small orchestra (this included using an upright piano that had to be wheeled in and continually tuned to compensate for the varying atmospheric conditions in the giant hangar!).

FONAC's band (Lt J M Ware) was on board HMS *Hermes* and shared the ceremonial duties including two transfers to HMS *Ark Royal* when other ships of the Fleet arrived. *Ark Royal's* band paraded on the quarter-deck with the Guard mounted to greet senior officers arriving to call on C-in-C Fleet whilst FONAC's band was on the Flight deck for the salutes to foreign ships as they took up their positions in the Review Lanes. During the weekend before the Fleet Review FONAC's dance band played for a ball in *Hermes* hangar. This was followed by Beating Retreat on the Flight Deck when, as ordered by the C-in-C, the ships of the Fleet took their time from the bugle call as Lt Ware conducted A C Green's '*Sunset*' and lowered their ensigns together.

A short distance away, on Southsea Common, displays by the Royal Navy and the Royal Marines were a prelude to the Fleet being 'lit up'. On the occasions that the Royal Yacht left and re-entered Portsmouth Harbour, Royal Salutes were provided by a Guard and Band on both sides of the harbour. The C-in-C Fleet Band, and the Queen's Colour of Naval Home Command, were at HMS *Vernon* the Torpedo School, whilst the Band of the RMSM, and the Queen's Colour of Submarine Command, were at HMS *Dolphin*. An RM Band was also on board HMS *Fearless*. The bands of the RMSM and C-in-C Fleet also took part in the Tattoo on Southsea Common[18].

At this time bands from the Army took part in a military musical pageant in Wembley Stadium every two years in June. The Silver Jubilee Musical Pageant followed the normal format but included bands from the Royal Marines and the RAF. The bands of Commando Forces, Flag Officer Plymouth, Commando Training Centre RM and BRNC were under the command of the Senior Director of Music Capt W W Shillito. Over two thousand performers from seventy bands, Pipes and Drums, Buglers, Corps of Drums etc assembled for the finale. The Massed Bands of the Royal Marines also provided one of the major attractions at the Royal Tournament.[19]

"The main Corps event to mark the HM The Queen's Silver Jubilee will be an Inspection of the Royal Marines by Her Majesty in Plymouth on August 5, 1977. The Inspection should be a colourful and memorable occasion." So instructed the CGRM exactly one year before the date of the inspection. The ceremony had to last for one hour and ten minutes and comprised a Royal Guard of Honour provided by 42 Cdo with their Queen's Colour; a march, drive and fly-past of detachments of Commando Forces to demonstrate the Corps roles world wide and its equipment; a band display; a series of 'tableaux' designed to illustrate as many abilities and skills as possible and to enable the Queen to meet as many men as possible. Once again Capt W W Shillito directed the bands of Commando Forces and Flag Officer Plymouth.

The event was a major success, but 1977 was not all ceremonial for the Band Service. In September, and at other times when the Commandos were deployed there, the band of the Commando Forces moved to Ireland to entertain the Units. Flakjackets and berets were the order of the day on those occasions.

December 1977 took some members of the Band Service even further away from their musical role. Two thousand men of the Corps were deployed on fire fighting duties (Operation *Burberry*) as men of the Fire Service went on strike. This force included musicians from the bands of the RMSM, Commando Forces and the Commando Training Centre RM who were sent to the Midlands and to the Glasgow area. Since the engines and equipment of the Fire Service could not be used, old fire engines were pulled from military stores and made ready. Coloured green they soon became known as 'Green Goddesses' after the green leotard clad TV keep-fit guru of the time. Equipment was poor and the stories of fires being started deliberately in order to win an insurance claim were rife. Before the days of Health and Safety in the Services the musicians used the simple technique of keeping close to the floor as they approached the seat of the fire. A Glasgow school was burnt down by its pupils and the Band Service had to do the best that it could with its 1½" canvas hoses that burst all too frequently[20]. There was also the famous story of the call-out to rescue an old lady's cat from a tree. Following the rescue the old lady supplied tea and cake for the Band Service fire-crew. Unfortunately as they drove away they ran the cat over and killed it! The firemen's strike lasted thirteen continuous weeks taking them well into 1978, the 75th Anniversary of the Band Service and the 25th Anniversary of the appointment of the Duke of Edinburgh as Captain General, Royal Marines. To celebrate that appointment Prince Philip directed that 'The Prince's Badge' would be given each year to the best Musician or Bugler at the RMSM provided that the candidate had attained the necessary standard. It was the Band Service equivalent of the Corps King's Badge and would be worn by the recipient throughout his career in the Royal Marines no matter what rank he attained. It replaced the Commandant General's Certificate of Merit. The Prince's Badge was first awarded in 1978[21].

The Combined Bands of Commando Forces and Commando Training Centre RM with the Band, Pipes and Drums of the 1st Bn The King's Own Scottish Borderers, the Band and Bugles of the 2nd Bn The Royal Green Jackets and six State Trumpeters from the Life Guards rehearse their display. The bands were on a tour of Iran in support of the British Cultural Festival, October 1977.

The two Anniversaries made Beating Retreat on Horse Guards Parade even more important than usual but Lt Col Neville resisted the temptation to make radical changes for the celebrations and concentrated on a high quality performance of a traditional ceremony. The Royal Albert Hall Concert, attended by HM The Queen, the Captain

General and the Earl Mountbatten of Burma was also an opportunity to celebrate and included in the programme were the joint winners of a competition for a march to celebrate the 25th Aniversary of the Captain General. The joint winners were *Virgo 57* by Musn S Reid and *Royal Salute* by Sgt R Waterer.

On the 1st October Lt Col P Neville retired as PDM and Commandant. His career had spanned thirty-five years and he had experienced life in all areas of the Band Service from the Royal Naval School of Music on the Isle of Man, through ships' bands to the modern Band Service that he had led so effectively for the past ten years. His pride in the men of the RNSM who served in ships throughout the world was immense and he felt that the work they did was never fully understood nor appreciated. His men were firmly of the belief, and many still are, that his greatest achievement was the standard at which the RMSM Orchestra performed under his baton. His successor was Maj J R Mason who, like Lt Col Neville, was a product of the RNSM.

41 Cdo[22] supported by the Staff Band of the RMSM carried out Ceremonial Duties in London from the 4th - 30th November mounting guards on Buckingham Palace, St James's Palace and, on this occasion, the Tower of London. The last time that the Corps had performed London Duties was in 1935 when they shared duties with the 2nd Bn Coldstream Guards and 1st Bn Scots Guards. In 1978 duties were again shared with the 2nd Bn Coldstream Guards. Unlike 1935 when Their Majesties were not in residence during the Royal Marines tour of duty, Her Majesty the Queen was in London and witnessed the Guard Mounting from the Palace windows. The RMSM was under the direction of the new Principal Director of Music, Major J R Mason, and was led by the Corps Drum Major WO2 D Buchanan.

1979, the final year of a decade that had been one of great change for the RMBS, was overshadowed by one event. The 'Globe and Laurel'[23] carried the following announcement:

Admiral of the Fleet, The Earl Mountbatten of Burma
KG PC GCB OM GCSI GCIE GCVO DSO FRS

It was with deep shock that the Corps heard of the death of Lord Mountbatten on 27th August 1979. Lord Mountbatten was appointed by Her Majesty The Queen to the unique appointment of Life Colonel Commandant of the Royal Marines on 3rd August 1965. Not only during his period as Life Colonel Commandant, but throughout the whole of his Naval career Lord Mountbatten took a keen interest in the Corps and his wise counsels were greatly appreciated. We have lost not only a great man but a true friend. We offer our sincere condolences to his family on his death and also on the tragic deaths of the Dowager Lady Brabourne and his grandson Nicholas.

For his funeral the bands of C-in-C Naval Home Command, C-in-C Fleet and Flag Officer Scotland and Northern Ireland were to be massed under the direction of Capt G A C Hoskins whilst the band of Commando Training Centre RM under Lt K Sivyer would be positioned on the route. Rehearsals took place at Portsmouth, Pirbright and London and included a full dress rehearsal at 0530hrs on the morning of the 4th September.

At 1040hrs on the morning of the 5th September the funeral procession left St James's Palace. The steady beat of the muffled drums of the RM Massed Bands marching with seven files led the procession at a dignified pace[24]. The solemn music consisted of two Beethoven funeral marches, Handel's Dead March in *Saul* and the Corps slow march *Preobrajensky*. Unlike Churchill's funeral where the various bands were able to alternate,

Mountbatten's funeral required the Massed Bands of the Royal Marines to play continuously for the full fifty-minute journey to Westminster Abbey.

As the coffin was borne into the Abbey the fanfare *Supreme Command*, played on the Fanfare Trumpets of the RMSM and conducted by Lt Col J R Mason, rang through the Abbey with a brilliance that 'brought a poignancy and thrill to the moment'. Following the Naval Prayer, the Royal Marines Prayer, the Life Guards Prayer and the Prayer of Sir Francis Drake, ten Buglers from the RMSM under the Corps Bugle Major sounded the Last Post and Reveille. Following the funeral service at Romsey Abbey, a twelve-man detachment from 45 Cdo formed the firing party whilst two Buglers from the RMSM sounded the final Last Post and Reveille.

Sir Vivian Dunn was invited to write an appreciation of Earl Mountbatten for 'Blue Band' and he summarised the 'Farewell' as follows:

> The contribution of the Corps in the Ceremonial Funeral Procession and the Service in Westminster Abbey was exemplary, meriting the highest public praise. The playing of the Massed Bands under Capt G A C Hoskins, had an eloquence and unmatched solidity that effectively controlled the slow march through the procession. And the sounding of the fanfare '*Supreme Command*' by the Silver Trumpets of the Royal Marines School of Music directed by Lt Col Mason, together with the Last Post and Reveille by the Buglers of the Royal Marines (WOII A C Crofts) wrung the last vestige of beauty and sadness as the notes echoed through the marvellous acoustics of the Abbey. So, in these final moments, and at Romsey Abbey, the Corps and the Band Service devotedly passed their last farewell to one who had served them so faithfully.

A few months later BBC Radio Solent in conjunction with Southampton City Council presented a tribute to Mountbatten which took the form of a concert and simultaneous radio broadcast. This was followed by a recording. HRH The Prince of Wales was the guest of honour and the musical programme was played by the Band of Naval Home Command directed by Capt G A C Hoskins.

Buglers and Corps of Drums 1957 - 1980

This was also a significant period of development for the Buglers Branch. In 1958 Maj-Gen I H Riches (MGRM Portsmouth) wrote to the CGRM suggesting that Cavalry Trumpets should be purchased for the Buglers Branch to allow them to satisfy increasing requests to provide trumpeters for the old custom of sounding a fanfare and carrying the banners of the High Sheriffs when attending Assizes or other functions. The CGRM agreed to provide four such instruments to each Group for this purpose and asked for clarification with regard to whether the trumpets should carry the Sheriff's Arms. It was decided that the banners should be similar to those of the Memorial Silver Trumpets and should be used at all times. It was also decided to purchase a set of four for the Depot since they also received similar requests and the strict Rules contained in the Charter[25] would not allow the use of the Memorial Silver Trumpets. When Lt Col F V Dunn returned from the tour of Canada he expressed the opinion that simple Cavalry Trumpets were inappropriate for the Royal Marines and that the purchase of fewer, valved, trumpets would be of greater benefit. This view was not accepted and trials into the precise type of valveless trumpet indicated that the type known as a "Herald Trumpet with chased ball and ferrule" was the best option. It was decided that the banners should be scarlet, not blue as originally proposed, with the full RM insignia, as supplied in 1956 for the Memorial Silver

Trumpets, in the centre and two fouled anchor and Royal cipher designs in alternate corners. The CGRM decided against the designs in the corners and eight Herald Trumpets and banners were ordered for the two Groups only. Special mouthpieces based upon the Bugler's mouthpiece were provided. These were accepted into service in 1959 conditional upon them only being used when bugles would be inappropriate or inadvisable and that they should not be used with bugles. Four years later four more were purchased for the Depot. Since then the playing of Herald Trumpets has been part of the Buglers' duties.[26]

During the period of reduction and rationalisation the question of allocation and training of Drum Majors often arose and the opportunity was taken to develop a policy regarding their standards of drill and their use. In a letter to the Royal Marines Office the FRMO (Med) suggested that the Fleet should have a General Duties (GD) Drum Major, of which there were only three in the Corps at that time, instead of using a Band Sergeant who wore Drum Major's badges and was issued with his accoutrements. A few weeks later, in mid-December 1955, a minute was sent to the Commandant, RMSM, from the CGRM's Office stating that it was time to regularise the position of Drum Majors with RM Bands other than the Group Bands and the RMSM Staff Band. The suggestion was for a musician to be surrendered from the complements of the Mediterranean and Home Fleet bands so that a General Duty NCO could be appointed as Drum Major. His duties would include assisting with the training of drummers. The length of his appointment might be a problem and three and a half years was suggested to ensure continuity. During 1956 QMS L J Keefe, one of two Drum Majors trained especially for Massed Band commitments was appointed Drum Major to the Mediterranean Fleet Band where he served until 1959 when he returned to General Duties as a QMS. He was not replaced.

During early 1956 discussions again took place regarding the throwing of the Drum Major's staff. CGRM had earlier issued instructions that this should not occur in Bands under his control but now wanted it extended to all RM Bands and Volunteer Bands throughout the Fleet. This met with much disagreement and CGRM was only able to issue an RMRO[27] banning the throwing of the staff to Group and Staff Bands. [28]

The question of Drum Majors for the Bands of C's-in-C The Nore, Portsmouth and Plymouth was raised in 1956 but was deferred pending the results of discussions relating to the employment of the Band Service. Two years later a Drill Instructor Drum Major (Sgt G J Higham) was appointed to Junior Wing in order to free the Bandmaster, who was filling that appointment, and allow him to resume normal duties at a time when there was a shortage of Bandmasters. As well as acting as Drum Major he would teach drill and act as Provost Sergeant of the Junior Wing. It was intended that when QMS Keefe returned to the UK CSgt C Bowden would transfer from the Staff Band to the Mediterranean Fleet with Sgt Higham taking over the Staff Band.

Not only was the appointment of Drum Majors being carefully assessed but also the use of Drum Majors' equipment. In July 1958 the Admiralty reminded the Band Service that Drum Majors' equipment was only allowed to the officially recognised bands of the C-in-C, the RM Establishments at Portsmouth Plymouth and 3 Cdo Bde.

Drum Majors for the Bands of Cs-in-C The Nore, Portsmouth and Plymouth was a subject that was again raised in 1959 when a request for a Drum Major for HMS *Excellent* (Portsmouth Command Band, BM Pottle), which often combined with the *St Vincent* Band, was made. This was seen by CGRM's office as perhaps the thin end of the wedge and so it was decided that, in order to protect the reputation and standards of the four authorised Drum Majors who were especially selected for their bearing, appearance and ability, any potential Drum Majors should pass the same stringent tests as those already serving and that a syllabus and rules should be laid down for Drum Majors' examination and selection. CGRM requested Portsmouth Group Commander, who was responsible for all aspects of training, to investigate and advise, in conjunction with the Commandant, RMSM, the training and examination aspect. Following a period of discussion the proposal from the Commandant RMSM, with a few additions from elsewhere, was adopted. This stated that candidates should be selected from NCO volunteers in the General Duty and Buglers Branches who have at least five years to serve; training would be given at the RMSM and would comprise a six-week course that included band drill, use of the Drum Major's Staff, all aspects of ceremonial as it affects bands and band administration; finally, upon completion of the course candidates would be examined by a panel of Officers and those successful would await an appointment which would be of a minimum three-year duration. This provided an opportunity for CGRM, through the Admiralty, to put an end to the practice of locally appointed Drum Majors wearing Drum Major's chevrons and full dress uniform. Henceforth these would only be issued to qualified Drum Majors and, even then, payment for items such as ceremonial tunic, Wellington boots and overalls would have to come from non-public funds. Following suitable training CSgt Dillon was appointed Drum Major Portsmouth Command, for band of C-in-C Portsmouth based at HMS *Excellent* in 1961. The first Bugler to be appointed as Drum Major was CplBug (Acting Sgt) Colin Bowden as Drum Major at Eastney.[29] It was then decided to appoint a Drum Major to the band of C-in-C Plymouth at HMS *Drake*. Details of the Drum Major's course were finalised and, in 1962, an RMRO was issued that detailed the length of tenure of Drum Majors' appointments.[30] A year later an RM Instruction gave details of the selection procedure and the course detail[31].

In 1967 it was suggested that as well as GD and Buglers Branch candidates for Drum Major appointments, Band SNCOs should also be able to apply. This was duly incorporated into an RMRO[32].

In 1961 an instruction had been issued to change the buglers' stick drill[33] when coming to attention. The pause between coming to attention and bringing the sticks across the body was to be eliminated and the two movements combined into one.

1979 was a year of great importance to the Buglers since it was the year in which they were fully integrated into the RMBS. The Walden Report had drawn attention to the changing patterns of employment of the bugler, particularly the fact that he no longer spent a high proportion of time away from the bands. This integration was not popular with many buglers since they valued their independence and their close links with the Corps and the Royal Navy. Many still came into the Branch from various organisations such as orphanages and sea schools as a result of tough or unpleasant childhoods. Sometimes they only had a choice of the Services or the Merchant Navy if they were to avoid homelessness. As a result, whilst they were institutionalised, they were also independent and used to an ordered life of discipline and duty.[34] An Order[35] stated that whilst the buglers would become part of the RMBS they would remain as separate sections of the technical branch of the Corps and would retain their own promotion rosters. WOs and SNCOs in the Buglers Branch would still be entitled to become candidates for selection for promotion to Officers on the RM Special Duties list.

This most important period was drawing to a close. The planning, the discussions and the changes that had so characterised the last ten years were very necessary in order to ensure, as far as possible, the future of the RMBS at a sensible and practical size and with the necessary resources. That process was still in hand and would continue to be of major importance. During this period the Band Service had nevertheless continued the work for which it was best known. Apart from the 'routine' work of Royal Tournaments, Edinburgh Tattoos, Beating Retreat and an extensive programme of concert work the bands had toured extensively, continually showing the flag in various parts of the world with, in addition to the work of the Royal Yacht Band, tours and visits to Tasmania, Canada, the United States, Seychelles, Iran and elsewhere.

Corps Bugle Major A C Crofts retired from the Royal Marines in 1983. He was the first member of the Buglers' Branch to be appointed a Warrant Officer 1st Class, Colin Bowden being the first to have been appointed Warrant Officer 2nd Class.

20th May 1981. 41 Commando finally disbands and the Royal Marines School of Music becomes the only incumbent of the huge barracks at Deal.

Band of HM RM Royal Marines School of Music, Drum Major J Griffith, march along Jubilee Drive, South Barracks in October 1990. The Officers' Mess is behind the band.

Band of HM Royal Marines Commander-in-Chief Naval Home Command, Drum Major G Naylor, on Eastney Parade for biennial inspection, 1989.

Royal Yacht Dance Band play on Veranda deck during a 'Sea-Day' lunch (Sea-Days were trade days). Dance Band wears the Divisional Tunic retained for Band use on the Royal Yacht. The saxophone player is the Royal Yacht Bandmaster. Note the lightweight drum kit that could be easily carried through hatchways.

Beating Retreat 1991, Horse Guards Parade. The Massed Bands under Corps Drum Major M Saywell marching from Wellington Barracks to Horse Guards Parade.

On the way to the Falklands the Task Force stopped at Ascension Island for training. Whilst there the Band of HM Royal Marines Commando Forces Beat Retreat.

Rehearsal for Beating Retreat on Horse Guards Parade with the Massed Bands in the distinctive Lovat uniform.

The Band of HM Royal Marines Commander-in-Chief Fleet (Drum Major D Archer) march under Admiralty Arch and up the Mall at the head of the Royal Marines Association on the 26th April 1987.

The Band of the Royal Marines Commander-in-Chief Fleet (Drum Major BA Walton) in shirt-sleeve order rehearse with the ship's company of HMS London in Jebel Ali, United Arab Emirates 1990 (deployment to Iraq on RFA Argus).

A traditional feature of the annual Festival of Remembrance at the Royal Albert Hall is the display by the Royal Marines.

Kosovo Band's Corps of Drums combined entertainment with their medical and other duties. December 2000. (Photograph courtesy Blue Band)

201

1983 Edinburgh Tattoo featured the massed bands of the Royal Marines (Lt Col G A C Hoskins) supported by the Massed Pipes and Drums.

The Massed Bands of the Royal Marines (200 strong) led by Corps Drum Major D Dawson at the 1987 Royal Tournament when the theme was 'Neptune, God of the Sea'.

Despite the first night of the Royal Military Tattoo 2000 being marred by rain the whole event was a technical and musical success. Here the Tri-Service bands led by RM Corps Drum Major AD Bridges and conducted by Lt Col RA Waterer can be seen wearing capes for the first night performance. (Photograph courtesy RMBS).

12th July 2001. Plymouth Hoe. Two Bugle Majors, Buglers and bass drummers, under the command of the Corps Bugle Major march on to retrieve the piled drums following the Presentation of Colours to 40, 42 and 45 Commando. (Photograph by author).

The 1999 Mountbatten Festival of Music at the Royal Albert Hall is the annual showcase for the Royal Marines Band Service. Here the massed bands, playing 'Star Trek Generations', are conducted by Lt Peter Best. (Photograph courtesy Blue Band).

Royal Beat Retreat 2003. To mark the 50th anniversary of the Duke of Edinburgh's appointment as Captain General Royal Marines the Massed Bands Beat Retreat in the garden of Buckingham Palace. The Corps Bugle Major (WO2 C Lawton) conducts the bugle fanfare St Barbaras. (Photograph Royal Marines).

CHAPTER EIGHT

War, Peace and Violence through the Eighties

As the decade opened the RMBS had ten bands plus the RMSM and twelve Volunteer Band Instructors. This totalled five hundred and fourteen musicians and buglers and one hundred and twenty-four Juniors under training.

Band	DoM/Bandmaster
Royal Marines School of Music	Lt Col J R Mason
C-in-C Naval Home Command	Capt G A C Hoskins
C-in-C Fleet	Capt T Freestone
Commando Forces	Capt H C Farlow
Flag Officer Scotland and Northern Ireland	Lt R J P Kempton
Flag Officer Naval Home Command	Lt W J P Rider
Commando Training Centre RM	Lt K E Sivyer
Flag Officer Plymouth	Lt M Goss
Britannia Royal Naval College	WOII C J Sheppard
Flag Officer Third Flotilla (FOF3)[1]	WOII R D Baker

Instructors were with the following Volunteer Bands:

Band	DoM/Bandmaster
HMS *Bristol*	BdCSgt P J Rutterford
HMS *Collingwood*	BdCSgt P W Fryer
HMS *Fisgard*	Mr B Oates
HMS *Neptune*	BdCSgt M Ashton
HMS *Norfolk*	BdCSgt F Bryson-Bassett
HMS *Caledonia*	BdCSgt A L Harwood
HMS *Heron*/HMS *Osprey*	BdCSgt S Waite
Portsmouth Royal Naval Volunteer Band	BdCSgt D Buberle
HMS *Hermes* [2]	
HMS *Sultan*/HMS *Dolphin*	BdCSgt S Richardson
HMS *Fife*	BdCSgt R W I Baker
HMS *Intrepid*	BdCSgt K Hargreaves

Training Company, RMSM, was under Director of Music Capt A C Finney. The Junior Musicians and Buglers were being increasingly used in support of the trained bands giving them valuable experience. This included a trip to Canada with the RMSM Band for the National Exhibition at Toronto. The band of BRNC also went to Canada where the RM Massed Bands paraded with bands from the United States, New Zealand and Canada and the Gurkhas. CTC band visited the United States and the band of FOF3, following a deployment with HMS *Intrepid* and summer leave, embarked in HMS *Invincible*.

Whilst, on the surface, all seemed normal for the Band Service at this time, further changes were being planned. The recommendations of the Walden Report began to take effect and this, combined with cuts to the 1981 Defence Budget, prompted Lt Col J R Mason to make this announcement to the Band Service through the 'Blue Band':

> Since World War II successive governments have found it necessary to streamline the Services to meet the changing needs of Britain in today's world structure. It was inevitable that the latest close scrutiny of the Defence Budget in January this year would result in proportionate changes in the structure of the Band Service, in line with the Corps and the Royal Navy in general. As we all know, the Band Service contribution to the savings target is a reduction in strength of three bands over a period of about five years. The reduction will be achieved by a carefully calculated withdrawal date for each band that will coincide with a numerical reduction in the overall strength of the Band Service caused by natural wastage, and a lower recruiting intake. There will be no redundancies and the regulations governing re-engagement will remain unchanged. The overall reduction in numbers will be approximately 100 all ranks, with proportionate reductions in the Director of Music, Bandmaster and Non-Commissioned Officer rank structures.

In the following issue Lt Col Mason was able to announce that it had been confirmed that there would be no further cuts to the Band Service, other than those already decided. He also emphasised that strict control of expenditure on travel and associated expense would be necessary and that this, combined with the lower manning levels that the Band Service was working towards, would cause concern about the ability to meet the demands of major ceremonial, and events such as the Royal Tournament, in future years. A decision to remain in Deal for the immediate future was taken and at the end of 1981 an announcement was made that the RMSM had become a self-contained unit within the Corps since 41 Cdo had finally disbanded. The unit comprised three companies, Headquarters, Band and Training plus a Commandant and Deputy Commandant. All other Corps Units had been relocated, mainly to the West Country. Immediate plans for changes to the Band Service during early 1982 were postponed as the situation in the South Atlantic began to deteriorate.

During their deployment on board HMS Hermes the Band of Flag Officer 3rd Flotilla (FOF3) visited Hamilton, Bermuda. During their display they 'formed lane' for beatings by the Corps of Drums.

The Bands in the Falklands War.

In March 1982 Argentine military forces invaded the Falkland Islands and South Georgia. The Government, after a suitable period of diplomatic discussion, decided to assemble and send a Task Force to the South Atlantic. On Sunday 4th April the Staffs of HQ Commando Forces and HQ 3 Cdo Bde briefed all Commanding Officers and Adjutants regarding the deployment to the South Atlantic. The Band of Commando Forces was added to the Brigade. Trained as stretcher-bearers and in First Aid, the intention was for the band to be based in SS *Canberra* initially and possibly come ashore later.[3] In the early hours of the morning of the 4th Capt J Ware, D of M of the Commando Forces, was asked to recall his band from leave. He expected that their duties would be as Barrack Guards, allowing the release of men from the units, and he was most surprised to learn that they would be embarking in the *Canberra*. Both Maj Gen J J Moore, commanding Commando Forces, and Brig J Thompson, commanding 3 Cdo Bde, wanted the band to function as a band as well as in its military role. To this end the band instruments had to be smuggled aboard in one of the large 'chacon' containers without the media being aware. First priority was to draw the necessary equipment and to begin training as part of Commando Logistic Regiment's Medical Squadron. The band left the barracks on the 8th April and joined the *Canberra* at Southampton. As the ship sailed it was played out by the Band of FOF3 (WO II T Attwood), also recalled from Easter leave. Prior to leave they had been on board HMS *Intrepid* and then HMS *Fearless*. FOF3 band then returned to Easter leave only to be again recalled, this time to fly to Gibraltar to join SS *Uganda*. This educational cruise ship was being hurriedly converted to a hospital ship and the band was soon thrown into the hard work of making the ship ready for its new role. Tons of stores had to be loaded and distributed and specialist equipment brought on board, fitted and made ready. They became part of Naval Party 1830, Surgical Support Team No. 4 but were better known as NOSH, (Naval Ocean-going Surgical Hospital) and underwent training for their stretcher-bearer role. The average age of this band was twenty-one. The ship's complement numbered one hundred and twenty plus the band and it was evident that, when organised into watches, the medical skills were spread very thinly. Medical training for the band was initiated and as she sailed towards Sierra Leone they became involved with exercising boat launch and recovery, flying stations and Replenishment at Sea. They designed and constructed CASEVAC (casualty evacuation) routes to help them in their role of quickly unloading casualties from helicopters on the landing pad and getting them down to the wards and the clearing station below. They also played for on-board Church Services and gave concerts, the band being augmented by Surgeon Lt Cdr D Baker, an accomplished flautist, and Nursing Officer Elizabeth Law who became resident vocalist.

The Commando Forces Band began by establishing themselves aboard the *Canberra*. They removed their instruments from the container in which they had come aboard and moved them to the band's new home, which turned out to be a Ladies' toilet. Periods of training and refresher courses in radio and signals procedure, the preparation of casualty control lists, Nuclear, Biological and Chemical Warfare (NBCW) updates and physical training on deck were all taken in the stride of the band. Rehearsals were fitted in and after a few days at sea they attended a Medical Squadron briefing about what would be done if things went badly. The band was impressed with the thinking that had gone into this plan, called Casualty Reception Action Plan and known by the inevitable and unfortunate acronym of CRAPLAN. Next evening a concert was given in the Stadium Bar. The band felt rather uncomfortable that the men watching their concert might be the same men who needed this room when the Stadium Bar assumed its emergency role of operating theatre.

Captain John Ware rehearses the Band of Commando Forces on board SS Canberra on the way to the South Atlantic. The scaffolding is part of the reinforcement to the ship's deck required to enable helicopters to land.

On the 16th the band received training for administering morphine and the level of training increased. Full-scale exercises for disembarkation took place with the 3 Parachute Regiment (3 Para) as guinea pigs and the musicians as marshals. The band also helped with the handling of loads being distributed, or redistributed, around the Fleet by helicopter. The band was cross decked to both *Sir Percivale* and HMS *Fearless* in order to give concerts. They were shocked by the conditions on board caused by the amount of stores and the additional men being carried. Another task given to the band was that of assisting with the air disembarkation. An exercise took place in which the whole of 3 Para were flown off the ship.

SS *Canberra* paused at Ascension Island for a busy period of stores rationalisation and training at the end of which the band gave a concert for 40 Cdo who were joined by their former CO, Brig J Thompson. The first item on the programme was the *William Tell Overture*, which began to a stunned silence. However the 'Lone Ranger' passage at the end broke the ice and a mighty roar went up. The troops were invited to join in, using various percussion instruments, as the concert progressed with Latin American numbers. Audience participation increased until the concert became a virtual sing-song. The concert ended with the band's special finale number - *Hootenanny*, a foot-tapping, hand-clapping selection of country and western tunes. The concert ended with the whole Commando on its feet. Lt Col M Hunt, 40 Cdo CO, told Capt Ware that "if he could have given his men rifles and put them ashore at that moment they would have walked right across and nothing would have stopped them."

The band was equally as impressed with the Commandos as the Commandos were with the band:

BdSgt R Ireland wrote:

We played for 40 Cdo and what a concert! The men of the Commando were entertaining the band with sing-songs, '*Zulu Warriors*' and anything else they could think of… the cheering and singing must have been heard at home. The men were so enthusiastic and the spirit they have is incredible. Brig Thompson could lead these men on a route march right through Argentina. Heaven help the Argies if this lot go ashore.

Whilst at Ascension the band disembarked and marched to Georgetown to rehearse for Beating Retreat but without instruments - the band sang, to the amusement of those who were watching! The real thing took place next day on the old garrison parade ground with the garrison church and the barracks that were built under the supervision of Royal Marines in the nineteenth century. The training and refresher courses continued whilst at Ascension and included weapon training, use of Arctic ration packs, a film of battle injuries in Vietnam to give an indication of what the band might have to deal with, a lecture on distress and bereavement and others. In the evenings they entertained with pop groups and concerts of various types[4].

Back in England the Commando Forces' band-room was turned into a coffee shop and information centre for all the wives of 3 Cdo Bde with Band Secretary, BdSgt R J Ward, and his rear-party holding coffee-mornings and dispensing cheerfulness at all times.

By the time that the Task Force had sailed 8,000 miles the Commando Forces Band on board *Canberra* had changed from a purely musical role to a fully-fledged medical one in an operational situation. The weather had changed from hot at Ascension to very cold with rough seas as they approached the Falklands. As *Uganda* sailed south she made for the Red Cross safe area, arriving there at 1700hrs on 11th May. The band stowed their instruments, and waited.

As the *Canberra* sailed south so the lectures and training continued: 'Aircraft Recognition', 'Falklands Weapons' and 'Eye Injuries'. On 15th May the ship came within striking distance of Argentine aircraft. Next day Surg Cdr R Jolly[5] briefed the band as part of Medical Squadron about the proposed invasion plans. Later the band spent several hours taking up floor tiles from the room to be used as an operating theatre, because of the fear of not being able to maintain sterile conditions.

It was decided that a landing should be made at San Carlos on the west coast of the island. In order for the attack to take place *Canberra's* Commandos had to be cross-decked to the Assault Ship HMS *Fearless*. The musicians were given the task of acting as guides by leading the various sub-units, fully equipped and armed, through the passageways of the ship and out to the boat-decks. This had to be managed carefully in order to get the men to the right place at the right time. On 20th May the band were mainly occupied with ammunition sentry duties until, at 1120hrs the emergency stretcher party closed up on deck and four members of the band carried down the first fatality to be brought on board the ship, one of the crew of a Sea-King helicopter that had crashed.

Friday the 21st was the most action packed day as far as the *Canberra* was concerned. The ship was under continual cannon and missile attack but the band continued to unload casualties from the helicopters and move them down to the reception area. The method that had been developed for this was to carry the stretcher from the helicopter to the head of a ramp. A musician on the deck would lower an injured man down the ramp using a rope pulley system. On the deck below would be two men ready to guide the stretcher down and to carry it to the ward or the theatre. Musn G Latham was on the deck lowering a wounded man down the ramp when the *Canberra* came under attack from what appears to have been three Argentine aircraft. He coolly continued to lower the wounded man and only took cover when he knew that his colleagues below had taken responsibility for the situation. During this time he was in a very exposed position. Later he recalled the sick faces of the men as he lowered them down the ramp. "Their faces were drained. You could not see their wounds because they were covered in blankets. But, there was blood on the ramp which had to be wiped off". The ship was at maximum alert all day and the Argentinian air attacks were almost continuous. The men continued these duties throughout the next day, working from 0100hrs, being woken after only two hours sleep to work through the night. They were relieved to hear that now that the landings were established the ship would sail from Falkland Sound and would return each day at dusk to evacuate casualties. Before this occurred the band were involved with the burial at sea of four Royal Marines. A member of the band prepared the bodies and then the small Church band played the *Naval Hymn*. Buglers Naylor and Smith sounded *Last Post*. On the 23rd the band shifted stores from 0900 until 1700hrs when it was too dark to see. They calculated that they had moved about 120 tons. The pop group then rigged up to entertain the survivors of HMS *Ardent* who had been brought aboard.[6] And so it continued; on 2nd June twenty-seven Argentinian casualties were brought on board. They were Special Forces and were considered dangerous so the musicians were issued with SMGs and live ammunition.

The band continued to move and unload casualties, help in the wards and provide stores moving parties. As the operation ashore progressed so the number of Argentinian prisoners increased. Four thousand had to be documented, de-loused, fed and guarded. Following the surrender on 14th June *Canberra* took on many more prisoners and the band was now armed at all times. The prisoners were then taken to Puerto Madryn in Argentina. During the passage the band threw all Argentine military equipment over the side of the ship. Upon return to the Falklands the band gave two concerts in Stanley Cathedral before leaving for the United Kingdom.

Whilst *Canberra* had seen action in Falklands Sound the FOF3 band in SS *Uganda* had also been heavily committed. The casualties started as a trickle but the flow soon increased, sailors with burns and flash burns and marines with gunshot and other wounds. The band carried them below, to the operating theatres and back to the wards, they took them to X-ray, they dressed their wounds and changed their beds. Each member of the band fought his own battle against exhaustion and BM Attwood's main task became one of carefully watching his own men. On several occasions he had to order his men to rest or get a meal. Then the Argentine prisoners came. Amongst them were boys of thirteen, who had all been living in the field for weeks and had dysentery and so they were bathed, reassured and guarded. The medical teams were fully stretched and the band lent a hand by removing stitches and, on one occasion, even hand ventilated a marine with breathing difficulties. The red crosses painted on the ship did not prevent the Argentine Air Force from 'buzzing' the ship. A total of seven hundred British and Argentinian casualties received treatment aboard *Uganda* during the operation.

847 Naval Air Squadron were surviving and working in a freezing tin hut at Navy Point. FOF3 band decided to provide them with supplies and some entertainment, both of which the Squadron greatly appreciated. Meanwhile, a few miles away, two Buglers were sounding *Last Post* as a burial took place on a wet hillside overlooking Ajax Bay. The band played for the return of the Governor, Rex Hunt, to the island and they also led an

Airborne Forces parade through Stanley and, finally, *Uganda*, with the band on board, returned to Southampton on 9th August.

The Commando Forces Band played every night during the journey back to England. This was an important phase for the returning troops since it allowed them to relax. On the last night at sea Capt J Ware's new march *San Carlos* was played during a Beat Retreat that ended, by popular demand, with *Hootenanny*. As *Canberra* sailed up the Channel, buglers sounded appropriate bugle calls from the ship's bridge. The band was playing as the ship neared the jetty then, after a final *Hootenanny*, the instruments were put aside and the band joined the others at the ship's rail as the Band of C-in-C Naval Home Command played *Canberra* alongside[7].

The two bands undoubtedly upheld the reputation of their predecessors who, during the two world wars, performed so well in action. Major Ewen Southby-Tailyour[8] wrote:

> John Ware (Commando Forces Director of Music) and his men organised what could only be described as a 'mini-prom' in the ship's concert hall. It was magnificent and as many of the embarked passengers as possible crowded into the theatre where the band Beat Retreat, the Corps of Drums countermarched and the audience took part. There were the usual songs straight from the Royal Albert Hall and the evening ended with the traditional Naval Sunset and Evening hymn. This was only a tiny part of the band's routines; for they were in demand non-stop with discos, pop groups, jazz groups, classical ensembles and even impromptu operatic arias. Let no one take them away from us for their presence in action is an integral part of the morale (including their medical support duties) of the Royal Marines, and morale has an irreplaceable role in achieving, and celebrating, victory.

On 12th October representatives of the Task Force, with FOF3 Band leading the RN contingent and the Band of Commando Forces leading the RM contingent, marched through the City of London to the Guildhall where they were entertained to lunch by the Lord Mayor. The bands proudly wore their Lovat uniforms and their green berets. It is believed that this, and a similar parade in Plymouth, was the only occasion when the Commando Forces Band wore the Prince of Wales Plumes as part of the cap badge in their berets.

Shortly after this, on 1st November, Lt Col J Mason retired and Lt Col G A C Hoskins, although originally gazetted to assume the dual responsibilities of Principal Director of Music, Royal Marines and Commandant RM Deal, became PDM whilst Lt Col D Watson RM became Commandant[9]. The reason for the Commandant General's decision to revert to the old system was the forthcoming changes of use, and possible expansion into a tri-service Defence School of Music, at Deal.[10]

The Falklands War had slowed the pace of defence cutbacks and, for a while, the Government found it difficult to restart them because of the strength of feeling that the country had for the Services. The embarrassment factor did not hinder the Government for too long and, in April 1983 the band of FONAC ceased to exist. This was a very popular band, a small band that achieved a great deal in the field of public relations. Regular appearances on the BBC 'Pebble Mill at One', at air days, in schools and in many concert halls all contributed to its popularity. The 'Blue Band' editorial comment ended with the simple phrase, "What a shame". Forty-three years' service to the Fleet Air Arm at HMS *Daedalus* and HMS *Heron* and on countless aircraft carriers ended when this band was disestablished. The first two band casualties of the Second World War had come from an aircraft-carrier's band.[11] From now on the Fleet Air Arm would have to rely on its own Volunteer Bands.

On the 20th May 1983 SS *Canberra*, having been completely refitted, sailed from Southampton for a cruise to Spain and back. It was appropriate that the Band of Commando Forces played for an hour on the quay as the passengers boarded and then went aboard themselves. The next day was San Carlos Day and the skipper, Capt D Scott-Masson, followed Royal Navy custom of parading a Baron of Beef to mark the anniversary of a successful engagement. In order to satisfy demand the band gave two consecutive concerts in the Stadium. They ensured that the music was patriotic and they received tremendous ovations. The Big Band played in the evening and, although it was intended they would only give two or three shows during the two-week trip they actually played almost every night - which meant that they missed a lot of evening dinners! Other combinations that played to entertain the passengers were the jazz quartet, the eight-piece dance band, a string quartet, the rock group, a full orchestra and a military band. It was intended that the band should Beat Retreat in Uigo, Spain, but the British authorities decided that the locals might not appreciate a British military band standing on Spanish soil on the anniversary of the Falklands War playing *Rule Britannia* so it was cancelled. A few months later the Commando Forces Band supported the visit of HM The Queen and the Captain General to Royal Marines, Poole.

The Service of Remembrance at the Cenotaph. The Corps Bugle Major and Buglers, with the RAF Trumpeters in rear, ready to take their traditional role in the annual Service. Capes are always worn for this occasion.

On the 2nd November 1983 the Band of C-in-C Naval Home Command marched a Naval Guard of Honour with the Queen's Colour of the Fleet along Birdcage Walk and took up position in the Horse Guards Approach Road close to Foreign Office Green. HM The Queen and most of the Royal Family gathered there for the unveiling of the statue of Admiral of the Fleet The Earl Mountbatten of Burma. The Band of the Life Guards played during the assembly and the Royal Marines, with the State trumpeters of the Life Guards played during the ceremony. *The Mountbatten March* was played to march on the Guard of Honour, and after the dedication the band played *Preobrajensky*, *Greensleeves* and *Where E'er You Walk*. To march off the guard the band played *Heart of Oak*, *A Life on the Ocean Wave* and *Under the White Ensign*.

The major events of 1984 were the tri-ennial Beating Retreat on Horse Guards Parade and the Royal Tournament. A look at the conditions behind the scenes of a Royal Tournament might be appropriate. This particular tournament featured the Naval Service and had the title '*A Day in the Life of a Naval Helicopter Pilot*'. The Massed Bands not only had to provide a display and the finale but also an orchestral spot. The bands congregated at Deal for a week of rehearsals before moving to London and Warwick Hall. Home for the next three weeks was on the dusty top level and consisted of a concrete floor, old metal bunk beds and one rickety locker between two men. Washing facilities were limited and taking a shower necessitated using the tradesmen's lift to get down to the basement followed by a journey through a maze of underground passages. An ability to make the best of whatever circumstances prevail is always apparent within the Corps and although they could not improve the showers they could build and run the 'Massed Bands Bar'. This was vital to the morale of the men and it became not only a place to drink but also a Citizens Advice Bureau and certainly a place to unwind and relieve the boredom. The coffee-boat was adjacent to the bar and this was also vital to the morale and well-being of the men. Both of these areas were staffed and stocked by volunteer members of the Band Service and often involved them in frantic changes of clothing between finishing a performance and providing this service. There was also a video parlour and occasional cabarets. Working extremely hard were two barbers, also from the Band Service. So cheap and so professional were all of these services that many of the other participants used them and the area became the shopping and entertainments centre of Earl's Court. On the first Sunday the massed bands were moved to Wellington Barracks, with all of the other participants, for the publicity parade past Horse Guards Parade and along the Mall. During the Earl's Court rehearsals carpenters, painters and electricians continued to build the sets. Once the real performances began a major problem was the waiting time between performances; not long enough to go anywhere but long enough to get very bored. The Tournament was a great success but, as always, the bands were pleased to come down from their hot, dusty temporary home - always far less comfortable than those occupied by the horses - and make their way home or to barracks.

At the end of 1984 the Band Service consisted of:

Royal Marines School of Music	Lt Col G A C Hoskins
C-in-C Naval Home Command	Capt P Heming
C-in-C Fleet	Capt E P Whealing
Flag Officer Scotland and Northern Ireland	Lt M Goss
Flag Officer Plymouth	Lt J R Perkins
Flag Officer Third Flotilla	Bm (WO2) A L Harwood
Britannia Royal Naval College	Bm (WO1) P Rutterford
Royal Marines Commando Forces	Capt J M Ware
Commando Training Centre RM	Lt R R Starr
RMSM Training Company	Capt W J Rider

The intended relocation of the RMSM to Eastney still had not taken place. Pressure from the Deal local community and its representatives for the maintenance of the status quo was extremely strong and the costs of moving to Eastney were rising. The plans for further reductions to the Band Service continued when, in 1985, the bands of Commando Forces and Commando Training Centre RM, formed in the early 1970s, were reconstructed. The Commando Forces band was a direct descendant of the Plymouth Group band and, as such, its members wore the Prince of Wales Plumes as part of their cap-badge and helmet plate. Transfer of the Plumes to what had been the other half of the split Plymouth Group Band at Commando Training Centre was approved by HM the Queen on 12th March 1985[12]. On 1st April 1985 the Commando Forces band ceased to exist and the band of Commando Training Centre became the Band of the Royal Marines Commandos, based at Lympstone with Capt J M Ware as the Director of Music. Because

The Royal Yacht Band, part of the Band of C-in-C Naval Home Command, on the Veranda Deck of the Royal Yacht during the 1986 Royal Tour. At this time (November) the Yacht was in Shanghai. During this period the Prince and Princess of Wales were embarked.

of this arrangement the band had full authority to wear the Prince of Wales Plumes as it was a direct and continuous descendant of the Plymouth Group Band.

During the period, September to November 1985, the band of the RMSM toured the United States with the Pipes and Drums of the Argyll and Sutherland Highlanders. The tour, which commenced with a press call on board the aircraft carrier USS *Intrepid*, covered 16,000 miles and seventy-three performances in sixty-eight major cities with only four free days during the three months' period. Lt Col Hoskins was the military tour commander with Lt D Cole as his assistant and principal arranger. BM T Attwood and a Piper travelled ten days ahead of the main party to carry out publicity interviews and to check each of the venues. Built in to the opening ceremony was the facility for having a local Colour Guard paraded. The USMC fully supported the tour by providing Colour Guards and uniformed attendance, including a number of persons to take the salute, at most venues. The tour ended with a performance in Madison Square Garden that attracted a remarkably complimentary review in the Arts Section of the *New York Times*.

1986 opened with HMY *Britannia* en route to New Zealand where the Royal Family came aboard. Having just passed through the Suez Canal news came through that civil war had broken out in Aden. The Queen agreed that the Yacht should assist in Operation *Balzac*, the evacuation of British nationals from Aden. The crew transformed the Royal Yacht into an evacuation ship, including a large sick-bay, and the members of the band were all assigned tasks for helping the evacuees when they came aboard. The Bandmaster (R C Grainger) and the Drum Major (J K Griffiths) were to be immigration officers with the remainder of the band divided into beach, stores and stretcher parties. HMS *Jupiter* and HMS *Newcastle* joined the Yacht and, when the situation ashore was felt to be at crisis point, the Yacht was ordered to move towards Khormaksar Beach, close to the British Embassy. BdSgt Salmon, who could speak some Arabic, BdCpl Oliver, Musn Morris and Bug Brown were attached to the RM Detachment. 152 people of 26 nationalities were taken aboard. The boats were unable to beach so the men from the Yacht had to carry the children and the injured from the beach to the boats. The fighting was getting heavier with tanks and artillery now engaged. Damage was widespread. The ship sailed for Djibouti to land the evacuees and, on the way, the band 'rigged up' and gave a concert on the Veranda deck. Next morning the band fell in for Colours only to discover that, with all the excitement, they had forgotten to set their watches to local time and were an hour too soon! The Yacht returned to Zinjibar where a further 200 people were taken off and transferred to HMS *Jupiter*. Over the next few days a further 441 people were embarked from Little Aden and returned to Djibouti. By the end of the emergency 1,068 men, women and children of 55 different nationalities had been brought aboard and, as always, the band had thrown itself into assisting in any way it could - from musical concerts and entertainment to carrying bags of rice and warming baby bottles[13].

Once again the Royal Marines undertook London Duties in 1986. This was the first time since 1978 and only the third occasion that this had occurred. This time 42 Cdo had the responsibility for mounting guard on Buckingham Palace, St James's Palace and the Tower of London. For the first time a guard was required at Windsor Castle so an extra band had to be provided. The RMSM supported L Company and Support Company in London whilst the Fleet Band from Northolt supported K Company at Windsor.

By now the frequent Commando tours of duty in Northern Ireland were supported by their own Cdo Forces Band and also FOSNI's Band would visit not only to entertain but also to recruit. 1986 found their visit to West Belfast coinciding with that of 45 Cdo. Apart from entertaining 'Royal' the band also carried out two public engagements. An extract from an article[14] describes how they worked together:

> The band did a couple of displays, one at Musgrave Park Hospital which was the base of 45 Cdo 'B' Echelon. For this gig we had most of the Company on the ground and our own clearance/close protection patrol while we worked. We fell in behind the main gate and the patrol went out doing the whole bit... taking good cover...ducking and weaving... total observation... 'Royal' at his best. One minute later the band went out doing the whole bit... regimental march... immaculate dressing...marks of expression... 'Bandy' at his best. Both sides of the Corps on the ground together doing what they do best and doing it well.

The last of the cuts initiated in the 1980's took place in 1987 when the Band of the Flag Officer 3rd Flotilla was disbanded. This was a milestone for the Band Service since it was the demise of the last of the sea-going bands. The band of FOF3 had travelled the world in support of almost all of the RN's major ships, had been one of only two bands used in a military role in the Falklands and was the last band in the Band Service to be commanded by a Bandmaster. The band gave its final concert in Portsmouth Guildhall on the 25th March, the proceeds of which were given to charity.

Later in the year a new Commandant arrived. He was Lt Col J J Thompson and in his first entry in the Blue Band[15] he commented that, unlike his predecessor, he would not be involved in the Defence School of Music since that project was dead and the RMBS was on its own. It was also announced that, as from the 26th October 1987 the Depot, Deal would become the RMSM, Deal, giving a new autonomy within the Corps. Other changes occurred but they were mainly as a result of retirements and promotions so that, by the end of 1987 the RMBS consisted of the following bands:

Royal Marines School of Music	Lt Col G A C Hoskins
C-in-C Naval Home Command	Capt E P Whealing
C-in-C Fleet	Capt M Goss
Flag Officer Scotland and Northern Ireland	Lt P J Rutterford
Flag Officer Plymouth	Lt J R Perkins
Britannia Royal Naval College	Lt R R Starr
Royal Marines Commandos	Capt W J P Rider
RMSM Training Company	Capt J M Ware

1988, although not quiet, was a fairly routine year. However, a few significant or unusual events occurred. In the middle of the year it was announced that Capt J Ware would assume the mantle of Principal Director of Music upon the retirement of Lt Col G A C Hoskins in 1989. Prior to this Capt Ware undertook a six-month sabbatical that included working with 'The President's Own' United States Marine Band. The band of the RM Commandos undertook a trip to Norway, not to entertain but to undergo Arctic Survival Training. An RAF Hercules took them to the north of Norway and then down to the south of Norway, a seven hour round trip. They were billeted in pleasant holiday chalet accommodation where the only drawback was the fact that the galley was five miles away. After a spot of skiing the band endured many lectures before spending the next part of their stay carrying Bergen rucksacks and learning to survive in tents at night in the Arctic as well as survival in snow holes, and under snow sheets. On their departure they fell in, as if in a band, with Drum Major H Roberts using a ski-pole for a staff with the Director of Music (Capt J Rider) alongside and marched across the car park singing marches!

The band finally took part in a Medical Squadron Exercise that involved them in acting as a decontamination unit at the hospital complex.[16]

Prior to 1987 SNCOs selected for commissioning as SD Officers attended an eight-week Special Duties Officers' Course and, on completion, successful students attended a post commissioning course followed by, in the case of Band officers, an acquaint with the various duties required by the Band Service. 1988 saw a change and successful candidates from the SD Officers Selection Board attended a sixteen-week course in Officer Training at the Commando Training Centre RM. The second course of this type included for the first time a Band Officer, Lt J Hillier, who went on to win the coveted Sword of Honour at the end of his course.

The 4th May 1989 saw the retirement of Lt Col G A C Hoskins who was known as 'the last of the Burford Boys'. During his six and a half years as Principal Director of Music the number of bands had reduced from eleven to seven, but all were large bands. John Ware became Principal Director of Music.

Six months later, Lt Col Ware found himself having to cope with possibly the largest tragedy that the Band Service had ever suffered. On the night of 21st/22nd September 1989 two Irishmen who had rented a holiday home in Deal, the garden of which bordered the barracks, made their way over the boundary wall and into North Barracks. They left undetected and then, at 0825 the following morning, as members of the RMSM Band were in the Recreation Room preparing to assemble on the Parade for rehearsals a massive blast occurred within the room. The walls were blown out allowing the solid concrete roof to fall in. Marines were obviously the first to the scene but were quickly followed by the emergency services. Members of Junior Band were rehearsing on the parade when the blast occurred and were amongst the first to arrive on the scene and they began moving rubble in an attempt to extricate those who were inside. Rescue attempts were hampered as the press hired helicopters and hovered over the heads of those listening for signs of life within the ruined building. Local hospitals were alerted and the injured were taken to Canterbury, Dover and Deal. The Irish Republican Army later admitted responsibility for the atrocity. In due course the Globe and Laurel[17] openly criticised politicians for expressing ill-advised views, possibly in an effort to attract publicity, and also the media for their insensitivity with regard to the lurid way in which they portrayed the event. Two days after the explosion Countess Mountbatten of Burma, Vice Lord Lieutenant of Kent, accompanying Prince Philip, as Captain General, visited Deal and the hospitals where the injured lay. He reminded everyone that the British had a long and proud history of not giving in to those who imagined that they could bomb us into submission. Next day Mrs Thatcher, the Prime Minister, visited the Barracks making it abundantly clear that she knew where the fault lay. Later, the Archbishop of Canterbury also paid his respects. Thousands of flowers were left at the Barrack Gates and it is possible that this was the first time that this practice, now so widespread, had occurred.

Lt Col J Ware later explained that he had been in Portsmouth when the news came through and that the first reactions of everyone were of shock, horror and disbelief. His abiding memory of that Friday was of meeting the survivors and through the shock and the numbness came the determination to get back onto the road and "do what we do best". From that came the decision to march through Deal. This had a three-fold purpose. Firstly it was an act of therapy for the band and secondly it was an act of intent to tell the world that the RMBS was going to continue in the manner for which it was famous. Thirdly it was an act of defiance to show that the bombing was a failure because the Band Service, the country and the world were determined that the bombers would not succeed.

A week after the event, on 29th September, the Junior Musicians and Junior Buglers marched along Canada Road, halted and laid a wreath and then returned to Barracks. A short while later, out of the prying sight of the media, Corps Drum Major J Griffiths called the Band of the RMSM to attention and then the band stepped off to *A Life on the Ocean Wave*. They marched out of the gates and halted as a mark of respect where the flowers had been laid. After a minute's silence the band led the parade through the town of Deal proudly bearing their scars. Gaps were left in the ranks of the band to show where they had lost their comrades. The Commandant General took the salute and, as they passed, Standards of a number of local Associations were lowered in respect. All the staff of the

School followed the band. The march was shown nationwide on television. As they marched they remembered the men who had been killed:

> BdCpl John (Andy) Cleatheroe
> BdCpl Trevor Davis
> BdCpl Dave McMillan
> BdCpl Dean Pavey
> Musn Mick Ball
> Musn Richard Fice
> Musn Richard (Taff) Jones
> Musn Chris Nolan
> Musn Mark Petch
> Musn Tim Reeves
> Musn Bob Simmonds

Afterwards the Commandant General, Sir Martin Garrod said, very firmly, that the men who had perpetrated this act:

> …were not freedom fighters nor idealists, nothing of the sort, we are talking about thugs, extortionists, torturers, murderers and cowards - the scum of the earth. The sacrifice of our magnificent musicians will not be in vain, our fine Band Service will play on and we will emerge stronger and more determined than ever before to end and destroy this foul and dark force for evil.

The Band of the Royal Marines School of Music (Drum Major JF O'Connell) with drums, staff and dress belt draped, at the funeral of their comrades killed in the Deal bombing.

A fortnight after the bombing the pre-planned Band Service Reunion and Memorial Service took place. Most of the serving Band Service attended plus three to four hundred retired members. A marquee had to be erected alongside the Church and the reunion venue was transferred to the much larger drill shed. A large Corps of Drums gave a magnificent display on the Saturday. On Sunday a composite orchestra played at the Church Service and then, as always, the Junior Band Beat Retreat. It was decided that, henceforth, the Reunion weekend and Memorial Service would be held on the weekend closest to the infamous 22nd September.

A Relief Fund administered by a Board of Trustees was set up to account for, and disburse, the assets of the Fund. By the third week in November three-quarters of a million pounds had been donated and a substantial amount had been paid out. The Band Service rigorously pursued a 'business as usual' policy and not one engagement was missed. A Memorial Service for those killed was held in Canterbury Cathedral on the 22nd October, an event of national significance that was attended by the Captain General and the Prime Minister. Before the service the orchestra of the RMSM played *In Memorium* (Sullivan) *Finale from Symphony No 11* (Lloyd)[18] and the Intermezzo from *Cavalleria Rusticana* (Mascagni). As the procession left at the end of the service they played the Finale from Beethoven's Symphony No. 5 in C Minor. The appearance of the RMSM Band and the Junior Choir at the Festival of Remembrance was particularly poignant as was the following Mountbatten Festival of Music when HM The Queen and Prince Philip attended.

It was at this time that it was finally decided that RMB Eastney would close with the band of C-in-C Naval Home Command due to move into the RN Barracks, HMS *Nelson*, later in 1989. This meant that Deal would remain open for the foreseeable future.

During the night of the 21-22 May 2003 the former Royal Marines concert hall at Deal was destroyed by fire. Firefighters managed to save the Deal bombing Memorial Garden plaque from damage.
Photo: F Yardley (Former RM QMS and First Drill).

CHAPTER NINE

Consolidation Through the Nineties

Funds were raised for the Deal Bombing Relief Fund through a host of events including many that were initiated or undertaken by members of the Band Service themselves. These mainly consisted of sponsored events but included the production of a special recording and lapel badges. An unusual event was the 'All Stars Concert' that featured one hundred and twenty ex-members of the Band Service under the leadership of Lt Col P Neville. Over £7,000 was raised from their concert at the Winter Gardens, Margate, which subsequently became an annual event.

Defence cuts included a moratorium on spending which delayed the closure of Eastney and the relocation of C-in-C Naval Home Command's band to HMS *Nelson*. This led to a postponement of the decision regarding the new location of the RMSM, which meant that Deal was expected to retain the School for perhaps a further five years. The 1990 Royal Tournament having the theme of 'The Sea Soldier' not only featured the band and a display by the King's Squad but also featured the 2nd Marine Division Band of the USMC, the Royal Netherlands Marine Corps and the Spanish Marine Corps Band and Drill Display team. The appearance of the latter caused the organisers to remove the battle-honour 'Gibraltar' from the large Corps crest that was suspended over the arena.

During 1990 a study into the size, deployment, terms and conditions of service, promotion and the military role of the RMBS was begun. This was the Hunt Report that was completed by the autumn of 1990 and resulted in a number of important changes. The Band Service was to undertake a modified Basic Fitness Test (BFT) and a new Military Training package was to be designed for implementation in April 1991. More musical tuition was introduced earlier into the initial training curriculum and Command Courses were graded instead of being pass or fail. Overall terms and conditions of service and the recruitment of women into the Band Service were to be the subjects of further studies.

On the 2nd October 1990 an advance party from C-in-C Fleet Band joined RFA *Argus*, the Primary Casualty Receiving Unit, at Plymouth in preparation for deployment to the Persian Gulf. Upon checking their accommodation they discovered that the mattresses were all 3" too long for the triple bunks and that the individual lockers were all too narrow for a coat-hanger! They were soon involved with the ship's routine and loaded stores, equipment and medical supplies[1]. Two days later the rest of the band under Capt M Goss joined - the largest formed body of Royal Marines to be deployed to the Gulf. Lt Col J Ware, veteran of the Falklands War, wrote:

> Engaged primarily as medical orderlies they will also be active in a musical capacity, providing the invaluable moral and psychological support which only a band can. Once again, as in the Falklands Campaign in 1982, the Band Service has the opportunity to prove that, even in modern times, there remains a need for a group of able musicians who are also intelligent and flexible enough to adapt quickly and efficiently to any task which may present itself.

Included amongst the pre-embarkation training was fire fighting at sea and, once at sea, training included first aid, Nuclear Biological and Chemical Decontamination (NBCD) and stretcher handling. Training and exercises continued on arrival in the Gulf and the band volunteered themselves as First Aid teams. Rehearsals and concerts were part of the ongoing routine of duties, including ship protection, and training. By mid-

The Band of C-in-C Fleet (Capt M Goss) on board RFA Argus, 1990.

December the ship was frequently at Action Stations although the Fleet Band's war did not start until January 17th when four potential air threats occurred. Capt Goss visited the bands of the Scots Guards, The Parachute Regiment and the Royal Anglians at the 33rd Field Hospital and Maj D Price came aboard *Argus* with a section of the Scots Guards Band to play for the crew. As the allies gained supremacy the ship sailed north and the band became involved in watching for mines. Shortly after this, Iraqi bodies began to be recovered from the sea and the band were involved in preparing them for burial at sea - a most unpleasant duty that moved the ship's Chaplain, the Reverend S Pickering to write:

> I know I am quite biased, but it is just an example of their fortitude, professionalism and dedication, all exemplified with their usual courtesy and good humour. A joy to work amongst and with. Thank you. Every Blessing[2.]

Following the cease-fire the ship moved south through the minefields again and two days later Capt Goss received a signal from C-in-C Home Fleet asking where his band was and why had it not returned home with the medics? Eight days later, and after Beating Retreat at the British Embassy at Abu Dhabi - possibly the last occasion when a RM Band wore green berets - they flew home to RAF Brize Norton.

Beating Retreat on Horse Guards took place at a time when manpower cuts amounting to a reduction of twenty-four musicians and buglers over the next six months had been announced. The result of these cuts was that the Commando Band at Lympstone was downgraded to a standard band of forty-one. Under 'Options for Change' the Band Service would number, by April 1992, four hundred and thirty-two divided between seven bands, the RMSM and other appointments such as Volunteer Band Instructors - a situation that compared very favourably with cuts to other services.

In the summer of 1991 links with the St Petersburg Admiralty Navy Band were established when Capt R Waterer visited Russia as guest conductor. At that time the band was still known as the Leningrad Admiralty Navy Band.

During October 1991 the Band of Britannia Royal Naval College (Lt J Hillier) was flown to Sebastapol to join HMS Fearless. The Russian Commander-in-Chief Black Sea Fleet paid an official visit for which a guard (from 4th Assault Squadron, Royal Marines) and band were provided.

On 31st October 1991 the last Royal Marine units still based at Eastney, led by the band of C-in-C Naval Home Command, marched out of the RM Barracks, the band being relocated a few miles to the west in Eastney Block, HMS *Nelson*. A display was given in the Guildhall Square as part of the closure ceremonies and the Corps flag at RM Eastney was hauled down for the last time, on this occasion by two members of the Band Service. On the 1st June 1991, the Band Service ceased to wear the green beret. Its wearing had been seen by many as an anomaly since the Marine has to fulfil certain training requirements to earn this badge of achievement whilst the musician does not. The move towards women joining was continuing and it was accepted that this would require fundamental changes. However it was stressed that the appearance of RM Bands would be largely unaffected. The official announcement was made in the House of Commons just before Christmas. Women would be accepted into the Band Service from September 1992.

For the 1991 G7 summit meeting of Heads and Representatives of Government the Royal Marines led a unique Tri-service event in the Inner Courtyard of Buckingham Palace.

Several changes occurred which had an effect upon life at the RMSM from 1992 onwards. The co-operation with the Royal Academy of Music changed as a result of the Academy taking the decision not to offer diplomas to outside students and, as a result, the

RMSM had to look elsewhere for its professional Military Band Conducting qualification. A partnership with the Associated Board of the Royal Schools of Music resulted in a very suitable curriculum and format being developed for the new diploma. A number of changes were made to the relevance of the Bandmasters Course syllabus in 1990/91 to make it appropriate to current educational thought and practice. The Band Musicianship course at University College Salford, taken as a Director of Music qualification, was upgraded from a two-year General to a three-year Honours Degree. Sixteen males and ten females joined New Entry training at Deal in September 1992 and, in another attempt to encourage recruitment and retention the Second Open Engagement (2OE) was introduced. This meant that service until the age of fifty could be approved for outstanding NCOs and instrumentalists.

A major deployment in 1992 was to the Far East with members of the band of C-in-C Fleet as a ship's band under the direction of WO2 BM S Morgan. A Hercules flew them and a RM Detachment of thirty-five to join HMS *Invincible* in Mombasa. The deployment covered Singapore, Japan, Korea and Hong Kong. In true ship's band style they performed as a military band, concert band, orchestra, jazz band, dance band and other small groups. Whilst on board *Invincible* they provided entertainment for the ship's complement including a final concert at which they combined with the ship's Volunteer Band. The band were then flown back to UK following a handover to the Band of Commando Forces in Singapore who continued the deployment in *Invincible* and RFA[3] *Olwen* through Malaya and back through the Persian Gulf to the UK.

Repercussions from the 'Options for Change' Government Strategy continued to permeate their way through all band services. The main cause of this strategy was the upheaval in Eastern Europe and a resultant need to change the Defence Policy. Another policy, mainly driven from the Treasury, was for things to be 'resource driven' rather than 'demand led', a policy that would have serious repercussions since military music is an expensive provision, difficult to define in terms of value for money and therefore a 'soft target' for Defence cuts. During the spring of 1993 the Army announced reorganisation and cuts of about 50% to its bands. The RN and the RM were to undertake a complete reappraisal of music provision and redundancies were inevitable. By the summer a DCI[4] outlining the RN's redundancy scheme had been issued and volunteers were called for. In parallel was a desire to reorganise the Band Service into fewer but sometimes larger bands that would be geographically located to areas of RN and RM concentration. A key factor in this would be the future of Deal but this would not be known until the Defence Training Committee made its report on a combined Defence School of Music. The redundancy programme was known during the late autumn and called for about ninety redundancies, of which many would be volunteers. However it was necessary to make about twenty-six people compulsorily redundant. In terms of proportion the Buglers' Branch would suffer badly. The Army continued to move towards a 50% cut whilst the RAF remained under review. The Defence Training Committee was still deliberating, which meant that the RMSM would remain at Deal until at least March 1996. Just before Christmas it was announced that the band of C-in-C Fleet would disestablish at the end of March 1994. This restructuring amounted to a cutback of about 20% and was the greatest change to the Band Service since the Leech-Porter Report. The future of the School of Music remained uncertain but it was a decision that remained fundamental to the future of the Band Service. As the Royal Navy concentrated at Portsmouth and Plymouth and the Royal Marines were nearly all in the West Country it was becoming obvious that Deal was becoming more and more isolated. In addition the cost of maintaining three aging and under-utilised barracks was extremely high. On 14th July 1994 the Secretary of State announced that Deal Barracks would close in March/April 1996. It was later confirmed that the RMSM would transfer to Portsmouth Naval Base in April 1996. The Navy Board approved the reorganisation of the RMBS with a complement of three hundred and fifty-eight Officers, men and women with a total of five bands located at Portsmouth, Plymouth, Scotland, CTCRM, BRNC.

Whilst all these discussions had been taking place the bands themselves had continued to go about their work. One of the first 50th Anniversary commemorations of notable World War II events was the Battle of the Atlantic Anniversary which took the form of a Tri-Service performance at Goodison Park, Everton in 1993. HMY *Britannia* was in Liverpool for the event.

The tragic event of September 1989 remained in the hearts and minds of the population of Deal and the surrounding area and supported by the Local Authority, funded by subscription and built by the National Round Table, a Memorial Bandstand was built on Walmer Green at Deal. On Sunday 2nd May 1993 the bandstand was handed over to the Bandstand Trust. Following a fanfare sounded by six buglers playing Herald Trumpets, the first concert was given by the Betteshanger Welfare Brass Band who played, as their opening piece, *A Life on the Ocean Wave*. On the Sunday of the Reunion weekend the Bandstand was dedicated and, prior to the first Royal Marines concert, the Fanfare Trumpets of the Band of C-in-C Fleet sounded Leon Young's Dedication Fanfare, *To Comrades Sleeping*.

On 29th July Lt Col J Ware retired from the position of Principal Director of Music, Royal Marines. His period of office had covered times of threat and great change. He was to be succeeded by Lt Col R Waterer who, like John Ware, chose to spend part of his sabbatical period with 'The President's Own' US Marine Band. He inherited not only the responsibility for the operation of a smaller Band Service with the same commitments as it had previously had but also the task of relocating the School of Music to Portsmouth and investigating the training of musicians at civilian colleges. At this time the RMBS was organised as follows:

Title[5]	PDM/DoM	AsstDoM/Bandmaster
Band of HM Royal Marines, School of Music	Lt Col R A Waterer	Lt C J Davis (Asst Director of Music)
Band of HM Royal Marines, Portsmouth	Capt D C Cole	
Band of HM Royal Marines, Plymouth	Capt J R Perkins	
Band of HM Royal Marines, Scotland	Lt B Mills	
Band of HM Royal Marines, Britannia Royal Naval College		WO2 D J Lindars
Band of HM Royal Marines, Commando Training Centre RM	Lt A D Henderson	
Royal Marines School of Music, Training Company	Capt D M J Rogerson (Chief Training Officer)	WO1 Bdmr R Metcalf (Chief Instructor)

For the RMBS the D-Day 50th Anniversary commemorations started when the Royal Yacht Band joined the remainder of the Portsmouth Band. A combined services Beat

Retreat led by the band of the RMSM at HMS *Excellent*, took place on the 4th June in the presence of HM Queen Elizabeth, The Queen Mother, in pouring rain. As well as the band of the Royal Corps of Signals there were also bands from the United States, Canada and France. In the evening the Royal Yacht Band performed as an orchestra at the Royal Banquet in Portsmouth Guildhall. The Queen and members of the Royal Family together with Prime Minister John Major, US President Bill Clinton and many other Heads of State and Government were present. The following day, in glorious sunshine, a Drumhead Service featuring the band of the RMSM was held on a very muddy Southsea Common in front of the Royal Navy War Memorial. The Royal Yacht component of the Portsmouth Band accompanied HM The Queen and Prince Philip and their many guests on the Yacht on its journey from Portsmouth Harbour, taking the salute from the 4,000 veterans at Southsea and then reviewing the D-Day Fleet at Spithead. The Royal Yacht then led the International Flotilla of ships to mid-channel where *Britannia* passed between the two columns of the International Fleet as each ship cast a wreath upon the waters. The International Flotilla anchored off Arromanches where, during the evening of the 6th June, the band of CTCRM with the bands of the Royal Artillery, the 1st Bn The Princess of Wales's Royal Regiment (Queen's and Royal Hampshires) and the Army Air Corps played on the beach for the march-past of about 7,000 veterans in the presence of the Queen and members of the Royal Family. All Royal Marines Bands were involved in D-Day commemorative events in various parts of the United Kingdom and France.

The RMSM band spent four weeks on tour in Canada. This included two weeks at the Nova Scotia Tattoo, the first time that Royal Marines had appeared at this event. During the autumn the Royal Yacht band accompanied HM The Queen to St Petersburg, the first visit of a British Monarch to Russia. President and Mrs Yeltsin and senior Russian officials were entertained to dinner on board and witnessed Beating Retreat.

A particularly important event for the Band Service occurred when the RMSM Band was invited to give the Gala Concert at the British Association of Symphonic Bands and Wind Ensembles (BASBWE) conference. The only professional symphonic wind bands in the UK are those of the Armed Services. The programme consisted of *Commando March* by Samuel Barber and conducted by Lt Col R Waterer,and the ambitious *After the Last Picture Show* by Bill Connors, transcribed from the original orchestral score and conducted by Bill Connors himself. This piece lasted almost an hour and relied upon the full resources of the wind band plus a saxophone quartet. The second half began with *A Short Ride in a Fast Machine* by John Adams and conducted by Lt C Davis, followed by the Trumpet Concerto by Arutjunjan transcribed and and arranged by the Assistant Instructor, Higher Training and played by BdCSgt J Yates. Lt P Rutterford then conducted Bruce Fraser's *Panache*, a piece of music commissioned by the Scotland Band and dedicated to Lt Rutterford himself. Jim Curnow's *Canticle of the Creatures* led to the final piece, *Fanfare and Allegro* by Clifton Williams and conducted by the PDM. Apart from providing the gala concert, which they did for the first time, the Band of the RMSM attended the conference as did the Staff of Higher Training, the Bandmasters' Course, Training Company Staff and Students and Supply Officer Music's Department as they had for the previous six years. As a result of the success of the concert the RMSM was invited back as guest band to give the concert the following year. On this occasion it was also used as a means of recruitment for the Band Service. In between these two occasions Lt Col Waterer had been invited to attend the largest band conference in the world, the 1994 International Band and Orchestra Clinic in Chicago, where over eleven thousand Band Directors, musicologists and senior Directors of Music of US and European Armed forces meet. At the Conference Lt Col Waterer was elected to the Board of Directors of the Sousa Foundation, the only British Director of Music ever to hold this appointment.

On the 18th September 1994 the Plymouth Band played at the Cenotaph for the 40th Anniversary of the Royal Naval Association. As they returned to Plymouth their coach left the M5 near Bristol and crashed. Musn Barry Holland was killed and ten members of the band were seriously injured. Forty-eight hours after the accident the band honoured a commitment to play at Plymouth Pavilions and donated their performance fee to begin a trust fund for Barry's family. A funeral service with full military honours was held at HMS *Raleigh*. The crash highlighted the amount of travelling that bands had to undertake to cover the workload of the disestablished C-in-C Fleet Band.

Early in 1995 HRH The Duke of Edinburgh visited the School and was given a tour of Training Company and the Musical Repair and Supply Departments. During February the 50th Anniversary of the Freedom of Deal was marked by a two-mile march through the town and, for the first time, girls under training were seen as armed sentries guarding the barracks.

On 3rd April 1995 Lt Col Sir Vivian Dunn died. His contribution to military music was enormous, a fact that was reflected not only by the attendance at his funeral on the 10th April and his Memorial Service at St Martin's-in-the-Fields on the 7th July but also in the wealth of correspondence and obituaries that followed the announcement.

In 1995 it was announced that a three-year trial of the Musician Bursary Scheme would commence in September. In January 1995 Major D Rogerson, Chief Training Officer at the RMSM, was also appointed as Tri-Service Project Manager of the scheme. The objective was to see whether it would be possible to obtain from civilian colleges all the military musicians necessary to sustain the three Services. The Services had already registered concerns with regard to the civilian sector's ability to meet the required standards and to develop and foster the necessary ethos. It had been decided, partly because of these reservations, to continue the Service Schools, in their current form, until the results of the trial were fully known.[6]

The main events of 1995 were to be the commemorations to mark anniversaries of various events leading up to the end of World War II. The first of these events that involved the RMBS was during May when the band of BRNC flew to Malta to take part in the island's celebrations. They were based in HMS *Illustrious* and their first task was to assemble on the after aircraft lift ready to be raised to deck level for a moonlit Beat Retreat. Next day began with Colours at 0745hrs. They then went to Pieta Marina Gardens for the unveiling of the Royal Navy Memorial. By 1100hrs the band was leaving the coach to march through Valletta to the Town Square where they played an hour's musical programme. They then marched back through the town, returned to change uniform, then Beat Retreat at the Lascaris War Rooms in Valletta before returning to the ship to prepare for a concert at the local old people's home. Next day they travelled to the island of Gozo where they carried out a marching display and, the following day, which was regarded as VE-Day on the island, began with Colours which was extended by the inclusion of the National Anthems of Malta, France, the USA and Greece. They then moved into Valletta for the VE-Day Beat Retreat which was carried out in front of a huge crowd. The Maltese provided the evening's entertainment but, later, the Clarinet Choir played at the British High Commissioner's reception. The final day again began with Colours and, in the afternoon, a concert was given in the old university for the Foundation for International Affairs.

The Victory in Europe Anniversary Commemoration in Hyde Park took place on Saturday the 6th May. By 1045hrs the bands were in position. The RMSM were centre with the Grenadier and Welsh Guards on their right flank and the RAF on their left flank. To either side were the Massed Pipes and Drums and, to the rear, were the Mounted Bands of the Household Cavalry. After the Veterans had assembled, the massed bands under Lt Col R Waterer played until 1125hrs when the surviving holders of the Victoria Cross and the George Cross assembled, followed by the arrival of the Clergy and Choristers. HM The Queen Mother arrived and the Drumhead Service began. The Drums used for this service came from the recently disbanded Foot Guards 2nd Battalions. During the religious service the RM Buglers sounded Last Post and the Trumpeters of the Household Cavalry responded with Reveille after the minute's silence. The veterans marched past after the service and then the Guards, RAF and Pipe bands countermarched whilst the RMSM band marched off to their front, wheeled and then, with the music drifting across the park, the white helmets could be seen cutting a swathe through the packed crowds. Unknown to many a very full rehearsal had only allowed enough time for a change of uniform before the bands had marched on at 1045hrs. The RMSM marched to one of the bandstands for an hour's concert. That evening a variety concert was given in the park. The military massed bands of the RM Plymouth Band, the RAF Central Band and the Guards joined the Central Band of the Royal British Legion under former RM Director of Music Captain E P Whealing.

Sunday 7th June had as its centrepiece the Ceremony of Peace and Reconciliation that would be attended by HM The Queen, Members of the Royal Family and many Heads of State and Government. For this occasion the massed bands comprised the RMSM, a combined band from the Grenadier and Welsh Guards, the Band of the RAF Regiment, the Pipes and Drums of the Royal Tank Regiment and the Scots Guards and the Fanfare Trumpeters of the Royal Military School of Music. Once again all were under the direction of Lt Col R Waterer.

The evening of Monday the 8th featured a VE Party in three sections with the military bands only being required for the central section. This was the Beacon Lighting Ceremony when the Queen lit a beacon that initiated the lighting of a chain of beacons around the country. The bands were the same as for the Saturday ceremony but were under the direction of Major S A Watts, Welsh Guards. The Pikemen and Musketeers of the Honourable Artillery Company and the Massed Bands, led by the RMSM, marched into position by the beacon and played music from the war years until the arrival of HM The Queen. After the ceremony was complete the Massed Bands marched away.

The story of the World War II commemorations ended with the weekend of 19th/20th August when events began with a Service of Remembrance and Commitment at Buckingham Palace. Following this service the band of the RMSM led the March Past from Wellington Barracks around the Queen Victoria Memorial and up the Mall where the Queen took the salute. The following evening the Queen and other members of the Royal Family attended a celebration on Horse Guards Parade where the massed military bands of the three services, an orchestra and a choir were assembled. The band of the RMSM once again represented the Royal Navy. Drummers of the 1st Bn Grenadier Guards sounded Last Post and, following the two minutes' silence, RM buglers sounded Reveille. Following this spectacular display the bands marched down the Mall to assemble in front of the Queen who was on a dais in the centre gateway for the Sunset ceremony which featured the Massed Bands and the RM buglers playing A C Green's arrangement of *Sunset*.

The Band of the Royal Marines School of Music, closely followed by the RAF, march into position to lead the Tri-Service March Past along the Mall. 19th August 1995. The band can also be seen on one of the giant screens.

An RMRO[7] was issued to confirm the closure of Deal under the "Front Line First" series of initiatives and to set out the programme of closure and relocation. The advance party was to move to HMS *Nelson*, Portsmouth on 4th March; the final Pass-Out Parade took place on the 21st March with a final public ceremony on the 22nd; between the 25th and the 29th March the RMSM would relocate to Portsmouth with the Barracks at Deal being closed on the 29th. By the 1st April rationalisation of the Band Service would be complete and training at the RMSM would recommence on 15th April. Upon arrival at Portsmouth the PDM was to assume the additional title of Commandant, RMSM. All RM personnel would be under the command of the Captain, HMS *Nelson*.

Friday, 22nd March 1996 was the day that the RMSM, Deal, officially closed. The School was the last unit to use what used to be the Depot, Deal and the inevitable day had arrived. At 1730hrs the Jubilee Gates were opened to allow the public in for the last time. The prospect of bad weather did not stop them coming and very soon all available space around the arena was full. The Closure Ceremony, including Beating Retreat, took place in heavy rain and began with a fanfare *Farewell to Deal* written for the occasion, by WO2 McDermott, and the Corps of Drums beating Drummers Call, Divisional Calls and Band Call. The augmented RMSM Band marched on to play a series of well known marches, during which the Corps of Drums Beat Retreat. The finale included the *Battle of Trafalgar*. The band then marched off to the Regimental March, *Auld Lang Syne*, *Will Ye No Come Back Again*, *Sarie Marais* and *Colonel Bogey* to form up for the march along Deal's seafront road, the Strand. Despite the heavy rain the crowds were massed on both sides of the road and cheered enthusiastically as the band marched to *Imperial Echoes*, *On the Quarterdeck*, *Voice of the Guns* and finally, as they marched back into the Barracks for the last time, *A Life on the Ocean Wave*.

The RMSM band was disestablished which meant that further responsibility would fall to the Portsmouth Band who, as well as meeting their usual commitments, would have to support the training programmes, particularly the Bandmasters' Course. The Students and Instructional Staff moved into what had been the Royal Navy Detention Quarters (DQ) inside Portsmouth Naval Base. Adjacent buildings housed a large rehearsal room, classrooms, offices and messing facilities and were clustered around an open area used as a parade ground. The cells of the DQ provided excellent individual training rooms for the students. HQ Band Service Royal Marines, including Supply Officer Music's Department, was located in Eastney Block with the Portsmouth Band. The very important Instrument Repair Workshop was located close by in Building 73. A strong case for retaining this facility, based on the fact that all repairs and overhauls to woodwind, brass, stringed and percussion instruments could be carried out, had been made. The point was made that both the Army and the RAF were envious of the system and that the Army had expressed an interest in the RM system for future restructuring.

During 1996 as well as the relocation of the School, the demise of the RMSM Band and the general restructuring of the Band Service the RMBS mounted the Mountbatten Festival of Music where the final night was attended by more people than attended the Last Night of the Proms, Beating Retreat on Horse Guards Parade to celebrate the Captain General's 75th Birthday and the Royal Tournament.

An additional item on the calendar was a Charity Concert in the London Guildhall. This concert was presented as a tribute to the late Sir Vivian Dunn with proceeds going to the Royal Marines Museum Bandroom Appeal. The Orchestra of the RM Portsmouth played the overture from Mendelssohn's *The Hebrides*; the intermezzo from Kodaly's *Hary Janos* Suite; two movements from Grieg's *Peer Gynt* and also accompanied the soprano Olivia Blackburn in a number of arias. After the interval a band concert was presented and then the audience proceeded to the Guildhall Yard where the CTC Band managed to overcome serious traffic problems to arrive in the nick of time to Beat Retreat. This concert was repeated in 1997 when the orchestral items included works by Mozart, Mascagni, Bizet, Elgar, Coates, and Sullivan.

Significant steps were taken with regard to all levels of training during 1997. The RMSM was transferred to the Flag Officer Training and Recruiting (FOTR)[8] making it part of RN Training. The CGRM still exercised functional authority through the Commandant, Lt Col Waterer but FOTR became responsible for the provision of all musical training through the Commandant and the Director of Music (Training) and his team. This covered the Initial Training Musician 3, Bugler 3 and Foreign and Commonwealth as well as the Musician 2, Bugler 2, Bandmasters, Drum Majors and Director of Music courses. The RMBS Military Training Team, part of the HQRMBS team, retained responsibility for New Entry Basic Military Training, RM Bands and RMSM Annual Military Training, RMBS Advanced Command Training and Sp to RMC[10]. The other significant change was the formalising of professional links with the University of Portsmouth. From September 1997 all courses run by the RMSM would be accredited by the University thus allowing RMBS musicians to gain professional civilian qualifications at each stage of Specialist Training throughout their careers. Following a validation process the School was accredited as a centre for degree study. The RMSM was compared very favourably with some of the most learned musical institutions in Britain.

PDM also took the opportunity to ensure that the Director of Music examinations were applicable to the new regime. This examination was laid down in Royal Marines Instructions[11] and consisted of two parts. Part 1 was a written examination covering (a)

Harmony, (b) History and Form in Music, (c) Orchestral Arrangement and (d) Military Band Arrangement. Part II was practical and consisted of (e) an aural test, (f) viva voce[12] and (g) conducting. The Royal Academy of Music (RAM) were the examining authority for a, b and e, whilst c and d were set, corrected and marked by a RM Director of Music. A Board consisting of the PDM, a representative from the RAM, and two RM Directors of Music conducted examinations in f and g. Failure in any one subject would result in that subject being retaken. Failure in more than one subject would necessitate the whole Part being retaken. This syllabus was used until 1997.

Once again musicians were at sea. The Plymouth Band joined HMS *Illustrious'* commission to Hong Kong via Gibraltar, the United Arab Emirates, Singapore, Pakistan, India, the Philippines, Japan and Australia. The Portsmouth Band attended the Nova Scotia Tattoo whilst the Royal Yacht contingent were on board for the world cruise that included visiting Hong Kong where they massed with Plymouth Band for the hand-over ceremony.

The Plymouth Band played host to the Captain General when he opened their new band complex on 25th July 1997. The purpose-built complex comprised the main rehearsal room 'Alford Hall', an orchestral rehearsal room, a small combination room, fourteen practice rooms, a purpose built music library, a recording studio, offices and a conference room.

HMY Britannia returns home to Portsmouth. Her paying-off pennant flies from her mainmast and the Band of Her Majesty's Royal Marines (Capt D Cole) play her into port for the very last time. 22nd November 1997.

The Royal Yacht Band was aboard when Britannia left Portsmouth for the last time on 20th October. They visited eight major ports around the UK including the Pool of London where she was used for a dinner for Senior Naval Officers and also accommodation for European Royal Families who had come to London for the Golden Wedding celebrations of The Queen and The Duke of Edinburgh. On 22nd November she entered Portsmouth flying her paying-off pennant and came alongside South Railway Jetty. On 11th December the Service of Thanksgiving and Decommissioning Ceremony took place. The finale was provided by the Royal Yacht Band and took the form of a traditional Beat Retreat. The final piece of music was *Highland Cathedral* featuring the RMBS piper. As *Sunset* was played the Commodore Royal Yachts saluted *Britannia* as the flags were lowered for the last time. But it was the Band that had the final, unspoken, word. At the end of the ceremony they stepped off, marched along the jetty playing *Heart of Oak*, countermarched towards the Queen playing *A Life on the Ocean Wave* and, as they approached her, the Director of Music Capt D Cole and the Drum Major CSgtBug G Naylor saluted the Queen, countermarched, and came out of the countermarch with the band playing *Auld Lang Syne*. For the first, and only, time the Director of Music and the Drum Major, marching at the front of the band, saluted the great ship as they marched her full length before leaving the jetty.

Following the ceremony the Queen and Prince Philip expressed a desire that the Portsmouth Band should retain its Royal Duty status by continuing to accompany Her Majesty on Royal tours. A few weeks later the Queen conferred the title 'Royal Band' upon the Portsmouth Band.

On 1ˢᵗ June 1998 a parade was held at the RMSM to commemorate the 50ᵗʰ Anniversary of the Dedication of the Memorial Silver Trumpets of the Royal Naval School of Music at Burford.[13] The parade was attended by, amongst others, Trevor Ford, a retired Bandmaster who had been present at the original Dedication.

In the same year the Scotland Band joined HMS *Ocean* for a commission to the US coast and the Caribbean. On the journey southwards the band entertained the crew and each other whilst the Corps of Drums earned special praise from the band for managing to slow march during Corps Birthday celebrations when the sea was so rough that everyone was having trouble standing still! After leaving the Virgin Islands the next scheduled stop was cancelled as *Ocean* was diverted to Nicaragua and Honduras to assist with disaster relief in the wake of Hurricane 'Tellar'. It was intended that the band would be used as boat crew ferrying supplies up and down the river or as medics at first aid posts ashore but, on arrival, it was discovered that casualties were few and only three musicians were required as boat crew. However 34 survivors from a fishing vessel had to be rescued and the band assisted with the care and medical treatment of these men, some of whom needed urgent medical aid.

In the UK one of the largest engagements for the Band Service was the International Festival of the Sea held in Portsmouth Naval Base.The Portsmouth and CTC Bands gave concerts and marching displays over the three-day period. 11,500 people attended the massed band concert on the Sunday evening.

A number of unrelated but important incidents occurred in 1999. On 1ˢᵗ July the ranks of RM Officers were aligned with those of Army Officers. Captain Directors of Music became Majors and Lieutenants became Captains. On completion of the Special Duties Officers' Course and the Director of Music Course, Lt P Weston was appointed DoM to the CTC Band. This was the first occasion that a holder of the Prince's Badge had become a Director of Music. A new Memorial to those who died in Service this century was placed in the Garden of Remembrance at the Royal Marines Museum and the Blue Band Magazine celebrated its fiftieth year of publication.

The CTC Band was flown to Naples to join HMS *Ocean* for the Ex-*Argonaut* deployment. On the journey through the Mediterranean the band entertained, rehearsed, played for Replenishment at Sea (RAS) and for Church Service and cross-decked to HMS *Edinburgh* for a ship's company concert. On 22ⁿᵈ September an Act of Remembrance for the tenth Anniversary of the Deal Bombing was held in St Christopher's Church, HMS

Ocean. The Reverend C W W Howard, who had been Chaplain at Deal in 1989 and was now Chaplain of HMS *Fearless*, officiated at the Service. Commodore N S R Kilgour RN and Brig D Wilson of 3 Cdo Bde read the lessons and Capt P Weston recited the Remembrance exhortation. A gun was fired to mark the two-minutes' silence throughout the Task Group. That evening the band performed their road-show in the hangar for the ship's company. Afterwards a collection for the ship's chosen charity was made. When Egypt was reached Ex-*Bright Star* involving 85,000 troops from 18 countries over a three-week period began. The band took part in a series of musical and military engagements ranging from playing for an Officers' dinner in the middle of the desert to acting as casualties to test the medical evacuation systems. In some cases they were exercise casualties for medics from BRNC Band who had been flown to Egypt as part of Medical Squadron, Cdo Logs Regt. They were split into two Troops and operated two Forward Dressing Stations (FDS) throughout the exercise. With the band running these two FDS it was shown that Medical Squadron could provide ample medical cover for 3 Cdo Bde and, by moving a FDS forward by road and air the optimum time for medical cover could be achieved. The Band Service was crucial to this achievement. During 'Distinguished Visitors Day' the Secretary of State for Defence made a point of telling CTC Band how much everyone was talking about the band's performances over the past few weeks. The band later assisted in preparing for an emergency landing on *Ocean* by a damaged Chinook helicopter.

The 1999 Beating Retreat on Horse Guards was unique in that it only required one word of command to step off. Apart from that, all movements were carefully synchronised to the music and the result was a high-quality performance from both musical and drill aspects. Members of the Portsmouth Band were tasked with musical support for the wedding of the Earl and Countess of Wessex. A fourteen-piece Fanfare Team under Capt J R Perkins were positioned at the West Door of St George's Chapel, Windsor Castle to play Capt D Cole's *Fanfare for Sophie* as the bride entered the Chapel. The organ played the last chord of the fanfare and continued with *Marche Heroique* as the bride walked the length of the aisle. The Fanfare Team then made their way to the organ loft to join with choir and organ for the last hymn, the anthem from *The Apostles* by Elgar, the Amen Chorus from *Messiah* and the Gordon Jacob fanfare that precedes the National Anthem. Later, four Buglers played a Herald Trumpet fanfare to announce the cutting of the cake and the toasts and, later still, at the reception members of the Portsmouth Band provided the dance music that included a spirited version of *"The Blues Brothers."* The other major musical event of the year was the final Royal Tournament.

CHAPTER TEN

The Modern Band Service 2000-2003

In 2000 the Edinburgh Tattoo was taken, as a complete show, to New Zealand. The Plymouth Band was the Royal Marines representative and the Principal Director of Music (Lt Col R Waterer) was the show's Musical Director.

2000 continued as 1999 had ended with the Royal Marines Band Service leading every major Tri-Service event. The Royal Military Tattoo 2000 (RMT2000) was a unique event and provided an opportunity for military bands in general and the RMBS in particular to show how they can adapt and use technology whilst maintaining the standards of drill and music for which they are famous. The Band Service Recording Engineer (BdCSgt K Peers) created a recording of all the music to be played, all the voice-overs and all the special effects. This was precisely set to the designer's events timetable. On top of the music he put a computer click-track and then produced a recording that would be used for the voice-overs. The computer click-track was then the key to everything that occurred, especially the conducting of the military bands. Lt Col Waterer used two earpieces as he conducted the bands; one of them was the computer click-track whilst the other was for him to hear cues from Wg Cdr R Wiffin, the RAF Principal Director of Music. The system worked very effectively and enabled the performance to be completely integrated to very fine tolerances. The bands were under the control of the Corps Drum Major (WOI A Bridges) and the ninety-minute timetable gave the Drum Majors a complex set of problems to overcome. The first problem was that, due to the time taken to compose, arrange, rehearse and record the music, they could not listen to the music until two weeks before the event. They then had to match the display to the music and to the rough sketches provided by the organisers - keeping in mind differences in service drill and the need to be able to see the conductor. Time for planning and practising the movements was reduced by using Royal Marines Band Service techniques, which consisted of the Drum Majors working out a routine and then getting the buglers onto the parade with the front ranks (only) from the other service bands. They marched through the routine, making alterations and adjustments as necessary, whilst singing the music, thus allowing the bands to continue practising elsewhere. Once the routine was proven the bands were brought out, without instruments, and taken through it, making notes on their music and concentrating on the drill. It was a unique tattoo and provided a fine example of how the modern Band Service leads not only musically but also in many other ways. They can now field a team of professionals capable of writing and arranging music for special events; planning and co-ordinating all aspects of display from parade work to concert work and, using their own technical ability, can provide lighting, stage management and recording skills.

The Massed Bands of all three Services were again on parade on Horse Guards, with a host of other musicians, choirs and organisations, for the 100th Birthday celebrations for HM Queen Elizabeth, The Queen Mother, on the 19th July. Once more they were under the baton of Lt Col R Waterer.

At the end of the year some of those who had led the way during RMT2000 found themselves leading the way in a different theatre; Op *Agricola* - Kosovo, as part of the Medical Squadron (Med Sqn) near Pristina. A specially formed band of thirty volunteers, known as K Band, underwent arduous training for this deployment. First Aid refresher courses were given at CTC and, for the SNCOs, training in Combat Stress Trauma Management. The School's Military Training Team (CSgt P Basford) took them to

Longmoor for a week's field training followed by a week's field exercises on Copehill Down. Lectures and exercises included fieldcraft, weapon training, map-reading and medical exercises using recruits from the School of Music as casualties. Lectures at the United Nations Training Advisory Team establishment on Salisbury Plain were followed by two and a half days' training in the FIBUA[1] village and an exercise to test the knowledge and experience that had been accumulated. They were flown into Kosovo in an RAF C130 Hercules and received an hour's lecture on the area and, in particular, minefields. Med Sqn then moved to Harden Lines[2] for the handover from 5 Medical Support Regiment RAMC to the sound of their own Royal Marines Band! Working with the undermanned Medical Staff they were split into two Troops each under a Troop (Band) Sergeant and their duties included driving, manning the Battlefield Ambulances and the Medical Stores. Ambulance Troop provided three-man teams consisting of a Vehicle Commander and a First Aider, both of whom were Musicians, and a fully trained Medic. The musicians were also rotated through other tasks including Op *Trojan* (escorting Serbian casualties who required medical treatment but were living in Albanian areas); Op *Sexton* (assisting United Nations Forensic Teams investigating war crimes through the exhumation of bodies); guard duties and armed escorts; manning vehicle check-points and emergency ambulance crews. They also went on patrol with Commando units in Pristina, Obilic and Kosovo Polje and, as part of KFOR, took packets (convoys) from Pristina to the Greek border and elsewhere - with musicians as Packet Commanders.

During the deployment to Kosovo members of K Band take a packet (convoy) from Pristina to the Greek border. Photo: BdCSgt I Davies.

They also entertained not only the troops but the local population, particularly the children. Eighty-six musical engagements were carried out in the six-month period. One engagement was a France versus Royal Marines rugby match when the band wore full Ceremonial Dress[3]. A campaign of hearts and minds has no finer assets than music and humour and the musicians and buglers proved they have both in abundance[4].

During the deployment to Kosovo members of K Band (Capt AP Thornhill), in full Ceremonial Dress provide pre-match entertainment before the rugby match. Photo: BdCSgt I Davies

On Thursday 12th July 2001 the Captain General presented new Colours to 40, 42 and 45 Commandos on Plymouth Hoe. The ceremony began with the Corps Bugle Major (WO2 C Lawton) and the Corps of Drums marching the Old Colours, Majors in Waiting and hassock bearers from the Citadel and onto the Hoe. The Massed Bands, formed from Plymouth, CTC and BRNC bands, then led the Parade onto the Hoe, countermarched and halted with the Corps Bugle Major and the Corps of Drums. Following the Captain General's inspection the Band trooped in slow and quick time before taking position in rear of 42 Cdo. With the hollow square formed the three Bugle Majors led three groups of buglers forward to pile drums. Instead of taking place to a series of commands the piling of drums was achieved by taking cues from the march, *Great Little Army*, being played by the massed bands. As the buglers marched off the Corps Bugle Major gave the signal for the Colours Officers to step off, setting the next phase of the display in motion. Two buglers were positioned at each of the sets of piled drums to hold the new Colours during the Service of Consecration. The drums were retrieved using the music *Army and Marine* to cue the various movements. On completion the band stepped off and assumed a position at the rear of the parade as it marched off the Hoe. The Band then led the parade on a march through Plymouth[5].

The 2001 Festival of Remembrance provided an opportunity for the Band Service to demonstrate to a wide audience not only their recent secondary role in Kosovo but also in the transmitting stations during the two World Wars. Whilst the Festival was taking place a detachment from Plymouth Band was in the desert taking part in Op *Argonaut* and Exercise *Saif Sareea II*. Conditions in the desert were uncomfortable and boring and there was very little opportunity for music.

As a result of reductions and reorganisations, a policy of Army bands having both a Director of Music and a Warrant Officer 1 Bandmaster for each band was introduced.

Presentation of Colours to 40, 42 and 45 Commando, 12th July 2001. The Corps Bugle Major leads the Corps of Drums off Plymouth Hoe. Photo: Author.

Parity was established when the RMBS Warrant Officer ranks were adjusted so that all RM Bands could also have a WO1 as Bandmaster. It was also announced that, due to a shortage of General List Officers the position of Staff Officer to the Band Service would, from 2003, be filled from the Band Service itself. Another milestone was reached when, during 2001, the first twelve members of the RMBS to gain BMus Degrees graduated.

Op *Tay Bridge* took effect on the 30th March 2002 when HM Queen Elizabeth, The Queen Mother, died. The Corps provided a marching detachment of four hundred, the same size as the Royal Navy, the Army and the Royal Air Force as well as three bands.

The Queen's Golden Anniversary celebrations took place in 2002, the final event being the Review of the Armed Forces at HMS *Excellent*. Lt Col R Waterer once again directed the music as Tri-Service Senior Director of Music and it was most appropriate that almost his final act as PDM was to conduct the RM Band as the Queen left Southsea Common. Lt Col C J Davis became Commandant RMSM and Principal Director of Music and was able to announce that the Queen had made his predecessor a Member of the Royal Victorian Order and, to recognise his achievements in music, he had also been awarded an Honorary Doctorate in Music from the University of Portsmouth. The new PDM's first engagement was the Edinburgh Military Tattoo that featured the Scotland Band. On returning the PDM was confronted with Op *Fresco*, the operation that required the military services to cover striking firefighters. Almost immediately two hundred members of the Band Service began training as Breathing Apparatus Teams, and drivers and crew for the Green Goddess fire appliances that were once again returned to service. Directors of Music, Bandmasters and Senior NCOs were given responsibility for Temporary Fire Stations which involved co-ordinating call-outs and deploying units to emergencies. This level of involvement meant that about 75% of engagements had to be cancelled and, in order to maintain the training programmes a composite band, known as the Rear Party Band was formed at Portsmouth from those not operational with Op *Fresco*.

In early 2003 the Band Service was again required to send musicians to Iraq as part of the build-up to an assault upon the regime of Saddam Hussein (Op *Telic*). A band (Capt N Grace) made up of thirty-nine musicians from all five bands was sent to RFA *Argus* which, as in 1990, was to be the Primary Casualty Receiving Unit. Their role was to consist of a number of tasks that included working in Resuscitation, Intensive Care, the General Wards and the High Dependency Unit in the ship's hospital; they also were to work as casualty handlers and decontamination specialists. They also continued their musical role providing all types of musical entertainment to the various messes as well as major concerts for the crews of RFA *Argus*, HMS *Ocean* and *Ark Royal*. Some members of the band joined at Oman having spent time training at a hospital in Birmingham and attending a Trauma Risk Management Course at Haslar.

Following a period of refresher training in the UK, a Decontamination Troop of thirteen musicians, was sent to Camp Gibraltar just outside Kuwait City as part of 3 Cdo Bde. They arrived there on the 7th February and remained for about four weeks before moving, with the Brigade, to Camp Viking on the Iraqi border where they remained for a further three weeks living in shell scrapes[6].

Scud missiles were fired at the camp, the closest landing within a kilometre of them. Three days after the Allied bombardment started they moved into Iraq. Half of the Troop, 'Decontamination Two' went to the port of Umm Qsar and were responsible to the Commando Forces Surgical Group (CFSG) for the total chemical protection of the port. The other half, 'Decontamination One' was deployed in support of 40 Cdo and, when the assault on Basra began (Op *James*), they followed the attack and were given the tasks of general protection and convoy escort duties and were provided with three Land Rovers, each equipped with a General Purpose Machine Gun, and a quad bike.

One of the three Land Rovers used by the musicians for protecting ambulances to the point of wounding. The vehicle is equipped with camouflage sheeting and towed a small trailer on which the musicians sometimes slept. As they had been told that they would be fulfilling this role for only eight hours they had left all of their kit, including sleeping bags and personal belongings behind. However, six days later...
Photo: BdCSgt I Davies

The role of the Troop gradually became one of a protection force for the battlefield ambulances that were escorted by a team of three from the decontamination team, each armed with an SA80 as a personal weapon, in one of the Land Rovers. What began as an eight-hour operation lasted six days as they remained on call and moved forward to collect casualties from the point of wounding. When Basra fell the Troop was with J Company, 40 Cdo, and were amongst the first into one of Saddam's Royal palaces. They later moved back to Al Zabia and then to Kuwait for recovery to UK.

The Royal Marines Band Service in 2003

So what is the structure of the current Band Service? Lt Col C J Davis, who is functionally responsible to the Commandant General, Royal Marines, currently fills the twin posts of Principal Director of Music, Royal Marines and Commandant of the Royal Marines School of Music. Through the latter role he is also responsible to the Flag Officer, Training and Recruitment. HQ RMBS is, like the entire Band Service, very slim with dual-roles being commonplace. Obviously the public is mostly aware of the five Royal Marines Bands:

Official Title[7]	Director of Music	Bandmaster
Band of HM Royal Marines:		
Portsmouth[8]	Major P F Watson	WO1 W G Tate
Plymouth	Major B Mills	WO1 G C Pumford
Commando Training Centre RM	Captain N J Grace	WO1 C B Gould
Scotland	Captain J A Kelly	WO1 M D Graham
Britannia Royal Naval College		WO1 S P Davis

Supporting these bands, either directly or indirectly, are a number of departments:

Appointment/Position	Holder	Responsible for
Staff Officer Band Service	Major A Thornhill	Military Training Team, HQ Administration Team
Supply Officer Music	Captain A Henderson	Central Music Library, Instrument Workshop and Store, Blue Band journal and other publications, Recording Engineer, Stage Manager, Purchasing
Staff Officer 3 Band	Captain P A Weston	Manpower commitments
	BdCSgt J Zawada	Drafting, Job evaluation
Corps Bandmaster and Branch Advisor	WO1 S Savage	Band Service administration
Corps Drum Major and Branch Advisor	WO1 A D Bridges	Major ceremonial
Corps Bugle Major	WO II C Lawton	Buglers' performance.
Staff Arranger	WO II M McDermott	Specialist arranger/composer

The Central Music Library[9] is recognised as a centre of excellence in the world of music libraries. It holds about 32,000 different titles, approximately 12,500 of which are original band and orchestral sets, original manuscripts, marches and 'buskers' books. Although each band has its own Music Library music is also supplied to them as well as to Volunteer Bands, other Service Bands, and civilian organisations including amateur and professional orchestras and even Conservatoires.

Music is prepared here for massed bands concerts and parades, especially tri-service events. Examples are the Edinburgh Tattoo, where music was supplied to the Scotland Band, two Army Bands and an RAF Band as well as bands in the USA, New Zealand, Australia, Netherlands and Tonga. Although music for Royal funerals is known in advance and is reserved, there is still a need to ensure that the music matches the allocation of musicians and such was the case when the library staff prepared for the Queen Mother's Funeral.

The staff of the Central Music Library also arrange copyright issues and this has included the negotiating, on behalf of the organisers, the rights for the compact disc recording, DVD, video, Internet and worldwide television, including satellite and cable, for the Royal Military Tattoo 2000. All music and training manuals for all levels of training are also prepared in this area.

The audio recording of Bandmasters under training has been utilised within the Band Service for many years but, whilst upgrading the system at Deal just prior to the relocation to Portsmouth, it was decided to record a compact disc for commercial sales.[10] This was a success and the next logical step was to create a facility that the entire Band Service could utilise for commercial recordings as well as for training purposes. As a result a VAT registered non-public fund was created in order to record compact discs under the name of "Chevron Recordings". The marketing of these recordings, combined with recording fees charged to bands, provides income for reinvestment in equipment and materials. Recordings can be made on location and editing is carried out at the recording studio at Portsmouth. BdCSgt K Peers, who is responsible for the facility, has made in excess of twenty recordings to date and is now totally responsible for the Mountbatten Festival of Music recordings. Mobility is an important part of the service provided and, partly due to this, recordings of Army and RAF bands have also been made[11]. MCPS licences, artwork, cover details and graphic design are all accomplished from within the Band Service. There are many other advantages to having this facility and RMT 2000 is a good example.[12]

Four civilian instrument repairers specialising in percussion, string, brass and woodwind instruments are employed in the Instrument Workshops. This is the only dedicated facility of its kind in the Ministry of Defence. Apart from silver plating, which is too demanding in terms of space and Health and Safety requirements, all instrument repairs are undertaken here. This not only provides a tangible cost saving but also, because of the proximity to the School of Music, fosters a culture of personal care and proactive maintenance on the part of the students.

The Royal Marines School of Music is under the command of the Director of Music (Training) Major P Best and WO1 Bdmr G R Martin. Before recruits enter the School they undertake a fifteen-week period of Basic Training. The Director, Royal Marines, through the Staff Officer Band Service and his Military Training Team, administers this. When this is successfully completed the recruits, now classed as Musicians or Buglers, join the School for either the Musicians M3 course of two years and eight months or the Buglers' B3 course of two years. Because of the high standard of many of the recruits it is possible for Musicians to "fast-track" through the School in a shorter time via a system called Fixed Mastery - Variable Time. The weekly timetable for the M3 course covers five days and includes Brass, String, Saxophone and Jazz Groups, Woodwind Quintets, String Ensembles, Parade Band work, Orchestral, Wind Band and Big Band rehearsals; Elements, Aural, Harmony lessons as well as Music History. Remaining time is used for individual practice, physical training and recreational training. The School is fully accredited for educating to Bachelor of Music with Honours level by the University of Portsmouth. On completion of M3 or B3 training Musicians and Buglers are placed with the bands.

Promotion to Corporal is dependent upon suitable progression in a number of areas including music. Each band has an Academic Instructor, usually a Band Colour Sergeant who is trained to Bandmaster level, who oversees the musical training of Musicians and Buglers preparing for the M2 and B2 (Corporals') course whilst with the bands. The Academic Instructors, with the Bugle Majors, are also responsible for the musical training of the Buglers. Following the successful completion of a task-book based course of ten lessons the Musician or Bugler returns to the School for a ten-day assessment and examination.

Training for the M1 and B1 course is undertaken at the School of Music. At the moment this course lasts twelve weeks for Musicians and eight weeks for Buglers but a twelve-week course for Buglers is currently under trial. The M1 and B1 course is also based upon a task book, assessment and examination programme and the Musician's successful completion satisfies Level 3 of the Degree Course for those who have chosen this route to accreditation. Buglers are no longer 'second class citizens' in terms of musical and academic training but now become highly qualified musically and, like the Musicians, are encouraged to gain academic qualifications at each stage of their promotion.

The Warrant Officer Bandmaster Course lasts a full year and, like the M1 course, is administered and taught in the Higher Training Department. Student Bandmasters undertake continual assessment, part of which is through the Winter and Spring Concert series. Trinity College at Greenwich and the Royal Northern College of Music are currently used for the musical training of newly promoted Directors of Music who, on successful completion, are awarded the Master's Degree. The SD Commission is now known as a Senior Officers Late Entry Commission. In order to be promoted to Captain the Director of Music has to complete his 'Passed Director of Music' (pdm) course at the School. Composition and arranging skills are assessed by PDM and leading civilian musicians and the conducting examination normally takes place during one of the Winter Concert series.

Summary

The Royal Marines Band Service enters its second century as a homogeneous organisation based upon the early years of the twentieth century when the Royal Navy entrusted the Royal Marines with the provision of not only its music but also a very important secondary role. During the intervening century both have developed to the point that the Band Service is acknowledged as one of the finest, if not the finest, in the world whilst it would also be difficult to find any military musicians who play such an integrated part when their secondary role is required. As part of a comparatively small but highly effective Corps that, by virtue of the development of modern warfare, is at the forefront of any activity that requires Great Britain's armed forces to be involved, the Band Service has to maintain the same efficient, highly-trained and streamlined profile as the Corps itself. This, like most things that are effective and successful, has not happened overnight but is the result of careful development and the recognition that, however difficult or inconceivable, adaptability and resourcefulness are essential commodities for survival.

So the current Band Service is a compact, streamlined organisation that is smaller than it has ever been during its history, a situation entirely in line with the general rationalisation of the services over the last forty or fifty years. Its role and duties have also changed. No more the need for permanent sea-going bands in support of the Royal Navy; no more tours with the Fleets or the Royal Yacht to outposts of Empire or Commonwealth. The demise of the Royal Tournament must be a warning that the days of such displays are numbered. Costs and availability of military bands and a reduced public awareness of this type of entertainment at a time when all appears to be geared to the young and to the electronic age are all contributing to a reduced demand for the military band generally. Yet all is not doom and gloom as the Mountbatten Festival of Music continues to go from strength to strength, links with professional musicians become ever stronger and the Band Service itself becomes ever more efficient, financially viable and an attractive career for young, and mature, musicians. As well as all that, rather like the jewels in the crown, the Royal Marines Band Service is renowned for its ceremonial role - and is instantly recognised through its distinctive uniform, its music and its élan.

The Royal Marines Band Service has, particularly in recent years, been carefully honed. Overheads have been slashed and resources have been concentrated but not at the loss of quality of musicianship or standard of performance, product or professionalism; quite the opposite has been effected through new approaches to training and the development of attractive facilities that help to improve self-reliance and efficiency. The introduction of women into the Band Service has been accomplished smoothly and the resulting integration, in the passing years, are proof that it has worked and that, whether male or female, all those joining the trained bands are fine musicians or buglers.

As the Royal Marines Band Service enters its second century it is a good time for its current members to reflect upon their forebears and the work that they did. Not always blessed with the finest of instruments, the best opportunities or even the greatest of talents they have, nevertheless, every right to be proud of being a part of the building of this organisation. It would be invidious to point the finger at individuals because as this book has been researched and as the story has been told in, hopefully, a balanced and fair way it has been realised that no one individual deserves to be raised above others. The Band Service has been blessed with having a great number of individuals who have been in the right place at the right time, whether that be the concert hall, the transmitting station, the Royal Yacht, Horse Guards Parade or the deserts of Iraq. Long may it continue.

APPENDIX ONE

The Band Service Memorials

The original War Memorial Charter of 1946 was as follows:

ROYAL NAVAL SCHOOL OF MUSIC

The War Memorial Charter

1. THE BOOK OF REMEMBRANCE.

 The BOOK OF REMEMBRANCE will form the permanent Roll of Honour and will be placed in the Chapel of St Cecilia at the Royal Naval School of Music.

2. THE TRUMPETS AND BANNERS.

 These shall be called "The Memorial Trumpets of the Royal Naval School of Music" and this title shall on no occasion be abbreviated.

3. CUSTODY.

 The War Memorials shall be in the custody of the Quartermaster (Music) at the Royal Naval School, who shall keep them in safe storage and issue orders covering their safety when in use.

4. USAGE OF THE TRUMPETS.

 The Trumpets are never to be played by any but R.N. School of Music personnel and when performing in public will always be conducted by a R.N. School of Music Officer.

5. FEES.

 Fees will normally be charged even if the object of the function is to raise money for charity.

6. FANFARE TRUMPETERS.

 Trained Fanfare Trumpeters will be maintained continuously at the Royal Naval School of Music as far as is possible. If circumstances prevent the maintenance of a team of the highest class, no engagements will be accepted, since the trumpets reflect the reputation of all ranks, past and present.

7. DRESS.

 The dress for the Fanfare Trumpeters will be Royal Marine Band Ceremonial Dress with the addition of dress cords and white gloves.

 Caps will be worn as it is not possible to play the trumpets when wearing Royal Marine uniform helmets.

8. INSURANCE.

 The Memorials are to be covered by a comprehensive Insurance Policy the cost of which will be met by the R.N. School of Music Band Fund.

9. THE 1914-1918 SILVER MEMORIAL DRUMS

 It is hereby decreed that all or any charter, rules or regulations drawn up in connection with the Silver Drums shall be cancelled and the provisions of this Charter, in so far as they shall apply, shall also govern the usage of the Silver Memorial Drums 1914-1918.

10. DECIDING AUTHORITY.

 Subject to the provisions of this Charter, the Commandant of the Royal Naval School of Music will be vested with final decision as to the use of the Instruments mentioned herein. In this connection, it is hereby recorded that they belong collectively to the Royal Naval School of Music, as opposed to being public property, and, as a War Memorial, they shall be used only with dignity and pride.

11. MEMORIAL DAY.

The War Memorial Committee recommend that the "Dedication Fanfare" composed by Mr Leon Young shall be sounded with due ceremony by the Fanfare Trumpets on the First of June each year.

End of the Charter.

There then followed a description of the Memorials:

THE SILVER DRUMS.

These consist of a set of five silver side drums and one silver finished bass drum. They were purchased by voluntary subscription of all ranks to commemorate those Royal Naval School of Music ranks who gave their lives in the War of 1914-1918. The bass drum is emblazoned with their names, whilst the side drums carry the names of the ships in which the men died.

THE BOOK OF REMEMBRANCE.

This beautiful Book, in parchment bound in blue leather tooled in gold, contains the names of the 225 ranks of the Royal Naval School of Music who lost their lives during the War of 1939-1945.

THE FANFARE TRUMPETS

The set comprises 14 silver trumpets as follows:- E flat soprano, 2; B flat treble, 7; B flat tenor, 3; G bass, 2. The names of the ships in which the men died are engraved inside the bells of the trumpets, whilst the following inscription appears on each instrument:-

"These Fanfare Trumpets were purchased by the voluntary subscription of their comrades in memory of the two hundred and twenty-five NCOs and Men of the Royal Marine Band Service who lost their lives in the World War, 1939-1945, whilst serving in His Majesty's Ships and Shore Establishments".

BANNERS[1]

The banners were of Royal blue velvet with gold lace fringes. In the centre was placed the Foul Anchor with the letters R.N.S.M. above the stock. The whole design was surmounted by a Royal crown[2].

At some point between the writing of this Charter and the 1950 amalgamation Rule 4 was changed by the addition of the following sentence. "They will normally be played only on important occasions such as National Ceremonies, Royal Naval or Royal Marine Corps occasions". No further changes appear to have occurred until 1953.

Whilst the 1953 Royal Tour was in progress the War Memorial Charter was updated to suit the new organisation and fully approved by the Commandant General. The new Charter was as follows:

ROYAL MARINES SCHOOL OF MUSIC THE WAR MEMORIAL CHARTER

THE WAR MEMORIAL

1. The Memorial to all ranks of the Royal Naval School of Music who gave their lives in the War of 1939-1945 consists of a set of 14 Silver Trumpets with Banners. The following inscription appears on each instrument:-

   "These Fanfare Trumpets were purchased by the voluntary subscription of their comrades in memory of the two hundred and twenty-five NCOs and Men of the Royal Marines Band Service who lost their lives in the World War 1939-1945, whilst serving in His Majesty's Ships and Shore Establishments"

THE TRUMPETS

2. These shall be styled "The Memorial Silver Trumpets of the Royal Marines School of Music" and this title shall on no occasion be abbreviated.

THE BOOK OF REMEMBRANCE

3. The Book of Remembrance containing the Roll of Honour of the 225 ranks of the Royal Naval School of Music who lost their lives during the War 1939-1945 shall be retained in the Church of St Michael's and All Angels' at the Royal Marines School of Music, The Depot Royal Marines, Deal.

THE USE OF THE TRUMPETS

4. The Trumpets shall only be played by personnel of the Royal Marines School of Music and will at all times be conducted by an Officer, or specially deputed Bandmaster, of the Royal Marines School of Music. Subject to the general direction of the Commandant General Royal Marines, the trumpets will be played on occasions appropriate to their use at the discretion of the Commandant, Royal Marines School of Music.

MEMORIAL DAY

5. On the 1ˢᵗ June each year the *"Dedication Fanfare"* composed by Leon Young shall be sounded with due ceremony to mark the dedication of the Memorial Trumpets which took place on 1ˢᵗ June, 1948, at the Royal Naval School of Music, Burford, Oxon.

FANFARE TRUMPETERS

6. A team of Fanfare Trumpeters will be maintained at the Royal Marines School of Music. If circumstances prevent the maintenance of a team of the highest class, no engagement will be accepted, since the Trumpets reflect the reputation of all ranks, past and present.

DRESS

7. The Dress of the Fanfare Trumpeters will be No.1 Order of Dress. Caps will be worn in order to obviate the difficulty of playing in white helmets.

THE WAR MEMORIAL SILVER DRUMS 1914-1918

8. The Rules and Regulations concerning the Memorial Silver Drums 1914-1918 are hereby incorporated in this Charter to establish that their use shall be similar to that of the Memorial Silver Trumpets. The Memorial Silver Drums 1914-1918 comprise a set of five silver side drums and one silver finished bass drum. This Memorial was also voluntarily subscribed by ranks of the Royal Naval School of Music to commemorate those ranks who gave their lives in the War 1914-1918. The bass drum is emblazoned with their names, the side drums bearing the names of the ships in which the men died.

Although no longer part of the Charter, the covering letter from the Commandant General's Office did confirm two points regarding the Charter. Firstly, "The Memorial Silver Trumpets of the Royal Marines School of Music comprise - E flat soprano, 2; B flat treble, 7; B flat tenor, 3; G bass, 2." Secondly, "Custody - The Trumpets shall be in the charge of the Supply Officer (Music) at the Royal Marines School of Music who will be responsible for their security, and will give directions for their safe keeping when in use. The Trumpets are to be fully insured by Comprehensive Insurance cover, the cost of insurance and maintenance being borne by the Royal Marines School of Music Band Fund.

The alterations to the Charter had taken account of the amalgamation and their new location. From now Buglers' Dress Cords (Properly known as 'Dress Cords Royal') were not to be worn[3]. Investigations were put in hand for the design of gold dress cords for the Fanfare Trumpeters but they were never produced.[4]

When the Charter was finally approved by the Commandant General it was printed on suitable paper and the details promulgated as an instruction from the Commandant General.

It would appear that in 1955 an attempt was made to again change the wording on the Memorial Charter. The Commandant RMSM met with Lt Col Dunn, and Lts Gale, Fitzgerald and Ough. The major changes proposed in the Minutes and the draft document were that decisions regarding the use of the Memorial Trumpets should become the responsibility of the Commandant and two Officers of the Royal Marines Band Service; fees would be charged even if the function was for charity and the proceeds would go to the maintenance of the instruments; it was firmly stated that "Caps will be worn as it is not possible to play the trumpets when wearing Royal Marines uniform helmets" and, most importantly, it was proposed that the restriction that only the full complement of trumpets should be used and played should be withdrawn. The changes to the Charter do not appear to have been adopted since, in 1959, the Assistant Adjutant General wrote a file minute that confirms that the Charter still invested the responsibility for their use with the Commandant of the RMSM but not with Officers of the RMBS. Then, in 1963, Major Ian Wray had a telephone conversation with Lt Col Dunn who wanted Portsmouth Group Band to use some of the Fanfare Trumpets instead of the Herald Trumpets. Major Wray reminded the Colonel that the Charter precluded the use of the Trumpets on such a relatively minor occasion and that all fourteen had to be used.[5] It would therefore appear that the 1953 version of the Charter was the final version. In 1954 the text of this Charter was produced in an illuminated form on vellum.[6] It was signed by the Commandant General and the Commandant of the Royal Marines School of Music and then framed for hanging in North Barracks, Deal. Photographic copies were made and distributed to RM Barracks, Plymouth and RM Barracks, Eastney, as well as ITC[7] RM, the Boys' Wing of the RMSM, the RMSM and the Royal Marines Office. The original is now in the Royal Marines Museum.

By 1956 it was felt that the original banners had become worn and faded to the extent that it would not be right and proper to continue using them. A committee comprising all of the Band Officers of the RMSM serving in 1956 produced a new design for the banner. The Commandant General subsequently approved the design and the new banners were made and fitted to the Fanfare Trumpets. They were markedly different being red with a Corps crest in the centre and this design caused distress to some of those who had served with the Royal Naval School of Music. Letters of complaint were sent to the School, to the Commandant General, to the Chaplain of the Fleet and to the Admiralty. The RMSM claimed that, since the original banners were purchased by the Admiralty, unlike the Trumpets themselves which were purchased by the men, the design could be altered. The opposite opinion was that the Trumpets and the Banners together were described in the

Charter as being the War Memorial. The RMSM felt that the new banners were in keeping with the current title of the School. However, despite approving the design and providing them, the Admiralty decided that the new banners would continue in use until they wore out, "when they will be replaced by banners of the original design". The Commandant of the RMSM expressed the view to the Commandant General that "Since it is expected that these banners will last for a period of over fifteen years, it is not a matter which is desired to alter in any way, and probably by the time that replacements are necessary, other views will have been expressed"[8].

During 1957 it was realised that the Memorial Silver Drums were not being used at Church Parades due to insufficient numbers of Musician or Junior Musician percussionists being available to use the complete set. Because of this situation the Band Officers' Conference decided that the Memorial Silver Drums should normally be kept in a glass case and only used on St George's Day, the 1st June and Armistice Day. However, if the Memorial Silver Drums were particularly required for a special Church Parade and insufficient Musicians or Junior Musicians were available then Junior Buglers could be used to complete the full team.

In 1965 the Memorial Silver Trumpets reached the point where they were neither mechanically nor musically reliable and replacements were obtained. The Memorial Silver Trumpets were dressed with their original Royal Naval School of Music banners and were laid up at the Depot, Royal Marines. The replacement trumpets, since they are not War Memorials, are not subject to the Rules laid down in the Charter.[9] In 1973 the Commandant General agreed to the suggestion that both the Memorial Silver Drums and the Memorial Silver Trumpets should be transferred to, and permanently laid up in, the Royal Marines Museum at Eastney. They are now retained at the Museum in showcases in the Band Memorial Room but each year they, and the Silver Drums, are returned to the RMBS for the Service of Remembrance at Portsmouth Cathedral.

A final story relating to the playing of the fanfare trumpets concerns the change to the headgear worn. Following the 1970 Beating Retreat on Horse Guards Parade Earl Mountbatten mentioned his disappointment that the fanfare team wore caps and not helmets to the Commandant General. At the subsequent reception Earl Mountbatten introduced the CGRM to the Queen, immediately repeated his preference for helmets and not caps and asked the Queen for her opinion. The Queen replied that she thought he was correct and, when the CGRM explained that it had always been considered that playing the fanfare trumpets with helmets was very difficult, she suggested, "I am sure the Royal Marines can overcome that problem."[10] As a result the Commandant of the RMSM was instructed to investigate the matter bearing in mind the War Memorial Charter. The latter was unnecessary since the Memorial Silver Trumpets were laid up and their replacements were not Memorials. Trials were undertaken at Deal, official photographs were taken for comparison and, as a result, it was considered practicable for the helmet WP to be worn by ranks playing the fanfare trumpets. This information was sent to HQ Training Group Royal Marines who endorsed the findings. CGRM then wrote to Earl Mountbatten informing him of the situation and asking him to solicit the thoughts of the Captain General. As a result of Prince Philip's agreement, which Mountbatten reported as being "At last! Thank God!! I have been trying to get the Royal Marines to do that for years", an instruction was issued which stipulated that fanfare trumpeters should wear the helmet when paraded with a band wearing similar headdress, on all other occasions they should wear caps.[11]

APPENDIX TWO

Music of Historical Importance to the Royal Marines

The Quick March of the Royal Marines. - 'A Life on the Ocean Wave'
Originally written as a song with words by the well-known singer and songwriter Henry Russell, to a tune composed by an American, Henry Epps Sargent, in New York during 1838 *A Life on the Ocean Wave* immediately became popular. It is now one of the most famous Regimental Marches in the world and is instantly associated with the Royal Marines.

The Royal Marines had used *British Grenadiers* until 1855 but, after that date, the selection of a march for this purpose was very much at the whim of the Commandants at each of the Divisions. Several marches are known to have been traditionally or semi-officially used during the period 1855 and 1882. Chatham Division used *Hoch Hapsburg* by J N Kral whilst the Portsmouth Division played the Coronation March from *Le Prophete* by Meyerbeer. Chatham Division is also believed to have used *Dashing White Sergeant* as a Regimental March. From its inception in 1862 until 1882 the Royal Marine Artillery used Gounod's Soldier's Chorus from *Faust*. When it was decided to have a regulation March Past several marches were considered for the purpose[1]. *Rule Britannia* was obviously an appropriate choice but it was already in use as the march-past of the Norfolk Regiment and they protested very strongly when it was suggested for the Royal Marines. Another possibility was the popular song *Wings* until it was realised that the Royal Engineers were considering using it. A third possibility was *The Defiler* written by Thomas Winterbottom until it was realised that it had been adopted by the York and Lancaster Regiment and was simply known as *The York and Lancaster*[2] "The Deputy Adjutant General, Royal Marines, called upon the bandmaster at each Division to arrange a march, if possible, on a Naval Song. Mr Kappey, Mr Winterbottom, Mr Kreyer and Mr Froehnert each submitted a march".[3] Mr Kappey, (Chatham Divisional Band) had arranged *A Life on the Ocean Wave* as a march that, prior to 1882, was occasionally used as a form of Regimental or Divisional march - as were many other marches. He had added a segment from the Naval Song *The Sea* as the trio. Another arrangement of this tune was in use with *White Wings* as the trio.

Kappey's submission was chosen and, in 1882, an official War Office publication[4] confirmed it as the march of the Royal Marines. In 1921 the following statement appeared: "…This march was in use by the Corps prior to 1882, and in this year an official War Office publication (103/Gen No.) allocates "A Life on The Ocean Wave" as the march of the Royal Marines. It was also officially recognised in MO 1524/1920 by the Lords Commissioners of the Admiralty as the March Past of the Corps"[5] In 1944 Major Ricketts made his own arrangement of this march and this is the version in current use. Staff Arranger WOII McDermott also made an arrangement of this march in 2001.

The Slow March of the Royal Marines. - 'The Preobrajensky March'
Prior to 1935 the only semi-official Slow March was *Galatea* used by the Royal Marine Artillery but written by George Miller of the Portsmouth Division RMLI[6]. In 1934 Commander The Lord Louis Mountbatten RN offered the *Preobrajensky March* as the

official slow march of the Royal Marines, an offer that was politely declined. However, the offer had engendered an interest in the subject that coincided with a need for a Slow March for the 1935 London Duties.

The Adjutant General suggested that Capts P S G O'Donnell, Ricketts, Fairfield and Lt Dunn should each contribute an arrangement, or an original composition, for selection. B Walton O'Donnell, now with the BBC Military Band and formerly Director of Music at the Depot, Deal was also invited to submit a composition. Capt O'Donnell was placed in charge of organising this event and he wrote to Lt Dunn to say that he was going to arrange a couple of 17th Century tunes and suggesting that Dunn might also follow this course[7]. As it happened Dunn's adaptation of *Early One Morning* as the trio to his march which, by August 1935 he had titled *The Globe and Laurel*, was selected and used. However the Adjutant General was not impressed by it, telling O'Donnell that the trio was fine but the opening was 'un-original' and suggesting that the three Directors of Music get together to write another march using just the *Early One Morning* part of the Dunn march. O'Donnell wrote to both Dunn and Ricketts on this subject but there is no evidence to suggest that anything other than the matter being 'lost in the mist of time' occurred.[8] *The Globe and Laurel* remained the Corps Slow March until 1964 when Earl Mountbatten of Burma presented the *Preobrajensky March* to the Corps at Buckingham Palace during the Tercentenary Year[9]. It was first played on the 10th June 1964, the Captain General's Birthday:

> The march was already in the Royal Naval School of Music repertoire at the end of the First World War, being used as a parade march entitled *Russian Parade*. It also had a military band selection called *The Glory of Russia* in which the march appeared as the *Preobrajensky March*. This was published by Hawkes & Son in the year in which the Preobrajensky Regiment was disbanded, 1917. As *Russian Parade* the march was featured many times whilst Beating Retreat in the 1930s by the bands of the Mediterranean Fleet, in which Lord Louis Mountbatten was, at the time, Chief Wireless officer in HMS *Queen Elizabeth*. In 1931 King Alfonso XIII of Spain abdicated, and not long after, became the guest of his cousin, Mountbatten, in Malta. During his stay, it is said he watched Beating Retreat, and on hearing *Russian Parade*, told his host and the attending Captain Robert Neville10 RM that he had the original score. Apparently this march had been the ceremonial slow march of His Majesty's Halberdier Guards. Captain Neville stated that King Alfonso told him that he had obtained the score from the Kaiser, but how the Kaiser acquired it, assuming this is true, remains a mystery. Having been presented with this score, it was not until 1942 that Lord Mountbatten arranged for the first band of the Royal Marines to come under Combined Operations command to play it as an inspection march for a guard of honour, and not until 1964 did it become the regimental slow march. During this period though, other arrangements were about: the Bandmaster for HMS *Queen Elizabeth*, Major[11] G C Keen RM did an arrangement just after the score had been acquired. Later, a new expanded version appeared being played by the Royal Marine Band of HMS *Glorious* on frequent flight deck parades (according to Captain Neville). Major Young, one time Bandmaster of the Duke of Cornwall's Light Infantry scored a version in B[b] for bugles (the Hawkes edition of 1917 being in A[b]) c. 1934, and an arrangement by Hackenburger appeared on a recording by the German Military Staff Band of the Bundeswehr entitled *Marsch aus St Petersburg van Leib-Garde Preobrajensky-Regiment*.
>
> As regards the date of origin of the march, it is, as yet, unconfirmed. As far as the exiled survivors of the Preobrajensky Regiment are concerned, Ernest Donajowski (1845-1917) takes the credit for the 'modern' march. It had been suggested though that the Russians had acquired the primary form of the

march from the Swedish Army after the Russian victory at Poltava 1709. Subsequent researches by Swedish correspondents state though, that individual regiments of the Swedish Army did not have 'Regimental Marches' so it would seem unlikely the march could have been so dramatically 'captured.' Upon researching Swedish Military music, to find a possible ancestor to the march, the 'Bjorneborgarnes' March is said to have similarities to the Preobrajensky, and this is of Finnish extraction! But, the researchers of the 'Swedish connection' seem to point to Ferdinand Hasse, the Guard Inspector of Music in S[t] Petersburg c.1800 as the most likely source of the Russian march.

The history of the Preobrajensky is somewhat inconclusive but there can be little doubt that the score presented to Lord Mountbatten by Alfonso XIII was not the only one!"[12]

The Quick March of the Royal Marines Commandos. –'Sarie Marais'

Written by Toonsetting and arranged by Dunn in 1937. Officially adopted in 1952. There is a report that the band of 3 Cdo Bde, in Malta, was using *The Lincolshire Poacher* for this purpose until the CGRM instructed the Officer Commanding the Brigade Band to replace it with *Sarie Marais*[13] Brigadier Wills claims that 3 Cdo Bde officially adopted *Sarie Marais* in 1947. Wills made this suggestion to the CGRM (Dallas Brooks) who was extremely keen on the idea. 3 Cdo Bde appear to have used an arrangement by their own Bandmaster Dixon.[14]

The Quick March of the Commando Logistic Regiment - 'Army and Marine'

Written by Zehle[15] and arranged by Hewitt this was first played as the adopted Regimental March of the Commando Logistics Regiment at the Regiment's inaugural parade on the 11th June 1972.

The Quick March of 29 Commando Regiment Royal Artillery - 'Soldiers' Chorus' from *Faust*

The Royal Marines presented the old march of the Royal Marine Artillery to the Royal Regiment of Artillery as an official quick march on 11 July 1994. The march was to be used by 29 Commando Regiment to celebrate the long-standing relationship with the Royal Marines.[16]

The Royal Marines Band Service Memorial Fanfare - 'To Comrades Sleeping'

"The Spirit of Joy and Thanksgiving for Victory, and Meditation for those who gave their lives in its cause" composed by Leon Young, a wartime survivor of HMS *Hermione*, and known simply as *To Comrades Sleeping* or *The Dedication Fanfare*. Initially composed for the ceremony to dedicate the World War II Silver Memorial Fanfare Trumpets in 1948. This fanfare is always sounded on Memorial Day, the 1st June, and at the Band Service Memorial Service as laid down in the Charter.

Marches associated with Regiments that served as Marines

Villiers' Marines, Fox's Marines and Saunderson's Marines were three of the six Marine Regiments raised in 1702. They became the 1st Bn. East Surrey Regiment, the 1st Bn. Duke of Cornwall's Light Infantry and the 1st Bn. East Lancashire Regiment respectively.[17]

The marches of The East Surrey Regiment, *A Southerly Wind and a Cloudy Sky* (Trad arranged Retford), and The Queen's Royal Regiment (West Surrey), *Braganza*, (a regiment that also served as Marines) are regarded as being associated with the Royal

Marines. Similarly, *British Grenadiers* is appropriate to the Royal Marines since Marines were once regarded as Fusiliers.

The story of *Braganza* is particularly interesting. A battalion of The Queen's Royal Regiment served as marines in HMS *Queen Charlotte*,[18] *Royal George, Defence, Majestic* and *Russell* at the battle of the Glorious First of June 1794. As a result the Regimental Colours bear a Naval Crown. There has been a close relationship between the two ever since and each year a two-day cricket match and dinner were held, alternately, in HMS *Excellent* or at the Queen's Depot. In 1923 Cdr P Macnamara joined HMS *Excellent* and quickly decided that the establishment should have its own Ship's march to a good rousing tune. Lack of musical knowledge on the Commander's part made selection very difficult. When the Queen's came down for their annual cricket match and their band played their Regimental march at dinner the Commander thought, in his own words, "It seemed a very good noise to me" and so he asked if the establishment could adopt it. Everyone thought this was a fine idea and the march was officially presented at a ceremony on the lawns of HMS *Excellent*.[19] The Band and Drums of the Queen's were drawn up facing the Royal Marine Band of HMS *Excellent*. The regimental Band marched through the Royal Marine Band playing the march then countermarched so that both bands could play it together. Mr Buckle, the Bandmaster of the Queen's, then handed a silver cylinder containing a parchment giving HMS *Excellent* permission to use the march.

The Royal Navy

Royal Navy March Past:	*Heart of Oak*	Boyce
RN Advance in Review Order:	*Nancy Lee*[20]	
Naval Hymn:	*Eternal Father*	

Corps Marching Songs

At the turn of the twentieth century, when the Corps marched almost everywhere, Marching Songs were very popular with the men and with concert audiences. Listed below are a few examples:

Soldiers of the Sea
Composed by Mr George Miller. Mus. Bac. Oxon. Bandmaster RMLI. Words by Oxenford.
Royal Marine Marching Songs
Composed by Mr George Miller. Mus. Bac. Oxon. Bandmaster RMLI.
The Blue and Red Marine
Composed by Mr B S Green, Bandmaster RMA. Words by Mrs Aubrey Cox.
The British Lions Awake
Composed by Mr B S Green, Bandmaster RMA.
Join the Red Marines
Words and music by Edward German
The Battle of the Falkland Islands (Sung to the tune of *The Girl I Left Behind Me*).
Words by Bd/Cpl R J Connell (HMS *Cornwall*) (1914)

Musical Salutes

Prior to 1927 the musical salutes were printed on two march cards that bore the title *"Naval Brigade Ceremonial Music"* and a statement saying they were Admiralty Approved and, on card 1, was the notation "Arranged Kappey". The cards had the following music on them.

Card 1.

March Past:	*A Life on the Ocean Wave*
Advance in Review Order:	*Boys of the Old Brigade* (At the double)
Double:	

Card 2.

Royal Salute:	*National Anthem*	
General Salute:	*Rule Britannia*	
Alternative Salute:	*Garb of Auld Gaul*	
For Inspection:	12 bars Bugle	Arrgd Miller.
	Rule Britannia	
	12 bars Bugle	
	Scipio	

There was also a General Salute, "Norma," for 'Other Flag Officers, Governors, etc'.

The 1927 changes to salutes are described elsewhere and resulted in the following:

Royal Salute - the Sovereign:	*National Anthem*	Complete
Royal Salute - Royal Family:	*National Anthem*	First six bars.
General Salute, Admirals and C-in-Cs:	*Rule Britannia* (Arne)	
General Salute, Other Flag Officers:	*Iolanthe* (Sullivan)	
General Salute, Governors etc:	*Garb of Auld Gaul*	
Unit Commanding Officers and VIPs - not Flag Officers.	*Alert/Drum Ruffle/Carry On*	

In 1988 another salute was added.

Royal Marine General Officers[21]:	*Preobrajensky*	First eight bars in quick time.

The Royal Marines use the Army Advance in Review Order:

	British Grenadiers	Trad arr Kappey

APPENDIX THREE

The Mountbatten Festival of Music[1]

C GRM approved Major P Neville's suggestion of a high-profile concert to raise funds for, and awareness of, the Royal Academy of Music Appeal as an acknowledgement of the work done by the RAM for the RMBS. It would also give the Corps considerable publicity. Major Neville had made two suggestions. Either a military band charity concert in London or a symphony orchestra charity concert in the provinces or Portsmouth would be appropriate. The CGRM gave permission for the proposed concert to take place as a Category I duty engagement. A military band concert in London was agreed with the RAM being the sponsors and the date of 6th February 1973 was set.

The bands taking part were C-in-C Naval Home Command, HMS *Ganges* and the RMSM, guest vocalist was Owen Brannigan and the concert was introduced by Richard Baker. The Principal of the Royal Academy of Music was most appreciative of the effort that the Corps had made towards the appeal and also of the standard exhibited by the Band Service.

In 1973 the Royal Marines Museum launched an appeal to raise the funds necessary to allow it to move into the building that once housed the Officers' Mess at Eastney. The pattern set by the Royal Academy of Music was used and on the 5th February 1974 the massed bands of the RMSM, Commando Forces, CTCRM and C-in-C Naval Home Command gave a concert at the Royal Albert Hall that raised £2,800 for the Museum.

The soloist was John Lawrenson and the compere was, once again, Richard Baker. A fitting tribute was paid to Captain A C Green, composer of the famous setting of Sunset. Having received news of his death earlier that day the Band Service dedicated this performance to him.

In 1975 the concert was given in aid of the Malcolm Sargent Cancer Fund for Children, which the Corps continues to support, and Royal Marines Charities. This concert followed a similar format to its predecessors featuring a mixture of marches and fanfares, film and classical music as well as opportunities for soloists. Guest soloist was Alan Civil, Professor of Horn at the Royal College and an ex-Royal Artillery Bandsman. Richard Baker played an even greater part in this concert as not only did he act as compere and help to produce the show but also narrated two items. One was *Tubby the Tuba* which featured Band Corporal David Cole on tuba. The other was the first playing of Albert Elms *Battle of Trafalgar* with a narration written by Richard Baker and spoken by himself and the fine actor, Kenneth More.[2] Bands involved, in addition to the Royal Marines School of Music, were from C-in-C Fleet and HMS *Ganges* plus, taking part in the finale, the Corps of Drums from Deal. The 1975 concert set the pattern for the next five years in terms of the beneficiaries. The concerts became known, albeit colloquially, as the 'Sir Malcolm Sargent Fund Concerts'. However, the content did not become set, for the hallmark of these concerts has always been their progress and development in terms of content and entertainment.

1976 Theme was the 200th Anniversary of the American Declaration of Independence and featured guest appearances from the Director and solo trumpet of 'The President's Own'

1977 Programme reflected the Silver Jubilee of the Queen's Accession. Corps of Drums featured for the first time.

1978 25th Anniversary of the Duke of Edinburgh becoming Captain General and the 75th Anniversary of the Royal Marines Band Service were celebrated in music. It was Lt Col Neville's final concert and also the first to be broadcast on radio.

1979 Marine Band of the Royal Netherlands Navy (Capt Koops) were featured guests.

1980 Concert extended to two nights. Featured a finale dedicated to the late Earl Mountbatten with Sir Vivian Dunn as guest conductor.

1981 Concerts renamed Mountbatten Festival of Music. 100th Anniversary of Kenneth Alford's birth was celebrated. First of Lt David Cole's special arrangements featured.

1982 Tchaikovsky's *Fourth Symphony* was the finale.

1983 Military role of the bands in the Falklands was highlighted.

1984 All previous attendance records broken. The Band Service Memorial Fanfare *To Comrades Sleeping* featured as part of the finale. Bandmasters conducted in Mess Dress for the first time.[3]

1985 BdCpl Henry Monaghan became the first Royal Marine solo vocalist at the MFM.

1986 Following a joint tour to the United States the Pipes, Drums and Dancers of the Argyll and Sutherland Highlanders shared the concert platform.

1987 An innovation was the singing of the massed bands to Wilhousky's *Battle Hymn of the Republic*.

1988 The concert was extended to three nights and, for the only time, it was recorded on video.

1989 Marine Band of the Royal Netherlands Navy (Maj Buitenhuis) shared the concert.

1990 Richard Baker gave a poignant introduction to a special arrangement dedicated to the men of the Band Service killed by the terrorist bombing of Deal. Richard Baker's final MFM concert.

1991 Desmond Carrington joined Susannah Simons as Richard Baker's replacement. A 'traditional' style concert featured an '*Evening Ceremonial*'.

1992 'The President's Own' US Marine band paid its visit to the UK specifically to share this MFM that also featured the Pipes and Drums of the Argyll and Sutherland Highlanders.

1993 A mixture of old and new that included the Junior Choir of the Royal Marines, the 'All Stars' Band and *Concerto for Clarinet* by jazz virtuoso BM Martin Dale.

1994 The RM Symphony Orchestra played *Cavalleria Rusticana* and accompanied vocalist Beverley Humphries.

1995 For the first time the concerts were produced, directed and recorded entirely by the Band Service. Col John Bourgeois of 'The President's Own' was guest conductor.

1996 The Ceilidh Band playing *Riverdance* was a huge success that was enhanced by the Corps of Drums and their very complex and fast stick drill.

1997 25th Anniversary of the original 1973 concert. Only one man, CSgt Jon Yates, had featured in all of them. He had also played solo trumpet, cornet or flugelhorn in many of them.

1998 Final appearance of Captain David Cole; first appearance of a RMBS piper and the Corps of Drums appeared in period costume for *The Last of the Mohicans*.

1999 A Royal Navy theme showcased the stunning music especially composed and arranged by the Staff Arranger (WO2 M McDermott) for *The Festival of the Sea*.

2000 The RMBS Production Team included a dance troupe and traditional Irish dancers in a show business concert that celebrated the new millennium.

2001 A traditional style concert that featured the RMSM Choir and marches, new and old.

2002 A tribute to the Queen and to the Royal Yacht were features of 2002.

2003 Due to the Fire-fighters strikes and an escalating situation regarding Iraq this concert was nearly cancelled. It required all possible musicians, including Drafting Office staff and Volunteer Band Instructors, to take part.

APPENDIX FOUR

The Royal Tournament and the Edinburgh Tattoo.

Royal Marine Bands at the Royal Tournament.

The Royal Tournament began life as 'The Grand Military Tournament' in 1881 but when a Royal Marine Band took part for the first time in 1919 (the year before it became 'The Royal Tournament') it was called 'The Royal Naval, Military and Air Force Tournament'. Only a resident band was used until the late nineteen-twenties since most of the displays were concerned with feats of arms and physical, and military, training. There were no Tournaments during the years 1915-1918 or 1940-1946 and the last Royal Tournament took place at Earls Court in 1999.

The following list indicates the years in which Bands of the Royal Marines featured:

1919 (Resident Band) Plymouth Division, RMLI. (Mr P S G O'Donnell).

1924 (Naval Pageant: Heart of Oak) RNSM (BM 1 A C Green LRAM and BM F G Stagg).

1931 RNSM Band supported a display of 17th Century Pike Drill by the Royal Marines, Depot.

1939 RM Chatham Division augmented from Portsmouth and Plymouth Divisions.

1947 RM Chatham Group augmented from Portsmouth, Plymouth and the RNSM with Drill Display by the King's Squad, RM.

1948 Staff Band of the RNSM augmented by ranks from the fleets and from shore establishments.

1949 Bands and Trumpeters of the RNSM. Display with the King's Squad, RM.

1951 Royal Marines School of Music. Drill Display by the King's Squad.

1953 Massed Bands of the Royal Marines including RMSM. Display by the King's Squad, RM

1954 Massed Bands including Plymouth, and the RMSM. (Capt W Lang).

1957 Massed Bands including Portsmouth, Plymouth; HMS *Daedalus*; RMSM and The Memorial Silver Trumpets of the Royal Marines School of Music. (Lt Col F V Dunn)

1959 Band of RMSM with drill display by the King's Squad, Royal Marines.

1960 Massed Bands of C-in-C, The Nore; Flag Officer Air (Home); Britannia Royal Naval College; HMS *Raleigh*; HMS *St Vincent*: Portsmouth Group and the RMSM (Lt Col F V Dunn).

1962 Massed Bands of HM Royal Marines. HM Royal Marines, Flag Officer Air (Home); HM Royal Marines HMS *St Vincent*; HM Royal Marines, HMS *Raleigh*; HM Royal Marines, Portsmouth Group; HM Royal Marines, Plymouth Group; HM Royal Marines (Royal Marines School of Music). (Principal Director of Music: Lt Col F V Dunn CVO OBE FRAM RM).

1963 'Drill as a Means to an End' with 43 Cdo RM. - The Massed Bands of Plymouth Group and C-in-C, Plymouth. (Capt L H A Arnold).

1964 Massed Bands of Plymouth Group; C-in-C, Portsmouth; C-in-C Plymouth; C-in-C Home Fleet; Flag Officer Naval Air Command; HMS *Condor*; HMS *Raleigh*; HMS *Thunderer* and the RMSM (Lt Col F V Dunn).

1968 Massed Bands of Plymouth Group; Portsmouth Group and the RMSM (Lt Col F V Dunn) Display included the RM Symphony Orchestra and the RM Dance Orchestra.

1971 Massed Bands of Portsmouth, Plymouth and the RMSM. (Major P J Neville).

1974 'The Battle of Trafalgar' - Massed Bands of C-in-C Naval Home Command, Commando Forces, Commando Training Centre, Britannia Royal Naval College, HMS *Ganges*; HM Royal Marines and the RMSM. (Lt Col P J Neville).

1977 'The Queen's Silver Jubilee - A Royal Review' -Massed Bands of C-in-C Naval Home Command; C-in-C, Fleet; Flag Officer Scotland and Northern Ireland; Flag Officer Naval Air Command; RMSM (Lt Col P J Neville).

1980 'The Centenary of the Royal Tournament' - Massed Bands of the Three Services. Royal Marines School of Music, Irish Guards with their Pipes & Drums, Central Band of the Royal Air Force (Lt Col J R Mason).

1981 'The Battle of Trafalgar' - Massed Bands of Flag Officer Plymouth, Flag Officer Scotland and Northern Ireland, Flag Officer Naval Air Command, Commando Forces, Commando Training Centre and the RMSM (Lt Col J R Mason).

1984 'A Day in the Life of the Royal Navy' - Massed Bands of C-in-C Naval Home Command, C-in-C, Fleet, Flag Officer Scotland and Northern Ireland, Commando Forces, Commando Training Centre and the RMSM. (Lt Col G A C Hoskins) Included the Orchestra of HM Royal Marines (Lt D C Cole).

1987 'Neptune, God of the Sea' - Massed Bands of C-in-C Naval Home Command, C-in-C, Fleet, Commando Forces and the RMSM. (Lt Col G A C Hoskins) Included the Dance Band of HM Royal Marines (Lt D C Cole).

1988 'The Drum' - Corps of Drums of the Royal Marines.

1990 'The Sea Soldier' - Massed Bands of C-in-C Naval Home Command, C-in-C, Fleet, Flag Officer Plymouth, Flag Officer Scotland and Northern Ireland, Commandos and the RMSM (Lt Col J M Ware).

1993 'Victory at Sea' - Massed Bands of C-in-C Naval Home Command, C-in-C Fleet, Flag Officer Plymouth, Flag Officer Scotland and Northern Ireland, Britannia Royal Naval College and the RMSM (Lt Col J M Ware).

1996 'Rule Britannia' - Massed Bands of Portsmouth, Plymouth, Scotland, Commando Training Centre (Lt Col R A Waterer).

1999 'The Royal Tournament 1880-1999' - The final Royal Tournament. - Massed Bands of RM Plymouth and RM Commando Training Centre. This was the final Royal Tournament and featured bands of all three Services under the Senior Director of Music for the Royal Tournament, Lt Col R A Waterer.

Royal Marine Bands at the Edinburgh Military Tattoo. 1950-2002

1951 Royal Marines School of Music (Capt W Lang).

1956 Royal Marines School of Music (Lt Col F V Dunn).

1959 Royal Marines, Plymouth Group (Capt W Lang).

1960 Royal Marines C-in-C Portsmouth (Sqn Ldr H J I Cash. RAF).

1962 Royal Marines School of Music (Lt Col F V Dunn).

1965 Royal Marines School of Music (Lt Col F V Dunn).

1969 Royal Marines School of Music (Maj P J Neville).

1975 Massed Bands of Commando Forces, Commando Training Centre, Flag Officer Scotland and Northern Ireland (Capt W W Shillito).

1983 Massed Bands of RMSM, Flag Officer Plymouth, Flag Officer Scotland and Northern Ireland (Lt Col G A C Hoskins).

1992 Massed Bands of RMSM, C-in-C Naval Home Command, Flag Officer Scotland and Northern Ireland (Lt Col J M Ware).

1997 Massed Bands of Plymouth, Commando Training Centre, Scotland (Lt Col R A Waterer).

2002 Royal Marines, Scotland (Lt Col C J Davis).

APPENDIX FIVE

Recordings of the Royal Marines

The first commercial recordings appear to have been made by the Massed Bands of the Portsmouth Command, directed by Bandmaster G C Keen, for Columbia in 1936. It was three years later that the Divisional Bands went into the recording studio when Major Ricketts and the Plymouth Band recorded a series of Alford marches for HMV. When Major Dunn became Principal Director of Music he took control of the recording policy and, with the exception of military tattoos, allowed no band except the RMSM to make recordings. This policy remained in place until Lt Col Dunn's retirement in 1968, apart from one made by Captain McLean and the Portsmouth Band in 1961. Recording companies were beginning to understand the potential in terms of re-issues and re-releases. They held the copyrights for the recordings and were able to produce re-issues which then competed with, and reduced sales of new recordings. With an increase in the number of bands recording came a broadening of the type of music being played. Lt Col Neville introduced collaboration with choirs when he combined with the Morriston Orpheus Choir.

With the introduction of the compact disc came the opportunity for the record companies to dip into their archives and release compilation after compilation of recordings that were cheap to produce and buy and gave no benefit to the RMBS except Royalties. The reissue and compilations became prolific and each World War II anniversary produced a fresh crop. In years to come Lt Col Waterer had the foresight and imagination to support the formation of an RMBS recording capability complete with its own recording engineer. This had the effect of 'locking-up' the copyright of all new recordings thereby gradually draining the recording companies of the ability to issue compilations of more recent material. Linked to the ability of the Blue Band staff to produce the artwork for the compact disc inlays, the RMBS have a powerful in-house tool that will be developed even further.

On a number of occasions, bands and orchestras of the Royal Marines have been involved in making recordings that were not for commercial gain. The most obvious are the recordings made during World War II for the entertainment of Allied troops. These are far too numerous to list here. There are also reports of recordings being made in the very early days of recording technology. Although no such recordings have been found the mere fact that data in the form of written reports exists is a fair indication that such recordings were made. We are, after all, dealing with not only a rare commodity, but also a very fragile one.

In an 1893 issue of 'Globe and Laurel' appears the following report:

About ten of the most accomplished performers of the Band of the Royal Marines Chatham Division are carrying out a novel engagement. They are attending the establishment of Mr Edison in London at stated times and give forth a number of martial airs, the tunes of which are received in phonographs. These instruments, thus charged, are sent to various parts of the world. The other day two of them were transmitted to the Pope whilst others have been transmitted to the reigning Princes of India, and to the different crowned heads of Europe, who thus have the opportunity of listening to lively marches, etc., originally played by instrumentalists hundreds of miles away

The following lists show the recordings made by Royal Marine Bands, Divisional Bands and Orchestras and Bands of the Royal Marines Band Service. Compilations and re-issues are not included and, whilst the lists are as extensive as possible, it is not claimed to be absolutely complete. Included are a few recordings that have eluded all attempts to date them accurately.

The Commercial Recordings

Date	Title of Recording	Band/DoM or Bmstr	Type	Recording Company
1936	Nautical Moments Pt 1 & 2	Portsmouth Cmd/Keen	78	Columbia
1936	Sea Songs Medley/Ship Ahoy	Portsmouth Cmd/Keen	78	Columbia
1939	Thin Red Line March/Colonel Bogey	Plymouth/Ricketts	78	HMV
1939	On the Quarterdeck/HM Jollies	Plymouth/Ricketts	78	HMV
1939	Smithy, The - Pastoral Fantasy/ Two Dons	Plymouth/Ricketts	78	HMV
1939	By Land & Sea - Ceremonial March/The Middy	Plymouth/Ricketts	78	HMV
1939	Country Life Suite - The Hunt Part 1/Part 2	Plymouth/Ricketts	78	HMV
1939	Vanished Amy/A Life on the Ocean Wave/The King	Plymouth/Ricketts	78	HMV
1939	Chase, The - Posthorn Solo/Posthorn Galop	Plymouth/Ricketts	78	HMV
1939	Stars & Stripes/Semper Fidelis	Plymouth/Ricketts	78	HMV
1939	Colonel Bogey on Parade - Pt 1/ Pt 2	Plymouth/Ricketts	78	HMV
1939	Carmen Selection pts 1& 2	Plymouth/Ricketts	78	HMV
1940	Amparita Roca/ La Belle Pense	Portsmouth Orch/Dunn	78	Columbia
1940	Temple Bells/Less Than the Dust	Portsmouth Orch/Dunn	78	Columbia
1940	Kashmiri Song/Till I Awake	Portsmouth Orch/Dunn	78	Columbia
1940	Life on the Ocean Wave/Heart of Oak	Portsmouth Orch/Dunn	78	Columbia
1940	Standard of St George, The/Royal Review	Plymouth/Ricketts	78	HMV
1940	Nautical Moments/Hornpipe Bill the Bosun	Plymouth/Ricketts	78	HMV
1940	August Bank Holiday 1915/ Voice of the Guns	Plymouth/Ricketts	78	HMV
1940	Contemptibles/Great Little Army	Plymouth/Ricketts	78	HMV
1940	Dunedin/Phantom Brigade	Plymouth/Ricketts	78	HMV
1941	Grasshoppers Dance/Turkish Patrol Op83	Portsmouth Orch/Dunn	78	Columbia
1941	A! Frangesa/El Abanico	Portsmouth Orch/Dunn	78	Columbia
1941	Merry Widow Selection Pt1/Pt 2	Portsmouth Orch/Dunn	78	Columbia
1941	La Caprice De Nanette/Demande Et Response	Portsmouth Orch/Dunn	78	Columbia
1941	Un Sonnet D'Amour/Tarentelle Fretillante	Portsmouth Orch/Dunn	78	Columbia
1942	Skaters Waltz/Estudiantina Waltz	Portsmouth Orch/Dunn	78	Columbia
1942	Dance of the Comedians/Perpetuum Mobile	Portsmouth Orch/Dunn	78	Columbia
1942	Gypsy Love Selection Pt1/Pt 2	Portsmouth Orch/Dunn	78	Columbia
1950	Salute to Amethyst/Pompey Chimes, The	Portsmouth/Dunn	78	Columbia
1950	Royal Vanguard/Springbok March	Portsmouth/Dunn	78	Columbia
1950	Prelude to the Morning/Sunset	Portsmouth/Dunn	78	Columbia
1953	Life on the Ocean Wave/Heart of Oak	Portsmouth Orch/Dunn	45	Columbia
1953	Music by the Band of HM Royal Marines, Portsmouth	Portsmouth/Dunn	LP	HMV
1954	Marching With The Marines	Portsmouth/Dunn	10"LP	GramCoLtd
1954	Huntsman/Waltzing Matilda	Portsmouth/Dunn	78	
1954	Sailors Holiday/Army of the Nile	Portsmouth/Dunn	78	
1954	White City Searchlight Tattoo 1954	Massed/Lang	LP	EMI
1954	Under the White Ensign/Captain General, The	Portsmouth/Dunn	78	HMV
1954	Globe & Laurel/Life on the Ocean Wave, A	Portsmouth/Dunn	78	HMV
1954	Waltzing Matilda/March from Suite No 3 (Holst)	Portsmouth/Dunn	78	HMV
1954	Brass Buttons/Amethyst March	RMSM/Dunn	78	Philips
1955	Band of HM Royal Marines Plymouth[1]	Plymouth/Lang	LP	Capitol
1955	Blaze Away/Washington Post	Portsmouth/Dunn	78	HMV
1955	Cockleshell Heroes/Royal Review	RMSM?/Dunn	78	HMV
1956	White City Searchlight Tattoo 1956	Massed/Dunn	10"LP	EMI
1957	Royal Tournament 1957	Massed/Dunn	LP	EMI-Columbia
1958	Listen to the Royal Marines Band	RMSM/Dunn	LP	
1958	Band of HMRM - RM School of Music	RMSM/Dunn	EP	EMI-HMV

Year	Title	Performer/Director	Format	Label
1958	Band of the Royal Marines	RMSM/Dunn	LP	
1959	Colonel Bogey Marches On	RMSM/Dunn	LP	CSD 1282
1959	Marching with the Royal Marines (No 1)	RMSM/Dunn	EP	EMI
1959	Marching with the Royal Marines (No 3)	RMSM/Dunn	EP	EMI
1960	Edinburgh Military Tattoo 1960	CinC Portsmouth/Mason	LP	Waverley
1961	Music of the Sea	RMSM/Dunn		
1961	Beating Retreat and Tattoo	RMSM/Dunn	LP	EMI
1961	Life on the Ocean Wave, A	Portsmouth/McLean	LP	
1961	Nightfall in Camp	RMSM/Dunn	EP	EMI
1961	Life on the Ocean Wave, A	Portsmouth/McLean	EP	
1961	Marching On With the Royal Navy	RMSM/Dunn	EP	EMI
1961	Songs of the Sea	RMSM/Dunn	EP	EMI
1962	On Land and Sea	RMSM/Dunn	LP	EMI
1962	Edinburgh Tattoo 1962	RMSM/Dunn	LP	Waverley
1963	Splendour of the March	RMSM/Dunn	LP	EMI
1963	Sound of the Royal Marines, The[2]	RMSM/Dunn	LP	Liberty
1963	Bath Military Tattoo	CinC Plymouth/Haigh	LP	Waverley
1963	1812 Overture[3]	RMSM/Dunn	LP	Columbia
1964	300 Glorious Years	RMSM/Dunn	LP	EMI
1964	Finest Hours/Longest Day	RMSM/Dunn	45	HMV
1964	Finest Hours, The	RMSM/Dunn	EP	HMV
1964	Churchill March/March of the Victors	RMSM/Dunn	45	HMV
1964	Marching to Victory	RMSM/Dunn	EP	HMV
1964	Mountbatten TV Series Music	RMSM/Dunn	45	HMV
1964	Frederick Harvey Sings West Country Songs	RMSM/Dunn	EP	HMV
1965	Edinburgh Tattoo 1965	RMSM/Dunn	LP	Monitor
1965	Great War, The	RMSM/Dunn	EP	HMV
1966	Both Sides of the Globe	RMSM/Dunn	LP	EMI
1966	Art of the Military Band	RMSM/Dunn	LP	EMI
1966	1812 Overture and Music by Tchaikovsky[4]	RMSM/Dunn	LP	EMI
1967	Worlds Great Marches	RMSM/Dunn	LP	HMV
1968	Royal Tournament 1968	Massed/Dunn	LP	EMI
1968	Royal Marines Play Sousa	RMSM/Dunn	LP	EMI
1969	Young Winston	RMSM/Dunn		Starline
1969	Music of Pomp & Circumstance	RMSM/Dunn	LP	EMI
1969	Edinburgh Tattoo 1969	RMSM/Neville	LP	EMI
1970	Magnificent Marines	RMSM/Neville	LP	HMV
1970	Band of HM Royal Marines Portsmouth	Portsmouth/Lambert	LP	Philips
1971	On the Square	RMSM/Neville	LP	EMI
1971	Excerpts from Festival Concert	Plymouth/Shillito	LP	?
1971	Sounds of Majesty	Portsmouth/Lambert	LP	Philips
1972	By Land and Sea	Cdo Forces/Shillito	LP	Decca
1972	Colonel Bogey on Parade Vol. 1	CinCNavHom/Mason	LP	Polydor
1972	Festival of Brass 1972	Fanfare Trumpets/Dunn	LP	EMI
1972	By Special Request	RMSM/Neville	LP	EMI
1972	Colchester Tattoo 1972	HMS Ganges	LP	Drum Major
1972	Milton Glee Club[5]	Ports Orch/Mason	LP	Solent
1973	Warship	RMSM/Neville	LP	EMI
1973	Around the Globe	Cdo Forces/Shillito	LP	Decca
1973	Rule Britannia	CinCNavHome/Mason	LP	Polydor
1973	Warship/Colditz March	RMSM/Neville	45	Columbia
1974	Her Majesty's Royal Marines	CinCNavHome/Mason	LP	Polydor
1974	Royal Tournament 1974 'Trafalgar'	Massed/Neville	LP	EMI
1974	Royal Marines Play Burt Bacharach	RMSM/Neville	LP	EMI
1974	Royal Marines Play Pops & Classics	Cdo Forces/Shillito	LP	
1975	Best Foot Forward	CinC Fleet/Sumner	LP	RCA
1975	1812	RMSM/Neville	LP	EMI
1975	Best of British	Cdo Forces/Shillito	LP	Decca
1975	Salute to Heroes	CinC Fleet/Sumner	LP	EMI
1975	Colonel Bogey on Parade Vol II	CinCNavHom/Mason	LP	Polydor
1975	Edinburgh Tattoo 1975	Massed/Shillito	LP	EMI/Waverley
1975	Victory at Sea	CinCFleet/Taylor	LP	Readers Dig
1975	The Best of the Royal Marines	Cdo Forces/Shillito	LP	

1976	A Grand Night for Singing (Morriston Orpheus Choir)	RMSM/Neville	LP	EMI
1976	Best of the Royal Marines	CinCNavHome/Mason	LP	Polydor
1976	On Land, Sea and Air	CinCNavHome/Mason	LP	Polydor
1976	British Are Coming, The	Cdo Forces/Shillito	LP	Monitor
1976	Alford Conducts Alford (The British March King)	Plymouth/Ricketts	LP	EMI
1976	Love is a Many Splendoured Thing/Life is Good[6]	RMSM/Neville	45	EMI
1977	Marines on the March	Cdo Forces/Shillito	LP	Decca
1977	Victory at Sea	RMSM/Neville	LP	EMI
1977	Tasmania Military Tattoo	CinC Fleet/Taylor	LP	
1977	Wembley Military Pageant	Massed/Shillito	LP	Pye
1977	Royal Tournament 1977	Massed/Neville	LP	EMI
1977	Sailing	HMS Ark Royal/Sheppard	45	
1978	Very Best of the Royal Marines, The	CinC Fleet/Taylor	LP	EMI
1978	Famous Concert Marches	CinCNavHome/Mason	LP	States
1978	Concert Programme, A	RMSM/Neville	LP	EMI
1978	Sailor	HMS Ark Royal	LP	BBC
1978	Very Best of Gilbert & Sullivan	RMSM/Neville	LP	EMI
1978	Songs of Land & Sea[7]	RMSM/Dunn	LP	EMI/HMV
1979	RAH Concert 1979	Massed/Mason	LP	RMA
1979	Imperial Echoes	RMSM/Mason	LP	EMI
1979	Lord Louis Mountbatten Tribute	CinCNavHome/Hoskins	LP	BBC
1979	Last Farewell, The	HMS Ark Royal & FOP	LP	BBC
1979	Last Farewell, The	HMS Ark Royal/Whittal	45	BBC
1979	Aldershot Tattoo 1979	Massed	LP	Orch&Rec
1980	RAH Concert 1980	Massed/Mason	LP	RMA
1980	Something Different	CinC Fleet/Freestone	LP	Foldback
1980	Say It With Music	RMSM/Mason	LP	EMI
1980	Royal Tournament 1980		LP	EMI
1980	Great Marches of the World	Cdo Forces	LP	Decca
1980	Once Upon A Time/Manhatten Skyline	CinC Fleet/Freestone	45	Foldback
1981	Sailor II	?	LP	BBC
1981	RAH/MFM 1981	Massed/Mason	LP	RMA
1981	Royal Tournament 1981	Massed/Mason	LP	Craighall?
1981	Plymouth Pageant 1979	Britannia/Sheppard	LP	DR Records
1981	La Traviata	HMRM/Mason	LP	
1982	Best of the Royal Marines, The	CinCNavHome/Mason	LP	Polydor
1982	RAH/MFM 1982	Massed/Mason	LP	RMA
1982	Tribute to the Task Force	FOP/Cole	LP	EAI?
1982	The Falklands Overture	Kent Concert Orch(RMSM)	45	Cinque Port
1983	RAH/MFM 1983	Massed/Hoskins	LP	RMA
1983	And the Band Played On	Commando Forces/Ware	LP	EMI
1983	Stars and Stripes Forever (Sousa Marches Vol 1)[8]	RMSM/Hoskins	LP	EMI
1983	Berlin Tattoo 1983	CinCNavHome/Heming	LP	Craighall?
1983	Edinburgh Military Tattoo	Massed/Hoskins		
1984	Hands Across the Sea (Sousa Marches Vol 2)[9]	RMSM/Hoskins	LP	EMI
1984	RAH/MFM 1984	Massed/Hoskins	LP	RMA
1984	Old Comrades-New Comrades	RMSM/Hoskins	LP	Grasmere
1984	Royal Tournament 1984	Massed/Hoskins	LP	Polydor
1985	Band of HM Royal Marines CinC Fleet	CinC Fleet/Whealing	LP	MusicMasters
1985	Spectacular Sound of HMRM+Argyll & S'land H'ers	RMSM/Hoskins	LP	EMI
1985	RAH/MFM 1985	Massed/Hoskins	LP	RMA
1985	Plymouth's Own	Cdo Forces/Ware	LP	Grasmere
1985	Men of Action	CinCNavHome/Heming	LP	Bandleader
1985	Marching to Glory[10]	CinCNavHome/Heming	LP	Pickwick
1986	By Land and Sea	Cdo Forces/Ware	LP	Bandleader
1986	Band of HM Royal Marines CinC Fleet	CinC Fleet/Whealing	LP	MusicMasters
1986	RAH/MFM 1986	Massed/Hoskins	LP	RMA
1986	Band of HM Royal Marines	CinCNavHome/Heming	LP	Fidelity
1987	Band of HM Royal Marines CinC Fleet	CinC Fleet/Goss	LP	MusicMasters
1987	Brass in Blue	CinCNavHome/Heming	LP	Fidelity
1987	Celebration of Christmas	CinCNavHome/Heming	LP	Bandleader
1987	Under the White Ensign	FOP/Perkins	LP	Raleigh
1987	Solid Men To The Front (Sousa Marches Vol 3)[11]	RMSM/Hoskins	LP	EMI

Year	Title	Band/Director	Format	Label
1987	RAH/MFM 1987	Massed/Hoskins	LP	RMA
1987	Plymouth Sound	FOP/Perkins	LP	Raleigh
1987	Royal Tournament 1987	Massed/Hoskins	LP	?
1988	Portsmouth	CinCNavHome/Heming	LP	Bandleader
1988	Its...The Royal Marines	CinCNavHome/Whealing	LP	MusicMasters
1988	RAH/MFM 1988	Massed/Hoskins	LP	RMA
1988	Beating Retreat	Massed/Hoskins	LP	RMA
1988	Finlandia	FOSNI/Rutterford	LP	MusicMasters
1988	Royal Tournament 1988	Buglers	LP	Craighall
1988	Eastney Searchlight Tattoo	CinCNavHome/Whealing	Cass	Stephan George
1989	Britannia	Britannia/Starr	LP	MusicMasters
1989	RAH/MFM 1989	Massed/Hoskins	LP	RMA
1989	Globe and Laurel	RMSM/Hoskins	LP	Bandleader
1989	Tribute, A	CinCNavHome	45	Ocean Sound
1989	White Cliffs of Dover with Vera Lynn	?	EP	Decca
1990	Music from the 100th Royal Tournament	Massed/Ware	LP	Bandleader
1990	Celebration	FOSNI/Rutterford	LP	MusicMasters
1990	Concert Performance, A	CinCNavHome/Whealing	LP	MusicMasters
1990	Navy Blue	FOP/Rogerson	Cass	MusicMasters
1990	RAH/MFM 1990	Massed/Ware	LP	RMA
1990	Fleet Review	CinC Fleet/Goss	CD	MusicMasters
1990	Great Berlin Band Show	CinCNavHome/Whealing	CD	Bandleader
1991	Beating Retreat & Tattoo	RMSM/Ware	CD	Grasmere
1991	RAH/MFM 1991	Massed/Ware	LP	RMA
1992	Anything Goes	Britannia/Hillier	CD	MusicMasters
1992	Men of Music	FOSNI/Rutterford	CD	MusicMasters
1992	Kaleidoscope	Commandos/Cole	CD	Bandleader
1992	RAH/MFM 1992	Massed/Ware	CD	RMB
1992	Sound the Alert	RMSM/CinCNavHome	CD	RMB
1992	Edinburgh Military Tattoo 1992	Massed/Ware	CD	EMT
1993	Battle of the Atlantic Suite[12]	CinCFleet/McDermott	CD	Conifer
1993	Marches of the Sea	Cdo Forces/Perkins	CD	Clovelly
1993	Battle of the Atlantic	Massed/Ware	CD	Bandleader
1993	RAH/MFM 1993	Massed/Ware	CD	RMB
1993	Christmas with the Royal Marines	RMSM/Ware	CD	Bandleader
1993	Complete Marches of Kenneth Alford	Cdo Forces/Perkins	CD	Clovelly
1993	Royal Tournament 1993	Massed/Ware	CD	Bandleader
1993	Toronto International Tattoo	FOSNI/Mills	CD	Lismor
1994	Admiral's Regiment, The	CinC Fleet/Waterer	CD	MusicMasters
1994	That's Entertainment	Britannia/Hillier	CD	MusicMasters
1994	RAH/MFM 1994	Massed/Ware	CD	RMB
1994	D-Day: 50th Anniversary	CinC Fleet/Whealing	CD	Souvenir
1994	Highland Cathedral	Scotland/Mills	CD	MusicMasters
1994	Twenty-First Mountbatten Festival of Music	Massed/Ware	CD	Grasmere
1994	For Those in Peril on the Sea	Plymouth/Perkins	CD	Clovelly
1994	Martial Music of Sir Vivian Dunn	Plymouth/Perkins	CD	Clovelly
1994	Nova Scotia International Tattoo 1994	RMSM/Ware	CD	?
1995	Mountbatten Festival of Music 1995	Massed/Waterer	CD	RMB
1995	Ashokan Farewell	Plymouth/Perkins	CD	Clovelly
1996	An Outdoor Overture	RMSM/Waterer	CD	RMB
1996	Mountbatten Festival of Music 1996	Massed/Waterer	CD	Blue Band
1996	The Big Band Sound	Plymouth/Perkins	CD	Clovelly
1996	Royal Tournament 1996	Massed/Waterer	CD	Bandleader
1997	Britannia Vol 1 - In Concert	Portsmouth/Cole	CD	Foldback
1997	Britannia Vol 2 - The Marches	Portsmouth/Cole	CD	Foldback
1997	Britannia Vol 3 - Royal Blue and Gold Leaf	Portsmouth/Cole	CD	Foldback
1997	The Chosin Few	Britannia/Watson	CD	Foldback
1997	Mountbatten Festival of Music 1997	Massed/Waterer	CD	Blue Band
1998	A Musical Journey - Trains, Planes, Autos	Scotland/Davis	CD	Chevron
1998	Mountbatten Festival of Music 1998	Massed/Waterer	CD	Blue Band
1998	International Festival of the Sea	Portsmouth/Plymouth	CD	Chevron
1998	The Music of Gilbert and Sullivan	Plymouth/Rutterford	CD	Chevron
1998	A Night in Concert	Britannia/Watson	CD	Chevron

1999	Beating Retreat	Massed/Waterer	CD	Chevron
1999	The Last Run - Royal Tournament 1999	Massed/Waterer	CD	Bandleader
1999	Mountbatten Festival of Music 1999	Massed/Waterer	CD	Blue Band
1999	Music for the Millennium	Plymouth/Rutterford	CD	Chevron
1999	Songs of the Sea	Portsmouth/Perkins	CD	Clovelly
1999	A Christmas Festival	Portsmouth/Perkins	CD	Clovelly
1999	Wind Machine	Portsmouth/Perkins	CD	Clovelly
1999	The Pride and Passion	Portsmouth/Perkins	CD	First Night
1999	1999 Open Day Concert	RMSM/Davis	CD	Chevron
2000	The Final Countdown	Various/Cole	CD	Chevron
2000	Mountbatten Festival of Music 2000	Massed/Waterer	CD	Chevron
2000	Royal Military Tattoo 2000	Massed/Waterer	CD	DD Video
2000	A Night at the Movies	CTC/Weston	CD	Chevron
2000	Just Marches	Plymouth/Mills	CD	Chevron
2001	International Festival of the Sea II	Plymouth/Waterer	CD	Chevron
2001	Mountbatten Festival of Music 2001	Massed/Waterer	CD	Chevron
2001	Trafalgar!	Britannia/Thornhill	CD	Plantagenet
2001	Celtic Salute	Scotland/Best	CD	Plantagenet
2002	The King's Squad	CTC/Grace	CD	Plantagenet
2002	Mountbatten Festival of Music 2002	Massed/Waterer	CD	Chevron
2002	Dancing Men	Britannia/Thornhill	CD	Plantagenet
2002	Adventures for Band	Plymouth/Mills	CD	Obrasso
2002	The Founders	Various	CD	IMMS/Chevron
2003	Mountbatten Festival of Music 2003	Massed/Davis	CD	Chevron
?	Two Dons, The/Carmen Overture	Plymouth/Ricketts	78	HMV
?	Washington Post/Blaze Away	Portsmouth/Dunn	45	HMV
?	Tattoo Highlights - SSAFA Searchlight Tattoos	Massed/Lang	EP	HMV
?	Military Band Favourites	Plymouth/Ricketts	EP	HMV
?	Band, Bugles & Orchestra of HM Royal Marines	Portsmouth/Dunn	EP	Columbia
?	True and Fair and other Tunes		LP	
?	Here Come the Marines		LP	Musicmasters

The Non-Commercial Recordings (Other than the ENSA recordings of World War II)

Date	Title of Recording	Band	Type	Recording Company
1893	?	Chatham/Wright		Edison?
1910	Queen Alexandra	RMA/Green		Pathe
1910	Voices of the Past	RMA/Green		Pathe
1910	The Jolly Coppersmith	RMA/Green		Pathe
1925	Bacchus	HMS Calcutta Orch/Allen	78	ACME
1925	Cavalleria Rusticana	HMS Calcutta Orch/Allen	78	ACME
1934?	Hungarian Dance	Portsmouth Orch/Dunn		

APPENDIX SIX

The Prince's Badge

On 9th March 1978, His Royal Highness The Duke of Edinburgh, to mark the occasion of the 25th anniversary of his appointment as the Captain General Royal Marines and in recognition of the service provided for him by the Royal Marines Band Service, directed that the best all-round Musician or Bugler from each annual intake should be awarded a badge consisting of his Royal Cypher surrounded by a lyre and referred to as 'The Prince's Badge', the recipient to wear the Prince's Badge throughout his service in the Royal Marines in every rank.

The Captain General Royal Marines further directed that the recipient should be referred to as 'The Prince's Badgeman'.

YEAR	AWARDED TO
1978	Musician P A Evans
1979	Musician P J Ryan
1980	Musician G H Smith
1981	Musician James Macgregor
1982	Musician P A Weston
1983	Bugler M E Stephenson
1984	Musician N J Grace
1985	No award
1986	No award
1987	Musician Wayne Riley
1988	No award
1989	No award
1990	Musician Terry Holland
1991	Musician P O Thomas
1992	Musician Matthew King
1993	Musician G A Wright
1994	No award
1995	Musician P F Trickett
1996	Musician Huw Williams
1997	Musician H A Munsey
1998	No award
1999	Musician R A Hunt
2000	Musician Ann Jonassen
2001	Musician Andrew Harvey
2002	No award
2003	Musician M J Walker

APPENDIX SEVEN

Drums and Staffs

Royal Marine Instructions (BR1283) contain, under Section 3: Ceremonial, Serial 10229, the following. 'When on parade with bands of other Services the Royal Marines Band is to form as a complete unit. There is to be no intermingling of ranks with other bands and the Corps of Drums must always be at the front.' Serial 10230 states that correct Royal Marines drill movements are to be adhered to at all times whilst Serial 10236 sets the minimum size of a Royal Marines Band for ceremonial in London at fifty.

The bands of the Royal Marines represent the Royal Navy – the Senior Service – and always take precedence when the Royal Navy or any Royal Naval Auxiliary Forces are on parade. This is set out in Queen's Regulations. When the Royal Navy are not on parade then they take their position according to Army precedence, a curious anomaly that does not take account of the fact that the Corps is now almost entirely a part of the Royal Navy. However, the Corps does not challenge this and, in practice, when there is no tradition to follow the Principal and Senior Directors of Music agree who will lead at each event. Within these Regulations we have the parameters for the classic ceremonial event featuring a Royal Marines Band or Royal Marines Massed Bands.

There are a number of symbols of great significance at the forefront of a Royal Marines Band. They are the Drum Major's staff and dress belt and the drums and their emblazonment. Each of them feature the emblems, symbols and Honours of the Corps in the same way as the Colours.

The Drum Major's Staff

In 1926 it was decided by the Royal Naval School of Music that a standard staff should be acquired for the School and for the bands of the Cs-in-C at Portsmouth, Plymouth, the Atlantic Fleet, the Mediterranean Fleet and the China Fleet. The design consisted of a Malacca cane with a tapered silver ferrule, a silver grip and a silver two-part head. The upper part of the head was a dome upon which was mounted a silver Imperial crown and a crowned lion. The lower part carried the Corps crest with lyre surmounted and, around the circumference, the wording "ROYAL NAVAL SCHOOL OF MUSIC". At the junctions of the various parts were silver rings with laurels engraved upon them. The Malacca cane was embellished with silver chains. These staffs were made by Hawkes and Co.[1]

By 1934 a further staff had been added for use by the Recruits Band for Recruits and Trained Soldiers Church Parades.[2]

It was decided to standardise the style of staff being used at the Royal Marine Divisions and so, during early March 1929, the Adjutant General called for sketches of the staff in use at each of the Divisions for selection of a standard. A drawing of the staffs supplied to the Depot and to the RMA[3] in 1899 was submitted. This showed a silver crowned lion on a Victorian crown mounted on a silver globe with continents of gilt.[4] On the silver grip was a scroll carrying the name "Gibraltar" and the words "Per Mare Per Terram" over which was an anchor superimposed upon the Royal Cypher of George IV.[5] Above this, on the Depot version, was a bugle horn whilst the Royal Marine Artillery model carried a bursting grenade. The Chatham Division was of a completely different style. It had a golden lion and crown mounted on a silver globe engraved with the continents, oceans and meridians. This was mounted on a golden dome engraved with a row of oak leaves and acorns then, in silver letters, the words "FIRST DIVISION - ROYAL MARINES". Below this was a further row of oak leaves and acorns and then, below a narrow space, a floral design consisting of roses, thistles, shamrocks and their leaves over a scroll with the words "Per Mare Per Terram" and a series of Prince of Wales' Plumes. The Malacca cane was fitted with cords instead of chain and these terminated in two tassels above the long tapering brass ferrule.[6] The Plymouth Division staff was much plainer and consisted of a gilded brass lion, crown, globe and shank. The latter was partly covered by a buff grip. The Malacca cane was fitted with cords and tassels at both the grip and ferrule ends. The ferrule itself was of gilded brass.

A decision was taken to adopt the style of the Portsmouth Division, Plymouth Division and the Depot, all of which were very similar, but with certain alterations to bring them into line. These were that all crowns were to be Imperial crown; chains were to be used, not cord, and would be of sterling silver and not gold; the bugle on the shank to be deleted above the anchor and ciphers were to be removed and the Royal cipher was to be standardised as George IV. It was also intended that the continents were to be shown on the globe. The Depot responded by stating that they would not alter their staff since it was originally the Woolwich Division staff and therefore of historical importance. However, the Adjutant General was able to show that this staff was originally purchased for the Depot in 1892 or 1894. The Brigadier commanding Plymouth Division wrote to urge that the Portsmouth staff should be used as the pattern since its dimensions and weight gave it a better balance. A new staff based upon the Portsmouth design was subsequently ordered and supplied by H Potter & Co of Charing Cross Road and so the original RMA and Depot design of 1899 became the basis for the current Royal Marine Drum Major's staff.

The Drum Major's Dress Belt

In 1925 the Adjutant General standardised the design of the dress belt. This was as a result of the amalgamation of the Royal Marine Artillery and the Royal Marine Light Infantry. On the front face of the belt the upper scroll carrying the name "GIBRALTAR" was to be gold on a blue background. Below this was the Imperial crown and then the foul anchor on the GRIV Cypher. The globe surrounded by a laurel wreath was positioned below the anchor with a scroll beneath it bearing the words "PER MARE PER TERRAM" in gold on a blue background. Below this was the Royal Cypher GRV. On the demise of the Crown this was to be changed to the cipher of the reigning Sovereign. The design of the buckle on the rear of the belt was slightly changed. The buckles of the RMLI had a crown at each side and a bugle at the bottom. These were replaced with roses as were featured in each corner of the buckle. It is presumed that the RMA buckle had a bursting grenade. The buckle also featured the crowned lion over the crown upon a globe and a scroll bearing the motto "PER MARE PER TERRAM" with laurel wreaths linking the components. All gold lace was to be wire[7].

At some time a lyre superimposed upon an anchor replaced the foul anchor on the GRIV Cypher. In 1960 new Dress Belts were required for the Drum Majors who would lead the massed bands Beating Retreat on Horse Guards Parade and the Corps decided to seek advice from the Royal College of Heralds with regard to the correct arrangement of the Royal and Corps insignia. As a result the order became, from the shoulder, "GIBRALTAR" in a scroll; the crown, Royal Cypher and Foul Anchor (as on the Sovereign Colour); the Globe and Laurel wreath; the words "PER MARE PER TERRAM"; the Royal Academy pattern lyre and the drum at the lowest point. Sufficient space had to be left for miniature medals to be worn above the upper scroll and the two ebonised miniature drumsticks having gold plated crowns, caps and bands enclosed the Royal Cypher and Foul Anchor as was customary.[8]

Drum Emblazonment

In 1961 the Captain General commented upon the imitation wood veneer that formed the rear part of the drum shell and suggested that the blue background to the emblazonment might be continued all the way around the drum. At the time there were about 350 drums within the Corps so this presented quite a problem. Trials took place on two of the rod-tensioned drums that had been introduced in 1960 and the Commandant General, after seeking advice from Band Officers, decided that the wood veneer should be replaced or covered with a scarlet paint finish.

During 1965, whilst obtaining transfers to re-emblazon a bass drum, it was realised that the drum did not carry a scroll with "GIBRALTAR". Tenor and side drums were checked for standardisation and correctness. Historically there were large variations, and little official guidance, in the painting of badges and emblems on drums and it would appear that the design and purchase of new drums had been the responsibility of the Divisional Drum Majors. The Royal Cypher GRIV had often been included as well as that of the reigning monarch - a practice used on the Regimental Colours. Following the 1950 amalgamation, the Royal Naval School of Music practice of using the Royal Cypher was adopted but with additional adornment in the form of the Corps crest, or parts of it.[9]

With investigations being inconclusive the matter lay dormant until 1967 when further stocks of the transfer were required and the omission of "Gibraltar" was again raised. Having decided to remedy this fault further criticisms were raised with the result that a local study team, led by Major G Manuel, was given the remit to produce the perfect emblazonment by 1971. The College of Heralds ruled that the practice of omiting the Royal lion and crown from the Corps crest because there was one in the Royal crest was incorrect. The lion and the crown was placed above "Gibraltar", EIIR was to be in the correct style and the layout on the bass drum was arranged so that the foul anchor was not obscured. These designs were then sent to the Royal College of Heralds for approval before being sent to the Department of the Commandant-General. The Lancaster Herald (Deputy Inspector of Regimental Colours) was most praiseworthy of the efforts made and gave access to the sealed pattern of the Royal Arms for the emblazonment. By this time the Queen had authorised Garter King of Arms to be responsible for not only Colours but all forms of military heraldry which included Colour Belts, drum emblazonment etc.From this it can be seen that all changes in heraldry in the Corps must be approved and recorded by the College of Heralds when the Royal Arms are included[10].

In 1971 Clarenceux King of Arms, in discussion with Chester Herald, the Advisor on Naval Heraldry, and Garter King of Arms agreed the designs for the drums of the Royal Marines and also for the drums of the Royal Navy Volunteer Bands. Paintings of the designs were laid before Her Majesty and approval for their use was given in November 1972.[11]

Notes

Chapter 1

1 Royal Marine Artillery Fraser & Carr-Laughton RUSI 1930
2 Mariners Mirror 1926
3 Papers of Capt A C Green and C Sanderson interview.
4 Order-in-Council (OIC) 28 March 1889
5 Mariners Mirror 1926
6 Interviewed by Lt A C Finney 1970
7 Unpublished papers of Capt A C Green
8 Charles Sanderson interview
9 Mariners Mirror 1926
10 Mariners Mirror 1926

Chapter 2 Part 1

1 Copy of Order-in-Council
2 Letter from BM Hammond to A C Green
3 Service Papers of Arthur William Shepard
4 In 1910 Lidiard signed a declaration to say that his name was Henry Ernest Lidiard, not Harry Lidiard
5 A C Green believed this to be H Lidiard
6 Navy List 1903
7 Globe and Laurel 1903 p91
8 Letter in RMM Archive
9 Admiralty Circular Letter N. 7327/1903 of August 1903 'New Scheme for the Organisation and Training of Bands for His Majesty's Fleet'
10 This became Channel, Atlantic, Mediterranean and China Fleets in 1905
11 In 1905 these became string bands and only efficient bandsmen of long service and pensioners seved in them.
12 Examinations were begun by Mr Stretton on the 20/8/1903 when he examined a BM2 and a BdCpl. From Report Book covering 1903-1904 in RMM Archive
13 See p116-117 for a full account of the 'Miller debate'
14 Globe and Laurel Vol X1 No 101
15 GORM 15/04 of February 1904
16 BM Hammond letter to A C Green and "The Log of HMS Crescent 1904-1907" by M E Donoghue
17 Copies held by RM Museum
18 Original letter in RMM Archive
19 Letter from Commandant RNSM to DAG 1/10/1904
20 RMM Archive
21 Source does not state what full marks were
22 CSM Baines recollection to A C Green
23 "Uniforms of the Royal Marines"- Stadden et al
24 Educational notes by Instructor Lt Cdr F J Wilkins (Rtd) - Blue Band Editor 1951-1954
25 Globe and Laurel 1906 Jan
26 Account by Lt Col Evans - RM Museum
27 GO 90/09
28 RMB729 M Booth recollection to A C Green
29 In 1908 The Prince of Wales went to Canada in HMS Indomitable with Mr H Reeby and an RM Band
30 GO/78 Nov 1908
31 No 33 RM361/09 and No 98 N 9422/1909
32 GO/90 of November 1909
33 A Silver Medal has been presented to the RAF since 1955
34 From the notes of J Trendell
35 Recollections of CSM Baines, given to A C Green
36 Naval manoeuvres required a large team of Umpires to oversee the 'battle' and judge the outcome
37 Reports sent back to UK. (Originals in RMM Archive)
38 Globe and Laurel and A C Green notes
39 'Flying Marines' by Major A E Marsh

Chapter 2 Part 2

1 Lt Cdr B Witts, HMS Excellent Museum Curator
2 Diary of J Allen and Blue Band articles 2000/2001
3 The Royal Naval Division D Jerrold 1923

4 With the Royal Naval Division on board HMS Crystal Palace and Elsewhere - A Souvenir 1915, and issue No 2
5 Diaries of J Allen. RM Museum
6 'Marcher' article - Blue Band journal
7 'Marines from the Medway' Lt Col B Edwards RM, RMHS Special Publication Number 20
8 The British Fleet consisted of 28 Dreadnoughts, 9 battle cruisers, 8 armoured cruisers, 26 light cruisers, and 75 destroyers 'The Royal Navy Day by Day' A B Sainsbury
9 Many of the gun's crew were killed. Maj Harvey, despite serious wounds, was able to order the crew of the cordite magazine to flood it thereby preventing an explosion in the main magazines. He was awarded a posthumous VC. 'The Royal Marines and the Victoria Cross', M Little
10 'British Battle Cruisers' - P Smith
11 Communications would only be routed through this area if the main electrical systems were damaged
12 Letter to A C Green
13 Naval Operations Vol IV (Official History of the War) Newbolt
14 It is not known if his death was related to any particular incident, neither is it known if he and the Band were involved in the action against the Germans in Togoland. The Regiment were certainly involved in the campaign that culminated in the destruction of the German radio station at Kamina
15 For whom he worked until his death in 1928
16 Captain Stoner's recollections written for A C Green
17 Footnote added to A C Green's Roll of Honour

Chapter 2 Part 3

1 GORM GO184/1920
2 GORM GO184/1920
3 In 1949 WOs would be re-titled Branch Officers. The junior grades were all titled 'Commissioned…' and wore a small star on their shoulder. The senior grades were titled 'Senior Commissioned…' and wore a large star on their shoulder
4 A blue diamond similar to the red one awarded to RM recruit Section Leaders
5 GORM 174/1920
6 GORM 127/1921
7 'Proposed Alterations to RM Band Clothing' ADM1/8629/131-PRO, Kew
8 RM Band. Band Ranks Uniform. PRO
9 As 7 above
10 Played in Excellent's Wardroom when passing the port
11 See Appendix 3
12 Official programmes
13 Recordings are in the RMM archive. H Berliner and the Cedo Company, whose trademark was "APEX", were experimenting in electrical recording from radio broadcasts - as opposed to placing a microphone in front of the radio loudspeaker. If these recordings are electrically produced they could be one of the first recordings, if not the first, made by this method in the world
14 Correspondence in RMM Archive
15 A C Green unpublished papers and Globe & Laurel
16 Globe and Laurel 1926 p102
17 The story of the Silver Bugles will be told on p130
18 Three sailors were especially embarked as Pipers. They brought two sets of pipes with them, a third set was purchased by the Wardroom and a fourth set was brought on board by the Drum-Major of the Portsmouth Division the night before Renown sailed. The fourth set was for a Scotsman in the RM Detachment. The drummers were trained to accompany the Pipers
19 "In the evening the band carried out a private engagement at the Town Hall. The fee charged was £50.

The Band Fund received 5%, the Musical Director 20%, the two Bandmasters shared 5% and the remainder divided equally between the members of the band"
20 Notes relating to the tour of HMS *Renown* were, mainly, taken from the Report of the OCRM, Maj T L Hunton
21 Percy Barnacle remained the modest, shy, man throughout his life. He moved to Plymouth, became involved with the Plymouth City Silver Band and an RM Band. He moved to the Deal area to become Bandmaster, at the recommendation of the RNSM, of the Betteshanger Colliery Band. He later became an Instructor at the RMSM and died aged 92. ["The *Royal Oak* Affair" by R Glenton]
22 A large hill between Telford and Shrewsbury
23 Educational notes by Instructor Lt Cdr F J Wilkins
24 'Music for HM Ships, C-in-Cs Bands and Shore Establishments 1931-1938' in RMM Archive
25 * First commission that was allowed a band. (Although the total bands 1931 - 1932 had risen by only three, four additional ships were given bands. One was offset because the battleship *Barham* went to Reserve). The reason for these ships being given bands appears to have been as a result of the "drafting manoeuvres" that had been carried out to ensure that ratings with suitable musical ability were on board and able to form 'volunteer bands' These new bands, allowed to *Leander* and 'D' Class ships, were smaller than those allowed to a Capital Ship or a larger cruiser. If acting as Flagship they had a Bandmaster, a Band Corporal and thirteen Musicians but as a 'Private Ship' the Musicians would be reduced to ten
26 Letter from A C Green 24/3/60
27 Article in 'Sheet Anchor' by M G Little
28 Licentiate of the Royal Academy of Music
29 The plotting table in the Transmitting Room
30 Superintendent Lt Col McCausland's Report on the Band Service 1938 - 1941. RM Museum

Chapter 2 Part 4
1 Admiralty Mobilisation Return No 1 - Complements of HM Ships. RM Museum
2 Account sent to A C Green
3 K Metyear notes to A C Green
4 Telephones used for communication in gunnery control
5 As chapter 2 part 3 number 30
6 Information given to A C Green by Musn Penfold
7 Globe & Laurel 1940 p397
8 A Howden information to A C Green and Blue Band
9 Notes to A C Green by T Bridle
10 *Barham* was actually 31,000 tons
11 Blue Band Spring 1987
12 Notes to A C Green by T Parnell
13 Lt T C Merrett's notes to A C Green
14 Information given to A C Green by Musn Penfold
15 Programme held in the RMM Archive
16 Navy List
17 HMS *Penelope* was the model for HMS Artemis in C S Forester's book 'The Ship'
18 'Our *Penelope*' (HMS *Penelope*) by her Company 1943
19 RM messdeck was always known as the RM Barracks
20 Information to A C Green by R Palmer, a band member, and from "The Ship That Torpedoed Itself"
21 Information supplied by BM Upstell to A C Green
22 Information from Musn A H G Kidd to A C Green
23 Musn P Herring to A C Green
24 Official War Logbook of RNSM - RMM Archive
25 Musn G Lillford information to A C Green
26 Adjutant General Royal Marines 1939-1943
27 Blue Band Winter 1984
28 HO's were men enlisted for the duration of the war
29 Musician Penfold to A C Green

30 Scarborough newspaper cuttings
31 Hunton Report. PRO ADM1/1191
32 "Passed School of Music"
33 R H Plowman - letter to the author
34 Letter from Musn Penfold to A C Green
35 Account given to A C Green by Musn J Clark
36 No explanation has been found for Musician Denness being on board a corvette - a ship too small to carry a band
37 Main armament is known as LA
38 Control Position
39 From a diary kept by Musns Webster and Baker who passed the diary from one to the other as watches changed
40 Lt Col Neville recalls BM 'Doc' Compton making them march to football practice wearing the helmets!

Chapter 2 Part 5
1 Scotland
2 Report in RM Museum
3 It is not known what contribution Woods made to this parade. The bands may have played Wood's march 'St George's Day'. See p72
4 Educational notes by Instructor Lt Cdr F J Wilkins
5 R A Hobbs (RMB/X214) to A C Green
6 J Trendell's notes
7 HMS *St George*. Barracks for training Short Service Ratings
8 HMS *Royal Arthur*., Butlins Holiday Camp at Skegness, was paid off in 1946
9 Correspondence - RMM Archive.
10 According to Brig Wills, Dixon's version of "Sarie Marais" was officially adopted by 3 Cdo Bde. See Appendix 2 p249
11 Band forms two files based upon the outer files of the band, leaving a large space, or lane, between.
12 'Marcher' article Blue Band Spring 1998
13 Globe & Laurel and Official Tournament Programme.
14 Article in 'Warship World' Vol 8 No 3
15 This was the march past of the RM Artillery until 1883.
16 Although not officially adopted until 1952 the march 'Sarie Marais' had been used by the Commandos for a very long time. It had been arranged by Lt FV Dunn of the Portsmouth Division in 1937
17 Details of the move to Deal covered later
18 This soon became the Commandant General's Squad
19 From 'Commandant's Report' (Papers of A C Green)
20 The King's Badge is awarded to the best recruit in the senior squad (known as the King's Squad.) Recipients are known as King's Badgemen and wear the badge on their upper left arm throughout their service
21 It is believed that Spencer of the RNSM led the parade as Senior Drum Major
22 Silver Bugles described on p130
23 G&L 1950

Chapter 2 Part 6
1 V = Victualling; M = Music
2 Report in RM Museum
3 Adm 1/21947/50 in PRO
4 'The Royal Marines' (Revised edn) Maj Gen J L Moulton
5 Agenda in RM Museum
6 RNSM had their instruments supplied and repaired at public expense. Group Bands received annual Admiralty Grant subsidised by Officers' subscriptions and 10% of the profit from private engagements. RNSM instruments were at greater risk since they were taken all over the world. Because they were supplied from the public purse RNSM instruments were not of the same quality as those belonging to Group Bands
7 It was later ruled that AFO 3174/47 applied equally to Group and RNSM Bands

8 War Office was revising allowances to Army Bands and believed that if Bands undertook private engagements some profit should return to the public. Proposal was 10% for jobs up to £2000, 15% for jobs over £2000

9 Volunteer Bands comprised RN Officers and ratings

10 Report in RMM Archive. 'The Band' refered to was RNSM Band

11 Commandant General Royal Marines

12 'Musical Progress and Mail' June 1948

13 Report in RMM Archive

14 RMRO 384/1949

15 Major General Royal Marines. (In command of a Group)

16 Later Quartermaster Sergeant

17 Leech-Porter Report - PRO - ADM 201/121

18 'Fiddler on the March' - D Oakley

19 Globe and Laurel

20 * = Class A Bands, remainder Class B

21 Public Record Office - ADM 1/21947/50

Chapter 3

1 Gosport Forton Barracks

2 There had also been a Division at Woolwich

3 GO/3 of January 1892

4 Six Buglers and four Gunners or Privates

5 Three Buglers and two Gunners or Privates

6 GO/46 of 1895

7 Royal Marine Artillery Vol. I p313

8 Trendell p18 & Tanner's unpublished papers

9 Tanner unpublished: papers

10 Random Records of the Royal Marines p52 - Order Book for the Chatham Division

11 Trendells dates. Tanner says 1845 - 1857

12 Globe and Laurel 1893

13 Records of Portsmouth Division of Marines 1764-1800

14 RM Records 1755-1792 (RMHS Special Pub No 2)

15 RM Records 1793-1836 (RMHS Special Pub No 4)

16 Royal Military Academy was at Woolwich, Royal Military College was at Sandhurst. Amalgamated in 1947

17 'Music and Musicians at the Edinburgh International Exhibition 1886' by R A Marr

18 Whilst S Griffiths was commissioned on the 24/12/1890 and A Stretton on the 25/03/1896 - both as Director of Music Kneller Hall where they held teaching posts. Zavertal, C Godfrey and Miller were the first in charge of bands to be commissioned since D Godfrey. Miller was the first military musician to become a Bachelor of Music (1892)

19 Maj G Turner (History of British Military Bands Volume I) states Thomas Winterbottom was appointed in 1845

20 Tanner's encyclopaedia

21 Blue Band July 1974 p91

22 Globe and Laurel p4, 1921 (Referring to 1816)

23 Records of the Portsmouth Division of Marines 1764-1800

24 RM Records 1793-1836 . RMHS Special Pub No 4

25 Official record and presentation inscription

26 Random Records of the RM. Blumberg & Field

Chapter 4

1 Miller reverted to Honorary Rank when promoted Maj and Green reverted to Honorary Rank when promoted Lt in 1914 - from Navy Lists of the time

2 The Warrant rank, similar to that in the RN, had been introduced into the Corps by an Order-in-Council in 1881 and the four Bandmasters became Warrant Officers. This was followed in 1898 by G Miller's promotion to Honorary 2nd Lt and then, in 1899, he was made 2nd Lt - the first RM Bandmaster to be commissioned

3 A description of this Tour of Duty is in the Chatham Division section of this book since the band was under the direction of Capt PSG O'Donnell, DoM Chatham Div

4 RMRO 1372/1946

5 GORM GO/34 March 1901

6 GORM GO/31 March 1902

7 Port Admirals Bands were only orchestral at this time.

8 The Daily Graphic 20th September 1921 (This was the father of Earl Mountbatten. The Marquess had played an important part in reforming Royal Navy music)

9 From official programme

10 Tattoo programmes

11 G&L Supplement 1935

12 G&L Supplement 1935/Household Brigade Magazine/ The Royal Marines - A Record of the Tour of Duty in London/Brigade Orders

13 Letter to Brigade Major, Royal Marines from Capt O'Donnell 3 Dec 1934 - RMM Archive

14 See Appendix 2 p248

15 Recently promoted

16 'Coronation Orders for RN and RM in London' RMM Archive

17 This occurred shortly after. The Bugle Major and 10 Buglers of Chatham Band were at the ceremony

18 Maj Gen Royal Marines

19 Random Records of the RM 233-236

20 Gen Blumberg who, at the time, was Adjutant of RMLI Portsmouth Division. "Random Notes'

21 *Alberta* carried the body of Queen Victoria whilst the *Victoria and Albert III* followed with the King

22 GORM (GO/43 March 1901)

23 Globe and Laurel 1901 p27-28

24 Correspondence and memorandum - RMMArchive

25 Extra Equerry to King George V

26 'Scheme for Band for HM Yacht' - RMM Archive

27 Abbreviation used in original quotation

28 'Band for HM Yacht' - RMM Archive

29 Original hand written draft in RMM Archive

30 Tanner's unpublished encyclopaedia

31 The Musical Times 1st Aug 1919

32 GO 44/02 and G & L 1902 Editorial and pages 40/41

33 'Western Weekly Mercury' 24th Sept 1910

34 GORM GO/206 Dec 1920 - helmet plates not mentioned.

35 Coronation Orders for RN and RM in London - RMM Archive

36 Later RM Armoured Support Group

37 All documents relating to this - RMM Archive

38 Globe and Laurel 1944 and 1946

39 GORM GO/64, July 1904

40 Letter to HM Yacht *Victoria and Albert*, dated 20/1/1911 in RMM

41 GORM GO/64, July 1904

42 From "To India With the King and Queen"

43 Private Secretary and Equerry to the King

44 All correspondence in the RMM Archive

45 Refer to 'Fiddler on the March' by D Oakley

46 Some of these have been released on compact discs by RMHS/Eastney Collection

47 From official programme

48 Documents in RM Museum

49 'The Story of Colours in the Royal Marines'

50 'Marcher' article Blue Band Spring 1998

51 JT A Life on the Ocean Wave p23

52 Deal, Walmer and Sandwich Mercury 3rd Nov 1928

53 His brother was the Bugle Major at the Depot

54 'With Full and Grateful Hearts' RMHS Publication

55 Sgt Maj C E Lidiard was the cousin of Major H E Lidiard. He served at Gallipoli and was the Bugle Major at the unveiling of the London Cenotaph

56 In 1969 a RMRO stated that they should not be used again. They are now held at the Officers Mess, Plymouth (8), CTC (6) and 42 CdoRM (2). The HQ RMBS and the RM Museum hold eight each. All 32 were gathered together for only the fourth time at the Special RMBS Exhibition at the RMM 2003-2004

57 GORM 128/1929

58 Jack returned to the Band Service in 1964 as Professor of Trombone, a position he held for twelve years until 1976 when he retired at the age of 74

59 RMRO1457/1946

60 RMRO576/1947

Chapter 5
1 'Fiddler on the March'

2 'Fiddler on the March'

3 'A Life on the Ocean Wave'

4 AFO 7588/1950

5 Mentioned-in-Despatches in 1945

6 This was later changed

7 AFO3422/51. File in PRO, Kew

8 Unless stated otherwise all information regarding the Korean War period is from G & L and Blue Band

9 *Ocean* was working up in the Mediterranean when her band joined. She was quarantined because of a polio outbreak

10 Unless stated otherwise, all information about service in Malaya has been taken from G & L and Blue Band

11 3 Cdo Bde comprised 40, 42 and 45 Cdo RM

12 The Lancers having relieved the Hussars

13 These cruises were intended not only to fly the flag but to give opportunities for the crew to exercise their wartime roles

14 Whilst the author is not credited the report has the style of the earlier report by Capt Stoner. RMM Archive

15 The Flagship Bandmaster was also Fleet Bandmaster therefore Cd BM Ough was Commissioned Bandmaster, Mediterranean Fleet

16 'The Story of Colours in the Royal Marines.'

17 Mrs Marjorie Green, Blue Band Vol 28 No 2 p79

18 'Fiddler on the March' and documents in the RMM

19 This was the only Colour that had also been on parade at the 1937 Coronation

20 Globe & Laurel and Brigade Orders for the RN and RM

21 When he died the title was changed to Colonel-in-Chief and given to the Duke of Cornwall and York, who subsequently became The Prince of Wales and then King George V, on the 1st Jan 1901. The title then passed to Edward as Colonel-in-Chief then, after the abdication, to King George VI who changed it to Captain General

22 'Fiddler on the March' by D Oakley

23 From 'Blue Band' Winter 1993

24 From 'Blue Band' Winter 1993 and report in RMM

25 Some buglers of Plymouth Group played pipes at this time

26 Detachment and Band transferred from *Vanguard* to *Tyne* when *Vanguard* went to refit

27 Rope or cable rigged between two ships under way along which a traveller block with suspended load can be hauled

28 Globe and Laurel

29 Royal Ceylon Navy

30 Royal New Zealand Royal Marines Band Service

31 The title 'Corps Drum Major' was not used until some time in the 1970s

32 HMS *Eagle* was in dry dock and did not require the band

33 'Minature Medals for Drum Majors' file in PRO, Kew

34 All supporting information is within the RMM Archive

35 Men whose duties did not involve standing watches

Chapter 6
1 Report in RMM Archive

2 Report in RMM Archive

3 RMM Archive

4 Band withdrawn, ship having major overhaul.

5 RMM Archives

6 Lt and Capt are combined because, at that time, a Lt was automatically promoted to Capt after eight years. This was altered to selection after a qualifying period

7 AFO1585/60(U)276

8 RMM Archive

9 This duty had been carried out by a General List officer with Band Service staff

10 The RMBS is responsible for Volunteer Bands, providing an Instructor, usually a BdCSgt, who trains, rehearses and administers the band. This provides good experience and training for the VBI

11 RMM Archive

12 Mess functions etc

13 RMM Archive

14 RMM Archive

15 All bands except HMS *Ganges* and BRNC would have Band Officers. This figure does not include those under training, instructors and others

16 Title to be Band of HM RM Commando Training Centre

17 Title to be Band of HM RM Commando Forces

18 Blue Band Vol 23 No1 p3

19 Blue Band

20 RMM Archive

21 1956. Recommendation was "Not only would no economy result from co-operation by the services in the training of musicians, but that there would be additional expense with less satisfactory results, than under existing system". Further investigation in 1963 when RAF had a large expense to rebuild the HQ of RAF Music Services and RAF Central Band at Uxbridge. Was raised again in 1967

22 Would eliminate the Army's need to use seventeen sites.

23 The Corps was under great pressure to quickly close one establishment and the Depot was the likely choice

24 Higher Education Test

25 Lt Col Dunn first introduced this as a means of assessing Bandmasters for promotion. The qualification lapsed for a while but was re-introduced by Lt Col Waterer in 1999.

26 File in RM Museum

27 RMM Archive

28 The Walden Report 1977

29 Globe and Laurel

30 RMM Archive

31 RMM Archive

32 RNAS Yeovilton. (Replaced RNAS at HMS *Daedalus*)

Chapter 7
1 Beat Retreat file in RMM Archive

2 Lt C G McLean and nine members of the band elected to remain in New Zealand upon their retirement in 1960

3 The 'official' drums of Portsmouth Group were kept in the Officers' Mess. Buglers used a set of brass shell drums for practice and day-to-day use. When the official drums were required the buglers were marched into the Officers' Mess through a rear door to collect them. (Colin Bowden)

4 The bands were conducted by either Capt Arnold or Capt Pottle throughout the course of the Tournament allowing Lt Col Dunn to participate in the Tercentenary events

5 File in RMM Archive and "1664-1964 An Account of the Royal Marines Tercentenary Celebrations"

6 See Appendix 1

7 File in RMM Archive

8 Played when RM Guard of Honour received Churchill with a General Salute when he was installed as Lord Warden of the Cinque Ports in 1941

9 Naval Personnel Department Two

10 File in RMM Archive

11 HMS *Hermes* was not converted until 1973

12 File in RMM Archive

13 Correspondance with Lt Col P Neville (Feb 2003)

14 As quoted in Minutes - should be DoM, Royal Military School of Music. This was Lt Col C H Jaeger

15 File in RM Museum

16 File in RMM Archive

17 A few months later the Government reversed its decision and 41Cdo RM was reformed at Deal

18 Account taken from author's contribution to 'Sound the Trumpets, Beat the Drum'

19 Programmes

20 Article by Maj B Mills, Blue Band Winter 2002

21 See Appendix 6

22 41Cdo RM were at Deal having been reformed following the Government's decision not to disband them

23 Sept/Oct 1979 issue

24 It is traditional that the unit that 'leads' a military funeral is closest to the gun-carriage and not leading the procession

25 See Appendix 1

26 Account taken from official file in RM Museum

27 RMRO 246/1996

28 Official file in RM Museum

29 Not to be confused with Drum Major Charles Bowden who, at this time was with the RMSM

30 RMRO352/1962

31 BR 1283

32 RMRO 228/1967

33 RMRO 229/1961

34 Conversations with ex Corps Bugle Major D Dawson who joined as a Boy Bugler in 1960

35 RMRO105/1979

Chapter 8

1 On board HMS *Hermes* at this time

2 Responsibility of FOF3 Band whilst aboard Hermes

3 'No Picnic' Maj-Gen J Thompson

4 '*Canberra*: The Great White Whale Goes to War.' (Diary kept by BdSgt Ireland)

5 Surgeon Cdr R Jolly who commanded Medical Squadron of 3 Cdo Bde

6 HMS *Ardent* was hit by four Argentine bombs. Fire and explosion damage was so great that the order to abandon ship was given and the crew transferred to *Canberra*

7 'Our Falklands War' G Underwood

8 'Reasons in Writing - A Commando's View of the Falklands War' Maj Southby-Tailyour

9 Lt Col G A C Hoskins correspondence

10 Tri-Service Training of Musicians was raised throughout this decade, and was the subject of a detailed Parliamentary debate, but these files are not yet open to the public

11 HMS *Courageous* 1939

12 RMRO 52/85

13 It is believed that this is the only time that the Royal Yacht was used in her originally anticipated 'dual role'

14 Blue Band Vol 37 No 3 page 76

15 Blue Band Vol 38 No 3 page 66

16 Blue Band Autumn 1988 p 45

17 Sept/Oct 1989 Editorial

18 At the event the 2nd and 4th Movements, including the march HMS *Trinidad*, were played and the Finale was played as an instrumental anthem during the service. The march was written in 1941 to commemorate George

Lloyd's ship, known as the ship that torpedoed herself, and never published or played after that date. The composer arranged the march for military band following the service and it was played at the 2003 Mountbatten Festival of Music

Chapter 9

1 Diary of Bug M Williams

2 Blue Band Autumn 1991 p40

3 Royal Fleet Auxiliary

4 Defence Council Instruction (DCI)

5 These official titles had been used since 1st April 1994

6 It was decided that the trial was not a success and, by this time, the RMBS had alternatives in place

7 RMRO 010/96

8 RMRO 064/97

9 F&C. Foreign & Commonwealth

10 Sp to RMC. Support to wider RM Command

11 RMIs 0793, 0794 and 0795 of BR1283/62

12 Technique of Instruments - General knowledge

13 See Appendix 1

Chapter 10

1 Fighting In a Built-Up Area

2 LCpl H E Harden VC RAMC was awarded a posthumous VC whilst serving with 45 Cdo in WWII

3 The Royal Marines won!

4 Conversation with BdSgt I Davies, Troop Sergeant

5 When Gen Sir Peter Whiteley took the salute at the rehearsal "Garb of Old Gaul" was not played as the General Salute because, when serving, he had adopted a 'personal' Musical Salute - the first six bars of Grieg's "Homage March Sigurd Jorsalfar"

6 Two-person dug-outs with sandbag walls and a tent-like cover over the top. Very low and offering good protection

7 RMRO 082/1998. Also gives the official, shortened titles as Portsmouth Band, Plymouth Band, CTCRM Band, Scotland Band and BRNC Band this is also the Order of Precedence

8 RMRO064/1998: At the decommissioning ceremony of the Royal Yacht *Britannia*, the Queen and Prince Philip expressed a desire that the Portsmouth Band should retain its Royal Duty status by continuing to accompany Her Majesty on Royal Tours and to retain its distinctive uniform, the Divisional Band Tunic and Royal Yacht shoulder flashes. In April 1998 Her Majesty the Queen agreed that the Portsmouth Band continue to provide Royal Duty in the form of a Royal Band for the Royal Family. A change to the existing Royal Yacht shoulder flash would be made to read 'Royal Band'. This would be worn by the entire Portsmouth Band on all uniforms. The Royal Band was to wear the Divisional Band Tunic when on Royal duty

9 Some information taken from Blue Band articles written by the Corps Bandmaster, WO1 S P Savage

10 As 9 above

11 "The Founders" compact disc

12 See beginning of this chapter

Appendix 1

1 The only known surviving copy of this original Charter is torn at this point so no official description of the banners can be given here

2 Description from inspection of original banners in the RMM

3 RMRO316/1953. "In future only Royal Marines Buglers are to wear Dress Cords Royal. The issue of Dress Cords Royal to Royal Marines School of Music ranks is to cease forthwith"

4 Minute Sheet - RM Museum

5 Maj I Wray made an official record of this telephone conversation. RMM Archives

6 Blue Band - 1954

7 Infantry Training Centre, now Commando Training Centre, Lympstone

8 File in HQRMBS and also Blue Band

9 File 6/6/181 (Minute from Asst Adjt Gen) in RM Museum

10 File Note to Asst Adjt Gen from CGRM 16/6/1970 "For the record - Royal Marines Trumpeters Headgear" RMM Archive

11 All correspondence is in RMM Archive (RMM6/6/19)

Appendix 2

1 Article by Capt F V Dunn for G & L suggests the alternatives that were considered

2 According to Maj Turner in 'The History of British Military Bands' Thomas Winterbottom of the RM Plymouth Division wrote the Regimental march 'The York and Lancaster' - the same march? There is also a theory that 'The York and Lancaster' was originally written in 1867 as 'Long Valley Stride'. Long Valley was where Aldershot Garrison was reviewed by Queen Victoria

3 From The Regiment 2nd Feb 1901, quoted by Col. C Field, 'Britain's Sea Soldiers Vol II'. Could Winterbottom's entry have been 'The Defiler'?

4 103/Gen No

5 GORM GO/45 1921

6 'The Band' BBC radio programme. Statement that 'Galatea' was Slow March of the RMA is unconfirmed.

7 'By Land and Sea' was submitted by Ricketts but it would not fit the appropriate part of the ceremony

8 O'Donnell's letter to Dunn in RMM

9 AFO 143/64; QRs & AIs Art 1305, Clause 1f

10 Later Major General

11 Rank upon retirement

12 Article written for the RMHS by M Little, RMM Archivist and Librarian

13 Capt G H Hennessy in conversation with Maj A J Donald

14 The Globe and Laurel 1967 p126

15 Bandmaster of the 2nd Seebattalion (German Marines)

16 Letter from Lt Cresswell Royal Artillery 13 Jan 2000. Also official letter to the Master Gunner from CGRM

17 The other three Regiments were later disbanded

18 This ship's successor became the third HMS *Excellent* in 1859

19 From "The House that Jack Built" by R T Young. 1955

20 Words to Nancy Lee are believed to have been written by M Maybrick who published under the name of S Adams.(In the programme for the 1948 Royal Tournament, during the 'March On' phase of the display, is stated "Nancy Lee... Adams". This was used as a quick troop). Music was written by M Weatherley, probably in the 1870s

21 Suggested by Maj A J Donald

Appendix 3

1 Information taken from 'Blue Band' articles by Marcher.

2 Kenneth More had been a Lt in the RN during WWII and Richard Baker was still a Lt Cdr in the RNR

3 Bandmasters usually wore tunics and caps when conducting the opening fanfare, a tradition taken from the Deal Winter Concerts

Appendix 5

1 Issued in N America

2 US version of 'Splendour of the March'

3 Accompanying Philharmonia Orchestra

4 With Bournemouth Symphony Orchestra

5 With RMSM/Neville

6 With Russ Conway

7 With Fred. Harvey

8 Later released on compact disc

9 Later released on compact disc

10 One track only

11 Later released on compact disc

12 Fanfare trumpet team only

Appendix 7

1 Information taken from the PRO File ADM1/8808 and from example presented to the Royal Marines Museum by the Royal Marines Band Service 26th June 2003

2 Letter from the Depot Commandant, 3rd December 1934. PRO File ADM1/8808

3 Being used by the Portsmouth Division

4 The silver parts of these staffs could not be hallmarked because of the use of gilt. An item has to be completely silver to be hallmarked

5 This was in deference to the King who had conferred the battle honour of the Globe upon the Marines in 1827

6 This staff is now in the RM Museum although prior to its arrival at the RMM the silver globe had been lost

7 File ADM1/8808 in PRO

8 File in RMM Archive

9 The Corps Crest, as laid down in the Navy List, consists of "The Globe surrounded by a Laurel Wreath and surmounted by the crowned lion and crown with "Gibraltar" on a scroll. The foul anchor is placed on the wreath below the Globe with, below, the motto "Per Mare Per Terram". This crest was devised shortly after the Corps amalgamated in 1923

10 Corps Historian's report to HQ Portsmouth Group. RMM Archive file

11 Information from file in RMM Archive. (RM 97/218)

Bibliography

Brooks. Richard - **The Long Arm of Empire** - Constable 1999

Clowes. William Laird - **The Royal Navy Volume 7** - Chatham Publishing 1996 (Reprint)

Donaghue. M E - **The Log of HMS Crescent 1904-1907** - Westminster Press, 1907

Edwards RM. Lt Col Brian - **Marines from the Medway.** - RMHS Special Publication No 20 1998

Fraser & Carr-Laughton - **The Royal Marine Artillery 1804-1923 Vols. I & II**, -RUSI 1930

Fremantle. Admiral Sir Sydney - **My Naval Career** - Hutchinson & Co 1949

Furness. A W - **To India with the King and Queen 1911-1912**. - Westminster Press (Gerrards Ltd)

Glenton. Robert - **The Royal Oak Affair** - Leo Cooper 1991

Jellicoe. Lord - **The Grand Fleet 1914-1918** - Cassell 1919

Jerrold. Douglas - **Royal Naval Division**. - 1923 - Hutchinson 1923

Little. M G - **The Royal Marines and the Victoria Cross** - RMM 2003

Lowe - **Records of the Portsmouth Division of Marines 1764-1800** (Portsmouth Record Series)

Marr. Robert A - **Music and Musicians at the Edinburgh International Exhibition 1886**

Marsh RM. Major A E - **Flying Marines** - Privately Published 1980

Nalden. Charles - **Half and Half** - Moana Press

Newbolt - **Naval Operations Vol IV (Official History of the War)**

Oakley. Derek - **Fiddler on the March** - RMHS

Owen. Charles - **Plain Yarns from the Fleet** - Sutton Publishing 1997

Page. Christopher - **Command in the Royal Naval Division** - Spellmount 1999

Pearce. Frank - **The Ship That Torpedoed Herself** - Baron Jay Ltd

Roskill. Capt - **History of the Second World War** - The War at Sea Volume 1 - HMSO 1954

Rowe. Robin - **Sticky-Blue** - Devonshire House 1995

Sainsbury. A B - **Royal Navy Day By Day** - Ian Allan

Scott. Admiral Sir Percy - **Fifty Years in the Royal Navy** - 1919

Smith. Peter - **British Battle Cruisers** - Almark

Southby-Tailyour. Ewen - **Reasons in Writing** - BCA / Leo Cooper 1985

Stadden, Newark and Donald - **Uniforms of the Royal Marines** - Pompadour Gallery 1997

Swales MBE. Joffrey - **We Blew and They Were Shattered** - Singing Saw Press 1993

Thompson. Maj-Gen J - **No Picnic** - Leo Cooper 1985

Trendell. John - **A Life on the Ocean Wave** - Blue Band Magazine 1990

Turner. Gordon & Alwyn - **History of British Military Bands Vols I, II and III** - Spellmount

Underwood. Geoffrey - **Our Falklands War** - Maritime Books 1983

Wells. Capt J - **The Royal Navy, an illustrated social history 1870 -1982** - A Sutton & the RN Museum. 1994

Wilson. Col L - **Bands, Drums and Music of The Queen's Royal Surrey Regiment, its Forebears and Successors**

Young. Cdr R Travers - **The House That Jack Built - The Story of Whale Island** - Gale and Polden 1955

Our Penelope (HMS Penelope) - By Her Company published by Charles Shribner's Sons

British Forces in the Korean War - Ed Cunningham-Booth and Farrar

British Commonwealth Naval Operations. Korea 1950-53 - Naval Staff History 1957

Royal Marines Records RMHS Special Publication No 2, 4 and 5

Bid Them Rest in Peace - A Register of Royal Marine deaths 1939-1945 RMHS

Canberra - The Great White Whale Goes to War 1983

With the RND on Board HMS Crystal Palace & Elsewhere - a Souvenir 1915 & Issue 2

Unpublished papers of Capt A C Green, John Trendell and Tanner

Mariners Mirror - Development of Bands in the Royal Navy W G Perrin OBE

Naval and Military Record 20/06/1917

Admiralty Circular letters; Admiralty Orders-in-Council; RM Orders and Instructions; Kings Regulations and Admiralty Instructions; MoD Navy Dept Orders-in-Council, Navy List (various)

Gunnery Training Manual Vol. I 1937

The British Survey 1950

Mobilisation Return No 1 - Complements of HM Ships - Admiralty Personal Services Dep't. 1939

Diaries of Musn. L P Donne, Wm D Craig and Bugler M Williams.